The Media in America

Books by John Tebbel in the Field of Communications

The Media in America
A History of Book Publishing in the United States (Vol. I)
The American Magazine: A Compact History
A Compact History of the American Newspaper
Makers of Modern Journalism (with Kenneth N. Stewart)
The Life and Good Times of William Randolph Hearst
George Horace Lorimer and *The Saturday Evening Post*
An American Dynasty
The Marshall Fields
Paperback Books: A Pocket History
Open Letter to Newspaper Readers

THE MEDIA IN AMERICA

By JOHN TEBBEL

THOMAS Y. CROWELL COMPANY
New York Established 1834

Manufactured in the United States of America

ISBN 0-690-00500-8

Library of Congress Cataloging in Publication Data

Tebbel, John William, 1912-
    The media in America.

    Bibliography: p.
    1. Mass media—United States. I. Title.
P92.U5T4   301.16′1′0973   74-9891
ISBN 0-690-00500-8

2   3   4   5   6   7   8   9   10

Contents

Introduction

THE LITERATURE OF JOURNALISM is not as rich with historical studies as it should be. Today, sadly, they appear to be out of fashion. Nevertheless, the monuments stand out: large-scale studies like Frank Luther Mott's *American Journalism;* Edwin Emery's *The Press and America;* Mott's *A History of American Magazines;* Erik Barnouw's three-volume history of broadcasting (*A Tower in Babel, The Golden Web,* and *The Image Empire);* and if I may be permitted an immodesty, my own three-volume history of book publishing in the United States, the first volume of which was published in 1972.

In all the literature, however, there does not exist a study which attempts to synthesize the history of the media—books, newspapers, magazines, and broadcasting—and project it against the backdrop of political and social history. That is the intention of this book, with the added intent of doing so from the perspective of today's attitudes and viewpoints.

I would be the last to claim it as definitive. Several more volumes would be necessary to give that claim any validity. But I hope it will be useful, not just to university and college students studying both journalism and American cultural life, but to the broader audience for which it is primarily intended, the intelligent reader who sees and hears a great deal of talk about the media but knows little or nothing of their history and the major role they have played in the making of this country. Unless he was a journalism student, he was probably not exposed to the major studies I have mentioned when he was in college. Much of the material in this volume, I think, will be new to him even if he has a good general knowledge of American history, and I believe he will be startled by the parallels between the past and contemporary history.

For this study I have drawn freely on my own ten volumes in the field of communications, listed on a previous page, but much new material and reinterpretation has been added, particularly in the area of press and government relations. The section on the media in the twentieth century draws on numerous contemporary sources.

Even if the book pleases and informs the general reader and the student, it quite possibly may irritate a great many other people, a circumstance for which no apologies are made. It will certainly not please those who want passionately to prove that the media are destroying the fabric of American life, nor will it please those who believe that criticizing the media is more important than trying to save them from government control and public hostility. While the book takes what could be called an unorthodox view of American history, it will not please the revisionists, who insist on seeing that history only in economic terms, nor the quantifiers, who think the history of human beings can be better understood by viewing them as statistics. "True history," as one historian wrote recently, "is the product of historical thinking, and historical thinking is critical thinking about the past." That is the viewpoint of this book.

The twentieth-century concept of a free press in a democratic society rests on the ideal of fair and accurate reporting, that is, the attempt to be as objective as possible in covering the news. It is the attempt to be so that counts, not the inevitable human failures.,

The governments of authoritarian countries share the belief that the ideal of objectivity is reactionary. There is no slightest pretense of objectivity in the press of those countries. They argue that there is no association of news and truth in the newsroom; consequently they impose their own truth on the news.

Further, the authoritarian press does not believe in reporting competing viewpoints for what they are worth, but it is just this kind of reporting that those who demanded a First Amendment had in mind. They meant to make it possible for every viewpoint to be heard, for all the facts that could be gathered to be laid before the people, who would then make up their own minds. This is the essence of the press's role in a democracy. If it has not worked as well as the Founders hoped it would, the fault is ours, not theirs.

These basic concepts are what I have attempted to trace in the pages that follow, beginning with the establishment of the media and carrying on to the present, showing how the concepts have both triumphed and failed, been attacked and defended, and yet survive as the continuous thread linking past and present.

To this study I have brought what I have learned from forty-six years of daily association with the media, beginning at fourteen with the smallest of small-town weeklies and ranging to the New York *Times*, two national magazines, a book-publishing house, and both teaching and administrative work at two universities. While I have never worked directly in broadcasting, I have appeared frequently on both radio and television since the early forties, have been associated in various ways with many of the people in the medium, and have helped to train many others who now occupy prominent positions in it. Besides writing for the media as an employee and teaching media practice, full and part time, for twenty-nine years, I have written, among many other books, eleven volumes of media history, including this one, and for a decade contributed every month to the Communications Section of the *Saturday Review*.

Those are my credentials for the present work. I cite them here in lieu of the usual acknowledgments to libraries and other sources. This book has come directly from my own writing and experience, and represents whatever insights and knowledge I have gained from them.

JOHN TEBBEL

New York City
April 1974

Part One

The Media and the Idea of Freedom

1

How the Media Began

ONE OF THE MOST STRIKING CHARACTERISTICS of the media in late-twentieth-century America is the freedom enjoyed by books, magazines, newspapers, and broadcasting. It is not only a freedom guaranteed uniquely by the First Amendment, but, deriving from that, a freedom to play a social and political role which is not enjoyed in quite the same way by any other nation.

In the darkening world of our time, the American media stand out like torches against the shades of authoritarianism, on both right and left, that threaten to engulf us. With all their faults, real and imaginary, they remain in vivid contrast to the media of other countries which have already been swept under tight controls, or are much more severely curtailed than our own.

Most Americans would regard this view of the situation as excessively melodramatic. They are largely indifferent to, or unaware of, the state of the media, when they are not downright hostile. They are profoundly ignorant of media history, and few have any idea of how the means of communication work, although they are abundantly supplied with misconceptions. This is not alone the ignorance of those without adequate schooling, whose numbers are formidable enough, but a lack of knowledge displayed by those judged to be informed on other matters of public interest, as well as by some of the most distinguished critics of the press, in and out of government.

We have come to accept widespread criticism of the media as a fact of life, and some regard it as a salutary feature of democracy.

3

The attacks come with equal fervor from both right and left, rich and poor, young and old. Everyone wants a different kind of reform; few are concerned with alternatives. The advent of television has sharpened the struggle because it has revived, on a vastly larger scale in a different medium, the political importance that the print media had in the nineteenth century.

In a little more than two hundred years, we have come around nearly full circle from where we began. First there were the tight political and social controls on the media in colonial times. These were followed by the excesses of the eighteenth century after controls were largely removed. Then came the steady growth of responsibility through the nineteenth and early twentieth centuries, and now we see the agonizingly slow eclipse of everything that has been gained. The public attacks on the media are only the most visible evidence of that process.

Paradoxically, the media which so many people today are quite willing to beat into the shapeless gray mass of uniformity and conformity have been prime shapers of our culture and political development, to an extent never witnessed before in human history. An understanding of how that happened, particularly when viewed in the light of our contemporary political and social ideas, provides us with some perspective on the future—to see where we are going, and determine whether we want to go there.

A starting point for the inquiry might well be the often quoted statement of Sir William Berkeley, governor of Virginia in 1671, who wrote home to his sovereign, Charles II, describing his difficulties with the colony but nevertheless finding a glimmer of hope in the fact that, as he said, "I thank God, there are no free schools nor printing, and I hope we shall not have these hundred years; for learning has brought disobedience, and heresy, and sects into the world, and printing has divulged them, and libels against the best government. God keep us from both."

Nothing so epitomizes the establishment mind of the seventeenth century as this dogmatic denial of freedom. Yet Berkeley was not the old fool Charles thought he was, because his estimate of the power of printing was an accurate one, and so was his appraisal of knowledge in the hands of the masses. It takes no radical turn of mind to see now that authoritarian systems up to that time had maintained their repressive and exploitive power in the same way they do today—that is, by means of loyal armies and control of what was taught and read. They counted on illiteracy, poverty, and the suppression of free thought in any form to stay in power, just as dictators of every persuasion do today.

In this conspiracy, which was the common way of governmental life, church and state were more often allied than not. Prelates and kings had a common philosophical cause. Consequently it is not surprising that when Fray Juan de Zumárraga, first bishop of Mexico, arrived in Mexico in 1528, he soon perceived that if the church could establish a printing press in the new colony, his task of making converts of the Indians would be made immeasurably easier, and the press, the enemy of illiteracy, would be firmly controlled. After Gutenberg's European invention of printing demonstrated by his Bible of 1456, it was clear to both Catholic and Protestant leaders that God had sent them an instrument of conversion of unexampled importance. For the first time, books could be reproduced exactly and printed in quantity.

The implications of Gutenberg's discovery were understood by political leaders as well, and under the powerful dual impulse of church and state it took only a quarter of a century to establish printers in France, the Netherlands, Spain, and Italy. By the time the sixteenth century began, printing was virtually an industry, with standardized type and a range of specialties, and less than a century after Gutenberg's original invention, printing was brought to the Americas, a part of the world unknown fifty years earlier.

Father Zumárraga was responsible for the negotiations that brought Juan Pablos, an Italian from Brescia, to the New World as its first printer. Pablos had been working for Seville's leading printer, Juan Cromberger. He printed his first book in Mexico City in 1539, although there is some scholarly doubt about whether it was the first in the New World; one may have been printed three years earlier. In any case, Pablos' primitive equipment had turned out thirty-seven books before he died in 1560, and he had created the kind of cottage industry in printing and publishing which prevailed in North America for the next 250 years. The technology he used changed so slowly that no really substantial breakthrough occurred until the early nineteenth century, and the cottage-industry character of publishing did not begin to change in the American colonies until after the Revolution transformed them into states. Meanwhile, both printing and learning were firmly in the control of the church during the early years of North American colonial development.

Those in Europe who supposed that the relatively low degree of literacy among workers and peasants would save them from "disobedi-

ence and heresy," as they put it, were astonished when the peasants
talked about "the rights of man" in the list of the grievances which
they drew up on the eve of the French Revolution. Long before that
time, the rapid growth of newspapers had guaranteed that such subversive ideas, generated from the growing revolt against misgovern-
ment, would be circulated and eventually trickle down to those who
were still unable to read.

As the historian Herbert J. Muller has pointed out, the bourgeois
played a key role in this development. Not revolutionary people by
nature, they nevertheless provided most of the writers and readers
who created public opinion. Pamphlets, newspapers, reading clubs,
and private societies were the instruments by which they spread the
new ideas about religious, intellectual, political, and economic freedom.

It was the bourgeois, too, who determined the establishment of the
media in America. These were the men of comfortable means who
settled on the banks of the James River in Virginia. In the Massachusetts Bay Colony, the first settlers included an unusually high percentage of university-trained men, although William Brewster was the
only man among the earlier Plymouth settlers who had gone to college, and he had never graduated. But in the first decade after Governor John Winthrop led the pioneers ashore, nearly a hundred of the
25,000 settlers who followed were Oxford and Cambridge graduates,
fifty had advanced degrees, and six had been appointed fellows.
These were the intellectual elite, who determined what would be
done with printing.

They were not imbued with the idea of democracy. Winthrop
called democracy "the meanest and worst of all forms of government." At the beginning, it was made clear by these refugees from
Old World tyranny and oppression that the new freedom they were
establishing was meant only for themselves, and opposition from
those who dissented would not be tolerated. In the case of religious
freedom, this kind of authoritarianism did not last long. Dissent was
in the bones of these men, and Roger Williams' insistence on full freedom of conscience, not mere toleration, was only the first step in a
process of revolt that led to widespread religious freedom in the colonies.

Not so in the case of the media. The colonial political leaders drew
on the experience of religion and concluded that authority and loyalty were best guaranteed by control of the printing press, and they
controlled it rigidly for a long period of time. The press had a dual

advantage for those in authority: it confirmed and propagandized at the same time.

It is hardly surprising, then, that the first item to emerge from a press in America was the Freeman's Oath, to which every resident over twenty who had been a householder for at least six months had to subscribe before he could become a citizen of the colony. The uncompromising voice of ecclesiastical and civil authority is heard in its language: "I do solemnly bind myself in the sight of God, when I shall be called upon to give my voice touching any such matter of this State, in which freemen are to deal, I will give my vote and suffrage as I shall judge in mine own conscience may best conduce and tend to the public weal of that body, without respect of persons, or favor of any man."

No one saw any incongruity in the use of words like "freemen" and "judge in mine own conscience" in a document prescribing the conditions for citizenship. It was only the first of a long line of similar documents based on the ancient but erroneous belief that loyalty and allegiance can be compelled by the swearing of oaths. The judiciary knew better. It coupled the giving of evidence under oath with severe penalties for lying.

Similarly, the early colonial authorities learned not to put all their trust in the Freeman's Oath. They ensured the loyalty of printers first by forbidding anyone to own a press or publish anything on it without a license, and then by regulating the flow of ecclesiastical and governmental job printing, on which the printer's income was nearly completely dependent, so that only the loyal got the work.

As a consequence, the establishment of printing in America, and the resulting rise of the media, was slow and sometimes painful. The beginnings are still a matter of controversy, but the facts, briefly, appear to be these:

In the early summer of 1638, the Reverend Jose Glover sailed out of London, bound for Boston, on the ship *John*, together with a company of fellow Puritans in flight from Archbishop Laud's attempt to purge the Anglican faith of all Nonconformist elements. In the hold was a printing press Glover had bought for twenty pounds, paper worth another forty pounds, and a font of type. In the company was a locksmith, Stephen Day (sometimes Daye), who was not a printer but a man ambitious to establish an iron foundry in the New World.

Stephen Day was long regarded as the man who operated the first press, but it appears possible that a printer, name unknown, was on board and died on the way over, not before teaching his craft to

Day's eighteen-year-old son Matthew, and his brother, Stephen, Jr. The Reverend Glover also died en route. and soon after the ship docked in Boston in mid-September 1638, his widow married the first president of Harvard, John Dunster, who set up the press as an adjunct of the new college in Cambridge, with the Days in charge.

This was the celebrated Cambridge Press, which established book publishing in America, the first of the media to come into existence. Its production under the Days and their successors, primarily the numerous Green family, was notable for many things, but chiefly for the first book to be printed in America, after the press had turned out the Oath and an almanac. It was the *Whole Book of Psalmes,* better known as the *Bay Psalm Book,* which appeared in 1640, and remains the prime bibliographical treasure in America today.

Glover originally intended the press to be a fountainhead for Puritan tracts, but the long struggle ended in England with the deposing of Archbishop Laud and the outbreak of civil war, so that the Puritans were relieved temporarily from persecution and censorship, and no longer needed a new power center in the Massachusetts Bay Colony. As a result, Harvard became a provincial college instead of a Puritan propaganda factory, and the press was turned to local uses, supplying the needs of the college and the community. It was under the college's general supervision until 1662, when the General Court (as the legislature was called) set up a licensing board to run it.

Before the Cambridge Press came to an end in 1692, it turned out more than two hundred books, pamphlets, and broadsides. Its importance lies not so much in what it printed, although the *Bay Psalm Book* had its particular significance, but in the fact that it existed at all, and so soon. Canada did not have a press until 1751, and the press in Cambridge was functioning before printing was practiced in many of the major cities of England and Scotland. If we measure by the number of imprints, rather than by quality, Boston was the second publishing center of the British empire by 1700.

Nevertheless, as the first of the media in America, book publishing was slow to rise as an industry. What was produced accurately reflected the character of the society. More than a third of the output was theology, a fifth of it was literature, and a little less than a half is categorized as social science, meaning collections of laws, proceedings of the assembly or government proclamations, along with a scattering of essays and treatises. Sermons comprised most of the theology. together with pamphlets and a few books of theological doctrine.

Most of these early books were paperbacks, for the practical reason that paperbacks were cheaper, as they are today. Some of them anticipated modern paperbacks in their use of the "skyline," the phrase or sentence on a cover which summarizes the content, and in effect is a selling message. "The happiness and pleasure of unity in the Christian societies considered," reads the skyline above the title on a Boston sermon.

For a century or more, the sermon publishing business was dominated by that "great Mather copy-factory," as the critic and historian John T. Winterich once called the prolific Mather family, the most notable of whom were Richard, Moses, Increase, and Cotton. The Mathers produced no less than 621 published works; Increase and Cotton between them accounted for 546 of these. Cotton, writing in seven languages, alone produced 444. Many were translated into Indian tongues.

Little creative literature appeared on the early publishing lists during the first fifty years of the colonies, and there was a similar and simultaneous lack in post-Elizabethan England. In America, the reason was a simple one. The authorities who controlled the press used it as a civil and ecclesiastical tool, and were not interested in employing it to promote *belles lettres*. Those few colonists who were concerned with literature sent their work to London to be published.

Colonial America, however, was not devoid of literary culture. It flourished in the private libraries of those affluent citizens who were able to import a wide variety of books through the local booksellers. An intellectual like Cotton Mather had a library of more than three thousand volumes, one of the largest in the world.

The Mathers published their own work because they were motivated by the powerful urge to proselytize. Other intellectuals disdained to see their own efforts in print, and in fact looked down on printing and publishing as a grubby business, on a par with the theater and even lower in social status. To preserve dignity, these people had their literary manuscripts copied and circulated among their friends, if they were not sent to London. Oddly enough, then, anti-intellectualism where the media were concerned did not originate in the lower classes in America, but among the upper-level intellectuals.

This reluctance to support local industry was not the greatest handicap to the rise of book publishing, however. Government control was the real deterrent. The Massachusetts General Court was so afraid of "the general diffusion of printing" that it gave the Cambridge Press a half century of monopoly before it began to license other printers. There was an attempt to establish a press in Pennsylvania near the end of the seventeenth century, but the authorities quickly ended it. No printing was permitted in Virginia, of any kind, until 1730.

Only the rise of an intellectual community among the better-educated university men of the Massachusetts Bay Colony, who followed after the farmers of early Plymouth, made the continued growth of book publishing possible. Poetry, history, and biography in time began to appear on lists which once included only theology, schoolbooks, official publications, Harvard theses, almanacs, and proselytizing religious books in the Algonquin language.

As the output of the Cambridge Press began to broaden in the hands of the Day family's successors, notably Samuel Green and Marmaduke Johnson, the authorities were increasingly anxious about what it was printing. Attempts were made by the General Court to restrict what little liberty the press enjoyed. In the legislature's law of 1665, establishing anew a board of licensers, who were really censors, there was a clause forbidding any printing press in a Massachusetts town except Cambridge. Johnson himself was censured in 1668 for publishing an innocuous fictionalized book of travel, not for what was in it but because he had published it without permission. In the same year, the General Court forbade the press to print a translation of Thomas à Kempis' *Imitation of Christ* unless it were properly expurgated of its papal doctrines. The licensing board refused to carry out this order, and the controversy seems to have been a clash between rural legislators and the college community as well as a conflict over the principle of censorship.

When Samuel Green retired from the Cambridge Press in 1692, leaving his son Bartholomew to move the press and types into Boston and set up for himself, he brought to a temporary end the unique and hardly admirable distinction Cambridge enjoyed as the only town in the English colonies to have a printing press.

Beyond that testimony to civil and religious restraint elsewhere, however, the press had a profound importance. As Samuel Eliot Morison, perhaps this century's most noted American historian, has said of it, "Almost every printer and publisher in New England and many of the great houses of New York can trace their ancestry to the little college printery operated by the Days and the Greens. . . ."

With the moving of the press from Cambridge to Boston, the prospects for independent printing improved because, for the first time, publishing began to move away from religious control. At the same time, a new generation of printers and booksellers was beginning to develop in Boston, which would soon make it the media capital of the colonies. By the end of the seventeenth century, in fact, book publishing in America had begun to forecast what it would become.

It was in the hands of printers, who were sometimes publishers themselves, and at various times practiced their trade on behalf of others, usually booksellers, who again might or might not be publishers as well. Copyright was unknown in America, and censorship was rigid. But the evidence of things to come was in the variety of work emerging from these presses. Most of the categories of modern publishing were in existence, and the growing population guaranteed that an even wider variety of publication would soon be demanded. But the technology of bookmaking was advancing scarcely at all, and the products of the press were not distinguished for their craftsmanship or beauty.

At the end of the seventeenth century, book publishing was still a century away from the rise of the modern industry; only the groundwork existed. What was needed primarily was freedom from restrictions of every kind so that books could become the free forum in an open society they were obviously destined to be.

It would be wrong, however, to view the colonial printer as the protagonist in a constant struggle between freedom and tyranny. It is easy to look at it that way now, with the advantage of contemporary hindsight, and to fall prey to the popular mythology that freedom was an early and indigenous preoccupation of the American colonists, leading to the Glorious Revolution. Unfortunately for the romanticists of history, that was not the case.

The instances of conflict already cited merely illustrate the nature of the controls. Most of the early printers did not look at them as a form of tyranny. They were loyal citizens who would not have thought of printing without a license, or of offending the authorities in any other way. For the most part, they were faithful and loyal subjects of the King. Defiance and rebellion came later.

The Crown itself, in fact, rarely intervened directly with printers in what they printed. Local government exerted the controls, especially the royal governors, who represented the Crown and conducted its affairs in constant fear of losing their positions of power.

Control from London rested in the seventeenth century on the Parliamentary Press Restriction Act, forbidding the publishing of anything to which the printer's name and the place of publication had not been signed. Among those in England who most vociferously opposed this act and disobeyed it whenever they dared were the Quakers, yet it was these same Quakers who in 1693 charged the first

Philadelphia printer, Andrew Bradford, with violating that act in printing pamphlets concerning a religious controversy. When they could not prove the charge, the Quaker authorities put Bradford in jail anyway, and paradoxically, it took the governor to release both him and his impounded equipment, after which he moved to New York.

In Massachusetts, the General Court's order of 1662 forbidding any printing except by license was a direct result of fear that the King might be displeased by something printed. His displeasure would most certainly be incurred by anything which intimated popular sovereignty, and so the Massachusetts authorities, in order to preserve their own power, deliberately stifled the only source that might threaten it. To this motivation can be added the fears of religious dissent which led at least partially to the suppression of the *Imitation of Christ*, and fear of deviation from established morality, which resulted in suppressing the *Isle of Pines*. In the latter case the complaint was not so much against anything contained in the book, but against Marmaduke Johnson, for publishing it without permission. As late as 1723, church and state joined in seizing and burning Thomas Maule's *Truth Held Forth*, a book regarded as both heresy and unauthorized for publication.

Some printers felt so confined by the heavy hand of Massachusetts authority that they went elsewhere in the hope of finding a better climate. Others were content to stay and share in the well-being of this most prosperous of the colonies. Only a relative few chafed against the ruthless and complete suppression of press freedom which prevailed well into the eighteenth century.

The most celebrated among those who offended the authorities is Benjamin Harris, who is credited with printing the first newspaper in the colonies. Harris was a complicated man, better remembered for his enterprise than for his bigotries. He began his career as a printer in Bell Alley, London, where he published his first book, an antipapist tract, in 1673. For a time he prospered as a book publisher, attacking the Catholics and Quakers, and as the proprietor of a Whig newspaper, ultimately suppressed in 1681. He joined Titus Oates in "exposing" that imaginary conspiracy known as the Popish Plot, an invention of the Whigs designed to convince citizens that the Catholics meant to kill all the Protestants in London and burn the city. For publishing a seditious pamphlet in 1679, Harris was sentenced to stand in the pillory and fined five hundred pounds, which he could not pay, and so was sent to King's Bench Prison. Illegally discharged with forged papers, Harris resumed his Pope-baiting with a coffee-house, where he sold books, patent medicines, and playing cards with antipapist propaganda on their backs. But when 5000 copies of *English Liberties*, a book he had published, were seized by the authorities, he told his friend John Dutton that England had become an "uneasie ... Place for honest men," and fled to Massachusetts, where his Anabaptist faith would be more welcome.

Not his notions of freedom, however. Arriving in Boston in 1686 with his son Vavasour and a stock of books, he set up a bookstore on the south corner of State and Washington Streets, brashly offering himself as competitor to seven other booksellers already established in the neighborhood. From this location, described in his imprint as "by the Town Pump near the Change," he published his first book in 1687, an almanac compiled by John Tulley. Samuel Green printed it.

Harris attempted to re-create in Boston some of the life he had left behind in London. In 1689, he expanded his bookshop by adding a counter from which he sold coffee, tea, and chocolate, and with the addition of a few tables, established what he called the London Coffee House, a resort so respectable that even ladies attended it to talk, sip the temperance drinks, and possibly buy books.

No doubt encouraged by this lively and ostensibly free atmosphere, a contrast to his self-invited oppression in London, Harris on September 25, 1690, brought out the first newspaper in America, which he called *Publick Occurrences both Foreign and Domestick*. Like the first newspapers in London, it was essentially an extension of his Coffee House, full of the gossip and information he picked up there from those who frequented it. It had no more than appeared, however, before it was suppressed, after only one issue. The primary reason was the familiar one: Harris had neglected to get a license from the authorities. Perhaps he also believed, mistakenly, that the new comparative freedom of the press which had accompanied Protestant King William's accession to the throne extended to the colonies.

Beyond this basic mistake was the irritation of the authorities over two items in the paper. Significantly, they had to do with the government's foreign and domestic policies. One concerned the mistreatment of prisoners taken captive by the Mohawk Indians during the sanguinary border warfare between the colonies and Canada. No one doubted this story unless it was Harris himself, who noted, "'Tis possible, we have not so exactly related the Circumstances of this business, but this Account, is as near exactness, as any that could be had, in the midst of many various reports about it." Nevertheless, the recital of atrocities would certainly displease the Indians who heard about it, and whom the authorities were, for the moment, trying to enlist on their side against the French. Harris referred to them as "miserable Salvages [an old word for savages]."

The other item was more embarrassing, both politically and in terms of conventional morals. "France," Harris reported, meaning the King, "is in much trouble (and fear) not only with us but also with his Son, who has revolted against him lately, and has great reason if reports be true, that the Father used to lie with the Sons Wife."

In themselves, these items would not have been seriously damaging except that everyone was aware that nothing could be published in the colony without a license, and since the public had no way of knowing that Harris had not taken the trouble to get one, it would have to be assumed that these stories were printed with the government's knowledge and consent. People reading *Publick Occurrences* in England, France. or elsewhere, consequently, would have reason to believe that the authorities had countenanced the insulting of valuable Indian allies and the French monarch in a single issue. No wonder it was suppressed, and all but a few copies destroyed.

Harris made no further attempt at newspaper publishing, but even so his career in the colony was remarkable. He had come to Boston as a stranger and he left it eight years later, to return to England, as the colony's leading printer, bookseller, and coffeehouse proprietor, as well as the compiler and publisher of the most successful book of the century in America. That was the *New-England Primer*, issued in the same year as his newspaper fiasco, and one of the truly remarkable volumes in publishing history. Sometimes called "The Little Bible of New England," this teaching tool for the secular alphabet and religious morality continued to sell for nearly two centuries and profoundly influenced the minds of generations of Americans. It laid the foundations for children's literature in America. Millions learned to read from it, and at the same time were indoctrinated by such familiar rhymes as "In Adam's fall / we sinned all." From later editions they learned to say, "Now I lay me down to sleep. . . ."

The *Primer* was Harris' lasting contribution to the media in America, far more than his abortive attempt to establish a newspaper, which won him a permanent place in the history of American journalism. But the lesson of the paper's demise was not lost on his contemporaries. Obviously, the publication of news had to have official sanction, and while there was an obvious necessity to disseminate information as the colony grew and word of mouth no longer sufficed, no one appeared anxious to·publish an approved gazette. It had taken nearly seventy years of colonizing to produce Harris' paper, and it took fourteen more before someone dared try again.

It required even longer for magazines, the third member of the print media triumvirate, to establish themselves. They were the last to appear, a full century after the publication of the *Bay Psalm Book*, and fifty-one years after the brief appearance of *Publick Occurrences*.

There were good reasons for the delay. The other media had risen out of necessity, but there was no immediate need for magazine reading, which was essentially a leisure-time occupation of the upper classes. Books had come first because there was a need for printed laws and proclamations, and for volumes that would advance both the religious and political interests of the colonies' founders. Newspapers were the response to a population grown too large for information to be conveyed by word of mouth. Magazines had to wait until the literary and practical arts in America had developed enough to create an audience sufficiently large to justify their publication.

That moment came specifically in 1741. Whether the idea for the first magazine originated in the fertile mind of America's universal genius, Benjamin Franklin, or in the lesser brain of Andrew Bradford, Philadelphia's first printer, is a matter of conjecture. We know that Franklin was planning his periodical, *The General Magazine, and Historical Chronicle, for All the British Plantations in America,* in 1740, but it did not appear until January 1741. Three days before its publication, Bradford issued his *The American Magazine, or a Monthly View of the Political State of the British Colonies.*

These two rivals, Franklin and Bradford, had been contesting virtually every field of publication. They had been rivals in newspaper publishing, rivals in getting books for their printing establishments to publish, and rivals for the postmastership of Philadelphia. In the latter case, Franklin had been appointed to the job when Bradford was fired from it. The two men can hardly be compared as individuals, however; printing and publishing were only two of Franklin's many interests.

Presumably both examined the same statistics before they launched their publications. Looking about them, they saw a Philadelphia with a population of 13,000 people, and a Pennsylvania colony with more than 100,000. Only a relatively small number of these people could be expected to become magazine readers. They would have to be educated and cultured men—ministers, lawyers, historians, educators, doctors. The publishers and editors of magazines would also have to be drawn from their ranks—people like Isaiah Thomas, Thomas Paine, Noah Webster, and Mathew Carey, coming on after Franklin and Bradford had paved the way. In a sense, then, magazines in the eighteenth century were intellectual forums where men of letters and learning could talk to each other.

In these circumstances, it is easy to see why magazines were incomparably better purveyors of knowledge and entertainment than the colonial newspapers. At the same time, they were far less indigenous, heavily dependent as they were on their British counterparts. The first ones, in fact, were put together largely with scissors and paste-pot, and the help of the mail from London. While the editors had no illusions about what they were doing, they were anything but apologetic about it. They meant to put America's best foot forward by serving the interests of cultivated men and providing a broad spectrum of subjects for them; consequently they considered their work an important element in advancing the state of culture in America. Many thought of their magazines as extensions of books, and hoped that readers would bind the issues and add them to their private libraries.

Magazines had to struggle hard to put down roots. In the eighteenth century, subscribers never exceeded 1600 for any one magazine, and the average was closer to 500. It was 1780, or later, before the total number of copies printed at any one time exceeded 2500. Mechanical limitations were severe. Paper and ink had to be imported, and the handpresses, relatively unchanged since the fifteenth century, were painfully slow to operate. They printed one page at a time, after which the type had to be redistributed. Newspapers and book publishing shared these limitations, of course, but their audiences were quickly larger and their survival chances were much better. With so few subscribers and little advertising, magazines made a negligible economic dent in the publishing industry.

Bradford's magazine lasted for only three issues, while Franklin's, although it was much better and had the inestimable advantage of its publisher's own writing and editing, ran for only six issues, a total of 426 pages, of which a little less than 10 per cent was original material. Franklin lost money on it, and thought so little of it he did not even mention it in his *Autobiography*. The fact of the matter was that it had little to offer beyond what the weekly newspapers were already carrying.

Most of the first magazines were short-lived. The greater number disappeared after a year or less, and only two lasted as long as eight years in the period before 1800. But the printers, editors, and publishers persisted in the face of every difficulty, driven on partly by national pride, partly by the intellectual's urge to preserve and advance culture, and no doubt occasionally by the demands of their own egos.

The realization of their hopes and ambitions did not come until the nineteenth century, when magazines became almost overnight, so it seemed, one of the most important factors in American social and cultural life, and soon a vital political influence as well. They were still struggling at the end of the eighteenth century, afflicted by an alarming mortality, still heavily imitative of English models, but gradually developing the special function that would make them a prime element among the print media.

Meanwhile, book publishing and newspapers, and particularly the newspapers, dominated the eighteenth-century stage in the struggle for independence and its aftermath as the new nation emerged.

2

The Development
of Freedom

IT WAS LOGICAL that the Boston post office should begin again where
Ben Harris had left off in the publishing of a newspaper. John Campbell, the sober Scot who functioned as postmaster at the turn of the
century, was a man who served at a pivotal point in the city. The post
office was the news center, as it would be in American small towns
from that day to this, a place where news and gossip were traded
freely. Campbell also possessed an instant means of distribution in
the postboys who carried the mail.

The civil authorities considered a postmaster a safe choice as publisher, since he owed his job to them and consequently was unlikely
to print anything that might offend. In Campbell's case there was
little danger. He was a conservative bureaucrat who was pleased to
print in large type under the title of his Boston *News-Letter*, when it
first appeared on April 24, 1704, "Published by Authority." In the
"ears," those boxes on each side of the title, were the insignia of his
distribution methods. The one on the left depicted a sailing ship, signifying that most of the news, or at least the news not already known
to the *News-Letter*'s readers, came from abroad. It was already four
months old by the time it got to Boston. In the other ear was the
figure of a galloping postboy, soon a familiar symbol on the front
pages of colonial newspapers.

Campbell had no trouble with the authorities, as might be
expected, but his paper was soon in other difficulties. The local news,
since it had been duly approved, was dull and most of it had been

conveyed by word of mouth before it appeared. As for the news from abroad, a certain insularity had developed in the colonies. Letters from home kept the colonists apprised of what was happening to friends and relatives left behind, and they had lost some of their interest in the larger affairs of England and the Continent. At home, in the world outside Boston, no large events were occurring in the continuing struggle with the Canadians and their Indian allies, and George Washington had not yet led his Virginia militia into the bush skirmish that would touch off the American phase of the Seven Years' War, or the French and Indian War, as later generations of Americans were taught to call it.

As a publisher, Campbell conducted his newspaper business with one hand, and with the other he ran the affairs of the post office and his other private interests. As these interests prospered, the *News-Letter* continued to be unprofitable; it had few readers and fewer advertisers. Nevertheless, when Campbell lost the postmastership in 1718, he refused to turn over his newspaper, along with the job, to his successor, William Brooker. He ran the paper in an even more desultory way until 1722, when he sold it to his printer, Bartholomew Green, whose father had been the proprietor of the Cambridge Press.

Brooker was so angry with Campbell for not relinquishing the *News-Letter* that he started his own paper, the Boston *Gazette*, which proved to be fully as dull as its rival. He gave the printing contract to a young Bostonian, James Franklin, but it was a brief arrangement because Brooker lost the postmastership in less than a year. He was succeeded by Philip Musgrave, who inherited the paper and transferred the printing contract to a friend. Now it was Franklin's turn to be angry. He immediately founded his own newspaper, the *New-England Courant*, on August 7, 1721, and suddenly there were three newspapers in Boston and the newspaper business in America had begun.

The *New-England Courant* was the first American newspaper worthy of the name, and for good reason. It was in the hands of James Franklin, an excellent printer, and in James's sixteen-year-old apprentice, his brother Ben, the press had acquired its first real writer. Some of his friends had tried to talk James out of starting the paper, Ben recalled later, deeming it "not likely to succeed." James persisted, however, and his brother, "after having worked in composing the types and printing off the sheets," was "employed to carry the papers through the streets to the customers."

As it happened, the newspaper saved James's struggling business, which had been trying to compete with several other printers in a community of no more than 12,000 people, where there was not enough job printing to go around. Since Ben had come to him as an apprentice at the age of twelve in 1718, the brothers had been compelled to turn out all kinds of odd jobs, including Ben's ballads, the issuance of pamphlets, and even printed linens, calicos, and silks.

The *Courant* arrived on the scene at a critical moment in the colony's history. For the first time, there was serious dissent against ruling authority. It was not yet political. The dissenters were finding the iron rule of the Mathers, allied with the civil administrators, stifling to religious freedom. Congregationalism had been the most powerful force in the colony from the beginning, but now there were enough Episcopalians, Deists, Baptists, and others to form a core of resistance. Two of these dissenters helped Franklin launch his paper. They were John Checkley, a bookseller and apothecary who had already been in trouble with the authorities, and William Douglass, a Scottish doctor, whose medical degree (earned in Edinburgh, Leyden, and Paris) had been the only one in America when he arrived in Boston.

Checkley and Douglass had seen how valuable the press could be as a propaganda medium. Dull as the *News-Letter* and *Gazette* had been, they were obviously effective as an arm of government. Presumably the dissenters had also observed that the printer could be a useful fellow in a variety of ways. Operating within a pattern that would persist for decades, he was a publisher whose output included books, pamphlets, broadsides, job printing, and now newspapers. In a short time, as we have seen, magazines would be added to this list.

All these activities attracted a broad variety of people to print shops, from intellectuals anxious to circulate their ideas in some form, to businessmen engaged in advertising. Other citizens came, too, because the front of the shop shared display space among not only books and newspapers, but candy, violin strings, and many of the sundries that would soon be the stock of a general store, and later of that great American institution, the drugstore. The press usually occupied its own space at the rear of the shop. This was the pattern of the colonial print shop, which was repeated in town after town as the presses moved westward to the Pacific during the eighteenth and nineteenth centuries.

Obviously, the products of such a shop could be no better than the talents and character of the man who operated the press; consequently some were typographically admirable, printed on excellent paper, while others were merely competent. The newspapers which came off these presses, since they were written primarily by the printers themselves, or by the postmasters, before Franklin arrived, were badly done, quite innocent of syntax and grammar.

As the media began to develop, the printer became more and more the operating craftsman, while the content of what he printed was more and more the province of editors and writers. The editors of the newspapers, as the eighteenth century advanced, were likely to be young intellectuals with a talent for writing, who gathered around themselves men of their own stripe. As young men, they were quite naturally in revolt against the establishment. First they defied the local civic and religious authorities, and later the Crown itself. When there was no editor as the focal point, the young dissenters simply used the printer as the tool of their dissent.

In the case of the *Courant*, it was Checkley, Dr. Douglass, and their friends using the paper against the Mathers, but ironically, the issue on which they chose to oppose their powerful enemy in the first number of the paper was one of the few on which the Mathers happened to be indisputably right. The *Courant* appeared for the first time in 1721 on an August day in the middle of a steaming summer during which smallpox had been rampant. The authorities had been fighting it with an inoculation Cotton Mather had heard about from one of his slaves, who had known of it in Africa. Following this lead, Mather had discovered in a London newspaper that the inoculation was being practiced in Constantinople, and obtaining some of the serum, the liquid from a smallpox pustule, he had persuaded a Boston doctor, Zabdiel Boylston, to inoculate two of his slaves and his six-year-old-son—seventy-five years before Edward Jenner scratched with his first inoculating needle in London. Dr. Boylston's inoculations were so successful that he had to set up a clinic, and became the hero of the hour.

Instead of attacking the substance of the inoculation, Dr. Douglass, in the *Courant*, opposed the "doubtful and dangerous practice" of inoculation itself. He quickly acquired the support of doctors, selectmen, and other citizens, who used the *Courant* as a club to beat Dr. Boylston and Mather, whose lives were threatened during the controversy.

James Franklin tried to stay a little above the struggle and assert a printer's impartiality. When the Mathers struck back through the pen of Increase's grandson, Thomas Walter, he printed Walter's broadside, *The Little-Compton Scourge; or, The Anti-Courant*. The language of *Courant* and *Anti-Courant* set the tone for the next hundred years or more of American journalism. Walter asserted that the *Courant* appealed only to "men of passion and resentment." Checkley, in the *Courant*'s third issue, called Walter an "obscene and fuddling Merry-Andrew," a drunkard and a debauchee.

It is hardly surprising that Cotton Mather found the *Courant* intolerable. He dubbed its writers the Hell-Fire Club, and characterized them in terms that would make the language of latter-day authoritarians seem unimaginative. He declared passionately that "the practice of supporting and publishing every week a libel on purpose to lessen and blacken and burlesque the virtuous and principal ministers of religion in a country, and render the services of their ministry despicable, even detestable, to the people, is a wickedness that was never known before in any country, Christian, Turkish, or Pagan, on the face of the earth."

As the smallpox died down, so did the passions on both sides. The *Courant*'s scant space—it was only a single sheet, printed on both sides—was devoted to shipping reports, snippets of information from neighboring towns, letters from Europe, and the material that was its real substance—letters to the editor from the Boston wits, poking Addisonian fun at the city's morals and manners, although being circumspect in what they said about the authorities.

These letters were signed with pseudonyms in the fashion of the day, conceits like "Timothy Turnstone," "Tom Penshallow," "Ichabod Henroost," "Abigail Afterw\`.t.' One that appeared on April 2, 1722, was the first authentic prose that can be attributed to Ben Franklin. He signed himself "Silence Dogood," and promised to provide the paper's readers once every fortnight "with a short Epistle, which I presume will add somewhat to their entertainment." Ben suspected correctly that his brother "would object to printing anything of mine in his paper if he knew it to be mine"; consequently he slid his contributions under the shop door anonymously.

It was a measure of how far press freedom had come since Harris' day that the authorities made no immediate attempt to stop it. They had reason enough, but the colony was larger now, the paper enjoyed some popular support, and the magistrates felt they had to be wary. Nevertheless, they waited only until they had a good enough reason to suppress it. They believed they had it with the publication of a fictitious letter from Newport which satirized what the young Boston intellectuals considered the establishment's bureaucratic slowness in dealing with public problems. The letter reported pirates off the coast, and added that the government was fitting a ship to go out after them, "to be commanded by Captain Peter Papillon, and 'tis thought he will sail some time this month, wind and weather permitting."

This, at least, was contemptuous, the Council thought, and it had James Franklin arrested and thrown into jail. He apologized within a week, and got out in a month when the *Courant's* erstwhile enemy, Dr. Boylston, certified that his health had been impaired in prison. While James was incarcerated, Ben had operated the shop and gained considerable recognition with his Dogood papers, which were written in the style that would soon make him one of the most admired colonial writers.

James was liberated but unrepentant. He began to attack the magistrates and the religious authorities again. In January 1723 he went too far once more. "There are many persons who seem to be more than ordinary religious," he wrote, "but yet are on several accounts worse, by far, than those who pretend to no religion at all." The Council had no doubt who the "many persons" were meant to be, and it reverted to the harsh kind of control that had always been exercised with dissenters. James was forbidden not only to publish the *Courant*, but "any other pamphlet or paper of the like nature, except it first be supervised by the Secretary of this Province."

The *Courant's* influential friends rallied around. At their suggestion, James made his brother publisher, giving him a release from his indenture for the purpose, so that if the authorities charged that the apprentice was merely acting for the printer, Ben would have a duly executed paper to show them. Privately, however, James insisted that his brother sign new indentures, although there is no record that he did.

In Ben's hands, the paper took on a different tone. "The present undertaking . . . is designed purely for the diversion and merriment of the reader," he assured his readers blandly. He had the overwhelming talent to fulfill that promise, and at the same time to keep on prodding the authorities so deftly that they scarcely knew they were being prodded. At seventeen he was, as Carl Van Doren has put it, "the best mind in Boston and . . . the best apprentice in the world." His excellence, at once made plain in his editing and in the Silence Dogood papers, earned him extravagant praise, and it proved too much for a jealous older brother. There were quarrels, the situation became intolerable, and, as Ben wrote later, "I took upon me to assert my freedom." He left secretly at night aboard a sloop bound for New York and Philadelphia, where he would soon make further contributions to media history.

What had happened to the *Courant* was not lost on dissidents there and in other parts of the colonies. James Franklin had shown how a printer could be used to attack authority, if he had the support of determined and able men. Should he be thrown in jail, it was clear, the paper need not die: its friends could guarantee its continued existence simply by transferring it to other hands. The friends, by preserving a discreet anonymity, were not likely to go to jail. The printer took the risk. He could be persuaded to take it either by his need for money, the most probable cause, or through the courage of his own convictions.

This idea was now to be tested again in New York City, where the inhabitants suffered under a rule far more oppressive than anything the intellectual Mathers might have conceived. Governor William Cosby was perhaps the worst of the colonial administrators the Crown had sent to America. Lazy, lecherous, and dissolute, he ruled by whim through his sycophants and favored cronies. He had antagonized the middle-class merchants with excessive taxes, and the respectable lower classes (who, one might add, were more respectable in the appearance than the act) were offended by the public display the governor made of his debauchery. It was not so much the immorality, but the fact that they were financing it.

Like so many arrogant rulers, past and present, Cosby went a step too far by deposing one of the colony's best-loved elder statesmen, Chief Justice Lewis Morris, and then appointing to succeed him young James DeLancey, the son of Oliver DeLancey, a rich merchant who was one of Cosby's friends. This appointment of a young man only recently returned from his training at Temple Bar, London, to replace a veteran jurist of high reputation affronted almost everyone.

Morris and his friends were outraged, but there was no legal recourse. The *New-England Courant* had shown them another way, however; they could take their case to the people through a printer. Unfortunately, the choice was not a wise one. William Bradford, rescued from the Quaker persecution in Philadelphia, had come to New York in 1693 as official printer, and in 1725 had started the city's first newspaper, a poorly printed two-page affair so official in character that its rival, the *Weekly Journal*, launched eight years later, was quite justified in describing it as filled with "dry, senseless Stuff, and fulsome panegyrics." Nothing could be expected from Bradford as a defender of Morris; his profitable business would be far too valuable for him to risk.

There remained John Peter Zenger, a poor printer who had arrived as an immigrant refugee from the Palatinate, then served a term as

Bradford's apprentice until he could set up for himself. He printed Morris' side of the story in a pamphlet following the Chief Justice's ouster, and the jurist's friends saw their opportunity. They helped him establish the *Weekly Journal* in November 1733.

Zenger has been so idealized in the annals of journalism that his real contribution to the historic case that bears his name has been obscured. He was an untalented writer and an indifferent printer, but he had fled from authoritarian rule in Europe and he had the courage to place his struggling business and possibly his life as well at the service of Morris and his friends. It was not an inconsiderable risk, to be a stalking-horse for determined men who meant to make an assault on a royal governor. James Franklin had used his friends as much as they had used him to poke dangerous fun at the rulers of Massachusetts, and while he faced jail and suppression for his actions, at least he had the knowledge that the clergy and magistrates of Boston were not monsters. No one could predict what a savage tyrant like Cosby might do.

At first Cosby did no more than conduct a countercampaign against the *Journal* through Bradford's *Gazette*, but it was an uneven contest. The *Gazette*'s heavy-handed vituperation, in the accepted style of the day, was no match for the satiric pens of Morris' friends, particularly the real editor of the *Journal*, an accomplished young lawyer named James Alexander, who drew on Cato's *Letters*, Swift's *Tale of a Tub*, and Addison's essays to score his points. Through the columns of the *Journal*, like a bright thread, ran the appeal to freedom from tyranny, the plea for representative government.

Cosby did not miss these implications and in time his patience, scant at best, ran out. He tried through DeLancey to get a grand jury indictment for libel against Zenger, but the jurors, ordinary citizens who hated Cosby, refused to hand it up. Frustrated, the governor instructed his handpicked Council to do the job, and it obediently issued a warrant on its own behalf which sent Zenger to jail. He was charged with criminal libel, much more serious than the civil variety since it involved imprisonment as well as a fine. (Since Zenger's day, it has been invoked only twice in New York City, the last time as recently as 1963.)

Once they had the printer in jail, Cosby and DeLancey persecuted him mercilessly. Reasonable bail was refused, and when his lawyers made a desperate effort to attack DeLancey's commission so that he would be prevented from sitting on the case, DeLancey disbarred them and appointed one of his friends to represent Zenger. This lawyer was not without conscience, however; he asked for a month's delay to prepare his case, a standard procedure DeLancey could not very well deny.

During that month, while the Morris faction plotted their course, the pending case became the talk of the colonies. Whatever the legal issues might be, even the most illiterate citizen could understand the morality of the situation: an unpopular, tyrannical governor opposed to a respectable judge with no ties to the ruling class, and a poor printer made the victim of their quarrel.

Zenger's disbarred lawyers interested Ben Franklin in the case, and probably it was Ben's persuasion that stirred his friend, Andrew Hamilton, the great liberal Philadelphia lawyer, then in his eighties, to the point of accepting one more battle for liberty. Hamilton rode to New York on horseback in the blazing summer heat of August 4, 1735, and sat quietly in the back of the room while the jury was being impaneled, and while John Chambers, the attorney appointed by DeLancey, entered a plea of "not guilty" to the charges. Then, with the sense of drama that marked his courtroom appearances, he rose and came to the bar, a striking figure with his white hair falling to his shoulders, his ancient body erect, and his eyes keen. DeLancey and his fellow justice, Frederick Philipse, who were hearing the case, had to greet him with respect, and could hardly deny his request to appear for the defense.

Turning his body so that he was addressing the jury as much as the justices, Hamilton began in his resonant actor's voice: "I cannot think it proper to deny the publication of a complaint which I think is the right of every free-born subject to make. Therefore I'll save Mr. Attorney the trouble of examining his witnesses to that point; and I do confess (for my client) that he both printed and published the two papers set forth in the information. I do hope in so doing he has committed no crime."

Those in the courtroom who were familiar with law turned to each other in astonishment. Under the statutes, the jury had only to decide whether the publications had actually been made by the defendant, yet Hamilton had opened his case by admitting it.

Puzzled but grateful, the attorney-general replied, "Then, if your honors please, since Mr. Hamilton has confessed the fact, I think our witnesses may be discharged; we have no further occasion for them." With publication admitted, he went on, there was nothing further for the jury to do but to bring in a verdict of guilty.

"Not so, neither, Mr. Attorney," Hamilton answered coolly. "There are two sides to that bargain. I hope it is not our bare printing or publishing a paper that will make it a libel. You will have something more to do before you make my client a libeler. For the words themselves must be libelous—that is, false, malicious, and seditious—or else we are not guilty."

On this point of law, Attorney-General Bradley and Hamilton stood before the bench and argued. The old lawyer cited the Magna Carta and the abolition of the Star Chamber. Bradley simply said that the law was the law. He was right, but Hamilton's superb courtroom manner had even the partisan justices momentarily hypnotized. It was only when he asserted that "the falsehood makes the scandal, and both the libel," and added he would "prove these very papers that are called libel to be true," that DeLancey interposed. Young and unqualified though he might be, he had been to Temple Bar and he knew something about English law.

"You cannot be admitted, Mr. Hamilton," he admonished, "to give the truth of a libel in evidence. The court is of the opinion you ought not to be permitted to prove the facts in the papers." He was correct, and he cited a long list of precedents to prove it. Hamilton listened patiently. He knew the citations by heart.

"Those are Star Chamber cases," he said, when DeLancey had finished, "and I was in hopes that practice had been dead with that court."

Confused and angered by this unexpected reply, DeLancey responded to it as a young man in his special circumstances might. "The court have delivered their opinion," he said coldly, "and we expect you will use us with good manners. You are not permitted to argue against this court."

It was the answer Hamilton had been waiting for. He knew he had no case in law, but he had provoked DeLancey into acting in the arbitrary way every man on the jury would recognize as Cosby's. Taking his cue, Hamilton then proceeded to give a magnificent, historic performance.

Bowing to the Chief Justice with a courtly "I thank you," he turned his back on both judges and addressed the jury in a ringing voice. "Then it is to you, gentlemen," he began, "that we must now appeal for witnesses to the truth of the facts we have offered, and are denied the liberty to prove. . . . I beg leave to lay it down as a standing rule in such cases that the suppressing of evidence ought always to be taken for the strongest evidence, and I hope it will have that weight with you."

DeLancey interrupted. Doggedly, he pointed out that the jury had no right under the law to do any more than decide whether Zenger had published the papers. It was the prerogative of the judges to decide whether they were libelous. Hamilton continued:

"A proper confidence in a court is commendable, but as the verdict (whatever it is) will be yours, you ought to refer no part of your duty to the discretion of other persons. If you should be of opinion that there is no falsehood in Mr. Zenger's papers, you will, nay (pardon me for the expression), you *ought* to say so; because you do not know whether others (I mean the court) may be of that opinion. It is your right to do so, and there is much depending upon your resolution, as well as upon your integrity."

The justices and every lawyer in the courtroom could see what Hamilton was doing. He was telling the jurymen to be freemen, to follow their consciences and assert the liberties guaranteed them by English law. His voice ringing in the tense courtroom, he confirmed those liberties for them in the words so often cited by press historians:

> Old and weak as I am, I should think it my duty, if required, to go to the utmost part of the land where my service could be of any use in assisting to quench the flame of persecutions upon informations, set on foot by the government to deprive a people of the right of remonstrating (and complaining too) of the arbitrary attempts of men in power. Men who injure and oppress the people under their administration provoke them to cry out and complain, and then make that very complaint the foundation for new oppressions and prosecutions. . . .
>
> The question before the court and you, gentlemen of the jury, is not of small nor private concern. It is not the cause of the poor printer, nor of New York alone, which you are now trying. No! It may in its consequences affect every freeman that lives under a British government on the main of America. It is the best cause. It is the cause of liberty, and I make no doubt but your upright conduct this day will not only entitle you to the love and esteem of your fellow citizens, but every man who prefers freedom to a life of slavery will bless and honor you as men who have baffled the attempt of tyranny, and by an impartial and incorrupt verdict have laid a noble foundation for securing to ourselves, our posterity and our neighbors that to which nature and the laws of our country have given us a right—the liberty—both of exposing and opposing arbitrary power (in these parts of the world, at least) by speaking and writing—truth.

DeLancey must have realized that he was defeated, after this moving appeal to the passions and prejudices of the jury, but he clung to what he knew. He gave what amounted to a directed verdict, insisting again that the jury could not go beyond deciding the fact of publication, which had already been admitted, leaving the question of libel to the justices. But the jury was transformed. In the afterglow of Hamilton's words, they saw themselves as freemen upholding the ancient rights of Magna Carta, and they brought in a unanimous verdict of not guilty.

The Chief Justice did not then do what he had the power to do. He could have set aside the verdict as being in direct contradiction to the law, as it was. He could even have cited Hamilton for contempt. That he did none of these things indicated that the British government in America, in spite of the excesses of men like Cosby, was inclined to move cautiously in its relations with the colonists at this point. It was plain to DeLancey that the verdict was not simply the result of Hamilton's histrionics; these had only been the key which unlocked the expression of a deep and intense popular feeling. He could see it in the faces of the inspired jurymen, and in the electric atmosphere of the courtroom, which erupted in riotous cheering after the verdict.

Hamilton's victory was no more than a moral one, however. The principle he argued—the jury's right to determine both law and fact—was not recognized either in England or America until more than a half century later. The verdict of the Zenger jury, as DeLancey maintained, was contrary to the law. In those days, the recognized principle was, "The greater the truth, the greater the libel."

Nor did the verdict have any immediate effect on the law. Truth as a defense was not recognized generally in America until 1804, when another Hamilton, the more famous Alexander, argued and lost a libel case which nevertheless stirred the lawmakers to belated reform.

Zenger might well have been rearrested after his trial, but Cosby too was cautious, primarily because Morris had gone to England to argue his case against the governor personally with the Crown. While Cosby was awaiting the result, he fell ill that winter and died the following March. Zenger published a verbatim account of the trial, which made him momentarily famous in the colonies and got him appointments as public printer in both New Jersey and New York, but he was not competent enough to take advantage of the opportunities that came to him, and died poor in 1746. Ironically, he was the one who achieved lasting recognition, while Andrew Hamilton, the real hero of the case, is known today only to scholars and students of American history.

If the trial established no legal precedents, it had a powerful effect on other juries, which were now emboldened to uphold critics of government, no matter what the law might be. This was particularly important in the turbulent decades before the Revolution, when partisan newspapers exhibited little, if any, regard for the truth in their propagandistic zeal. The Zenger trial also encouraged citizens to believe that colonial laws, as laid down and interpreted by the governors and their councils, were not immutable and could be changed by popular demand. In all this, the newspaper had emerged as the vehicle of popular revolt.

By contrast, the slowly developing magazines were the pleasure of the upper class, and if they reflected anything besides the imported interests of the British aristocracy, they provided a religious platform. Boston magazines, at the cultural hub of the colonies, exemplified both these characteristics. Bostonians felt themselves bound to the mother country by strong traditional and cultural ties; consequently they welcomed *The American Magazine and Historical Chronicle; for All the British Plantations*, which was a kind of *Reader's Digest* of several British magazines, with articles from the leading English periodicals abridged to provide a cross section of what was being talked about in London and Edinburgh.

Another Boston magazine, *The Christian History*, took advantage, when it appeared in March 1743, of the "Great Awakening," the revivalist movement that swept New England that year, battering at the doors of the conservative, established church. Several earnest and eloquent ministers contributed to this first religious magazine in the colonies, but it waned with the "Awakening" itself, and died after two years.

In New York, magazines were slow to catch on, although a few were started, because more than half its population was Dutch, with no interest in the English literary tradition, and many of the remainder were blacks who could not read, and whose white masters did not encourage them to learn. Around the busy little city itself, nestling at the end of Manhattan Island, stretched the manors of the Dutch patroons. Many of them were highly cultured men, but they had no particular interest in magazines, either British or American.

After Franklin abandoned his magazine, Philadelphia produced nothing of consequence until Andrew Bradford's nephew, William, began to publish in 1757 *The American Magazine, or Monthly Chronicle for the British Colonies*. Bradford was only the printer. The magazine's moving spirit was its editor, William Smith, provost of the

College and Academy of Philadelphia, later the University of Pennsylvania. This Scottish doctor of divinity was so outspoken in attacking the peace program of the Quakers in Pennsylvania, and in supporting new military action against France, that he found himself twice in prison after he began to edit the publication. Aside from its political stands, taking on briefly the character of the newspapers, Smith's magazine was different from the others because of its high literary quality. Its contributors came from the universities, for the most part, and several were Southerners. Their contributions made the *American* the most original and vital of the magazines published before the Revolution. The work of American poets like Francis Hopkinson appeared in its pages, and other native writers could be found among the foreign essayists. Nonetheless, like so many other magazines, it lasted no more than a year.

While the magazines had to wait for their flowering, and the newspapers were struggling with authority to establish their independence, it was clear in these decades before the Revolution that in spite of Governor Berkeley's fears and the efforts of governments to justify his anxieties, printing and publishing were beginning to be solidly rooted in the colonies. With the establishment of a press at Savannah in 1763, the last of the original thirteen colonies came into possession of a printing plant. It had taken publishing nearly a century and a half to travel from Cambridge to Savannah. By 1755, twenty-four presses were operating in fifteen communities in ten of the British colonies in North America. They were printing not only the newspapers and magazines, but a growing list of almanacs, chapbooks, reprints of English titles and sermons, and in fact most of the literary forms to be found in England, with the exception of imaginative literature; in that category, the output was so small it was scarcely worth recording. Politics, religion, philosophy, and science dominated the lists.

Publishing could not have survived and prospered without the clergy, who were the intellectual lifeblood of the colonies, and whose broad interests, as their writings attest, included virtually everything beyond the borders of their faith.

Politically, book publishing was profoundly stimulated by the dissent in the colonies before the Revolution, as well as by the events of the so-called French and Indian War, in which France and England fought for control of the North American continent. These events, beginning about 1755 and ending only a decade before the Revolution itself, produced a flood of books, some of them landmarks. The contest between the great powers forced the Americans to examine themselves for the first time, as a people and as the inhabitants of a continent. It compelled them too, for the first time, to consider the Indian problem as something more than a contest for land on the frontiers. The savage events of the war undoubtedly had much to do with hardening the attitudes of Americans toward the Indians, culminating in what was virtually a genocidal policy.

Meanwhile, there was much public interest in the treaties signed with the Indians before the outbreak of war with the French. Many of them were published and circulated also in England. where land speculators and politicians alike were intensely interested in the enormous areas of real estate being acquired, or else seemingly given away to the tribes. When Benjamin Franklin published the Lancaster Treaty of 1744, he printed an extra two hundred copies for the British market. There was, in fact, an entire literature of Indian treaties, published mostly between 1750 and 1763. Earlier, Cadwallader Colden's *History of the Five Nations,* published in 1727, was a landmark book in the literature about Indians. It went through a good many editions during the century.

One obscure pamphlet had unusual significance, *The Importance of Gaining the Friendship of the Indians to the British Interest,* by Archibald Kennedy, receiver general of the New York colony, published anonymously in New York in 1751, with a reprint appearing in London the following year. This perceptive work planted the seed of Franklin's Plan of Union, which he proposed at the Albany Congress during the following year, and thus set in motion the idea that the colonies could unite as a political body in their own interest.

Another obscure but important document came from the Williamsburg printer William Parks, who published the *Journal* of a young Virginia militia officer, George Washington, a rather laconic account of his futile and dangerous mission to the French commander at Fort LeBoeuf. Although this publication had no literary merit, it alarmed at least some of the colonists into realizing the nature of French intentions against them, and at the same time it helped to establish Washington's reputation for the first time outside his native Virginia.

Published evidences of the smoldering revolt against colonial rule were also appearing. Often, for obvious reasons, they bore no imprint and were published either anonymously or pseudonymously. Occasionally an unfortunate printer, like Daniel Fowle, in Boston, had his work seized and burned; Fowle, in addition, served three days in jail, after which he published an account of the whole episode, *A Total Eclipse of Liberty.*

Publishing was also making the colonists more conscious of the vast continent on which they had established little more than a foothold in the early eighteenth century. Lewis Evans, a Pennsylvania mapmaker, journeyed about his own colony and along the Atlantic coast, making observations and consulting reliable citizens. The result was his *Map of Pensilvania, New-Jersey, New-York, and the Three Delaware Counties*, published in 1749 in Philadelphia. That created a considerable stir, but not as great as his *General Map of the Middle British Colonies in America*, which emerged six years later under the imprint of Franklin & Hall. At the same time, Evans published a pamphlet intended as an "Analysis" of the map—sixty essays which proved that map publishing could be a political weapon as well as an informative guide, because in them he talked of the glories of the Ohio Valley, urged his countrymen to study the region, particularly the routes to reach it, and advocated that all those who dared to follow the routes should do so and drive out the French. The essays were a splendid mistake for Evans. They projected him into colonial politics, and a year after the map was published, he died in a New York City jail, where he had been taken after being charged with slandering Governor Robert Hunter Morris.

Evans' maps, however, touched off a public interest in their own country among Americans, which in time came to be a national obsession.

By the close of the eighteenth century, a publishing community had developed that would in the next quarter of a century take the general shape of book publishing as we know it today. Printers were still publishers, and so were booksellers, but publishing as a separate activity was beginning to emerge.

So the media stood on the eve of the Revolution: the newspapers, emerging from governmental restraint and becoming propaganda organs for the contestants; the magazines, struggling to establish themselves; and book publishing, still the most important of the three as a conveyor of both information and culture.

3
The Revolution and the Media

"FROM THE INCEPTION of the controversy," Professor Arthur M. Schlesinger tells us, "the patriots exhibited extraordinary skill in manipulating public opinion, playing upon the emotions of the ignorant as well as the minds of the educated."

That is a fair summary of the Americans as propagandists, and it would apply to the loyalist press as well, which was just as skillful but outnumbered. Revisionist historians who see the Revolution as an economic conflict fail to understand the deep fundamental emotions in men's minds which the newspapers of the time so clearly reveal. It was not greed for control of maritime commerce, or political arguments over the power to tax, that impelled writers to refer to their King as "the sceptered savage of Great-Britain," and to charge that he thirsted "for the blood of America."

It is true, however, that the use of the press as a propaganda instrument has distorted the character of the Revolution. To read the colonial newspapers, one would be justified in believing, as generations of schoolchildren have been taught, that the revolt against the Crown was the result of intolerable abuses suffered by downtrodden colonists, who at last rose up and defeated, ragtag and bobtail though they were, the best the British Army could offer, and so won their independence.

In this simplistic version of history, the redcoats and wicked George III are cast as villains, while the embattled farmers and their leaders are seen as heroes. In reality, the Revolution was an illegal and violent rebellion against constituted authority, in the opinion of

34

some modern scholars as well as that of some of the best minds in the colonies. The loyalists who opposed it, and they constituted a third of the population at the outset, were the victims of a savage reign of terror by the mob, all in the name of liberty, so that thousands had to flee, leaving little opposition except what was represented in British-occupied New York City, and later Philadelphia and parts of the South. The Declaration of Independence itself was, as the historian Herbert Muller puts it, "a revolutionary manifesto, asserting the right to revolution." Not all the revolutionaries were zealots for democracy. Many of their leaders fought against making the Constitution as much of a democratic instrument as the radicals wanted it to be, and the result was a compromise.

It was an extremely reluctant revolution from the beginning. A decade before the war broke out, there was very little sentiment for any kind of open rebellion, and nothing like a general demand for independence—although again, reading the press, no one would have believed it. When the skirmish at Lexington and Concord occurred, it precipitated a war which only a small minority of colonists really wanted. That was why the conduct of the war itself proved to be so difficult. There was little agreement on objectives, many of those who fought were halfhearted about it, and great numbers fled the militia at the first opportunity, leaving in the middle of a battle if that was when their terms of enlistment expired. The British had little more appetite for the conflict, and a good case could be made for the argument that this was a major reason for their ultimate defeat.

If the Revolution had an authentic hero, it was George Washington. Raging at his recalcitrant militia, dependent on the ragged ranks of the Continental Army, beset on every side by treachery and treason, in constant struggle with a Continental Congress so divided and weak that it could not provide him with the men and money he needed, lacking any real support from a population that was far more self-seeking than patriotic—against all this, Washington stood firm, a monument to patience and persistence. His army lost every major battle of the war except the two decisive ones, at Saratoga and Yorktown, and there is little doubt that the contest would have been lost entirely without the help of the French.

In these events of the Revolution (including those preceding and following actual warfare), the newspapers played a key role. The magazines were not yet strong enough to take a major part, and the impact made by book publishing was confined largely to pamphlets, if in fact one counts them as books.

Perhaps the easiest way to relate the situation of the colonial press before the Revolution to our own times is to imagine that the student radicals of the late sixties had gained control of the nation's leading newspapers, and were using them to attack the establishment. James and Ben Franklin had been the first of these young men, but their effort was a brief one. By 1748, James had long since moved to Newport, Rhode Island; he set up shop as a printer of books, issued a short-lived newspaper, printed odd jobs, and died there in 1735, while Franklin had gone to Philadelphia and made a small fortune as proprietor of the *Pennsylvania Gazette*. By a series of interlocking business partnerships in Connecticut, Georgia, the West Indies, and elsewhere, he had become the first chain newspaper publisher. But he turned away from journalism in 1748 and "retired," meaning that he switched to another of his several careers.

In New England, there were several young men at the head of lively newspapers, some in partnership with their fathers, others who had inherited their presses. In the South, William Parks was not yet thirty when he established the *Maryland Gazette* at Annapolis in 1727, and nine years later founded the *Virginia Gazette* in Williamsburg, Virginia. Having learned his art from the finest printers in England, and enjoying the benefit of an excellent education, Parks gave the educated English gentry who had settled in the tidewater South typographically superior, well-written newspapers, much appreciated by Washington, Jefferson, and other future leaders of the Republic who lived there.

There were other factors at work to make the newspapers a potent medium in the Revolution besides the youth of their proprietors. One was the fact that the Crown had given up trying to license them; consequently they had proliferated until, by 1750, there were fourteen weeklies in the six colonies with the highest population. They had become an essential part of colonial life, not only as transmitters of news but as the transmission belt between producer and consumer, although in an elemental manner compared with the role they play today. Nevertheless, they were becoming closely allied with the spectacular rise of business in pre-Revolutionary America; by mid-century, circulations were substantial enough, aided by advertising revenue, to make a few publishers reasonably rich. That kind of success made it possible to produce papers with more news in them, and to publish them more often, sometimes as frequently as three times a week.

The young publishers did not agree about what their new freedom and prosperity meant. The division of opinion appeared to be between those who were primarily or entirely printers and those who were editors as well. The former seemed to think that freedom of the press meant they were free to publish any submitted comment on a public issue, particularly if the writer paid for it. Franklin, a genuine editor and writer as well as a master printer, spoke out plainly against this theory, asserting that he was not operating a stagecoach with seats for everybody. Those who wanted to carry on controversies should do it through pamphlets, he said, and these he was prepared to print at the regular job rates.

At the time Franklin made this declaration, just before mid-century, pamphleteering was in fact the chief method of printed controversy, in much the same way it has been in nearly every Western country, and many of those in Asia, for centuries. But this condition would not prevail for long in colonial America. A single piece of legislation by the Crown in 1765 was enough to turn the newspapers, still half intimidated and self-censorious in spite of their ostensible freedom, into political organs of the most virulent kind.

The legislation, of course, was the Stamp Act. Often cited as a particularly unjust example of "taxation without representation," from the British point of view it was completely defensible, and in historical perspective it is not difficult to understand their reasoning. Britain had been bankrupted by the long war with France, during which their armies had unquestionably saved the Protestant colonies from coming under the rule of Catholic France, and their navy had opened up the sea again to American commerce. Tax money was absolutely essential to put England on its feet again, and the Crown turned to its colonies for taxes in no greater proportion than were levied against its subjects at home.

The colonists were not particularly grateful for what the British had done to save them from the French and their Indian allies. They were under the impression that they had saved themselves, with some help from the British, of course. Consequently, when the Stamp Act was passed, they were outraged. The levies fell on everyone; the notion that it was the tax on tea which precipitated the trouble is only another part of the American mythology. In reality, the blow fell heaviest on newsprint and legal documents, so the two most offended segments of the population were those capable of doing the most harm to the mother country—publishers and lawyers.

The publishers were divided on the question of resistance. A minority simply declared that they could no longer carry on their businesses profitably, and suspended their papers. Such actions roused up the citizens who relied on the pages of these journals to advertise their wares and get their news. The majority, however, fought the law by evading it. If a newspaper was published without masthead or title, it was technically not a newspaper, and therefore not taxable. A much bolder evasion was to publish without the required tax stamp on each issue, and to explain editorially that the publisher had tried to buy stamps but found none available. That was quite literally true in those places where angry mobs had succeeded in stopping the sale.

There was one thing the publishers agreed on. They agreed with near-unanimity that the tax was a direct assault on their freedom, and it is quite possible the King's ministers intended this to be an additional benefit. The *Pennsylvania Journal and Weekly Advertiser* proclaimed that the press was dead, and appeared in the shape of a tombstone with its column rules turned over to make heavy black divisions. The skull and crossbones appeared on the front pages of the Boston *Gazette* and the *Maryland Gazette*.

A polarization began to take place. It was not a simple division between the have-not mobs of Boston and New York against the privilege and position represented by the Crown and its rich friends in the colonies. Such a division existed and grew, whipped on by radicals like Sam Adams. But the tax was also an affront to these same rich friends, whose viewpoints were identical with those of conservative capitalists from that day to this, insisting on the sanctity of property rights and free enterprise. The arbitrary action of government, whether it was the King's, as in this case, or a provincial assembly's, was as much an affront to them as it was to the conservative community in the nineteen-thirties when Franklin Roosevelt proposed his social legislation.

It was these political ideas—Tory, Whig, and democratic (for lack of a more exact word)—which began to dominate the newspapers before the Revolution. Causes attract zealots, and the writers and editors attracted to these conflicting ideas of the social order were nothing if not zealots. With varying degrees of skill, even brilliance, they told what they were convinced was the truth, and at the same time denounced those who did not agree with them as liars and worse.

In the decade or so before the Revolution broke out in armed conflict, the war of ideas was easily dominated by the young editors who spoke for the democratic view. Their influence cannot be underestimated, although many historians have virtually ignored them. While they lashed out fiercely at the establishment, or Tory, papers, and at the embryonic Whigs who believed until the last moment that conciliation and compromise would save their properties, they argued their own cause with fervor and dedication, if not with much devotion to the truth.

It was not difficult to kindle the patriotism of those in the great port cities, where the British tax collectors, civil servants, and soldiers were constantly under everyone's nose. But the settlers who had moved into the interior were so occupied with their own hard lives that they would have had little knowledge of what was going on in the centers of revolt if the newspapers of Boston, New York, and Philadelphia had not reached them.

There was a conscious effort on the part of these city editors to woo the farmers and convince them of their cause. It was a propagandistic campaign in which truth was the first victim. One paper, for example, depicted the British as so hungry for tax money that they meant to tax kissing. What unity existed in the colonies for the war, when it began, was the result of such exhortations by newspapers, reaching out to the farthest settlements of the Ohio Valley, weeks or months late, where they were read by people who feared the Indians far more than they did the British. Nevertheless, slowly and painfully, the will to resist British rule was crystallized among large numbers of colonists.

The newspaper editors knew what they were doing in this collective endeavor, and they exulted in their mission. "The press hath never done greater service since its first invention," boasted the *New Hampshire Gazette,* and only the most sophisticated editors would have disagreed. Certainly it took a high degree of courage. The language of these papers was intemperate and defiant, to say the least, and there was no way of knowing when the authorities might be goaded beyond their reluctant tolerance. Moreover, it was a time when the mindless mob did not hesitate to invoke violent repression in the name of liberty. The anti-intellectual street people who had no compunction about burning Lieutenant Governor Thomas Hutchinson's magnificent library, or sacking a Tory newspaper office, were equally capable of destroying a patriotic press that they considered not patriotic enough, or dangerously deviationist.

Much of the newspaper war was collective and anonymous, since many of the best writers were afraid to sign their names (and the fashion of the day still favored pseudonyms), but the proprietors of the papers, whether they wrote for them or not, and most did, could not hide their identity. By the time war came, a few leaders had emerged.

In Boston, they were two young men, Benjamin Edes and John

Gill, natives of Charlestown, Massachusetts, who had grown up there as friends. Gill was married to Ann Kneeland, daughter of the noted Boston printer Samuel Kneeland; she was directly descended from John Alden's Priscilla. He was the printer of the partnership. Edes was a politician, poorly educated but nevertheless possessed of a talent for writing inflammatory prose which reflected his radicalism. When they came into control of the Boston *Gazette*, the city's second oldest paper, early in 1764, they boldly published it without license and quickly made its offices a gathering point for dissenters, who gravitated between the *Gazette*'s back rooms and the nearby Green Dragon tavern. Edes's friends, Sam Adams and James Otis, earnest and angry radicals, were among them, and began writing for the paper under pseudonyms. "Retreat or you are ruined," the *Gazette* advised Governor Sir Francis Bernard. It was a vituperative Otis assault on Hutchinson that led to the burning and sacking of the lieutenant governor's house, with its great library.

Only a few years earlier, the authorities would have found this intolerable, but when the governor tried to bring an action against Edes and Gill, charging a "breach of privilege tending to overthrow all government," the Council refused to act, on the ground that they would "only be rescued by the mob." It was the mob that ruled now, not the Crown's representatives, and the *Gazette* was its mouthpiece. Edes himself was a member of a little revolutionary group called the Loyall Nine, the operational brains behind the activities of the organized street gang known in Boston, as similar groups were elsewhere, as the Sons of Liberty.

Leading the revolt against the Stamp Act, the *Gazette* could claim at least a partial victory when the ministers retreated in May 1766 and repealed the part of it that applied to printers. There was jubilation and a growing sense of power in the shop at Court Street and Franklin Avenue, where the partners and their friends gathered to celebrate. These friends now included such other names, soon to be illustrious, as John Adams, Josiah Quincy, and Joseph Warren. Their collective labors, as John Adams described them, consisted of "cooking up paragraphs, articles, & occurrences &c, working the political machine!"

There was little opposition to them in Boston. The three other papers, two more or less kept alive by government printing contracts, were jointly, as John Adams described one of them, "harmless, dovelike, inoffensive." When the *Post-Boy* and the *News-Letter* issued a joint supplement, the *Massachusetts Gazette*, published on Mondays and Thursdays, it carried the old, familiar mark of government control, "Published by Authority," and was referred to derisively by the opposition as the *"Court Gazette."*

In this situation, the frustrated authorities got no help from the timid proprietors of the papers they controlled, and they were given no help from abroad, although they had generated a demand in Parliament to bring Edes and Gill to England for an examination of their part in the Stamp Act resistance. Nothing came of that move. Consequently, the Massachusetts officials of the Crown determined to start another paper, with a publisher who might be more successful in countering the *Gazette.* They chose John Mein, a pugnacious Scottish bookseller, whose loyalty was guaranteed. His Boston *Chronicle* appeared for the first time just before Christmas in 1767.

Within a month, the two papers were at each other's throats, and in the process set a pattern that persisted in the American press for the next century. The style was one of violent language, often followed by violent physical action, either by disgruntled readers or by the publishers themselves. In the first instance, the *Gazette* published a vituperative article attacking something the *Chronicle* had printed. Mein demanded the writer's name (it was probably Otis, signing himself "Americus"), and Gill refused, whereupon Mein came at him with a club, for which he was taken to court and fined.

The attacks continued under such names as "Populus" (Sam Adams) and "A True Patriot" (probably Edes). When Governor Bernard brought an action against Edes and Gill before the Council, the upper branch predictably supported him but the lower branch asserted that freedom of the press was "the great Bulwark of the Liberty of the People" and refused to act. A grand jury refused to indict, and the governor was compelled to withdraw his true bill.

Strengthened by these decisions, the publishers pursued Bernard relentlessly. Someone in the governor's office leaked to them the news that British soldiers were to be quartered in Boston to establish law and order, and the *Gazette* carried an account of it. Bernard pleaded with the Council to make Edes and Gill identify their sources, and disclose the names of their pseudonymous contributors, but the Council declined. Then an even more damaging leak occurred, in which the *Gazette* obtained, no one knows how, confidential letters the governor had sent to his British superiors in London, describing what was happening in the colony and referring in blunt, unflattering terms to the individuals, including several Council members, who were obstructing him. That resulted in a demand by the Council for his recall, and he sailed out of Boston Harbor for England on the first of August 1769, with the jubilant chiming of the church bells in his ears, celebrating his departure.

It was a victory for a free press, but hardly one for truth. The *Gazette* saluted Bernard's departure by describing him as "a Scourge to this Province, a Curse to North-America, and a Plague to the whole Empire." The governor was, in fact, an honest and conscientious public servant, a scholar with a talent for architecture; Harvard Hall, which he designed after a fire destroyed the college, is a present reminder of his abilities. Like Hutchinson, he was a cultured man, an able administrator in the British colonial system who no doubt regarded the Sons of Liberty in much the same light as college presidents looked upon the students who were trashing libraries, looting offices, and paralyzing administrations in the late nineteen-sixties.

If Edes and Gill represented the rough and ready patriot press, John Mein demonstrated that the Loyalists could answer in the same tongue. To him, John Hancock was "Johnny Dupe, Esq." and Otis a "Muddlehead." Worse language was employed in his *Chronicle* to answer the daily slander and libel in the *Gazette*. But he had no chance against the zealots who were crusading in the name of freedom; they intended the freedom to be for themselves, not for John Mein. They hanged him in effigy, boycotted his bookshop, disfigured his signs, and broke into his office at night with the intent to tar and feather him. After that, he went about armed, until he was attacked in the street one day by an organized mob, and during the scuffle, by ironic chance, he wounded a British soldier who happened to be passing by. Some patriots hypocritically seized upon this as an opportunity to swear out a warrant against Mein, and he had to flee by night to a British ship in the harbor, which took him to England.

There were men of larger talents who tried to bring reason to bear in the press, unsuccessfully. One was that giant of the century, Isaiah Thomas. His *Massachusetts Spy*, which he started in Boston when he was only twenty-one, was the work of a man who was a master printer and one of the finest scholars of his time. So poor that he had to be apprenticed when he was only six years old, to support his widowed mother, he rose to be the foremost book publisher of the post-Revolutionary era, a courageous newspaper editor, a noted historian, and the founder and first president of the American Antiquarian Society.

The *Spy* started out to be a voice of moderation, following the Whig line, and announced its good intentions in the same kind of language used by hundreds of papers in the next century, and abandoned with varying degrees of speed. A slogan under its masthead asserted that it was "A Weekly Political and Commercial Paper— Open to All Parties, but *influenced* by None." Perhaps no paper could have pursued such a policy for long in the tense years just before Lexington and Concord, but Thomas tried hard until he lost his faith in the possibilities of conciliation. More and more, the *Spy* took on the radical coloration of the *Gazette*, although it was much more reasoned, as well as better written and edited. Typographically, it was a work of art compared with its contemporaries.

Eventually, Thomas became a part of the underground conspiracy, as the open break with Britain came nearer (Paul Revere was one of his best friends), and the *Spy* joined the *Gazette* on the list General Thomas Gage's officers were compiling of places to be captured and destroyed when the troops occupied Boston. They were to pay special attention to "those trumpeters of sedition, Edes and Gill."

In the last hours before the occupation, these two trumpeters dissolved their business, loaded their press and type on a wagon at night, and escaped to Watertown, where Edes continued publishing, moving back into Boston after the British left in March 1776. Gill remained in Boston, was arrested, but later freed. Similarly, Thomas loaded up his type and presses two nights before the occupation and hauled them across the Charles River to Watertown. He did not pause there, going on to Worcester, where he would become, when the war was over, the new nation's leading publisher, with his newspaper, three magazines, and a distinguished list of more than four hundred books, including Blackstone's *Commentaries*, Bunyan's *Pilgrim's Progress*, Defoe's *Robinson Crusoe*, more than a hundred children's books, and (strictly under the counter) the first American edition of the erotic classic *Fanny Hill*, under its original title, *Memoirs of a Woman of Pleasure*.

Thomas's Worcester shop was the wonder of the printing industry in post-Revolutionary America. It had 150 employees and seven presses, supplied by its own paper mill, and possessing its own bindery. The apprentices Isaiah trained opened branches in eight other cities, utilizing his money and advice to do it. The *Spy* itself persisted until 1804.

The nearest counterpart to Thomas among the loyalist printers and writers was James Rivington, familiarly known as "Jemmy." If Thomas was the most distinguished newspaper publisher of his time, Rivington was the most exciting. His father had been the Church of

England's official publisher, as the family had been for generations, and Rivington grew up in the atmosphere of a united authoritarian church and state, which explains his Tory viewpoint and perhaps the rebellion that took the form of wine and women, if not song. He dressed flamboyantly, liked to see the horses run, kept several mistresses, and came to America in 1762 to recoup his fortunes, lost mostly at the Newmarket races. He began as a Philadelphia bookseller, prospered, and opened branches in Boston and New York, thus becoming the first chain store book operator in America.

Seeking other outlets for his ebullient personality, Rivington began to publish in New York, in 1773, *Rivington's New York Gazetteer, or the Connecticut, New Jersey, Hudson's River and Quebec Weekly Advertiser*. It circulated in all these and other places, as far as the West Indies and England itself, but most of its 3600 copies were distributed in New York City. Typically, Rivington asserted it circulated "thro' every colony of North-America, most of the English, French, Spanish, Dutch, and Danish West India islands, the principal cities and towns of Great Britain, France, Ireland, and the Mediterranean."

Its editorial policy was proclaimed in equally grandiloquent prose: "Never to admit any Performance, calculated to injure Virtue, Religion, or other public Happiness, to wound a Neighbor's Reputation, or to raise a blush in the face of Virgin Innocence." Rivington added that he would print both sides of public questions, and in the beginning at least, that was the one part of his policy he was scrupulous about, as Thomas had been.

Thomas had no reason to love his Tory rival, but he could not help admiring his abilities. "Few men, perhaps," he wrote, "were better qualified ... to publish a newspaper," and as for the *Gazette*, "No newspaper in the colonies was better printed, or was more copiously furnished with foreign intelligence." But all this was written long after the Revolution, when tempers had subsided.

As the war came closer, Rivington found it as hard to be objective in New York as Thomas was finding it in Boston. Then, in November 1775, a Sons of Liberty mob, in pursuit of freedom, swept down on Rivington's shop and destroyed it. He was understandably bitter, because he had been attempting to print both sides of public issues, as he had promised, in spite of his own Tory sympathies. He had even carried patriot versions of events from other papers when he knew them to be untrue. But the patriots disdained impartiality; for them there was only one truth, and that was their own. Completely disillusioned, and hardened in his own attitudes, Rivington went back to England.

He returned two years later, after the British had occupied New York for the duration, and when he resumed publication of the *Gazette*, it was an entirely different paper. Rivington turned the full force of his clever, vitriolic pen against the patriots and all their works, with telling effect. From General Washington on down, the rebels suffered from his savage wit, and were outraged by the paper's unprincipled charges against them. Rivington apparently had no compunction about printing the most scurrilous forgeries or spreading any kind of rumor which seemed likely to discomfit the Continentals. He created scandals that even such formidable figures of virtue as Washington were busy denying years later. No doubt it was his experience with Rivington which helped to form in Washington's mind a distaste for newspapers which became a passionate hatred when he was President. General Ethan Allen, whom Rivington pursued with ridicule through the war years, swore he would "lick Rivington the very first opportunity" he had when the conflict ended. He tried earnestly to carry out his promise, but Rivington disarmed him with two bottles of ten-year-old Madeira and soft words.

The patriots of New York, restored to power, were not so forgiving, although Rivington expediently apologized for his wartime conduct. Some of those who did not forgive him were journeymen printers, who remembered his opposition to their strike of November 1778, the first labor walkout in America. The other master printers had yielded almost at once; Rivington held out for five days. Another of the unforgiving was a patriot whom Rivington had ridiculed during the war. Encountering the editor in the street, this man set upon Rivington and beat him. Even his generosity earned him nothing but a cell in debtor's prison when those whose bills he had guaranteed failed to pay. People no longer patronized his newspaper, which was not as sharp and readable as it had been during the war.

Nothing could save him, not even the disclosure that he had been a double agent, one of Washington's spy network in New York, who had stolen the British Navy's signal code book, which, in the hands of Admiral de Grasse, the French naval commander at Yorktown, undoubtedly played a major role in the Franco-American victory. Although documentary proof of this activity did not come into the light of modern scholarship until 1959, it is almost as difficult to believe today as it was for Rivington's contemporaries to accept it in

1782. Probably the answer—at least the only reasonable one—is that his truly scurrilous attacks on Washington and the other Continental commanders, particularly the abuse and ridicule he heaped on the general himself, must have occurred before he accepted the double agent's role. But the motivation for that move is still lacking.

Rivington's newspaper career overshadowed his considerable accomplishments as bookseller and publisher. He imported books from London, pirated and published some on his own account, and, before the war, brought out American editions of *Robinson Crusoe* and other children's books. By 1776, he had published no fewer than thirty-eight books, pamphlets, broadsides, and almanacs.

After the war, at fifty-eight and with no other means of making a living, he turned once more to bookselling, and with considerable courage opened up a trade with his erstwhile enemy, Isaiah Thomas, and the rising young Philadelphia publisher Mathew Carey. He even opened up a second shop, and did a little publishing, but after he fell into debtor's prison as a result of the bad debts of others with whom he had done business, he never recovered. Not long after his release, he died on the Fourth of July, 1802, just before his seventy-eighth birthday.

Aside from the street in lower Manhattan named for him much later, Rivington left behind a reputation which has grown with the years. The series of political pamphlets he published were a considerable influence in the course of the revolution; his power as a publisher can be measured by the fact that so much of what he printed was destroyed by the irate patriots, and by the countless resolves passed against his newspaper. He was printer, publisher, stationer, King's printer, propagandist, and businessman, but more than any of these, he was a bookseller, with a sure instinct for knowing which books and magazines would be most popular with the public. He made a real contribution to American life in his time by providing that public with the best works, particularly those by British authors.

Another noted Tory editor was of a somewhat different stripe. He was Hugh Gaine, an opportunistic Irishman who had come to New York from Belfast in 1753 and founded the New York *Mercury*. As the war approached, he tried to maintain a nonpartisan stance, like Thomas and Rivington, but he too failed. His fantasy of obtaining revenue from both sides ended when the Sons of Liberty, those strident enemies of objective journalism, hinted at his total destruction if he did not advocate their cause.

As the British moved into New York after defeating Washington at

Brooklyn and White Plains, Gaine prudently removed to New Jersey, where he continued to publish the *Mercury* in Newark, as an exceedingly mild patriot paper. He was not happy there. Supply was difficult, and he missed the good friends and good drink he had left behind in New York. Surveying the military situation from the standpoint of ignorance, he concluded that the war would soon be over and the British would win it, so he concluded it would be best to switch to the winning side. He returned to New York and found a welcome from the British, who had been publishing their version of the *Mercury* in the same shop he had left. They were glad to turn it back to him as long as he printed it in their interest.

As a convert, Gaine proved to be more Tory than the Tories. Those who had known him as at least a mild patriot must have been astonished to read in the *Mercury* of December 16, 1776: "The shattered Remains of the Rebel Army, 'tis said, are got over into the Jersies. Humanity cannot but pity a Set of poor misguided Men who are thus led on to Destruction, by despicable and desperate leaders, against every idea of Reason and Duty, and without the least prospect of Success." His later versions of war news were so wildly partisan that it was difficult for even the British to believe some of them. In any case, he was not the kind of man to endear himself to the British leaders. A hardworking, serious, frugal man, Gaine was not particularly congenial to a British commander like General Sir William Howe, who felt himself much more akin to a man who loved drink and women, like Jemmy Rivington. Consequently, when Rivington returned, he got most of the Tory business and Gaine was left with precious little from his switch of allegiance.

Like Rivington, Gaine's newspaper career ended in failure, but his book publishing was more successful. Most of it occurred before the Revolution. He produced editions of the classics, poetry, and music, and an ambitious two-volume *Journal* of the votes and proceedings in the General Assembly.

While the most colorful editors of the Revolution were in Boston and New York, Philadelphia could boast three excellent newspapers during that period, and one of them had considerable distinction. It was William Bradford III's *Pennsylvania Journal*, which from the beginning made no attempt to be nonpartisan. Bradford, third in a line of famous printers, was an unabashed patriot. He fought the Stamp Act, was among the first to come out flatly for independence, and published the first of Thomas Paine's "Crisis" papers. On the side, he operated a coffeehouse, conducted a marine-insurance business, and published books. A man of conviction, this veteran of the French and Indian Wars enlisted in the Continental Army at fifty-seven, and ended the war as a colonel. But the British occupation of Philadelphia ruined his business, and field duty so impaired his health that he could never get started again.

Philadelphia also had an equivalent of Hugh Gaine, in the person of Benjamin Towne, publisher of the *Pennsylvania Evening Post,* one of three Tory papers. The *Post* had begun as a patriot organ, and was first in the city to print the Declaration, but when the British occupiers came, Towne switched his politics and began competing successfully with his old Tory rivals when they returned to the city. After the British evacuation, it was the turn of these editors to flee once more—all except Towne, who succeeded in selling himself to the returning Americans, who permitted him to keep on publishing.

As Gaine had discovered, however, it was easier to placate authority, particularly military commanders, than it was to erase the memories of common citizens. Advertisers did not return to the *Post* in any great number, and neither did subscribers. Patriot writers did not believe his protestations of reform and refused to write for him.

More and more, in fact, the censorship of newspapers had passed from governmental authority to public opinion, and some editors found it harsher than the old order. It was possible to conciliate, bargain with, or otherwise deal with governments, but there was no way to argue with an angry mob of patriots who insisted that a paper print only the propaganda of the cause.

By a wry turn of events, the government of Maryland, in 1777, found itself in the position of upholding freedom of the press against the mob rule of its own people. The victim in this case was William Goddard, a printer-editor of high principle, neither Tory nor Whig, but simply a man who believed that a newspaper ought not to close its columns to unpopular ideas. He was not a neutralist bent on printing both sides of public questions. Goddard believed that, as editor, he had the right to make the decisions about what went in his newspaper.

When the British offered peace terms to the Americans in 1777, Goddard wrote a piece for his *Maryland Gazette,* which he had established in Baltimore in 1773, suggesting in what was meant to be an ironic way that the terms be accepted. The Baltimore Whig Club failed to grasp the irony, and ordered Goddard to close his paper and get out of town within forty-eight hours. The editor turned to the government for protection, which he said must be granted if freedom of the press meant anything. Agreeing, the Maryland House of Representatives granted him protection, and at the same time rebuked the Whig Club.

Two years later, Goddard had the courage to print an article by General Charles Lee, that eccentric, moody officer who had so angered Washington that when their long quarrel came to a climax with Lee's insubordination at Monmouth, the commander in chief lost his temper and had him dismissed from the army. Lee's article in the *Gazette* was an angry defense of his conduct, coupled with a slashing attack on Washington, who in spite of all his difficulties was a national idol. Angered patriots descended on Goddard's office, pointed a pistol at his head, and compelled him to write and publish a repudiation of the piece. A few wanted to lynch him.

After they had gone, Goddard once more appealed to the state, and once more the legislature obliged with protection for his person and property. When he had it, Goddard denied his forced repudiation, and told how it had come about. Perhaps there were more reasonable men in Maryland, but when the war was over, Goddard was one of the few editors who had been in such trouble who escaped lingering political hatreds.

While the newspapers of the Revolution were valuable to each side in providing a unifying force and a platform for political conviction, they obviously divided the country even further by their unbridled partisanship. It may well be that the familiar saw "You can't believe everything you read in the newspapers" had its roots in the press of the Revolution, when people believed only what was in the papers that represented their own political convictions and not much of that. Such disaffection, along with the wartime difficulties of getting newsprint and paper, reduced the number of journals from thirty-seven in 1775 to twenty after the guns were silenced at Yorktown. That would not include eighteen started and discontinued during the war. But other new starters were more fortunate, so that the net loss was only two at the time hostilities ended.

Physically, newspapers did not improve during the Revolution as one would expect, but their quality was lifted because of the influx into journalism of young and talented men. Compare, for example, the typical notice of a local death in the New London *Gazette*—"Last Monday there died here Mr. Edward Ashby, a very inoffensive man, in the hundred and ninth year of his Age"—with Rivington's coverage of the same kind of event: "On Monday afternoon, the Spirit of that facetious, good-tempered, inoffensive Convivialist Mr. John Levine, ascended to the Skies."

One of the most astute observers of the role of the press in the Revolution was Ambrose Serle, in charge of the Royalist press in New York, who wrote home to Lord Dartmouth in 1776 about the American papers: "One is astonished to see with what avidity they are sought after, and how implicitly they are believed, by the great Bulk of the People. . . . Government may find it expedient, in the Sum of things, to employ this popular Engine."

Government did. As every politician could not help observing, the press had already exceeded the pamphlet and the sermon as a propaganda instrument, and people were beginning to depend on it for their information, right or wrong. It was a situation ripe for exploitation, and that was exactly what happened when the Revolution was over and the new nation began.

Part Two
Freedom Defined

4

The Birth of the
First Amendment

Nothing testifies to the vitality of the Constitution more than the continuing argument about what it means, particularly the meaning of the first ten amendments embodied in what we call the Bill of Rights. Supreme Courts interpret and reinterpret these amendments, the results sometimes depending as much on the political complexion of this body at any given time as it does on the depth of scholarship of the learned judges.

There are dissenting views in the Court, in the Congress, in the White House, and among the general population, but one thing on which everyone agrees is that the Constitution is a unique political document in the history of Western civilization, and that the First Amendment itself has given the press in America a privileged position not held by the communications media in any other country.

It is difficult, in fact, even for the most distinguished editors in other countries to understand how the American press functions under the First Amendment. When controversy broke out in June 1973 between the Senate committee investigating the Watergate scandal and the special prosecutor named to prosecute possible wrongdoers, over the issue of whether pretrial publicity would preclude the selection of an impartial jury if indictments were brought, the London *Times* was forthright in condemning the freedom assumed by the media. It acknowledged that the whole affair might have been successfully covered up if the Washington *Post* and the New York *Times* had not conducted their investigations (for which two *Post*

reporters were given the Pulitzer and numerous other prizes), but it
contended that the papers ought to remain quiet while the law took
its course. As for live television coverage of the Senate hearings, such
a thing would be simply incomprehensible in England.

This cousinly disapproval and misunderstanding only accentuated
the difference between the parliamentary and constitutional systems
of government, and underlined once more how dependent the validity of the political system set up by the Founding Fathers is upon the
maintenance of checks and balances. Under British law, the press is
subordinate to government, particularly the judiciary. In the American system, it is not. The difference is as simple as that. Senator
Samuel Ervin, chairman of the Senate investigating committee,
expressed the difference succinctly when he argued that it was better
for the American people to know what was going on in their government through full coverage of his committee's work by all the media,
than to have a selected few wrongdoers sent to jail through the cir-
cumscribed workings of the judicial process.

Leaving aside the mythology of the unbiased, impartial jury, to
which bar and bench cling because it is too firmly institutionalized
for serious challenge, and which the population accepts because the
judiciary says it must, the First Amendment and what it means ought
to be much better understood by Americans than it is. Their freedom,
quite simply, depends upon it. Yet not only do many of them fail to
understand it but, as the polls tell us, a substantial percentage would,
in effect, be willing to give it up in favor of government control.

To the average citizen, the Constitution and its Bill of Rights were
handed down to us almost in the style of Moses on the Mount. Lofty
intellects met in Philadelphia, decided to revolutionize the world's
systems of government, and after due deliberation produced the Constitution. Having overlooked a few things, the Founders made up for
these omissions in the first Congress by initiating a series of amendments, which were duly ratified by the states. As the polls disclose, a
good many people think the Bill of Rights *is* the Constitution.

It is no denigration of what was accomplished to say that the reality of the Constitution's creation was quite different. The founders
were men with widely differing opinions, and they performed something of a miracle at Philadelphia in creating a system of federation
which went beyond anything accomplished in the rise of a democratic Europe. Holland and Switzerland had both federated under a
constitution, but did not have the strong central government created
in America. England did not possess the elaborate checks-and-bal-

ances system. No government anywhere had the specific guarantees of the Bill of Rights, particularly those in the First Amendment, nor did they have the institution of the Supreme Court, entrusted with interpreting the meaning of the Constitution.

That this miracle was accomplished depended on the good sense and honest instincts of several men, and in the case of the Bill of Rights and First Amendment, it was the political realism of James Madison that was responsible, more than any other factor, for their passage.

In the wrangling over the details of the Constitution, which was essentially a quarrel between Federalists and anti-Federalists, between strong-central-government people and those who believed in Jeffersonian democracy, the idea of a Bill of Rights was not even broached until late in the convention. On a hot September morning in 1787, they were still arguing. One delegate thought it ought not to be necessary for Congress to muster three fourths of its members to override a presidential veto; two thirds would be enough, he asserted. Another member rose to demand jury trials in civil cases.

Everyone listened respectfully when George Mason, of Virginia, rose to speak. He had earned their respect through his work in drawing up a Declaration of Rights for Virginia in May 1776, which Jefferson had drawn upon freely to write the Declaration of Independence two months later. In that same year, Mason had composed most of the Virginia Constitution. Residing in the principal slaveholding colony, he nevertheless had the courage to oppose slavery. Freedom was in this man's bones; consequently the delegates listened when he observed, "I wish that this plan had been prefaced with a bill of rights."

Mason was supported immediately by Elbridge Gerry, a rich shipowner and merchant from Massachusetts who had suffered, along with the rest of the elite, from the ruinous economic policies of the King's ministers, and wanted his rights protected from a central government much closer to home. Gerry moved that a bill of rights be drawn up, and Mason seconded the motion, but Roger Sherman, of Connecticut, rose to say that he thought the bills of rights contained in the state constitutions—there were now eight of them—were enough, and the new Constitution would not repeal them.

Not so, Mason protested. When this "plan," as they were presently calling it, became a new Constitution, he said, it would be the law of the land, and the states' laws, including their bills of rights, would be subordinate to it. But that raised the question of states' rights all over again, and it was plaguing the convention as much as it does the body politic today. When a vote was taken, the delegates put their faith in the states and unanimously voted down a bill of rights. Even Mason's own state voted against it.

That was not the end of the matter, however. Two days later, James Madison, of Virginia, and Charles Pinckney, of South Carolina, moved a declaration asserting that "the liberty of the press should be inviolably preserved." But again Roger Sherman objected, this time on different grounds. Such a declaration was not needed, he said, because the power of Congress did not extend to the press. Once more the vote was called for, and this time it was seven to four against. With that vote, the idea of a bill of rights was dismissed by the fifty-five delegates as irrelevant. Mason was indignant about it. The conduct of his fellow delegates, he complained to Jefferson, had been "precipitate & intemperate not to say indecent."

Yet it was never a contest between good men and bad. In their own ways, all these delegates believed in freedom; they only disagreed on the best means to secure it. With the advantage of historical hindsight, we know that the core of their disagreement, Hamiltonian centralism opposed to Jeffersonian states' rightism, was no more capable of solution then than it is now. How contemporary the fears of both sides sound to us even today.

". . . As the fundamental rights of individuals are secured by express provisions in the State Constitutions; why may not a like security be provided for the Rights of the States in the National Constitution?" That was the Federalist, Rufus King of Massachusetts, speaking. "A bill of rights is what the people are entitled to against every government on earth, general or particular, and what no just government should refuse, or rest on inference." There was Jefferson, the anti-Federalist, speaking from Paris of the great fear that the people's liberties would be invaded by governmental power, from which only a bill of rights would protect them. "Why declare that things shall not be done which there is no power in Congress to do?" And that was Alexander Hamilton, asserting that a bill of rights would be downright dangerous, comparing such bills with documents like Magna Carta, "obtained by the barons, sword in hand, from King John." Such a process was unnecessary in America, where "We, the People of the United States" had surrendered nothing and therefore needed no agreement between rulers and governed.

As the delegates left Philadelphia for home, to continue the struggle in the state conventions which would have to ratify the new Con-

stitution before it could become law, nearly all of them were inclined
to agree with Hamilton. They did not, in any case, think they had
labored to produce a philosophy of government, a grand declaration
of the rights of man. They thought they had done no more than
devise a practical code by which the new nation could be governed,
and they were ready to fight any move to graft a bill of rights on it.

The whole country was soon involved in the argument, and it was
quickly apparent that the delegates had badly misjudged the temper
of the nation, except for the three who had refused to sign the Constitution—Governor Edmund Randolph of Virginia; George Mason, and
Elbridge Gerry. These three now found themselves supported by
many people who read the news from Philadelphia in their papers.
To most of these readers, what had come out of the convention was
something of a shock. They had thought the Articles of Confederation
would be amended in a mild way, and the country would go on in a
fashion not much different. Instead, the convention, working in secret,
had produced something large and frightening, something radical.

As the state conventions gathered to debate ratification, the controversy boiled over in the newspapers, people shouted at each other in
the taverns and on street corners, until it was clear that the fate of the
Constitution might well rest on the outcome of the Bill of Rights controversy. In general, the people were ready to approve what the delegates had done, with some reservations. It was what they had *not*
done that alarmed them. They wanted a Bill of Rights. A generation
educated by the press to believe in freedom of expression, no matter
how intemperate, was not ready to give it up, nor were people who
believed themselves delivered from tyranny ready to put their trust in
another government without adequate safeguards against it.

In vain the majority delegates pleaded their cause, employing both
logic and ridicule. In Connecticut, Roger Sherman wrote to a New
Haven newspaper: "No bill of rights ever yet bound the supreme
power longer than the honeymoon of a new married couple, unless
the rulers were interested in preserving the rights; and in that case
they have always been ready enough to declare the rights, and to preserve them when they were declared."

Noah Webster sarcastically advised the members of the New York
convention, when they argued for a bill of rights, that the delegates
should add to their list of "unalienable rights" a clause declaring that
"everybody shall, in good weather, hunt on his own land, and catch
fish in rivers that are public property ... and that Congress shall
never restrain any inhabitant of America from eating or drinking at

seasonable times, or prevent his lying on his left side, in a long winter's night, or even on his back, when he is fatigued by lying on his right."

In Philadelphia, Dr. Benjamin Rush, the fiery signer of the Declaration, asserted that he "considered it an honor to the late convention that this system has not been disgraced with a bill of rights. . . ." On the other hand, Jefferson wrote from Paris to General Washington that he was indignant over the omission of a bill of rights, and the anger of the grass roots could be heard in the words of Thomas Wait, a printer in Portland, in the territory that would be Maine, who saw "a certain darkness, duplicity and studied ambiguity of expression running through the whole Constitution which renders a bill of rights peculiarly necessary. . . ."

The three delegates who had refused to sign hastened to publish their reasons for it, touching off a new uproar of debate. There were many who thought the Constitution was in fact a consolidation, like the English system they had just been fighting. Had the Revolution been in vain? they demanded to know. Had they simply exchanged one establishment for another?

"The greatness of the powers given," declared the Virginian, Richard Henry Lee, "and the multitude of places to be created, produce a coalition of monarchy men, military men, aristocrats and drones, whose noise, impudence and zeal exceed all belief." He added ominously, "Either a monarchy or an aristocracy will be generated." The rhetoric of the great anti-Federalist orators reached new climaxes, and over them sounded Patrick Henry's angry question: Why not "We, the states" instead of "We, the people"?

In the furious debate over the Constitution, the country was torn apart by the issues it raised, with South pitted against North on some issues, farmers against the cities on others, and the back country against the Eastern seaboard on still others. In the document produced at Philadelphia there was something to alarm everyone, it appeared, including those who thought that the idea of a vice-president was "a dangerous and useless office." The notions of having a federal city and a national army were denounced as frightening. The fight for ratification was often bitter and sometimes violent. In Philadelphia, two anti-Federalist assemblymen were seized and brought in forcibly to their seats, raging and disheveled, so that the Assembly could declare a quorum present and thus vote in favor of a ratification convention.

Underneath the conflict, however, ran the consistent and universal fear that the Constitution would mean nothing without a bill of rights. The convention delegates who had dismissed it as unnecessary began to understand that a good part of the country did not agree with them.

It remained for Massachusetts to show everyone how the argument could be resolved. When its 355 delegates convened for the first time in the Brattle Street Church, Boston, the atmosphere on the bustling floor, and in the crowded galleries where the people sat, was anti-Constitution and anti-Federalist. Governor John Hancock was opposed to the Constitution "heart and soul," and stayed away from the convention at the beginning. Altogether, the anti-Constitution delegates numbered a majority of 201 as the convention began, but this opposition was not well organized and many of the fears they voiced in their excited, frequently wordy speeches seemed absurd.

The Federalists were patient, however. They listened to everyone, even when they were accused of all manner of things. But as the sessions dragged on week after week, it appeared the delegates might never agree—unless, as Sam Adams suggested, the anti-Federalists were given a chance to propose amendments to be submitted to Congress. These would be recommendations only, but they would express the doubts and fears of those who opposed the Constitution.

Nine amendments were offered, most of them proposals to limit the federal power. They could hardly be called a bill of rights, and in fact only one of them was included in the final bill, but they offered a means of compromise with the anti-Constitution people—a means that could be useful not only in Massachusetts but elsewhere.

John Hancock was persuaded to offer the amendments—Sam Adams called them the "Conciliatory Propositions"—to the convention. Part of the persuasion had been a promise that Hancock would be nominated as first president of the United States. With these and other bargains concluded, the governor duly appeared before the convention, packed to the doors that day. He had to be carried in, his legs wrapped around in bandages because he had been sitting at home suffering from the gout, and delivered a speech which someone else had written for him. It touched off a spirited debate that went on for six days. Toward the end of it, Sam Adams offered some more amendments, including freedom of the press, and guarantees against a standing army and unreasonable search and seizure. That led to a fresh outbreak of disorder because the delegates were afraid that if Adams had thought such measures were necessary, the Constitution must be setting up a government even more powerful than they had feared. Adams had to withdraw his suggestions. With that done, the vote was called for, and it was another close call for the Federalists. There were 187 delegates for adopting the Constitution, with recommendations for amendments, and 168 against.

In spite of the narrow margin, many of the delegates who had fought hardest against the Constitution made speeches promising to support it if it were adopted, and to try to persuade the people back home to do so. Everyone walked over to Faneuil Hall after the adjournment, while bells in the city rang out the news and salutes of cannon boomed along the waterfront. They celebrated, as one newspaper put it, with toasts which "were truly conciliatory, and were, we believe, drunk with sincerity by everyone present. All appeared to be willing to bury the hatchet of animosity, and smoke the calumet of union and love."

Massachusetts had shown the way. Historians today believe that if the state had not voted for the Constitution it would never have been ratified by the others. Now, slowly, the contest drew to a close in the other states, until it was clear that Virginia held the key to the final result. As Randolph observed, "the accession of eight states reduced our deliberations to the single question of *Union or no Union.*"

In the Virginia convention itself, the most eloquent orators of the day prepared their arguments. Patrick Henry and Henry Lee were foremost on the barricades in the rough battle on the convention floor, hurling invectives in the classic manner. Jefferson remained on the sidelines as a neutral observer, making it clear that while he might criticize the Constitution, he was not opposed to it. There was much behind-the-scenes maneuvering. Washington and Madison, for example, were influential in prevailing on Randolph, who had refused to sign in Philadelphia, to reverse his decision in Richmond, thus swinging one of the state's most popular figures to the side of the Federalists. But it was the quiet, persuasive, skillful work of Madison that eventually won the convention battle.

At Philadelphia, he had been among those who believed private rights were adequately protected by the states. But where the subject of amending was concerned, there was a certain ambivalence in him. When one of the Connecticut delegates argued at the convention that they were only obligated to do as much as was prudent and might safely leave future amendments to posterity, Madison called that idea "a dangerous doctrine." He pointed out that the Netherlands had tried four times to amend the nation's constitution and had failed every time. "The fear of innovation," he said, "and the hue and cry in favor of liberty of the People will prevent the necessary reforms." He did not have Jefferson's complete confidence in the ultimate wisdom of the electorate.

With the battle lines clearly drawn, the Virginia convention assembled at Richmond, in the new Academy on Shockoe Hill. Its delegates were conscious that they stood at the crossroads of the great debate. They were aware, too, of the Old Dominion's power. At that time, its territory stretched westward to the Mississippi, including the District of Kentucky and West Virginia, and boasting a fifth of the Union's entire population. The cosmopolitan character of that population was evident on the convention floor, where the polished citizens of the Tidewater sat with the fourteen Kentucky delegates, who came dressed in their rough frontier gear, with pistols at their belts, because they had ridden through hostile Indian country to get there.

At center stage was the aging figure of Patrick Henry, only fifty-two but his tall, thin body already stooped and besieged by ill health. Spectacles could not dim the fire still in his blue eyes, however, nor an ill-fitting brown wig diminish his dignity when he rose to speak. Physically broken as he was, fierce energy radiated from this brilliant, opinionated, powerful man. Contemplating him, Madison recognized him as the force to be overcome in the convention, and the political enemy whose influence he must subvert if he himself had any hope of sitting in Congress: Madison was running for the Senate.

The convention was in its fourth day before Madison rose to make his first extended speech. He had been preceded by the eloquent, well-reasoned oratory of the convention's presiding officer, Judge Edmund Pendleton, still an elegant, white-haired figure even though he had to stand on crutches, the painful result of a fall from his horse. Patrick Henry had replied to Pendleton with one of his theatrical performances, calling the Constitution a "tame relinquishment" of freemen's rights and coming to a rousing peroration: "It is said eight states have adopted this plan. I declare that if twelve states and a half had adopted it, I would with manly firmness, and in spite of an erring world, reject it. . . . Liberty, greatest of all earthly blessings—give us that precious jewel, and you may take everything else!" And then, lowering his voice to a sardonic half whisper, an effect straight out of the Williamsburg theater, "But I am fearful I have lived long enough to become an old-fashioned fellow."

Then, on the heels of elegance and passion, came Madison. Hugh Blair Grigsby, a subsequent vivid reporter of the convention's doings, describes him "handsomely arrayed in blue and buff," but so short that it "made it difficult for him to be seen from all parts of the house; his voice was barely loud enough to be heard throughout the hall. He always rose to speak as if with a view of expressing some thought that had casually occurred to him, with his hat in his hand and his notes in his hat; and the warmest excitement of debate was visible in him only by a more or less rapid and forward see-saw motion of his body."

Nonetheless, Madison was a masterful debater. He carefully picked apart Henry's arguments, making a formidable list of his inaccuracies and inconsistencies. He was clear and forceful, and in the end he urged the delegates to approach the Constitution with open minds and not judge it by Henry's standards, which he considered outmoded.

As it became more and more apparent that the Virginia convention would probably ratify the Constitution, the argument over possible amendments grew hotter, and the populace was split apart on that issue too. This alarmed Washington, who had been, like Madison, an opponent of amending; no issue, it seemed to him, was worth destroying the unity of the state, and possibly the country as well. Modifying his stand, he let it be known that he was coming around to the side of the amenders, although not on very profound philosophical grounds. Amendments, he told Madison, "can't do any harm."

As for Madison, he was fearful that the anti-Federalists meant to deadlock the convention until the debate on ratification would have to be adjourned, which would force the calling of a second constituent assembly, whose membership might be more to their liking. If it meant saving the Constitution, Madison was for reversing his own and the Federalists' stand and coming out for a bill of rights. Always sensitive to public opinion, he felt a strong popular support for amendments, expressing itself through popular leaders. If the public will was directed toward a bill of rights, it seemed reasonable to conclude, the public would not be likely to tolerate despotism; consequently such a bill would set up sound standards and no doubt, in the end, produce beneficial results.

So Madison swung around full circle on the amendment question, from opposition to support, and came to believe that two desirable ends could be gained by passing a bill of rights. First, such a bill might, in creating a standard of free government, also create a national tradition to "counteract the impulses of interest and passion." There was also the possibility that arbitrary acts of the government, rather than oppressive majorities, would turn out to be the real invaders of the citizens' rights. In that case, he said, "a bill of rights will be a good ground for an appeal to the sense of the community."

As the Virginia convention drew to a close, Madison was fearful that neither ratification nor amending would be accomplished. New York had not yet ratified and, as he told Hamilton, he was afraid that Henry and his friends were trying to spin out the session in the expectation that the New Yorkers might invite Virginia to join in seeking to reconvene the constitutional convention, or else, as he put it, "trick delegates into an adjournment without permitting a vote."

It was true that Henry did have a final maneuver in his bag of tricks. He proposed that a declaration of rights precede ratification, no doubt hoping (although it cannot be proved) that a struggle over this question would so deadlock the convention that the Constitution would be abandoned. But Madison, by this time convinced that his previous opposition to amending had been futile, announced that he himself would recommend some of the amendments Henry favored. He could not resist adding, however, that he was doing so not because he believed they were necessary, "but because they can produce no possible danger and may gratify some gentlemen's wishes."

The Virginia convention moved toward its final decision, believing that it had the opportunity to decide the ratification issue by becoming the ninth state to approve the Constitution—the decisive number. In reality, New Hampshire had ratified three days before the vote in Richmond, but the delegates did not know it. They heard Madison set forth the reasons for delaying no longer. If eight other states ratified and Virginia did not, he argued, then Virginia would be in the position of asking the others to believe they were wrong. If eight states ratified and Virginia refused to be ninth except on her own terms, the others would be compelled to call new conventions to consider those terms, which could only lead to further amendments offered by the other states and to the possibility of hopeless disagreements. Thus Virginia, by a negative vote, could end, or at least indefinitely postpone, the prospect of an American government. If the vote was affirmative, on the other hand, Madison said, it could bring about "one of the most fortunate events that ever happened for human nature."

Patrick Henry fought him to the end, hurling his oratorical thunderbolts until a real electrical storm broke over the Academy, so fierce that it "put the house in such disorder, that Mr. Henry was obliged to conclude." Next day, all the storms were over, and the vote came at last. By 89 to 79 the Constitution won, although it now included a declaration of rights containing twenty articles, drawn up by a committee, and twenty other amendments, which the convention voted to recommend to Congress to be acted on by the states in the manner prescribed by the Constitution.

That night the anti-Federalists held a mass meeting in Richmond to lay plans for resisting further, but astonishingly, their champion deserted them. Henry said he had argued against the Constitution in the only proper place to argue, the convention, and now, "as true and faithful republicans you had all better go home."

Later, before New York followed Virginia in ratification, the anti-Federalists burned a copy of the Constitution at a public rally, and there were other hostile demonstrations elsewhere, but in general there was widespread public acceptance. Now the drama shifted to New York, where, in the newly decorated Federal Hall, the First Congress was to meet, and the Federalists who controlled it could be expected to redeem their promise to enact and submit a bill of rights to the states.

Five states—Massachusetts, South Carolina, New Hampshire, Virginia, and New York—had ratified the Constitution "with recommendations," not many of which were expected to be considered seriously by the Congress. The Bill of Rights, however, was a different matter. Madison believed Congress should respond to the unmistakable temper of the country and offer every possible safeguard for popular rights, not only as "appeasement to the Antifederalists," he wrote, but "gracious acceptance of these amendments would separate the well-meaning from the designing opponents, fix on the latter their true character and give to the government its due popularity and stability."

Madison rose before the House and brought up the matter of the amendments on June 8, 1789. He expected little, if any, opposition, but an outcry arose at once. There were those who wanted to solve the urgent problems of organizing the government first, before getting on to amending. One congressman even argued that the Constitution ought to be given a thorough trial, and when defects became apparent, that was the time for amendments to cure them.

Madison was surprised, but he was determined not to give in to such opposition, after so long a struggle. In his mind, he had a clear mandate from Virginia and the people of the other states as well to guarantee them against any possibility of a federal tyranny. He did, however, have his own ideas about the amendments. He wanted a bill which would set forth a few general principles, taken from the bills of rights of Virginia and perhaps other states, rather than a long list of specific guarantees.

When he was finally able to present his amendments, after the debate-weary House consented to consider them on August 13, they won a mixed reception. Even Jefferson was not entirely pleased. But Madison had sensed the public mood accurately. After the substance of his amendments had been publicized and become widely known in the states, there was general approval of what he had offered. In the debate that followed, Madison stood firmly opposed to any further amendments that might diminish the force of the new government, particularly those anti-Federalist amendments which would have given the states more power in such matters as direct taxation and treaty making.

The language of the amendments Madison proposed was plain, even laconic. There were twelve of them at the beginning. The first two had to do with the scale of representation in the House and congressional pay. The others were the familiar ones we know as the Bill of Rights.

One amendment Madison proposed did not survive passage in Congress. It would have prohibited the states as well as the federal government from infringing the rights of conscience, freedom of speech, press, and trial by jury in criminal cases. As the historian Nathan Schachner has observed, if Madison had been able to get this amendment passed and ratified, "much of the constitutional history of the country would have had to be rewritten, and certain disastrous consequences might have been avoided."

In the end, twelve amendments went to the states for ratification. The first two were unable to make the hard journey through the legislatures, but the ten we know as the Bill of Rights were ratified and became part of the Constitution on December 15, 1791. Virginia, again, was the pivot. The anti-Federalists there accepted defeat and became the eleventh state to ratify. Three states—Connecticut, Massachusetts, and Georgia—refused. They did not give their consent until 1941, when the sesquicentennial of the Bill was celebrated.

For Madison, it was a personal victory; for the Federalists, a party triumph; for the country, an event of the greatest significance because the Bill, in itself a redemption of promises, reinforced the Constitution and helped the states toward that more perfect union which the document intended—and this at a time when both union and Constitution were not fully accepted by all the people. Within three or four years after it was adopted, the Constitution, with its Bill of Rights attached, was being acclaimed by men of every political persuasion, and before much longer it had passed from mere acceptance to outright veneration by the general population.

Large parts of the intellectual community, however, remained unconvinced. Jefferson believed it to be an "oligarchic" attempt to suppress democracy, and like some others who had been steeped in the philosophy of the Revolution, it seemed to him that the Constitution represented more of a conservative reaction to the event of the Revolution than a democratic document. Some of those who thought of it as a conservative manifesto went further and cited it as an elaborate plan concocted by men of property and wealth to preserve their interests. There was considerable basis for this conception. Most of those who had drawn up the Constitution were, in fact, men who believed in the prime importance of property, and who worried that they might become subject to the tyranny of the majority.

The majority of the population, indeed—farmers, artisans, proprietors of small businesses—were not represented in the Constitutional Convention, which conducted its business in secret. It was a half century before the details of its deliberations were given to the public. No wonder, then, that some believed the checks-and-balances system was designed mostly to check the common people, who could only elect the lower House directly, and did not even enjoy the benefits of universal suffrage, since women, blacks, and many of the poor were excluded from the voting booth—a direct repudiation of the principle of equality set forth so nobly in the Declaration, but which no one really believed in as a fact of everyday life. So many of the people had no direct representation in the ratification process that later historians have estimated that only about 5 per cent of adult males in the new nation were actually represented in the voting on the Constitution.

Nevertheless, the document that emerged from the convention was the foundation beneath a political idea that seemed more radical to most people at the time than it actually was. It was a mass of compromises—far too many, some thought. Yet it had made concessions to relatively powerless people and, unlike many of those in Europe, it had been ratified by representative bodies rather than proclaimed by fiat. If the Constitution was conservative in character, at least it was not wholly the product of conservative minds and reflected more an enlightened self-interest than it did an aristocratic elitism.

In brief, it made the United States the most democratic country of its time, and in the Bill of Rights it gave the American people a basic set of principles not enjoyed by any other nation. These and subsequent amendments directed America along increasingly democratic lines as time went on, so that what started out to be a "monstrous fraud," by liberal standards, as Lord Acton put it, produced eventually a community "more free than any other which the world has seen," as Acton added.

For the media, the most important result of the Constitution was the language of the First Amendment: "Congress shall make no law respecting an establishment of religion, or prohibiting the free exercise thereof; or abridging the freedom of speech, or of the press; or the right of the people peaceably to assemble, and to petition the Government for a redress of grievances."

Like the remainder of the Constitution, the First Amendment has come to mean what successive decisions of the Supreme Court have held it to mean. "Congress shall make no law . . . abridging the freedom . . . of the press." That seems to restrict interpretation to the actions of Congress, yet the Court has often based its findings on what it deems to be the intentions of the men who devised the Constitution. It is hardly surprising that there have been, and continue to be, disagreements about what those intentions were. If, for example, the matter had been left to the Constitutional Convention's delegates, there would have been no specific provision for freedom of the press at all. They believed it was implied in the document itself.

It should be remembered by those who discuss it today that the First Amendment, with its specific guarantee of press freedom, is in the Constitution only because it was demanded by a suspicious population, before the state legislatures considered ratification, who feared that the liberties they thought they had achieved were going to be abridged. They particularly wanted freedom of the press because they had seen at first hand what the printed word could mean to people struggling against an authoritarian government representing monarchy.

There should be no doubt about what freedom of the press means; both the language and the historical record are clear enough. But generations of interpretations by the Court, by constitutional lawyers, and by academic authorities on the subject—quite often derived from partisan politics—have obscured the basic meaning of press freedom in a fog of learned language which has only served to polarize the argument around two viewpoints. One, notably enunciated by Justice Hugo L. Black, affirms that the First Amendment gives the people an unlimited right to criticize their government. The other contends that the founders and framers meant to stop press freedom at the point of seditious libel, a legal tool that has always been used to stifle political dissent.

For a century or more, there was little testing of the First Amendment's meanings, except for the Jeffersonians' struggle against the Federalist-sponsored Sedition Act of 1798. As Professor William A. Hachten points out in his book *The Supreme Court on Freedom of the Press,* no national laws were passed to penalize dissenting opinion, at least, before the First World War, and there was no legislation in the states except for the spate of criminal anarchy laws after President McKinley was assassinated, so that, as Hachten says, "most of the law we need to know about freedom of the press has been made since 1917."

Nevertheless, almost from the moment the Bill of Rights was ratified, freedom of the press has been under attack by a wide variety of elements in American life, and it has centered on the question which has never been resolved, namely, whether government has any right whatever to control the press through regulation. That it does regulate, in various ways, is a fact, but whether government intervention in the broad interests of the First Amendment, in order to make the mass media responsible and responsive to the public interest, should be permitted is a matter of fundamental dispute, among constitutional scholars and laymen alike.

The role of the media in American life is inextricably bound up in all these considerations, and how that role was carried out in light of them is the substance of media history in the years after ratification of the Bill of Rights.

5

First Consequences of Freedom

WHEN THE FIRST AMENDMENT was ratified, guaranteeing freedom for the media within the limits of the libel laws and assuring an appeal to the highest court in case that freedom was infringed, it seemed a sufficient safeguard for the life of the nation. Some thought it was more than sufficient, as we have seen. But it omitted two considerations of such importance that the groundwork for endless controversy was laid.

One of these was unavoidable. Naturally, the convention delegates and the state legislatures could not foresee the rise of the electronic media in our time, and their social and political significance. We are only beginning to deal with that problem. The other omission was any mention of the fact that the press was to be responsible as well as free. The framers of the Constitution did not even discuss the subject, perhaps believing that responsibility was at least theoretically implied. Or it may have been that they were wise enough to understand that responsibility could not be legislated unless the government imposed some kind of control on the press, which would negate the letter and the spirit of the amendment.

There is a third possibility. Since the framers and the ratifiers were all politicians, they may have believed that the greatest use of a free press was to make it a platform for party politics, on which the two parties that were now formed (Federalists and Republicans) could take their stands and proclaim their cases to the voters while they denounced each other. Freedom, in that case, simply meant relief from any kind of government control, with moral and ethical standards left entirely to the newspaper proprietors themselves. Magazines were still not serious enterprises. Books had always been a free forum, once the presses were unlicensed, but they were not yet seen as political tools to any large extent.

There were few people in these post-Revolutionary years who thought of newspapers in terms of responsibility. They were carriers of news, but their news function was overshadowed by the editorializing, which of course was not in the form of editorials alone but permeated most of what the papers carried, since there was yet no clear distinction between editorials and news. The idea of trying to cover the news with as much objectivity as possible, to be as fair and accurate as fallible human beings could be, was a concept far in the future. The pre-Revolutionary pattern persisted long after the war was won and the Constitution, with its guarantee, established.

As a result, the press became no more than a tool in the hands of contending politicians, a means of disseminating political arguments. As such, it was not always merely a platform for propaganda. Great issues were argued in the pages of these papers, by some of the best minds of that or any other time. Jefferson (to a limited extent), Hamilton, Jay, and Adams were among those who discussed and debated the consuming issue of the time, the balance of power in the new Republic—an issue by no means settled today. The Founding Fathers believed that it could be resolved by reasonable men working together within the framework of the Constitution. In our time, with the advantage of nearly two hundred years of historical precedent behind us, the history of this issue can be seen as a continuing struggle for control in which one side or the other has an advantage for varying periods of time.

Today the debate centers on whether the executive branch has gained too much power at the expense of the legislative. With big government, big unions, and the industrial-military complex so intimately involved with the operations of both the executive and the legislative branches, it could well be argued that the electorate at large has lost its power, since no matter who is elected from either party, public officials are subject to the same pressures and entangled in the same alliances, in all of which the public good is too often simply ignored in favor of privilege and power.

As the Republic began, however, the struggle was almost exclusively over the degree of centralism a people recently freed from monarchic rule should permit. The ordinary citizen viewed this argument in practical terms—as little taxation as possible, as much local control as possible, as much individual freedom as could be obtained. To intellectuals like Jefferson and Hamilton at the center of the controversy, however, it was a fundamental struggle over the very nature of government, whether it was to be strong and central, or whether power was to be dispersed among the states and the wisdom of the electorate relied upon more than the judgment of those in public office.

In a deeply divided people, still not certain whether they had traded British rule for control by an American aristocracy, and even more uncertain about how best to govern themselves, the result was a relentless power struggle between the two factions, in which the press was used to convince and persuade. Unfortunately, the lofty persuasions of Hamilton and others were overshadowed by the unprecedented vitriol pouring out from both sides of the politically controlled press, so vicious and unrestrained that the period between 1789 and 1808 has often been called by journalism historians the "dark ages" of the American newspaper. That this scurrility was the work of lesser men did not entirely condone the activities of Jefferson and Hamilton, who permitted and even encouraged it in newspapers which they controlled. Like politicians of every era, they did not hesitate to deny that they had anything to do with these papers.

As soon as George Washington took office, Americans got a taste of what was to come, and it must have been shocking to those who believed that one already elevated to the national sainthood would be spared indignity. No man has since entered the presidency under circumstances of such universal veneration, and certainly none has entered it with such high standards, personal and public. Yet he was subjected to a vilification by the anti-Federalist press which was much worse than anything seen in the pre-Revolutionary days.

Washington was not unprepared for these attacks, although that fact did not make them easier to take. As a Virginia planter, he had regarded the press as an advertising convenience, offering land for sale, and noting the escape of two runaway slaves for whose return he promised a reward of twenty dollars each. As a commander in the field, however, he depended on the newspapers reaching him as a source of information, and in doing so began to develop his ambivalent attitude toward the press, which was repeated in the lives of most other presidents.

It was a simple ambivalence. Like those who were to follow him, Washington approved the newspapers when they were useful to his work, or helped to publicize his views; he was against them when they persisted in printing things which were not useful, or when they attacked him. Particularly, as a military commander, he disapproved highly of the freedom newspapers enjoyed to print news not authorized by himself or other commanders. Long before this issue came to a crisis state in the administration of Lincoln, he was writing to the President of the Congress in the dark days of 1777:

"It is much to be wished that our Printers were more discreet in many of their Publications. We see almost in every Paper, Proclamations or accounts transmitted by the Enemy, of an injurious nature. If some hint or caution could be given them on the Subject, it might be of material Service."

Before he became president, Washington complained that he was the recipient of too many "Gazettes," some sent without his subscription order. He had little time to read them, he wrote to a friend, and when he did, found them "more troublesome, than Profitable. . . ." He thought they were inaccurate and meddlesome, but on principle he felt compelled to defend them against any attempt to restrict their circulation.

Even when they were complimentary—and the Federalist press treated him like a deity—he did not trust the papers. As he became president, he observed gloomily that the day would soon come when "the extravagant (and I may say undue) praises which they are heaping upon me at this moment" would be turned to "equally extravagant (that I will fondly hope unmerited) censures."

That prophecy came true almost at once, as the anti-Federalist press revived the old charge that he had misappropriated Virginia property belonging to his old friend and patron, Lord Fairfax. But there was no open quarrel between the President and the newspapers until he was drawn unwillingly into the public battle between his two Cabinet members, Hamilton and Jefferson.

Few people in the country understood the press and what it could do as well as Hamilton. He had gotten about the colonies and read the papers from Boston to Virginia, observing that a government or a politician could have no better friend than a newspaper dedicated to party or personal interest. He saw, too, that the best way to be certain of a newspaper's dedication was to hand-pick its editor and control him. Consequently, in 1789, he established what became, in effect, the official organ of the Federalist administration, the *Gazette of the United States.*

This paper was founded with money supplied by Hamilton and his influential friends, who were always ready to supply more if it were needed. Hamilton himself was the paper's chief contributor, and he picked a man weak enough to control as editor—John Fenno, a New York printer who had kept General Artemas Ward's orderly book during the Revolution.

It is hardly surprising, given this kind of day-to-day director, that the *Gazette* was not distinguished for anything except what Hamilton and some of the other Federalist leaders wrote for it. It would hardly have survived even so, if Hamilton had not arranged for regular transfusions of government printing contracts. Naturally, President Washington approved of the *Gazette* because it published nothing except what the government approved, and consequently never said anything to irritate him.

Washington, in fact, was a firm believer in "managed news," in the phrase we use today. As a broad principle, he believed that the public should be kept informed, and he was against direct federal censorship except in time of war, as well as indirect censorship by means of post office regulations or taxation. On the other hand, he held at least partially the view that there were some government matters which should be kept secret, and he would decide which ones were to be withheld from public view. (He did not, of course, use the word "security.") Moreover, he was against the publication of any news that might hurt the image of the United States abroad, and again, he was to be the judge.

The anti-Federalists, then, had some reason to believe that the strong federal government had more power than was consistent with democratic principles. Yet no doubt many of them would have agreed with the President when he instructed his Secretary of War: "Orders or advertisements, which are intended to be put into the public Gazettes, ought to be well weighed and digested before they are inserted, as they will not only appear in all parts of Europe, but may be handed to the enemy. To publish beyond the limits of the army, or the vicinity of it, the dastardly behavior of one's own Troops, is not a very pleasant thing."

Washington made no attempt, however, to control the press, and whatever power he and the *Gazette* possessed was balanced by the paper Jefferson started when the government moved to Philadelphia. Alarmed by what he saw as a concentration of power in the federal establishment, he resolved to fight Federalism in print with a newspaper of his own, the *National Gazette*.

Jefferson's role in this paper remains a matter of controversy. Philip

Freneau, his editor, once signed an affidavit denying that the Secretary of State had ever had anything to do with the *Gazette*, but near the end of his life he swore to the opposite, charging Jefferson with authorship of some of the paper's most violent pieces, and producing a marked file to prove it. In the course of a four-thousand-word letter to Washington, defending himself against charges made by Hamilton, Jefferson explicitly denied any connection with the *Gazette*, and went to some lengths in explaining why it was that Freneau was also working in the State Department as a translator, at $250 a year. It was because Freneau was a "man of genius," he said, and he had been glad to help him as he had aided other such men.

Hamilton's charge had been direct. Writing to Washington, he declared: "I cannot doubt from the evidence I possess, that the *National Gazette* was instituted by him for political purposes, and that one leading object of it has been to render me, and all the measures connected with my department, as odious as possible."

Defending himself, Jefferson said of the *National Gazette*: "As to the merits or demerits of his [Freneau's] paper, they certainly concern me not. He & Fenno are rivals for the public favor. The one courts them by flattery, the other by censure, & I believe it will be admitted that the one has been as servile, as the other severe. . . . "

Jefferson went on to tell the President what he considered the role of newspapers to be in a democracy: "No government ought to be without censors, & where the press is free, no one ever will. If virtuous, it need not fear the fair operation of attack & defence. Nature has given to man no other means of sifting out the truth either in religion, law, or politics. I think it as honorable to the government neither to know, nor notice, its [sic] sycophants or censors, as it would be undignified & criminal to pamper the former & persecute the latter."

Jefferson's distinguished biographer Dumas Malone insists that his subject did not start the *National Gazette*, did not support it, and did not write for it. Neither he nor Frank Mott, the leading journalism historian, credits what Freneau swore to the contrary in his old age. Yet a nagging doubt persists. It is true that James Madison, Jefferson's close friend, persuaded Freneau to come to Philadelphia and start the paper, after Jefferson had failed to convince Benjamin Franklin Bache, proprietor of the Philadelphia *General Advertiser*, to make a national organ out of his paper. Neither is there any doubt that Jefferson subsidized Freneau with a job in the State Department and gave him access to government advertising. In the context of the times, and considering Jefferson's role as politician, there is good reason to believe that the *National Gazette* was "his" paper and that his support of it was necessarily disguised.

In any case, the *Gazette* was the chief journalistic cross that Washington had to bear. Freneau was a latter-day Rivington. He was a complicated man—a fierce idealist, a political writer of exceptional talent, a poet whose lyricism was an authentic American voice (he is sometimes called "the poet of the Revolution"), and a man torn all his life between his career on land and his love of the sea, where he sailed as a captain. At Princeton, he had been Madison's roommate.

More than once Freneau's slashing pen drove Washington into those fits of temper he sometimes found hard to control. Jefferson recorded one of these outbursts in May 1793:

> He adverted to a piece in Freneau's paper of yesterday, he said he despised all their attacks on him personally, but that there has never been an act of the government . . . which that paper had not abused. . . . He was evidently sore & warm, and I took his intention to be that I should interpose in some way with Freneau, perhaps withdraw his appointment of translating clerk in my office. But I will not do it. His paper has saved our constitution which was galloping fast into monarchy, & has been checked by no means so powerfully as by that paper.

Hardly the observation, one might add, of a man who asserted that the merits or demerits of the paper concerned him not.

A particularly vicious thrust of Freneau's so incited Washington on another day that, according to the often quoted entry from Jefferson's diary, "The President was much inflamed, got into one of those passions when he cannot command himself, ran on much on the personal abuse which had been bestowed on him, defied any man on earth to produce one single act of his since he had been in the govmt which was not done on the purest motives, that he had never repented but once the having slipped the moment of resigning his office, & that was every moment since, that *by god* he had rather be in his grave than in his present situation. That he had rather be on his farm than to be made *emperor of the world* and yet they were charging him with wanting to be king. That that *rascal Freneau* sent him 3 of his papers every day, as if he thought he would become the distributor of his papers, that he could see in this nothing but an impudent design to insult him. He ended in this high tone. . . ."

Not that Washington was entirely satisfied with the *Gazette of the United States*, in which Hamilton and Fenno were defending him.

With some justice, he deplored the Federalist organ's language and tactics as much as he did the opposition's. In a "plague o' both your houses" mood, he wrote to Edmund Pendleton: "We have some infamous Papers calculated for disturbing if not absolutely intended to disturb the peace of the community."

In spite of the *National Gazette*'s clear superiority, however, the "power of the press" it represented, long before the phrase was invented, did little to diminish the Federalist government. Nonetheless it was a constant irritant and there was no mourning when it suspended during the yellow fever epidemic of 1793, an interruption from which it never recovered, since Jefferson's retirement from the cabinet soon after led immediately to Freneau's departure.

It was more than matched by another weapon in the hands of the anti-Federalists, Benjamin Franklin Bache's *General Advertiser*, popularly known as the *Aurora*, the name of a well-known London paper which the *Advertiser*'s proprietor insisted on centering above his publication's real title. Bache, too, had another name by which he was more commonly known. Friends called him Benny, but Philadelphians referred to him as "Lightning Rod Junior," in remembrance of his distinguished grandfather.

Bache had been only twenty-one when he started the paper in 1790, and at first it seemed that he meant to improve the quality of journalism rather than debase it further. The *Aurora* was the first paper to make an attempt at providing a full account of the proceedings in Congress, at a painstaking length which the other papers did not emulate. But Bache was an angry young man, a strong anti-Federalist, and he soon began to devote his news columns to a virulent campaign against the President, the Federalists, and all their works far surpassing anything the *National Gazette* had attempted. It accused Washington of overdrawing his salary, professed to regard most of his acts as unconstitutional, and reprinted forged and long since discredited letters of Washington which the British had used in Rivington's paper in 1776.

The *Aurora* surpassed itself, however, when John Jay came back from London in 1795 bringing the treaty he had negotiated with Great Britain, ending the war crisis that began in the spring of 1774. Washington got this document on March 7, but it was so unsatisfactory he did not dare to submit it for ratification. What followed provides a vivid contemporary parallel with government secrecy in the Vietnam War, and in a sense, with the case of the Pentagon Papers.

This was the first real test of a newspaper's role in American life under the protection of the First Amendment. Washington considered the treaty a secret document, and it was his intention to discuss it secretly in the Senate (in those days, the President presided) before submitting it for a Senate vote whose outcome seemed doubtful. The anti-Federalists, as well as everyone else, knew that the treaty was in the government's hands, and they were highly suspicious of its contents. In a democracy, they believed, such a document ought to be the subject of public discussion and debate.

It was June 8 before Washington submitted the treaty to a special session of the Senate for private discussion, and meanwhile speculation about its contents had risen to a high public and political pitch. The situation exploded when Bache somehow learned of the treaty's contents, although he did not actually have a copy of the document itself, and published its substance in the *Aurora* of June 29. What Bache wrote was so full of inaccuracies that Senator George Mason, of Virginia, who had fought so assiduously for the Bill of Rights, made his own decision that it was unfair to argue the matter without having the actual facts and gave a copy of the treaty to Bache, who printed it in full, attacking it as fiercely as he had in the original version. Always a man with an eye for the odd dollar, he republished it as a pamphlet on July 2 and sold it in large figures.

The effect of this was to arouse and divide the public. A storm of criticism burst upon Washington and the administration. "I have brought on myself a torrent of abuse in the factious papers in this country," the President remarked gloomily to Gouverneur Morris, "and from the enmity of the discontented of all descriptions therein. . . ."

Administration stalwarts rushed to defend the treaty in friendly newspapers. Hamilton wrote long letters under the signature of "Camillus," and Washington urged that this defense be circulated as widely as possible. Meanwhile, the *Aurora* charged that he "had violated the Constitution and made a treaty with a nation abhorred by our people; that he had answered the respectful remonstrances of Boston and New York as if he were the omnipotent director of a seraglio, and had thundered contempt upon the people with as much confidence as if he had sat upon the throne of Industan."

Even this attack was surpassed by the open letter Tom Paine had published in the papers, which concluded: "And as to you, sir, *treacherous in private friendship* . . . and a *hypocrite* in public life, the world will be puzzled to decide, whether you are an *apostate* or an *impostor*, whether you have abandoned *good principles*; or whether *you ever had any?*"

The man who had entered office a national hero found himself now referred to in the *Aurora* and other anti-Federalist papers as one whose character was composed of "little passions," "ingratitude," "want of merit," and "insignificance," and whose fame was spurious. His trips North and South as president were, according to Bache, "a stately journeying through the American continent in search of personal incense." He was "a frail mortal, whose passions and weaknesses are like those of other men, a spoiled child, a despot, an anemic imitation of the English kings."

Nor was this attack confined to those papers nearest at hand, in Philadelphia and New York. The Republican press in Boston, Kentucky and the Carolinas, and elsewhere joined in with fervor. Washington's every official act was regarded with suspicion and accusation, his personal life (blameless though it actually was) came under free discussion, and no matter what he did or did not do in private or public, he was condemned.

Washington responded to all this more with outraged dignity than with anger as time went on, but inevitably the abuse of the papers contributed heavily to his decision to leave public life. There is something of a "you-won't-have-Dick-Nixon-to-kick-around-anymore" tone in this letter he wrote to Hamilton on June 26, 1796, declaring: "Having from a variety of reasons (among which a disinclination to be longer buffited in the public prints by a set of infamous scribblers) taken my ultimate determination 'To seek the Post of honor in a private Station' I regret exceedingly that I did not publish my valedictory address the day after the Adjournment of Congress."

Having decided to leave, Washington made a last attempt to frustrate his journalistic enemies by giving an exclusive on his Farewell Address to a Federalist paper, the *Pennsylvania Packet and Daily Advertiser*, published by John Dunlap and David Claypoole, which later became the first morning daily in America. The address was, of course, not meant to be given as a speech but to be published, as widely as possible, Washington hoped. He submitted a first draft to Hamilton, who was to polish the President's tortured prose and otherwise advise him.

In it, he lashed out for the last time at those "Gazettes" which had "teemed with all the Invective that disappointment, ignorance of facts, and malicious falsehood could invent, to misrepresent my politics and affections; to wound my reputation and feelings; and to weaken, if not entirely destroy the confidence you had been pleased to repose in me; it might be expected at the parting scene of my public life that I should take some notice of such virulent abuse. But, as heretofore, I shall pass over them in utter silence never having myself, nor by any other with my participation or knowledge, written or published a scrap in answer to any of them."

But in the rewriting he omitted this paragraph, characteristically reducing references to himself to an absolute minimum, here and elsewhere. The fact that he made no direct reference to the press in the final version did not soften the response to his address. Bache greeted its publication with these words:

> If ever a nation was debauched by a man, the American nation has been debauched by Washington. If ever a nation has suffered from the improper influence of a man, the American nation has suffered from the influence of Washington. If ever a nation was deceived by a man, the American nation has been deceived by Washington. Let his conduct then be an example to future ages. Let it serve to be a warning that no man may be an idol.

As Washington left Philadelphia in March 1797 for the welcome relief of Mount Vernon, he was followed by Bache's parting crow of triumph: "If ever there was a period for rejoicing, this is the moment —every heart in unison with the freedom and happiness of the people, ought to beat high with exultation that the name of Washington from this day ceases to give a currency to political iniquity, and to legalized corruption. . . . When a retrospect has been taken of the Washington administration for eight years, it is a subject of the greatest astonishment that a single individual should have cankered the principles of republicanism in an enlightened people just emerged from the gulf of despotism, and should have carried his designs against the public liberty so far as to have put in jeopardy its very existence. . . ."

It is understandable that Washington canceled most of his newspaper subscriptions when he left the presidency, although he renewed many of them in the quiet of Mount Vernon. Understandable, too, that he should have supported the infamous Alien and Sedition Acts enacted in the administration of his successor, John Adams. Yet, at the same time, he continued to believe that the public should be fully informed. He wrote to Secretary of State Timothy Pickering: "The crisis, in my opinion, calls loudly for plain dealing, that the Citizens at large may be well informed, and decide, with respect to public measures, upon a thorough knowledge of facts. *Concealment* is a species of mis-information; and misrepresentation and false alarms found the ground work of opposition."

In spite of everything he had suffered from the papers, Washington continued to believe in the broad principles of the Bill of Rights, including the First Amendment, and since he was also a firm believer in leaving his own conduct, in and out of office, to the ultimate judgment of history, he refused to use the press as a personal political weapon, and did not always approve those who used it in his behalf.

He spent the last evening of his life reading the papers. Tobias Lear, his faithful secretary, tells in his diary how he and the President sat up until after nine o'clock going through the gazettes which had just arrived from the post office. "When he met with anything which he thought diverting or interesting," Lear tells us, "he would read it aloud as well as his hoarseness would permit. He desired me to read to him the debates of the Virginia Assembly, on the election of a Senator and Governor; which I did—and, on hearing Mr. Madison's observations respecting Mr. Monroe, he appeared much affected, and spoke with some degree of asperity on the subject, which I endeavored to moderate, as I always did on such occasions."

A few hours later he was dead, and so great was the universal grief in the nation that even the opposition press was momentarily silenced.

The character of the press did not change in the least, however, with Adams' accession, nor could it, because it still had no prime reason for existence except to be the tool of the two political parties. Its news function, even a substantial part of its advertising, was subverted to that purpose.

Adams was a far different kind of man and a far different president. He was tougher-minded and more combative. As an excellent writer on his own account, he contributed to various newspapers for more than forty years of his life, although he had no formal connection with any of them. As president, he suffered most from what was happening in this third term of Federalist administration, which saw a growing consolidation of political and economic power in the hands of a relatively few people who were benefiting financially and politically from the government, while the anti-Federalists, still out of power and many of their supporters out of pocket as well, raged and snarled at what they conceived to be the triumph of the haves over the have-nots.

Like Washington, Adams believed that the press ought to present America in the best possible light, and he followed his predecessor's policy of public silence in the face of newspaper attacks. Similarly, he was against carrying on political controversies in the press.

In spite of his essentially moderate approach, he had to bear responsibility for the Alien and Sedition Acts passed in his administration, which were an extreme reaction to extreme partisanship in the press. It was not Adams' idea to have this legislation enacted, but on the other hand, he did not oppose it and signed it into law without protest. Three of these acts were designed to punish or otherwise deal with objectionable or dangerous aliens. Honest men could differ on these laws, but the fourth one, the Sedition Act, was the action of frightened and angry politicians who did not trust their own people. It was intended to punish native-born critics of the government, much as President Nixon's proposed amendments to the criminal code were meant to do in 1973.

The act was a response to violence in the streets as well as in print. A gang of Federalist hoodlums had wrecked Bache's shop, and a sympathizer of the President's whom Bache had slandered came into the editor's office later and beat him severely. As Bache continued to attack Adams even more fiercely than he had Washington, he provoked the President into having him arrested for libel, but was quickly released. Soon after, Bache encountered Fenno, his rival Federalist editor, on the street and the men exchanged words and blows. In little more than a year later, both men were dead, victims of the yellow fever which made Philadelphia a ghost city for a time, and the Federalist press danced with glee on Bache's grave. "The Jacobins are all whining at the exit of the vile Benjamin Franklin Bache," said *Russell's Gazette*, a Boston paper. "So would they do if one of their gang was hung for stealing. The memory of this scoundrel cannot be too highly execrated."

Bache's attractive Danish-born widow, Margaret, took up the paper's management and soon married its associate editor, William Duane, an angry Irish radical who combined a caustic style with a reckless courage. He made the *Aurora's* columns "an uninterrupted stream of slander of the American Government," as Pickering said.

In doing so, he led the anti-Federalist press in a salutary counterattack on Federalist policies which were dangerously wrong. He fought hard against the idea of a war with France, which threatened the new nation and would have been a disaster of the first magnitude, and in fact he helped to avert it by his marshaling of public opinion. He assaulted the Alien and Sedition Acts, and was a factor in their repeal. He survived two Federalist libel indictments brought against him, meanwhile living a life of constant wariness because those who could not bring him down legally hoped to do it by assassination if they could.

Adams tried to prosecute Duane under the Alien Act, but his case dragged on until it was finally dismissed. It was clear, even to some of the most ardent Federalists, that the Alien and Sedition Acts had been a mistake. There were few prosecutions and even fewer convictions, while their effect on the public was to stir up opposition and resentment, which culminated in the eventual downfall of the Federalists. Adams attributed the party's collapse partly to its own ineptitude, and almost equally to the attacks of "foreign liars" in the anti-Federalist press. "If we had been blessed with common sense," he wrote in a shrewd analysis, "we should not have been overthrown by Philip Freneau, Duane, Callender, Cooper, and Lyon, or their great patron and protector [meaning Jefferson]. A group of foreign liars, have discomfited the education, the talents, the virtues, and the property of the country."

After his retirement from office, Adams continued to write for the press, in the interest of better public understanding, as he thought, but he did not forgive the newspapers. He wrote to a friend in 1815:

> One party reads the newspapers and pamphlets of its own church, and interdicts all writings of the opposite complexion. The other party condemns all such as heresy, and will not read or suffer to be read, as far as its influence extends, any thing but its own libels. . . . With us, the press is under a virtual imprimatur, to such a degree, that I do not believe I could get these letters to you printed in a newspaper in Boston. . . . Have not narrow bigotry, the most envious malignity, the most base, vulgar, sordid, fishwoman scurrility, and the most palpable lies, a plenary indulgence, and an unbounded licentiousness. If there is ever to be an amelioration of the conditions of mankind, philosophers, theologians, legislators, politicians and moralists will find that the regulation of the press is the most difficult, dangerous, and important problem they have to resolve. Mankind cannot now be governed without it, nor at present with it. Instead of a consolation, it is an aggravation to know that this kind of ignorance . . . runs through every State in the Union. . . .

Jefferson had apparently learned something about the press from his years with Washington. He saw the uses of the newspaper as a partisan political weapon, and certainly the *National Gazette* had done a service for him and his party. But he was never comfortable with the virulence of Bache and the *Aurora*, and even less happy with Duane's fanaticism, mixed though it was with valuable insights into political cause and effect. Consequently, when Jefferson moved the seat of government from Philadelphia to Washington, he did not invite Duane and the *Aurora* to follow him.

What government attacks and two libel indictments had failed to do, presidential indifference from his own party succeeded in doing to Duane and his paper. Jefferson did not even give him a government contract for printing. Duane remained a supporter of Jefferson, but it is easy to understand why conviction gradually disappeared from the *Aurora*'s columns. It lingered on and died at last in 1822.

In cutting off such valuable support, Jefferson was not being ungrateful. It was simply that, as president, he hoped to place himself and his office above partisan squabbling in the gazettes, as Washington and Adams had not been able to do. It was a vain hope—ironically, because Jefferson did more for freedom of the press than any other president, yet he was assailed in the same terms that had tormented and damaged his predecessors.

Nothing appeared to shake Jefferson's belief in a free press, however. He defended the right of his detractors to print when others would have silenced them, and he rarely chose to defend himself. Basically, he believed it was more important to be informed than to be governed, an idea that has steadily lost ground in the late twentieth century.

One often sees him quoted: "The basis of our government being the opinion of the people, the very first object should be to keep that right; and were it left to me to decide whether we should have the government without newspapers, or newspapers without a government, I should not hesitate a moment to prefer the latter." The quotation usually ends there, but the real wisdom lies in the sentence that follows: "But I should mean that every man should receive those papers, and be capable of reading them." Jefferson understood that the effectiveness of the press in a democracy is in proportion to the number of people who are able to read its publications and take the time to do it. Those who choose to remain ignorant rather than informed deserve more government and less freedom of information.

Jefferson was profoundly opposed to the Alien and Sedition Acts. He was for freedom of the press, he said, "& against all violations of the constitution to silence by force & not by reason the complaints or criticisms, just or unjust, of our citizens against the conduct of their agents. . . ."

As president, nevertheless, Jefferson was first to have what amounted to an official paper. Having rejected the rough radicalism of Duane, he turned to an editor and a newspaper who would serve him with the moderation he hoped all the press would learn to practice. His choice was Samuel Harrison Smith, editor of the triweekly *National Intelligencer and Washington Advertiser*, whom Jefferson invited to follow him from Philadelphia to Washington and turn his paper to the service of the new administration.

In one sense, it was an unfortunate choice. Smith carried moderation to such an excess that the opposition was justified in calling the *Intelligencer* "Mr. Silky-Milky Smith's National Smoothing Plane." As such, it was no match for the paper that Jefferson's perennial enemy, Hamilton, was soon to start in New York. On the other hand, the *Intelligencer* foreshadowed the future. It was not shrill and viciously partisan, in the accepted style which had prevailed for so long, and it had better foreign and domestic news coverage than any other newspaper in Washington, or perhaps elsewhere. These solid qualities, while it made the *Intelligencer* appear bland in comparison with its contemporaries, enabled it to far outlast its rivals. Changed to a daily in 1813, it remained one of the best papers in America until its eventual demise after the Civil War.

Smith was not able to accomplish much for his mentor, who had to disavow his interest in the paper for the same reason he had forsworn any responsibility for the *National Gazette*. It is possible that Smith's attractive and charming wife, Margaret, did more for the Republican cause than her husband's newspaper, at her salons in their splendid country place, Sidney, where Catholic University now stands. Margaret Smith was the forerunner of those Washington hostesses—Perle Mesta, Evelyn Walsh MacLean, Gwen Caffritz, to name the most noteworthy—who knew how to organize soirees where people might find themselves eating and drinking with their political enemies. Smith, a connoisseur of food and wine, saw to it that his guests had the best basic ingredients for the advancement of quiet politicking.

In New York, Hamilton's answer to the *Intelligencer* was a new Federalist organ, the *Evening Post*. This time he had not been quite so bold about it. Like Jefferson, he disassociated himself publicly from the paper, but there is little question that he and his friends were the real founders, and he carried on his philosophical and political debate with Jefferson anonymously in its columns.

Begun on November 16, 1801, the *Post* is today the second oldest paper of continuous publication in the United States (the oldest is the Hartford *Courant*, established in 1764). Its beginnings were more modest than its Washington rival, since Hamilton, as representative of the party out of power, had not been able to raise much cash to launch it. The first issues had to be printed on an old secondhand press, but its quarter-size sheets found ready circulation in a city which by this time had grown to sixty thousand.

Its editor, hand-picked by Hamilton, was William Coleman, and a greater contrast to Smith could hardly have been found. Coleman would have been perfectly cast as Hollywood's idea of a big-city editor—a large, handsome man with a hearty voice, who loved women, alcohol, food, arguments, and politics. He had been a lawyer in Massachusetts in his early days, where he had been a rare combination of scholar and athlete, the kind of man who would read Greek in the morning and skate twenty miles from Greenfield to Northampton in the evening.

At the beginning, and setting a style that would be common for the next fifty years or so, Coleman began his career as editor on a note of high principle, declaring in the *Post*'s first issue that he abhorred "personal virulence, low sarcasm, and verbal contentions with printers and editors." He would not be swerved, he said, from "the line of temperate discussion." It was all window dressing, of a kind increasingly common as the new century wore on. Paper after paper appeared with high-minded declarations from the publisher on the front page of the first issue. These declarations were promptly forgotten in the interest of politics, and it was not long before Coleman was swinging his editorial ax with as much good will as the others. In doing so, he inadvertently opened the way to another major test of press freedom.

The long-continued violence of the partisan press had produced an inevitable reaction by this time. Having observed and opposed the serious mistake the Federalists had made in trying to throttle press opposition wholesale through the Sedition Act, Jefferson decided to apply Republican philosophy to the problem and encouraged the states to bring a few libel cases under state laws, as an example to the worst offenders.

The first opportunity to do so came in New York State, where Coleman had written a roundabout assault on Jefferson for the *Post*, in which he reported, without making any attempt to deny it, that "the burden of the Federalist song" was the party's charge that "Jefferson paid Callender [James Callender, the notorious editor of the Richmond *Examiner*] for calling Washington a traitor, a robber, a perjurer; for calling Adams a hoary-headed incendiary and for most grossly slandering the private characters of men he knew well were virtuous." He concluded defiantly: "These charges not a democratic Editor has yet dared or ever will dare to meet in an open and manly discussion."

This accusation, in spite of the devious way it was presented, was a serious one and the clumsy subterfuge was no protection whatever against its libelous content. It was picked up on "exchange" and republished by Harry Croswell, editor of the Hudson, New York, *Wasp*, a publication so vicious that the more respectable Federalists would have nothing to do with it.

It was exactly the kind of case Jefferson had been talking about. Here was one of the worst offenders, who could now be prosecuted under New York State law. Croswell was indicted on a charge of libeling the President and duly tried. Found guilty, he took the case on appeal to the State Supreme Court.

As had been the case with Zenger, Croswell found a distinguished advocate waiting to defend him—Alexander Hamilton himself. Like that earlier Hamilton, the Federalist stalwart made one of the most eloquent pleas for freedom of the press that had ever been heard in a courtroom. He argued that the press had "the right to publish with impunity truth, with good motives, for justifiable ends, though reflecting on Government, Magistracy, or individuals." Once more it was being argued that truth should be admitted as a defense in a libel action.

In Callender's case, the truth was that he had been indicted under the Sedition Act for a scurrilous pamphlet assailing Adams, the Federalists, and the act itself. Convicted, he was fined two hundred dollars and given nine months. Jefferson, seeking in his first week in office to right some of the wrongs inflicted by the act, had freed Callender, who looked upon this generosity as something that was only his due, insolently petitioned the President in strong terms for the postmastership of Richmond, threatened him with blackmail when he was refused, and then sold out to the very Federalists who had put him in jail. Far from Jefferson paying Callender to attack the Federalist leaders, it was those leaders who now paid Callender to attack Jefferson and his party.

Hamilton, then, had chosen an unfortunate case to advance a vitally needed reform in the cause of press freedom, and no doubt it was because of the weakness of the case that Hamilton lost it, the four justices dividing evenly. Nevertheless, his argument for truth as a defense in libel was so convincing on its own merits that the New York Assembly soon passed a law admitting it, and providing further that the jury could judge the facts as well as the law—the same points Andrew Hamilton had argued more than a half century before.

The melancholy by-product of the Croswell affair was Hamilton's death. It was while he was in Albany arguing this case that he made the remarks about Aaron Burr which led to the challenge from his old rival, and his subsequent death on the heights of Weehawken. The legal result of Croswell's conviction, apart from the New York Assembly's liberating action, was an epidemic of libel suits elsewhere, both seditious and civil, brought by both Republicans and Federalists.

As for Jefferson, in spite of every attack against him—and many were as vicious as those Washington and Adams had endured—he continued to interpret the First Amendment as absolute (within the libel laws) where the press was concerned. Privately, he advanced the novel idea that newspapers ought to divide their content into truths, probabilities, possibilities, and lies, but he closed the letter outlining this notion with an expression of "solicitude, that this hasty communication may in nowise be permitted to find its way into the public papers," so that he would not "volunteer away that portion of tranquility, which a firm execution of my duties will permit me to enjoy."

Press freedom and an orderly government were not incompatible, Jefferson believed. Margaret Smith told of how the Prussian minister once picked up a Federalist paper, and pointing to an article full of abuse of the President, asked Jefferson why he didn't have it suppressed and the editor punished. "Put that paper in your pocket, Baron," Jefferson told him, "and should you ever hear the reality of our liberty, the freedom of the press questioned, show them this paper—and tell them where you found it."

The measure of the President's conviction was his unfaltering refusal either to suppress or to punish, through two terms in which the Federalist press subjected him to attacks so obnoxious that even its own followers were shocked. Nothing, except for the attacks on Lincoln, have equaled it since, and even the most ardent defender of the First Amendment would have had a hard time deciding where freedom stopped and license began. Jefferson believed that public opinion would, in time, provide the counterbalance, and he was right, although he lived to see only the worst of the abuses corrected. Another quarter of a century and he would have seen his confidence vindicated.

As he wrote to Lafayette about the prospects for freedom in Europe, "The only security of all is in a free press. The force of public opinion cannot be resisted, when permitted freely to be expressed. The agitation it produces must be submitted to. It is necessary, to keep the waters pure." He was still talking about "the unbounded exercise of reason and freedom of opinion" as assuring the "blessings and security of self-government" in the last letter he wrote, only ten days before he died on July 4, 1826.

Eighteen years earlier, the response of public opinion to the excesses of the partisan press was already in evidence. "It is full time," the Washington *Monitor* observed in 1808, "that some effort should be made to purify the presses of the United States, from their froth, their spume, and their coarse vulgarisms. Newspapers of all descriptions teem with bombastic invective, with ridiculous jargon, and empty declamation. The popular taste becomes vitiated, and is prepared to receive the pestilential banquet of every noxious creature that wields a pen or controls a press."

Dr. Samuel Miller, in 1803, had diagnosed with some insight the reasons for the dismal character of the press, and why the initial post-Revolutionary pattern had persisted. In his *Brief Retrospect of the Eighteenth Century,* he had written:

> Too many of our Gazettes are in the hands of persons, destitute at once of the urbanity of gentlemen, the information of scholars, and the principles of virtue. To this source, rather than to any particular depravity of national character, we may ascribe the faults of American newspapers, which have been pronounced by travelers, the most profligate and scurrilous public prints in the civilized world. These considerations, it is conceived, are abundantly sufficient to account for the disagreeable character of American newspapers. In every country the selfish principle prompts men to defame their personal and political enemies; and where the supposed provocations to this are numerous, and no restraints are imposed on the indulgence of the disposition, an inundation of filth and calumny must be expected.
>
> In the United States the frequency of Elections leads to a corresponding frequency of struggle between political parties; these struggles naturally engender mischievous passions, and every species of coarse invective; and, unhappily, too many of the conductors of our public prints have neither the discernment, the firmness, nor the virtue to reject from their pages the foul ebullitions of prejudice and malice Had they more diligence, or greater talents, they might render their Gazettes interesting, by filling them with materials of a more instructive and dignified kind; but, wanting these qualifications, they must give such materials, accompanied with such a seasoning, as circumstances furnish. Of what kind these are no one is ignorant.

Large elements of truth exist in Miller's assessment, yet it does not produce the more balanced view that historical hindsight provides today. The "Gazettes," one must remember, were not in the hands of publishers and editors as we think of them now, but were rather controlled by the contending political parties and their leaders, from the highest to the secondary levels. These leaders, who mostly concealed their support, both financial and literary, comprised, generally speaking, the intellectuals of the day. Aside from Hamilton and the presidents, there were lesser figures who nevertheless qualified as men of intellect and culture—people like Noah Webster, whose *American Minerva,* representing only an episode in his varied life, was a Federalist organ whose invective was limited by Webster's own moderate personality. His defense of Jay's treaty, for example, was a model of public discussion in a newspaper. Moreover, his editorials, running in the same place every edition, were the prototype of the editorial page in America, while his semiweekly edition, the *Herald,* intended "for country readers," was the first bulldog, or undated, edition.

Duane, too, was a man of intellect, although expressed mostly in invective, and so was William Cobbett, the English political refugee who signed himself "Peter Porcupine," a prickly radical whose *Porcupine's Gazette* lived up to Cobbett's opening pronouncement: "Professions of impartiality I shall make none." His slashing pen—he described Ben Franklin as a "crafty and lecherous old hypocrite . . . whose very statue seems to gloat on the wenches as they walk the State House yard"—got him into endless trouble and he finally had to flee to England, but he no more fitted Dr. Miller's scathing description of newspaper proprietors than many of the others.

If the press was scurrilous, it was a reflection of the times. The presence of great men like Washington, Hamilton, Adams, and Jefferson obscures the fact that the American party political system was already producing lying, manipulating, cheating, violence, and the other dismal attributes which have always gone hand in hand with its virtues. These were at a disgraceful peak in the first three administrations because the system was new and unrefined, still far from enjoying the benefits of public-relations and advertising techniques.

When Dr. Miller asserted that more talented editors would fill their pages with "materials of a more instructive and dignified kind," he was expressing in the language of his time what we still hear as pleas to "print the good news, not the bad," to publish "what's right with America, not what's wrong." In fact, everything that was wrong with America can be found in the pages of the late-eighteenth- and early-nineteenth-century press. They reflect a nation that was still half civilized, violent, poorly educated, profoundly uncertain of how its newly devised political system ought to work, and deeply divided still on exactly what form the system should take. All this was in the newspapers, which have always faithfully reflected their times. The people were already cynical about their political leaders, great men though they might be. It was not lost on them that when these leaders deplored the excesses of the press, they seldom disavowed the papers that were excessive in their behalf.

The dark era began drawing to a close, however, with the departure of Jefferson at the end of his second term. By that time Washington and Hamilton were dead, Freneau had retired to his New Jersey farm, Fenno and Bache were both dead of yellow fever. Profound changes were stirring in the nation itself, and in another twenty-five years the media would be almost unrecognizable as the ones that entered upon the first full century of independence.

6

The Media as
a Social Force

IN THE FIRST QUARTER of the new century, before the Great Leap Forward after 1825, the media began to assume the role in national life that proved to be their most important influence in the long run. Newspapers had assumed an early dominance because of the epic political struggle fought out in them. Now the magazines, and particularly book publishing, began to make a far deeper impression on the American consciousness as educators, informers, and cultural shapers of morals and manners.

The nation itself was beginning to take shape, not only as a geographic entity but as a place with a characteristic national life of its own, sharply varied though it might be from the Eastern coastal cities to the advancing frontier. No factor was more important in defining America than the printing press. As the tide of migration and settlement moved west, presses and types were loaded into wagons, lashed onto barges, and even carried by hand. Everywhere the colonial pattern was repeated: the printer-proprietor turned out newspapers, pamphlets, local laws, commercial announcements, bills, legal forms, books, and sometimes magazines, although these were slower in coming at first and did not expand quite so rapidly. If the equipment was inadequate, and that was usually the case, the printer made do with whatever he had. In Alabama, for example, the first novel to be printed there, in 1833, *The Lost Virgin of the South*, was set in two different type sizes.

The westward advance of the media was as rapid as the migration itself. It began as early as 1786, when the first newspaper west of the Alleghenies, the Pittsburgh *Gazette*, began publishing in that city, then a settlement of only three hundred people. In the same year, a Philadelphia printer named John Bradford loaded his press on a wagon, and with the further aid of flatboat and packhorse made his way as far as Lexington, Kentucky, where he began publishing the *Kentucky Gazette* in August 1787.

As Jefferson was leaving the presidency in 1808, Joseph Charless crossed the Mississippi and set up the *Missouri Gazette* in St. Louis. In Texas, a Baltimore printer, Sam Bangs, was busy turning out propaganda in pamphlet, book, and newspaper form on behalf of the Mexican revolutionary movement against Spain. In 1834, the first press in California was set up by Agustin Zamorano, of Florida, who had come by way of Mexico City, and with his advent, printing spanned the continent. A dozen years later there were presses in Monterey and San Francisco, and in 1839 a missionary brought a press from Honolulu, at the instigation of the islands' Christian women, to establish printing in the Pacific Northwest for the specific enlightenment of the Nez Percé Indians.

By 1820, 512 newspapers were being published in the United States, 24 of them dailies, 66 semi- or triweeklies, and 422 weeklies. It must be remembered that the presses producing them were also turning out books, magazines, pamphlets, and a large quantity of job work for local governments and governing bodies. These products of the presses were read largely by the upper economic and social classes, who could read and had the money to buy them.

Culture was increasingly centered in the cities. Philadelphia, the largest in 1800 with 70,000 inhabitants, was also the publishing center of the nation, although it was soon overtaken by both New York (60,000 residents in 1800) and Boston (25,000); Charleston had 18,-000 people and Baltimore had 13,000. All these cities, the only ones in America with populations of more than 10,000, had printers and publishers, and generally speaking, they had the best ones. Nevertheless, printer-publishers in the old sense persisted for a long time in places like Litchfield, Connecticut; Norfolk, Virginia; Harrisburg and Pittsburgh, in Pennsylvania; Poughkeepsie and Plattsburg, in New York State; Walpole and Portsmouth, in New Hampshire; and Dedham, Massachusetts. Even in a hamlet as obscure as Northumberland, Pennsylvania, an ambitious pioneer printed and published four volumes of Joseph Priestley's *History of the Christian Church*.

While the printing press continued to serve multiple publishing purposes as it moved westward, the beginnings of specialization were already occurring in the East as the nineteenth century began. Book publishing was beginning to separate itself from newspaper publication on a large scale, while magazines, slowest to develop, were not as able to stand by themselves and were often the by-product of a press whose greatest thrust was toward books or magazines. The alliance with newspapers was rapidly coming to an end for magazines; increasingly, they were associated with book publishing, and as the century progressed, many of the best were the subsidiary properties of publishing houses.

Geography played a decisive role in establishing New York, Boston, and Philadelphia as the nation's cultural centers. Not only had they been the first to put down roots and establish themselves, but as the country developed, the books and magazines they published were carried into the interior by the natural waterways and consequently a trading pattern was established.

Scholars have pointed out that the New York media grew quickly and came to dominate the others because they had such ready access to the interior through the Hudson River and later the Erie Canal. Philadelphia survived because, similarly, it had control of the Susquehanna trade. But Boston was stifled because no large river flowed from it into the interior; Baltimore diminished in stature after a promising start for the same reason; Hartford, until 1830 as important as Boston in book publishing, found its trade aborted because the Connecticut River could not be successfully navigated above the Massachusetts border. New York and Philadelphia became cultural centers because they were better able to interreact with the inhabitants of the interior and consequently understand public taste. Rivers, roads, and eventually rails emanated from them to the whole country.

Important cultural differences among the regions also influenced the growth of publishing. In the South, for example, the peculiar nature of those whose economic life was based on slavery conditioned literary and other aspects of cultural life. Erudition was certainly far from unknown among plantation owners—there were superb multilingual libraries in some of the great mansions, particularly in Georgia—but the South nonetheless lived in its own private world, far surpassing the exaggerated insularity of the Boston aristocrats. Southerners did not read much, on the whole, even in the region's cultural center, Virginia. They lived in a world dominated by tradition, where anti-intellectualism was part of the way of life. Nothing in print was safe from Southern intolerance. Nothing, perhaps, with the exception of

Sir Walter Scott, who enjoyed an almost morbid popularity which Northern publishers and booksellers could hardly satisfy. Southerners responded passionately to Scott's unflagging devotion to the feudal past, to his celebration of a social order that remained immutable. (Southern intellectuals, however, were often immune to the Scott virus. Jefferson had no love for him, and in fact the only novel he is said to have read twice was *Don Quixote*, satirizing the feudalism which Scott exalted.)

Books, wherever they were published, continued a tradition already established, as did newspapers, but magazines broke new ground. They were helped considerably by the Postal Act of 1794, which grudgingly recognized them as a medium, stating that they "may be transported in the mails when the mode of conveyance and the size of the mails will permit of it." Before, they had been transported or not at the whim of individual postmasters, and that was one more handicap added to the high cost of distribution through an erratic mail service operating over roads that were usually no more than rough wagon trails. Postmasters and government alike gave little consideration to magazines. When they did, it was someone like Franklin, who was not above sending out his own magazine without paying the nearly prohibitive postal rates demanded of others.

Even after 1794, it was expensive to deliver periodicals. It cost eight cents a copy for a sixty-four-page octavo magazine to be carried more than a hundred miles. For shorter distances, rates fell slightly: six cents for fifty to one hundred miles, four cents for less than fifty miles. That meant the annual cost of distributing twelve issues of a magazine of these dimensions would be anywhere from forty-eight to ninety-six cents, depending on the distance. The subscriber paid this cost.

It is a melancholy fact, as true today as it was then, that nothing seemed to discourage the rise of postal rates. New roads were built, postal routes were extended, and transportation in general improved as the new century advanced, but after the War of 1812, postage went up 50 per cent for every category. But neither then nor later was America ever able to approach Western European postal systems for efficiency and relatively lower costs.

In spite of all these handicaps, magazines began to increase in number. There were a dozen of them at the turn of the century, where there had been only five in 1794. By 1810 there were forty, and the figure had climbed to nearly a hundred by 1825. These were the survivors at that date. Between five and six hundred had actually appeared in the century's first quarter, but most were ephemeral.

With the magazines came a new breed of editors—not printers, or publisher-booksellers, or political leaders and their friends using a medium as a vehicle, but workers and practitioners in what was still a new and virtually untried medium. The prototypical editor—the first magazine editor in the modern style—was Joseph Dennie, whose *Port Folio* dominated the field before 1825. Dennie, a man of immense charm and wit, was a Harvard graduate who had started as a lawyer but found himself drawn irresistibly to literature, and began writing and editing in 1793 the *Farmer's Museum*, a weekly newspaper in Walpole, New Hampshire. A rather short, slender man who dressed elegantly, Dennie signed his beautifully written essays with the pseudonym "Lay Preacher." He was described at work by Joseph T. Buckingham, a noted editor himself who began as Dennie's printer's devil on the *Museum*.

Buckingham reported many years later:

> Dennie wrote with great rapidity, and generally postponed his task until he was called upon for *copy*. It was frequently necessary to go to his office, and it was not uncommon to find him in bed at a late hour in the morning. His *copy* was often given out in small portions, a paragraph or two at a time; sometimes it was written in the printing-office, while the compositor was waiting to put it in type. One of the best of his lay sermons was written at the village tavern, directly opposite to the office, in a chamber where he and his friends were amusing themselves with cards. It was delivered to me by piecemeal, at four or five different times. If he happened to be engaged in a game when I applied for copy, he would ask some one to *play his hand for him while he could give the devil his due*. When I called for the closing paragraph of the sermon, he said, "Call again in five minutes." "No," said Taylor, "I'll write the improvement for you." He accordingly wrote the concluding paragraph, and Dennie never saw it till it was put in print.

The "Taylor" in whom Dennie put such trust was actually his friend Royall Tyler, also a former lawyer, whose play, *The Contrast*, was the first comedy to be performed on the American stage. Tyler was one of the literary friends Dennie gathered around him, who contributed to the *Museum* and later to the *Port Folio*.

A great change in Dennie's life came in 1799 when Secretary of State Timothy Pickering invited him to Philadelphia as his private secretary, and in return for this Federalist plum gave him the opportunity to devote some of his writing talents to Hamilton's *Gazette of the United States*. Dennie took on both jobs, but he had no intention of abandoning his "Lay Sermons," which had been so popular in the

Museum, and consequently cast them in a new form as a magazine, the *Port Folio*, which began publishing on January 3, 1801. It persisted until December 1827. Writing for it, Dennie assumed a new pseudonym, "Oliver Oldschool, Esq."

At five dollars a year, the *Port Folio* was worth the price. Besides Dennie's own polished prose, its pseudonymic contributors included John Quincy Adams, Charles Brockden Brown, Tyler, Gouverneur Morris, and others, besides such imported tidbits as unpublished letters written to Tobias Smollett by James Boswell, Samuel Richardson, and David Hume. That kind of quality commanded two thousand subscribers within four months.

The heart of the magazine, however, was Dennie's "Lay Preacher" essays, and seventy-seven of them appeared in its pages between 1891 and 1808. They reflected Dennie's diverse interests—literature, politics, morals, manners—and they were all graceful, witty, informed, and perennially entertaining. The other contributors wrote humor, travel, biography, comments on American speech, and satire. The general tone was English and vaguely anti-American. Politically, the magazine was Federalist, of course, and to some extent it took on the tone of emotional invective prevalent in the Federalist press. That brought Dennie into court in 1803, on an indictment by a grand jury, for seditious libel, but after numerous postponements he was ultimately acquitted in 1805, and unabashed, went back to baiting the democrats.

The *Port Folio* became nonpartisan after 1809; in time it dropped politics entirely. Dennie died on January 7, 1812, and the magazine in other hands was never the same again. It had been the vehicle of its gifted proprietor, who made it the most successful literary periodical of its day, and perhaps the first really successful magazine.

One of Dennie's contributors, Charles Brockden Brown, was equally talented as editor and writer, but less successful. Beginning in 1799, he edited a series of periodicals with various titles, none of which survived very long at a time. Brown made more of a name for himself in literary history as a novelist; his first novel, *Wieland*, was a popular success and Brown is sometimes cited as America's "first novelist," but that is a matter of definition.

Whatever else Brown may have been, he was certainly among the first voices in the media to be raised in the cause of feminism, at a time of entrenched male chauvinism. True, he was inclined to take a highly romantic view of women that would scarcely be accepted by today's movement zealots, but he did defend their rights as human beings at a time when few others were particularly interested in doing so. The prevailing view of women was expressed by a contributor to one of Brown's periodicals, the *Literary Magazine*, when he wrote: "All the virtues that are founded in the sensibility of the heart are theirs. Pity, the attribute of angels, and friendship, the balm of life, delight to dwell in the female breast. What a forlorn, what a savage creature would man be without the meliorating offices of the gentle sex!"

Now here is Brown himself, writing in another of his publications, the *Weekly Magazine*, and carrying on a dialogue about "The Rights of Women." He asks a hypothetical lady, "Pray, Madam, are you a federalist?" and she replies: "While I am conscious of being an intelligent moral being; while I see myself denied, in so many cases, the exercise of my own discretion, incapable of separate property; subject in all periods of my life to the will of another, on whose bounty I am made to depend for food and shelter; when I see myself, in my relation to society, regarded merely as a beast, as an insect, passed over, in the distribution of public duties, as absolutely nothing ... it is impossible I should assent to their opinion, so long as I am conscious of moving and willing. . . . No, I am no federalist." Gloria Steinem could scarcely have put it more plainly.

Brown had only to look within his own profession to see how little progress women had made as individuals. There were a few women printers like Ann Franklin, James's widow, and Dinah Nuthead, widow of a Maryland printer, who had inherited their husband's businesses and won some notice, but there were nowhere near the number of women printers, sixty of them, who had practiced in Great Britain in the seventeenth century alone. In America, they were usually the widows of printers, whose sons helped and eventually carried on for them, or they married other printers who took over the business and relegated them to the fireside. The fact that women could learn to work in printing at all rose from the fact that it was still a cottage industry until well into the nineteenth century, and a printer's family usually worked for him.

Nevertheless, a few women had made their marks. Mary Avery, of Boston, was the first American woman bookseller and a publisher as well. Elizabeth Short, of Connecticut, was the first woman binder in the colonies, and in 1714 had bound two thousand copies of *Confession of Faith*, better known historically as the Saybrook Platform. Catherine Zenger is still regarded as a heroine, although the help she gave her husband during his imprisonment has been romanticized and exaggerated. After his death, she operated his press for a time and printed several books until her stepson was old enough to take control. In Annapolis, Anne Catherine Hoof Greene not only published the *Maryland Gazette* but became public printer to Annapolis in 1767. Her three sons and several grandsons were well-known printers. More notable, perhaps, were the remarkable Goddard women, of Providence, especially Sarah, who helped her son William start the town's first newspaper and became his partner; and whose daughter, Mary Katherine, an expert compositor, took over the *Maryland Journal* from her brother and edited it through the Revolution.

There were others, but as the nineteenth century began, the number had diminished, and in all the media women were the extraordinary exception rather than the rule. It was the magazine, however, which soon gave them by far the greatest opportunities they were to have in that century.

In Brown's time, except for his own astringent defenses of their freedom, women were not depicted as the "intelligent moral beings" he wrote about, but as pretty butterflies pinned to the board and argued about endlessly in the magazines, and to a lesser extent in newspaper features. The general view was expressed in the January 1804 edition of the *Monthly Anthology*, where a writer commenting on the influence of French fashions grumbled:

"We have imported the worst of French corruptions, the want of female delicacy. The fair and innocent have borrowed the lewd arts of seduction. . . . What must we say of some, whom we daily observe, whose dress is studiously designed to display the female form? Why do they solicit our gaze? I will not charge them with the design of kindling a lawless flame. They will shudder at the suggestion. But I warn them. . . ."

Those who think of this viewpoint as a quaint relic of the distant past need only recall the turmoil over the miniskirt to understand that the idealization of women has not changed in a large segment of the population.

Some magazines seriously debated the subject of physical education for women. The *American Journal of Education*, for instance, deplored gymnastics as "unfeminine" but granted that riding and walking were not harmful, although it appeared to consider the best exercise for women to be spinning and household chores. The children in the family did not fare much better. Periodicals were emerging, but they were generally as humorless as the books provided for them, devoted mostly to teaching religion and morality, and written in a stilted, heavy-handed style. A literature for children was slowly developing in America, but meanwhile there was no lack of magazines concerned with how to educate them.

In discussing education, the chief argument in the magazines was over the standard classical curriculum, as opposed to the new studies in science and mathematics that, as some complained, were crowding Greek and Latin out of the colleges. Here again Brown was the most controversial of editors. He had a low opinion of colleges, and deplored what he called the "mania" for establishing them. "Three fourths of the colleges in the United States," he wrote, "have professors wretchedly unqualified for their station. . . . I have known young gentlemen going home with A.B. affixed to their names without being able to construe the diploma which certified their standing."

On this subject, Brown was profoundly wrong. He would have been on much sounder ground if he had been writing of higher education 150 years later.

Perhaps the most important factor in the magazine business as it began to take shape was its faculty for attracting the best writers as contributors, and occasionally as editors. Often the editors were excellent writers as well, like Brown, or even more so, like Washington Irving, who was briefly editor of the *Analectic Magazine,* begun in 1813. Some were poets, like Samuel Woodworth and George Pope Morris, young men (Morris was only twenty-two) who founded the *New-York Mirror* in 1823, a magazine that laid the foundations for the comfortable literary tradition that permeated what came to be known as the Knickerbocker Period in New York life in the eighteen-forties.

Imitation of English models was still a prevailing mode in magazine publishing, not only typographically and in general content, but in the tendency to attract coteries of intellectuals as editors and contributors, many of them from the universities. There was even a class of magazines, the eclectics, which were simply clip-and-paste potpourris from the British periodicals.

Religion had used book publishing from the first as a platform and propaganda machine to spread the faith, but in the America of the new century the churches added magazines to their arsenal, perceiving at once that this medium was even better adapted to their needs than books. Religions could have their own magazines, as they already owned book-publishing houses, and through them it was possible to extend their area of influence beyond the perimeters of publishing. Since it was an era of splintering and controversy among the religionists, with the established faiths not only contending among themselves but collectively fighting off the inroads of the free-form fundamentalists, it was no wonder that religious publications proliferated. By 1824 at least twenty-one of them were published monthly, coming from denominations which often also put out newspapers as well.

It was obvious that magazines as a medium offered everyone a chance to advance his own specialty or interest, and soon there were periodicals reaching out to specific new audiences—farmers, teachers, lawyers, doctors, musicians and theatrical people, college students, scientists, mechanics, and historians. Thus the essential character of the magazine business was established in substance before 1825. There was even a suggestion that periodicals were starting to conceive of themselves as something more than a medium of information and instruction. It was not lost on the print entrepreneurs that comic magazines were beginning to sweep the country, as their earlier rivals, the comic almanac and the jest book, had done. Book publishers were the primary producers of this genre.

In a large sense, however, magazine editors thought of themselves as engaged in a much loftier enterprise than simply entertaining the public. "We wish to impress upon every mind, a true value of the dignity of our national character. This dignity is promoted and upheld by nothing more than learning," wrote the editor of a magazine called *Portico* in the summer of 1816. It was the authentic voice of a new nation trying in literature, as well as politics, to present itself as a state worthy of taking its place in the older, established community of the Western world.

The country was full of serious doubts about itself, however, and nowhere is this more completely reflected than in the media of the early eighteen hundreds, particularly the magazines. In his book *The Unquiet Eagle*, Professor Fred Somkin reports that when the Marquis de Lafayette returned to America in 1824 for a triumphal tour, he appeared to set off a passionate reexamination of the national character and experience. There was nostalgia and regret in the look backward at where the nation had been, and a feeling of deep disquiet about where it was going. People wanted to retain the simplicities of the past within the framework of an increasingly affluent and complicated society which had already surged frighteningly past the average citizen's expectations. The fear was that they were in danger of losing the old values, of trading them in for a society in which the old communal ideal would be lost. All this was reflected in what was being written for the media. The parallel with our own time is obvious.

But along with the doubts about the future of such concepts as freedom and democracy, and a longing for the peaceful Jeffersonian agricultural life-style that now seemed slipping away, the magazines were trying to break away from British models and develop a national literature. Consequently the tone of many periodicals was doggedly patriotic and defensive against attacks on American culture. In an age of great orators like Henry Clay and John C. Calhoun, the oratorical style flourished in the magazines as well, both in prose and in poetry, and both were inclined to be long-winded and declamatory. Paradoxically, Noah Webster was going around the country trying to persuade editors of newspapers and magazines to abandon English usage in spelling and establish an "American language," but it was not easy. Even while they were boasting about America's "unshackled genius," many editors, by habit as much as by veneration of Old World standards, persisted in talking about the nation's "gigantic vigour."

For a long period there was a war of words between British and American magazine editors. "Who reads an American book?" the *Edinburgh Review* inquired disdainfully, expressing an attitude which is hardly unknown in British intellectual circles today, where American books are regularly clubbed to death in the British quality newspapers and periodicals, and American magazines are widely regarded as essentially vulgar, although some of them are widely read and two or three have had their formulas and formats adapted to the British market. The British *Quarterly Review*'s blunt observation that "Americans are inherently inferior" intellectually to Europeans would still find many Britons in agreement.

American editors struck back, advising readers to treat British "rhapsodies" about the "barbarism of the United States" with "laughter at their blunders, if made ingenuously and with commiseration, if they proceed from malice." Dennie denounced those English travelers who had returned to deride the promised land, calling them "unblushing miscreants—those slanderers by profession . . . ," while the *North American Review*, soon to be the leading intellectual periodical in America, declared angrily in 1816 that "the travellers who described us have with very few exceptions been so ignorant or so profligate, that we almost despair of an able and unprejudiced account of the United States from a European." There were those who thought the foreign critics were part of a paid conspiracy to ruin the United

States industrially and economically. Some patriots today firmly believe that critics of America are still in the pay of those same conspirators, who have meanwhile moved from London and Paris to Moscow.

American magazine editors were only slightly less hostile toward the French than the British. They often warned their readers about French novels and French "atheism," and spoke of French "literary decay." They were much more cordial toward the Germans. Several, like Edward Everett, of the *North American Review*, could read German literature in the original. Everett, in fact, helped make the work of such writers as Goethe and Schiller known to America, through the pages of his magazine. While deploring the French, it may be added, the editors reprinted both poetry and prose from France.

A major problem confronting the editors was the difficulty of finding enough able contributors. No writing class as such yet existed, no group of professional writers who made their living with their pens. Magazines were still less a business than a leisure occupation for gentlemen, and the bulk of the readers were still an educated elite. Writing, like acting, was not considered quite a respectable occupation. As Charles Brockden Brown put it, a gentleman might write for amusement and distraction, but to write for money would be vulgar. Usually an editor had to depend on his friends for much of the contributed material, and these friends were often members of a literary club that more or less supported the magazine they favored. Since articles were still unsigned or pseudonymous, there was not much incentive to write as an outlet for ego. Worse, editors exerted absolute control over what was printed, making any changes they thought were necessary. Payment was small and came when the contribution was printed, which sometimes might be a year or more later. Some gentlemen loftily refused the dollar-a-page rate that was standard for some time. Editors were often not paid at all, except for the few professionals whose salaries were so small they were scarcely more than honorariums. Consequently editing was a part-time occupation for most editors, and circulations were as small as the salaries. Two thousand was exceptional.

Yet the magazine business continued to expand, concentrating in Boston, New York, and Philadelphia, as the book-publishing business was doing, but proliferating also in Baltimore, Richmond, Charleston, Lexington (Kentucky), and Cincinnati. Even in the more remote cities, periodicals were beginning to be more attractive as an influx of

English engravers began to make noticeable improvements with illustration, and as the technology of pressmaking began to improve. Wood engraving was transforming the appearance of magazines by 1825.

Specialization by scientific, agricultural, and legal periodicals was proving itself useful in spreading knowledge across a diverse country, but the magazines were starting to show that they too, like the newspapers, could be a political force. There was already in 1821 an antislavery magazine called, in the grandiloquent style of the day, *The Genius of Universal Emancipation*, published in Mount Pleasant, Ohio, by Benjamin Lundy, who started his magazine with no capital and a subscription list of six. His publication was printed in Steubenville, twenty miles away, and Lundy walked there to get the printed product, carrying it home on his back. Later, he printed his little sixteen-page monthly in Greenville, in northeastern Tennessee, then walked all the way to Baltimore in 1824, where he reestablished the magazine. It did so well there that in two years he made it a weekly.

The *Genius* was not a radical magazine by today's standards. It advocated only gradual abolition, and the eventual colonization of black people elsewhere (an idea Abraham Lincoln also entertained). In the context of the times, however, that was enough to infuriate Baltimore slaveholders and dealers. One of them nearly succeeded in killing him. Undismayed, Lundy continued to publish, and also traveled on foot through the states, preaching abolition. On his travels he met young William Lloyd Garrison, soon to be one of the nation's leading abolitionists. Garrison began publishing an antislavery newspaper, the *Journal of the Times*, in Bennington, Vermont, in 1828, but it lasted less than two years. Lundy walked up to Bennington and persuaded Garrison to come down and be assistant editor of the *Genius.*

These men were the pioneers in what was to become an important magazine movement. The impetus behind the antislavery magazines was largely religious, just as the discussions of it in the general periodicals were far more sentimental than realistic. Religion was also implicit in the attack on drinking, which began in 1826 with what was probably the first temperance magazine, the *National Philanthropist*. The subject had already been debated in the general magazines, and smoking, too, was under assault in many periodicals. The magazines also sought, with no better success, to end dueling.

New kinds of magazines continued to emerge. Theatrical reviews appeared and vanished again as rapidly as many of the productions they criticized, but there was continuing drama criticism in the general magazines and newspapers. Another new classification was the comic periodical, equally transitory in the beginning, but later one of the mass audience's chief pleasures. The best of them, famous in its own right and serving as a model for those that came after, was the *Salmagundi, or, the Whim-Whams and Opinions of Lancelot Langstaff, Esq.* This distant ancestor of the old *Life* magazine, *Judge,* and ultimately the *New Yorker,* was distinguished by its writers and editors, which included Washington Irving, his brother William, and his brother-in-law, James Kirk Paulding.

This magazine lasted only a year, from 1807 to 1808, and did not appear regularly, but it was pleasantly filled with gentle satire, fun-poking comments on the theater and other institutions, a little verse, and some unflattering portraits of contemporary personalities. Its young entrepreneurs did not take it seriously. "I know you consider old Sal as a sort of saucy, flippant trollope," Paulding wrote to Irving, "belonging to nobody, and not worth fathering."

Otherwise, the arts were not well served in the magazines. Music had no magazine of its own until later, although some general magazines published music criticism and a few even made it a department. Art was neglected except for an occasional article or a piece of criticism.

Another kind of publication on the rise was the business periodical. It was slow to start before 1825, and it would take the sudden burst of technology preceding the Civil War to bring it fully into being, but it was on its way. Such publications traced their ancestry to the publications known as "price currents" appearing first in seventeenth-century Holland and England. Translated to the American colonies, they appeared first in Charleston, South Carolina, in 1774, and were virtually the only kind of business publishing until 1812. Philadelphia was the financial center in these years, and business publications naturally centered there. "Price currents" soon became the property of the newspapers, but other business information was the province of magazines, with exceptions like the *Daily Items for Merchants,* the first daily business paper, which began in New York in 1815. Real specialization started in 1825.

In the general periodicals, fiction was getting more attention, although it would be some time before it became the dominating factor. The short story, however, was already a staple in the weekly miscellanies, of which there was a plentiful supply, and in the magazines intended for women. But the progress of fiction was impeded by the same public intolerance, the same urge to control other people's minds in the name of morality, that still afflicts us today. The new bourgeoisie in the new nation was against actors, fiction, dancing, gambling, cockfighting and horse racing, with varying degrees of vehemence. A London periodical's article of 1797, "Novel Reading a Cause of Female Depravity," was widely reprinted in American magazines several years later. There were many sober, serious people who believed in this kind of nonsense, just as they believe today that there is a connection between pornography and crime in spite of the overwhelming evidence to the contrary.

In the light of these depressing beginnings of literary censorship, it is refreshing to find a writer in the *Western Review* of March 1821 referring in his breezy outlands way to the "bigots" who called the novel "the primer of Beelzebub." A few years later the same magazine termed the outcry against novels "mere wretched cant, utterly unworthy of the least pretension to mental enlargement, and fit only for men, who could have presided over a judicature for the trial of witches, or an ecclesiastical legislature to enact 'blue laws.'"

In an atmosphere of false morality, it is hardly surprising that magazine readers wanted, more than anything else, to read about duly certified and accepted heroes. Most of the periodicals ran biographical accounts of these great men, completely uncritical for the most part, and consequently infusing the national consciousness with erroneous, whitewashed views of history, supplementing a similar flood of biographies being issued by the book publishers. It is not too much to say that these well-laundered versions of American history, perpetuated in schoolbooks whose acceptance was controlled by ill-informed parents and school boards, laid the groundwork for the peculiar American innocence about the nation's political life which continues to cause such profound trouble.

The magazines were full of travel articles. Reassured constantly in all the media that their past was unequivocally glorious and the future stupefyingly unlimited, Americans turned their interest to the rest of the world. There were now many of them who had been born in this country, and who could not afford to travel. They read eagerly the accounts of those who could, like John Quincy Adams' narrative of his journey through Silesia, and the letters of other noteworthy people who were traveling in Europe. Much of the travel writing consisted of excerpts from books, of which there were nearly as many as there were travelers.

Since books of American poetry were infrequently published, in about the same ratio that they are today, the magazines became the chief outlet for poems. On the whole, the output was dismal, but not entirely without merit, and in some instances the best American work appeared first in the periodicals. Henry Wadsworth Longfellow, William Cullen Bryant, and FitzGreen Halleck were among these, and the first American appearance of "Thanatopsis" was in the *North American Review* for September 1817. But there were far too many pretentious outpourings like Alexander Wilson's "The Foresters," which had to be published serially in the *Port Folio* because it was two thousand lines long.

In any case, American poets were not much admired by Americans, who devoured the English poets both in book and magazine form. Burns was popular here before he was at home. Milton, Shakespeare, Pope, and Cowper were read in America by people who lived in farmhouses as well as by those in the fine Georgian houses of the cities and Eastern countryside. Tennyson, later, was "too dear for the cottages" in England because of comparatively higher prices there, but he was mass-distributed in America.

It was Scott, however, who eclipsed all others, British and American, in both poetry and prose. The *American Review* observed in 1811 that no poet's works had been "more widely circulated or read with more avidity in this country than those of Walter Scott, who is now as a poet, on the highest pinnacle of fame and popularity." He soon attained the same fame as a novelist, and was rivaled as a poet only by Byron.

Politics had made the American newspaper a distinctively American product by this time, but the magazines were still imitative of the English, and their contents were either English-written or English-oriented for the most part. Book publishing reflected the same situation. What turned everything around was the creation of a mass market as immigration exploded the population, and the mechanical means to reach it were developed. When that occurred, in the period between 1825 and 1850, the media, particularly magazines and books, began to play an entirely different role in national life than they had before.

7

Book Publishing Becomes
an Industry

EMERGING FROM ITS PROVINCIAL STAGE, in which it had languished for nearly two centuries, book publishing in the half century before the Civil War became a powerful force in American life, influencing the development of native literature and consequently doing much in a variety of ways to reflect and illuminate the American character. Growing phenomenally in a period whose chief characteristics were greed and ruthlessness, it developed nevertheless as a business that was widely known then, and since, as a profession for gentlemen.

Change of all kinds propelled the publishing business into a prominence it had never known before. Roads were becoming much better and more numerous; transportation and communication were improving dramatically, and were less costly; radical changes in printing technology were taking place, for the first time since the fifteenth century. Few inventions have so influenced American life as the advent of the steam-powered cylinder press, with the consequent use of stereotyped plates and cheaper methods of making paper and bindings. These devices opened the door to the mass market.

That market was building rapidly. By the eighteen-forties the rapid growth of education at all levels had produced the largest reading audience anyone had ever seen, an audience which virtually demanded books, although magazines and newspapers, of course, shared in the general expansion of the print media.

As soon as they were able to produce for the mass market, American publishers took advantage of the lack of copyright on foreign works, or, more accurately, the refusal of the American government to recognize foreign copyrights in this country. That touched off the great Age of Piracy, in which books of several European countries, but particularly English novels, were appropriated and published here in such quantities as to flood the market for a time. At first, publishers observed what they called a "courtesy copyright," in which the American reprinter had sole rights if he was the first to produce a book in this country, but this "courtesy of the trade," as it was more commonly known, was soon exposed as a pious fraud, and there was no longer even a pretense of ethical conduct as the competition became cutthroat.

Minor houses often succumbed to this competition, and even well-established firms had to withdraw to the safer ground of textbooks, theology, or some other specialization. Those that survived learned to estimate publication schedules in hours instead of days or weeks, and could make a quick profit simply by getting out a first edition of a new English novel a few hours earlier than their rivals. Some had agents in England who hovered like vultures over the bookstalls, or the printers whenever that was possible, to get sheets or books which would be shipped on the fastest boat available. In New York or Philadelphia, the copy would be rushed from the dock, or in some cases from a fast packet which had met the incoming boat offshore, to a publisher's composing room, where the speediest compositors would be employed and the presses would run day and night until the book was ready to be hurried to the stores, or sold on the street like fish. Some ingenious and enterprising publishers even had type set aboard ships while they were making the passage to America.

Newspaper and magazine publishers had not yet exhibited the fierce competitive enterprise these early book makers displayed in the struggle for the British novel trade. For example, M. Carey & Sons, of Philadelphia, had 1500 copies of *Quentin Durward* ready to go within twenty-eight hours after it came off the ship—forty-eight hours before the first opposition edition. It was enough, as they put it, "to have complete and entire possession of every market in the Country for a short time."

In 1836, when this same house was known as Lea & Blanchard, the firm paid an English publisher a substantial sum for an advance copy of Bulwer's *Rienzi*. Unfortunately, the ship that brought it carried a copy of the book destined for Harper & Bros. in New York, the Philadelphia company's chief rival. In a race to capture the New York market first, Lea & Blanchard rushed their copy to Philadelphia, distributed the sheets among a dozen printers, operated their presses all night, and had the reprinted sheets ready for the bindery by nine o'clock the next morning. Binding cases for the volumes had already been made and were waiting. By afternoon, Abraham Hart, another member of the firm, was on his way to New York in a mail stage in which he had hired every seat. He sat on only one; the others were fully occupied by five hundred copies of *Rienzi*. The edition went on sale in New York bookstores the next day, a day ahead of the Harper version.

It was not a case, one might add, of unethical American publishers as opposed to the moral British houses. Piracy proved to be a two-way street, owing to the vagueness of English copyright law and the universality of greed. Between 1841 and 1846, 382 American books were reprinted in England, and most of them had been pirated without permission or royalty payments. Even worse, from the standpoint of the authors, titles were often changed and texts freely altered to suit English tastes and prejudices.

There were conscientious publishers who tried to make token payments to English authors, or who sought to issue their works in "authorized" editions, with suitable payment, but the public would have none of it. Readers were not interested in the moral problems of the book business, if they even knew of them. They went on buying the pirated editions because they were cheaper, and a publisher who wanted to sell English novels in America had no choice but to pirate them under these competitive conditions.

The growth of the book business sometimes astonished contemporary observers. By 1855, America had already far surpassed England in sales, so that while it was most unusual to sell more than 10,000 copies of even the best fiction in Great Britain and Ireland, it was not at all out of the ordinary to sell 50,000 copies of even a moderately good book in America. "So rapid, and so great, has been the demand for books in the United States," marveled one trade journal in 1855, "that some of the leading publishing houses in this city, New York, possessed of princely fortunes, and transacting an unexampled amount of business, in Iron and Red-sandstone palaces, commenced business, certainly not much more than thirty years ago, with 'a feeble beginning' and, probably, small capital."

Such publishers were making a mockery of Sydney Smith's old taunt, "In the four quarters of the globe, who reads an American book?" which had so irritated the magazines. In America, at least, books by native writers were being read in very large quantities.

Washington Irving's works had sold 800,000 copies by 1860. More than a million of T. S. Arthur's books had been purchased, and Cooper's novels were selling at a rate of 40,000 annually. Bayard Taylor had recorded 150,000 copies, and of course there were the incredible sales of Webster's little *Blue-Backed Speller*, totaling 30 million by 1859.

Culture had moved westward, particularly to Cincinnati, by 1856. There, in a city less than a century away from its log cabin beginnings, were twelve publishing houses in 1850, employing 700 people among a population of 116,000, and grossing $1.25 million a year in books and periodicals. In Cincinnati, as in the East and elsewhere, people were reading the nation's own considerable body of literary figures—Irving, Cooper, Hawthorne, Thoreau, Melville, Emerson, Poe, Whitman, Longfellow, Whittier, Lowell. In one climactic year, 1855, America saw the first publication of *Leaves of Grass, Hiawatha, The Age of Fable*, and Bartlett's *Familiar Quotations*. American publishing had also produced a best seller still unsurpassed today in hardcover sales: *Uncle Tom's Cabin.*

By 1860, book production had assumed the general proportions it has today—that is, textbooks were the largest part, 30 to 40 per cent of the whole, a proportion that has risen to roughly 75 per cent in our own time. These schoolbooks had, like fiction, shifted gradually from British to American authorship, spurred by the spectacular success of Webster. In 1856, America was producing every year more schoolbooks than the entire continent of Europe. Even the classical works in use were nearly all published in America, and so were the elementary treatises on law, medicine, theology, and science, as well as the dictionaries.

But by far the most spectacular development in book publishing was the first paperback revolution, which had an impact on the public and on publishing itself so powerful that, in a sense, its effects are still felt today in the existence of what might be called a "permanent revolution" establishing paperbacks as an important division of publishing.

It began as an ingenious scheme by two young New York journalists, Park Benjamin and Rufus Wilmot Griswold, who launched in July 1839 a new weekly periodical called *Brother Jonathan*, with the backing of Wilson & Co., a printing firm. They avoided book postage rates by calling their publication a newspaper, and printing it in that large-page format. Instead of news, however, except for a few random items designed to give it the appearance of legitimacy,

Brother Jonathan contained pirated serials of British novels—Dickens, Bulwer, Marryat, and others.

After six months of gratifying success, the partners lost their paper because Benjamin H. Day, a shrewd entrepreneur in his own right, who had founded the New York *Sun* and introduced penny newspapers to America, bought into Wilson & Co. and fired them. Benjamin and Griswold then went to another printer, Jonas Winchester, who had been Horace Greeley's partner in producing a periodical called the *New-Yorker*, and persuaded him to start another pirate newspaper. The *Jonathan* partners had once worked on the *New-Yorker*, which was now in such financial trouble that Greeley was making other plans (they led him to found the New York *Tribune*) and Winchester was looking for a new venture. Now there were three partners, and in June 1840 they began publishing the *New World*, a twin of *Brother Jonathan* in nearly every way. It had a quarto, or "library," edition, which could be bound, along with its folio edition, forcing Day's *Jonathan* to publish a quarto edition two years later.

Popular as they were, there was a serious difficulty involved in both these publications, as their readers soon informed them. Long before the serials were completed, the books themselves were likely to be on the market, and in spite of the price differential, there were a good many people who preferred to read the whole book at once. Responding to this criticism, *New World* issued in July 1841 the complete first volume of Lever's *Charles O'Malley* in the same size and format, for fifty cents. It was called a "supplement," or an "extra," as it was popularly known. *Brother Jonathan* promptly brought out the same book in the same form, for twenty-five cents. By the middle of 1842, the supplements had become regular features of both publications. They were the prototype of the paperback book in America as we know it now.

The Napier and Hoe cylinder presses, which had already revolutionized newspaper production, were the powerful instruments behind the new supplements. Printed on these presses in as large a quantity as there was demand for, they were sold by newsboys on the streets as well as by mail. For the street sale, the proprietors put out an edition in paper covers in somewhat lurid color. Another edition went through the mails without covers, thus maintaining the pretext that these books were really newspapers.

The newspapers themselves saw that the supplement proprietors had a good thing, and soon the Boston *Nation*, the *Mirror* and the *Sun* in New York, and the Philadelphia *Public Ledger* were in the business. Book publishers were aghast at these developments. They were publishing the same books—English and French novelists, mostly—in well-printed clothbound volumes at anywhere from one to two dollars, a high price in those times, although not as high as the customary British price, twenty-one shillings.

Competition from the newspapers, added to that between the supplements themselves, brought the price of the supplements down to twelve and a half cents. At that figure, the book publishers had no choice, if they did not want to give up their own lucrative piracy, but to get into the battle themselves. Harper was first to join the combat, in 1843, bringing out a series of popular British reprints for a quarter. That was still too high to compete. The retail price was cut in half, with the booksellers given a one-third discount. Then other publishers joined the competition, and the price war soon reached a point of absurdity, where it was impossible for anyone to make money. Some titles had already reached that low point. In 1842, for example, both supplements and Harper's published Bulwer's *Zanoni* almost simultaneously, with the result that it could be bought for six cents a copy. During the following year, short books were selling for six and a half cents a copy. The next year, short books were selling for six and a quarter cents; longer ones ranged from eighteen and three-quarters cents to thirty-seven and a half.

The regular publishers were badly hurt by the supplements, especially houses like that of the Harper brothers, who had built a substantial part of their trade on the English reprints known as the Family Library of English Literature, which sold for a dollar, or sometimes a little more. They (and the others) must have been particularly galled when they read an "editorial" in the *New World* advising its readers, "You are not so green as to pay a dollar for what you can get for eighteen pence or a shilling—not you!" The *New World* loudly proclaimed, "We are friends of the people, and our motto is, 'The greatest good to the greatest number.'"

Park Benjamin, the editor of *New World*, took a cynical delight in the anguished cries that arose from Harper's. He quoted an imaginary English writer, the victim of American pirating, accusing the brothers Harper: "Ah, ha! you have caught it at last yourselves, have you? The robbers have been robbed; the filchers have had their pockets picked! ... We like to see the pirates made to walk the plank!"

But the pirates, and especially the Harpers, were not exactly helpless. They were rich and powerful enough to publish in competition and reduce prices with the supplements, and they were joined by others not as rich but determined to get as much of the low-price market as they could while the boom was on. At first, the supplement publishers professed not to take the competition seriously. "We welcome them to the field," *Brother Jonathan* said, "hoping they may 'turn their money quick,' as did the bright lad who purchased apples at two for threepence and sold them at three for twopence." But the inevitable result, which was just as inevitable in much later periods of paperback publishing history, was a glutted market, and by April 1843, *Brother Jonathan* was writing in a different key: "Literature is now a drug. All the markets are overstocked."

Even as these gloomy words were being read, the United States Post Office dealt the supplements a deathblow by suddenly ruling that they could not be carried at newspaper rates but must go at book rates. *Brother Jonathan* survived only seven months after that; it sold out to *New World* in January 1844, but it too was suspended in May 1845. The publishers had won, with the Post Office's help and by virtue of their superior resources.

The first paperback revolution demonstrated several things. It proved that good literature, along with the cheap, could be brought to a large new market of people who could not afford the clothbound volumes, and so a new class of readers had been created. More important, the revolution disclosed the new significance of the book as a mass medium, after years of serving a comparatively small elite. Cheap books, paperbound or not, were firmly established in the publishing scene, never to disappear. The immediate result, between 1845 and 1857, was the greatest boom the business had ever witnessed. Cheap books appeared in profusion from many publishers, some in cloth, others softbound, most selling for less than a dollar. Simultaneous publishing of titles in cloth and paper was common. Piracy did not disappear, but the publishers now drew heavily on American authors; perhaps 70 per cent of the new output was by native writers, who proliferated rapidly in the new atmosphere.

Besides the original promoters of the supplements, the first paperback revolution launched the careers of two publishers whose books had a lasting influence on American culture. Theophilus B. Peterson, of Philadelphia, emerged as the preeminent publisher of sensational fiction and cheap reprints. A descendant of Swedish immigrants whose arrival in the New World anticipated William Penn, and whose mother came from an old New England family, Peterson followed a pattern of nineteenth-century business success that was firmly established before the Civil War. Some of these successful

Americans were college graduates, but more were the sons of farmers or small merchants who started out with little or no capital and scant education and made fortunes of varying sizes. Peterson hated school so intensely that he left at thirteen to be an errand boy in a dry-goods store. After various jobs, and looking for a way to advance faster, he learned the stereotyping trade and by 1843, at eighteen, he was fore-man of that department on the *Saturday Evening Post*, then a strug-gling, rather nondescript magazine. At twenty, he was in business for himself as a bookseller and news agent, with $300 in savings and less than $100 in capital stock, after expenses had been paid.

Out of this came a remarkable enterprise. Sensing the great demand for books at low prices, especially cheap, sensational fiction, he set himself a policy of "small profits and quick sales," and went to work. His subsequent success was the result not only of his natural business abilities, but his astute feeling for public taste. That was best illustrated, perhaps, by his most popular author, Mrs. E. D. E. N. (for Emma Dorothy Eliza Nevitte) Southworth, whose first novel he pub-lished after it had been rejected, for legitimate literary reasons, by several other publishers.

Mrs. Southworth was the prototype of a publishing phenomenon of our time, the author whose work is condemned as meretricious by critics, but whose work nevertheless sells in spectacular figures. From Mrs. Southworth on, through a long list of these popular favorites (mostly women, although there have been more men in the category in this century), the chief ingredient shared by these authors has been a talent for storytelling, as ancient as the keepers of the oral tra-dition who have sat in bazaars and villages all over the world for cen-turies and entertained the spellbound throng.

The critics unanimously deplored Mrs. Southworth and the entire breed of writers of whom she was the acknowledged leader, and they did it in words which, with a little updating, could have appeared in last week's New York *Times Book Review*. Typical was the *National Quarterly's* complaint in June 1860:

> It is a truth, sadly attested by the times in which we live, that liter-ature, like human society, is growing more degenerate every year. At the present day the great mass of reading matter of the public is com-posed of the most worthless and enervating effusions of the many would-be authors whose names fill the annals of nineteenth-century literature. . . . Nine out of every ten (nay, we say ninety-nine out of every hundred) persons prefer the stories of Mrs. Southworth and Syl-vanus Cobb, Jr., to the noble productions of Miss Muloch and George

Elliott [sic]. *The Hidden Hand* and *The Gunmaker of Moscow* are far more universally read than *John Halifax* and *The Mill on the Floss*. Even the great Bulwer is rated a bore, while Emerson Bennett is considered charming.

The critics were unquestionably right about the quality of what was being printed and read so widely. One need only quote a brief excerpt from *Ishmael; or, In the Depths*, the novel Mrs. Southworth considered her best. Ishmael, a young man of unbelievable virtue, has just rescued Claudia, the daughter of a judge, from a runaway. Mrs. Southworth writes:

> "How do you feel yourself this morning, my lad?" he [the judge] inquired, putting the usual commonplace question.
>
> "Much easier, thank you, sir," replied the youth in the pure, sweet, modulated tones of a highly-cultivated nature.
>
> The judge was surprised, but did not show that he was so, as he said:
>
> "You have done my daughter a great service; but at the cost of much suffering to yourself, I fear, my lad."
>
> "I consider myself very fortunate and happy, sir, in having had the privilege of rendering Miss Merlin any service, at whatever cost to myself," replied Ishmael, with graceful courtesy.

With that kind of prose, Mrs. Southworth made a fortune for Peterson and herself. At one time, she was earning an unprecedented six thousand dollars a year in royalties. Peterson was still publishing her in 1877, when he brought out an edition of her works in forty-two volumes. In the second great paperback boom of the eighties and nineties, her books were sold in large figures, opening up a new public for the romantic novels that made her the second most popular woman writer in American publishing history. She was still widely read when she died in 1899, and Street & Smith had more than ninety volumes of her work in print in 1930, selling for ten cents. Of her fifty or more novels, nearly all sold at least 100,000 copies. As the Jacqueline Susann of the last century, with extravagant romance substituted for extravagant sex, Mrs. Southworth was a prominent example of the truism that mass readership (or viewing, in our time) means a proportionate lowering of the cultural level. The fact that she continued to sell for sixty years or more constitutes further proof that, in spite of the contention of some sociologists, prolonged exposure to reading will not raise that level to any degree.

Besides his exploitation of the mass market, T. B. Peterson, as he was known through his imprint, also contributed to the publishing scene the first notions of how advertising could be used effectively to sell books. Another of his original ideas was to issue a catalog with portraits of his principal authors, and biographical sketches of their lives and works, of the kind common on dust jackets today. Peterson may also have been the first publisher of cheap books to give himself a façade of respectability by turning out a few elegantly printed and illustrated books of real literary quality.

In spite of Mrs. Southworth's enormous popularity, however, perhaps the most enduring kind of book to emerge from the first paperback revolution was the dime novel. It had its roots in the cheap, sensational paperbacks put out by several different houses before Irwin and Erastus Beadle affixed their names firmly to this branch of popular literature. The story papers of the early nineteenth century were the true ancestors of the dime novel, and some of the tales they printed later reappeared in the Beadle and other lines of nickel and dime publications.

"Dime novel" does not mean what it seems to mean; in their heyday, during the seventies and eighties, these books sold mostly for a nickel. It is a genre phrase, meaning sensational, blood-and-thunder or detective tales, issued in pamphlet form. The first Beadle Dime Novels, however, did sell for ten cents. They were about a hundred pages long, clearly printed and bound in yellow wrappers, bearing a dramatic woodcut illustrating the content, at first in black and white, later in lurid color. They were inclined to be nationalistic and intensely patriotic, as well as sensational in tone.

The Beadle brothers—Erastus, Irwin, and James—came from Pierstown, New York, on the west side of Otsego Lake. Erastus, the real founder of the line, began at thirteen as a miller's apprentice, but at seventeen he learned a new trade as apprentice to H. & E. Phinney, printers and binders, in Cooperstown. With his brother Irwin he later went into the stereotyping business in Buffalo, and soon began to publish a magazine for young children. With various partners and after a move to New York, Beadle turned gradually toward his life's work with paperback song books, cookbooks, and other cheap literature of the same kind Peterson published.

His real career was launched on June 7, 1860, with this advertisement in the New York *Tribune*:

BOOKS FOR THE MILLION!
A Dollar Book for a Dime!!
128 pages complete, only Ten Cents!!!

BEADLE'S DIME NOVELS NO. I

MALAESKA:

Indian Wife of the White Hunter

By Mrs. Ann S. Stephens

128 pages, 12 mo. Ready Saturday morning, June 9

Thus, on a note of miscegenation, the dime novel began, and the firm of Irwin P. Beadle & Co. was launched. Erastus and Robert Adams, a Buffalo boy, were the partners. No sooner was the series well begun, however, than the Civil War erupted, and the books at first reflected its depressing effects, as all publishing was affected. The books were issued less frequently, sometimes at intervals of three or four weeks, instead of twice a month as they had been at the beginning. But at the same time the demand for them grew in the camps, where the soldiers were devouring all the reading they could get. The dime novels exactly suited their tastes, and it was not long before they were being shipped to the army in bales. Beadle & Co. gave away thousands of copies to soldiers, and advertised them as for sale by "all Booksellers, News Dealers, Country Merchants and Army Sutlers." A quarter of a century later, a popular magazine recalled, "The Dime Novels became not only household words in all sections of the country, but were the soldier's solace and comfort in camp and campaign, and contributed, in a wonderful degree, to ameliorate the trials and sufferings of army life—as every living member of the Grand Army will attest."

By the middle of 1865, Beadle & Co. had published more than 4 million dime novels, individual sales running from 35,000 to 80,000. Only two of them, *Malaeska* and *Seth Jones*, eighth in the series, became best sellers. *Malaeska* may have sold as many as 50,000, and *Seth Jones* perhaps even more. After the war, the house went on to new heights, starting series after series, attracting more and more competition but outselling most of it, until the proliferation of cheap "libraries" brought ruin to nearly all these lines, soon after 1875.

T. B. Peterson and the Beadles had their special importance in American life, but they were not typical of the publishing community that was growing up in New York, Philadelphia, and Boston before the war. The names of many of these men are perpetuated in the houses they began which still flourish today. As individuals, they represented a first generation of modern book publishers who gave it a tone and character which persist, at least in some degree, today.

Mathew Carey was the progenitor; his publishing career began with the new nation, and the publishing enterprise he launched in

1785 was the forerunner of the industry as we know it today. He was an aggressive Irishman, a radical in his youth, bright and quick, a shaker and maker from the time he was an adolescent, a man who refused to follow conventional patterns. His fellow publishers of the early nineteenth century were largely poor boys who struggled upward, but Mathew was born rich, the son of a Dublin contractor, a practical man who thought the literary world was nonsense. He offered his son a choice of twenty-five other trades, all of which Mathew declined, whereupon the father refused to look for a master printer who would accept an apprentice, which was the only job Mathew wanted. He found his own master at fifteen, and while he was learning began to experiment with writing, an occupation that soon got him into trouble with an anonymous pamphlet exhorting Irish Catholics to rebel against the British penal code.

Carey's radical attacks on the British, in this and other writings, made it necessary for him to depart the country for a while. That was the turning point in his life. He went to France, where a letter from a priest introduced him to Benjamin Franklin, then an aging American minister amusing himself with a small printing office in Passy during his hours away from diplomatic duties. That was where Carey learned his trade, from a real master.

Returning to Dublin, Mathew started a revolutionary weekly called the *Freeman's Journal,* which again got him into trouble with the British authorities. Brought before Commons on a criminal libel charge, he served a month in Newgate Prison before he fled at last to America, arriving in Philadelphia on November 1, 1784.

Carey began to print and publish books as early as 1785, and before he retired in 1824, accomplished so many noteworthy things that it is difficult to list even the most outstanding. Among them would certainly be his 1792 edition of Epictetus, the first time Greek type had been used in America. Two of his books, Guthrie's famous *Geography* and Goldsmith's *Animated Nature,* alone earned him at least $60,000. He sold 2500 copies of the former at $16 and 3000 of the latter (four volumes octavo) for $9. His various editions of Sir Walter Scott helped materially to establish that much-pirated writer in America. Carey also published the work of his famous traveling salesman, "Parson Weems," whose adulatory biography of Washington implanted such completely untrue tales as the cherry tree, and of throwing a dollar across the Potomac, in the willing American consciousness and still remain as cliché symbols. Mason Locke Weems may have originated myths about great men that platoons of scholars have failed to dislodge, but he was the greatest book salesman of his time, or probably any other, and a true original. He was everything Carey was not, extravagant and disorganized where his employer was frugal and disciplined, filled with jollity and gusto where Carey was sober and earnest, but these men needed each other for psychological as well as business reasons.

Carey's influence on publishing went beyond his list. His success as a bookseller, his efforts to organize the trade and to improve the distribution of books, were as notable as what he published. Like other publishers, he was concerned chiefly with issuing and selling his own books, but he also wanted to sell the books of other houses, both foreign and domestic. He was the first to see how a magazine and a book list could supplement and help each other in a publisher's establishment. He grasped at every opportunity to dispose of books. Playgoers who entered the lobbies of Philadelphia theaters in 1794 found themselves solicited by hawkers—Carey called them "itinerant stationers"—selling reprints of song hits from the play they were about to see, or had just seen—a kind of selling that survives today virtually unchanged.

Like so many young rebels, Carey ended his long career as a solid establishment figure. In 1802, he was made a director of the Bank of Pennsylvania, later worked hard for a renewal of the Bank of the United States charter, and was a charter member of the Philadelphia Society for the Promotion of National Industry. Carey aided this promotion through his protectionist books, pamphlets, and speeches on banking and the protective system. He fought hard for and undoubtedly influenced the protective-tariff bills of 1824 and 1828, but after the triumph of nullification, he became progressively disillusioned with the manufacturers. Retiring in 1824, although remaining for a time as adviser to the firm, he devoted his remaining years to public and philanthropic work. A prolific letter writer, he corresponded with the great men of his time, including Jefferson, Washington, Franklin, Lafayette, Hamilton, Adams, Madison, and Clay. Small wonder that when he died on September 16, 1839, at the age of eighty, his funeral was the largest ever seen in Philadelphia up to that time.

By that time the establishment of publishing dynasties was well begun. In New York, Charles Wiley had started, in the way so many others did, as a bookseller who also owned a printing press, and whose back shop, reminiscent of the colonial design, was filled with the best-known writers of the day, exchanging literary gossip. Wiley's most noted author was Fenimore Cooper, whom he had met casually as a traveling companion while he was selling books on the road in western New York State.

Cooper and Wiley were friends, but another publishing pattern appeared, for the first time, to mar their relationship. The first three of Cooper's novels were successful, but they did not make Wiley rich. Shortly before the publisher died in 1826, Cooper took his fourth book to another house. It was *The Last of the Mohicans* and it made a small fortune for Carey & Lea. The book was published as Wiley lay dying. His son John, then only twenty-one, took over the business, as sons were to do habitually in publishing for more than a century to come, and the house today bears the son's name. John Wiley proved to be a quiet but moving force in early-nineteenth-century publishing, particularly in his labors for an international copyright law.

While the Wiley firm was establishing itself under Charles, another and much more extraordinary family dynasty was being launched in New York. The story of the Harper brothers and the house they founded is certainly the most remarkable in the history of American publishing. The brothers were the sons of Joseph Harper, a Long Island farmer. They were brought up in a strict household which observed all the Methodist pieties and virtues. Circuit-riding preachers often stayed in this stronghold of Methodism.

James, the oldest brother, born in 1795, was a quiet, studious boy apprenticed to a good Methodist printer in New York. He was followed into the business by his brothers, John, Wesley, and Fletcher. It was James and John who started their own printing firm in a small, dingy room on Dover Street, as J & J Harper, in March 1817. They were well under way in the eighteen-twenties with the publication of seven of Scott's *Waverley* novels, and by 1825 the other two brothers had come into the firm. They now thought of themselves as publishers, not printers.

They were all Harpers, but they were not alike as people. James was a tall, affable man who made friends easily. He was the face the firm presented to the public, and the one every employee knew by sight as he knew them all by name. His blue eyes looked out humorously from behind the steel-rimmed glasses he always wore. He had dark hair and sideburns, which had been blond when he was younger. John was a big, square, broad-shouldered man, deliberate in his actions and not as outgoing as James. He was admirably suited by temperament for his job in the firm, which was to keep its financial affairs in shape. Wesley was more like him than the others, also a quiet man who found some of his closest friends in the composing room rather than among the authors or editors, although he was extremely well read in the English literature the firm published. Wesley became noted as the best correspondent in the book business.

Fletcher was regarded as the ablest of the four, and as chief editor he was in a position to be better known in the publishing world. This blue-eyed, extroverted, ambitious man, with a wry sense of humor, had curly, brownish-red hair and wore sideburns. He was a superb administrator, full of a driving energy, possessed excellent literary judgment, and knew how to deal with people.

These four men revolutionized the book-publishing business. They were first to use cloth over boards as a binding, first to make stereotyping a regular procedure, and they were well in advance of their competitors in terms of marketing. The idea of a series of books to be published as "libraries" was theirs, although Constable, in Edinburgh, had first used this form in 1825. They were probably first to use the phrase, "for sale by the principal booksellers throughout the United States," and they were also the first to employ editors—academic figures who were called literary advisers at first, but who did the kind of reading and working with manuscripts which was later commonplace.

While there were those who praised the Harper brothers for bringing literature to the masses with their "libraries" and so elevating the nation's intellectual life, others believed, as many do now, that there must be something wrong with anything so popular. Thoreau grumbled that Harper's was presuming to select what Americans should read.

By 1833, the firm had installed a steam press, which had just been invented, and the horse that had walked for years in circles around Daniel Treadwell's horsepower press was retired to the Harper farm on Long Island, where he gave a classic demonstration of the conditioning process by walking around a tree in the pasture from seven in the morning until six at night, his usual working hours. When the noon whistle blew at a neighboring factory, he took off his customary lunch hour.

In the year of the horse's retirement, the firm's imprint was changed to Harper & Bros., giving rise to the often repeated story of how, when they were asked which was Mr. Harper and which the brothers, they always replied, "Any one of us is Mr. Harper, and all the rest are brothers."

The Harpers overlooked nothing to promote their books, and in doing so they laid the groundwork for modern publicity practices by getting out a veritable flood of releases to reviewers and newspaper editors, particularly literary figures like Bryant and Greeley, who were known to be friendly to books and authors. These campaigns were not only good for the books, but they were good publicity for the firm, whose remarkable climb to the top of publishing in such a short time made fine copy for the magazines and newspapers, particularly when James ran for mayor of New York in 1844 and found himself elected—"the sublime triumph of the Bible," one newspaper called it, a reference to the firm's publishing of Protestant books and the church's subsequent support. The Catholics, who had fought the use of these books, opposed him.

By the end of the eighteen-forties, Harper's was the largest publisher in America and on the way to being the largest in the world. Its nineteen power presses, augmented by hand presses, were installed, along with the remainder of the business, in seven five-story buildings, and were turning out about 2 million volumes a year, employing nearly 350 people. In June 1850, the house launched *Harper's New Monthly* magazine, whose circulation rose from 50,000 to 130,000 in 1852. In January 1857, a second magazine, *Harper's Weekly*, was added, and it too quickly reached a circulation of 120,000. Both of these periodicals were to be important factors in the mobilizing of Northern opinion before the war, and their coverage of the war itself set new standards in journalism.

It was Harper's that introduced the Brontë sisters and Thackeray, among others, to the American public. They were not the first of Dickens' several publishers in this country, but they may have been the best. Melville was on their list, and so was Darwin. They were not only the leading house in America, and probably the world, by the end of the Civil War, but five sons of the four partners were already in the business, ensuring the continuity of family ownership for decades to come.

A splendid contemporary of the Harper boys was Daniel Appleton, who began his career with a dry-goods store in his native Haverhill, Massachusetts, but began to apply his good business sense and restless energy to book publishing in 1831. He established himself as a publisher of devotional and theological books, quickly expanding his business, not only in the United States but in the United Kingdom, Europe, and South America. Like the Harpers and most of the other large publishers, he operated a handsome retail bookstore as well. Daniel's son William took control of the house after his father's death in 1849, and after a reorganization bringing three other sons into the management, the house put out its famous *New American Cyclopedia*, which is said to have been the idea of Charles Anderson Dana, then managing editor of the New York *Tribune* and later founder of the *Sun*. These sixteen volumes were the first such reference work oriented to American life. Dana was the editor, with his *Tribune* associate editor as co-editor, the two directing a staff of 364 contributors, most of them Americans.

Launched in the Panic year of 1857, and concluded in 1863, the darkest year of the war, these sets were soon averaging 20,000 a year in sales, and with the help of a revised editon in 1876, they reached a sale of more than 3 million volumes, grossing nearly $6 million.

Appleton was also the publisher of Webster's *Blue-Backed Speller* after 1855, an acquisition that was something like discovering gold. By 1890, this book had sold more than 35 million copies; still in print in 1950, it had by that time reached the incredible total of 70 million copies. For years it sold a million copies annually, and only the Bible exceeded it.

Most of the antebellum publishers, including Appleton, were involved in textbook publishing, but one, A. S. Barnes & Co. (as the house is known today), was probably the first to establish itself as primarily an educational publisher, although it now has a general list. Alfred Smith Barnes, the founder, came from New Haven, the son of a farmer, and began his business in New York in 1838, working out of an office twelve by twenty feet, and possessing neither cash nor capital. From this barren beginning, Barnes changed the course of textbook publishing by refusing to follow the standard practice of selling to schoolbook agents, and instead going directly to the teachers himself, traveling from town to village, sometimes by stage, often on horseback with the books in the saddlebags, or in a horse and buggy hired for the trip. From this extremely modest start, Barnes had established a business by the end of the war that could boast a list of 218 textbooks, some of them selling in astronomical figures. One series of mathematical books alone sold 5 million copies. Barnes, too, had an able son to succeed him.

Still another major figure in publishing to put down his roots before the Civil War was George Palmer Putnam, who was not only fortunate in having sons to carry on the business but doubly fortunate in having one, George Haven Putnam, who was as outstanding a figure as his father. Starting as a bookseller's apprentice and later clerk, George Palmer got most of his education in the reading room of the New York Mercantile Library, where he could be found every night reading his way through most of the historical works in the English language. John Wiley gave this ambitious nineteen-year-old boy a start in his firm, in 1833; Wiley himself was only a year older.

George Palmer Putnam distinguished himself from other publishers almost at once by opposing book pirating. A firm believer in international copyright, he became in 1837 secretary of the first organization in the country formed to fight for such protection, and led the battle until his death.

The partnership with Wiley came to an end in 1847, and Putnam set up for himself, founding the house that still bears the family name. From the beginning, when Putnam was fortunate enough to get the reprint rights to Washington Irving's books, the house that would ultimately be known as G. P. Putnam's Sons was one of the best supporters of American literature. Poe, James Russell Lowell, Cooper, and Bayard Taylor were among the better known before the Civil War. But it was an unknown novel by a young girl, rejected by nearly every publisher in New York, that really established the house commercially in 1850. Susan Warner's *The Wide, Wide World* proved to be one of the wonders of publishing history. Putnam bought it because he gave the manuscript to his mother to read, and she told him, through her tears, that he must publish it if he never did another book. Dutiful but doubtful, the son obeyed. Frank Luther Mott has termed *The Wide, Wide World* "mawkish in its sentimentality and pious to a repulsive degree," a fair description. It was a huge success, selling more than 500,000 copies in America alone, as well as enjoying large sales in England, where it was almost as popular. More important, it touched off a flood of sentimental fiction that characterized publishing in the eighteen-fifties, most of it by women.

There were other members of that early publishing clan, putting down roots that flowered later. Moses Dodd got into the business in 1839, laying the foundation for the house that is now Dodd, Mead. The first Charles Scribner established himself in 1846, beginning another family dynasty that would end as Charles Scribner's Sons. Edward P. Dutton started with a partner in Boston, in 1852, but later he singlehandedly built the house now known as E. P. Dutton & Co. in New York.

In Philadelphia there was Henry Charles Carey, son of Mathew, who carried on the founder's business under several imprints, and with considerable imagination and initiative. There was also Joshua Ballinger Lippincott, who began his business in 1836 and by 1850, when he was only thirty-six, had established himself as a substantial

publisher of Bibles, prayer books, and general literature, while doing bookselling and printing on the side, and getting into the magazine business with his *Lippincott's* magazine and some professional journals. Later he became a diversified publisher of religious and medical books, gift books, deluxe editions and standard editions of favorite British authors, as well as becoming the first American publisher of *Chambers' Encyclopedia*. As the home of medical publishing, Philadelphia also saw the rise of such houses as the Blakiston Company, founded by Presley Blakiston, who began working for a book-auctioneering firm when he was only twelve and established his own house in 1843.

In Boston, publishing was directed largely to New England in the first half of the nineteenth century, accounting for its generally parochial character. But it was nevertheless always colorful and exciting. The personalities of the publishers and booksellers were engaging, sometimes eccentric, and the conduct of their business reflected the unique blend of literary culture and Yankee trading that is indelibly Bostonian.

The distinctive flavor of Boston publishing, so reminiscent of England, emanates pleasantly from such stories as Emerson's, related to Edward Everett Hale, of how in 1850 he took the first check he had ever received for any of his work to his publishers, Phillips & Sampson, and asked them if he was free to use it. Kindly, Phillips himself showed Emerson how to endorse the check.

Many of the Boston firms did not survive the century—even houses like Ticknor & Fields, which occupied the famous Old Corner Book Store between 1832 and 1865 and whose chief partner, James Fields, was one of the most striking personalities in the business in his time. It was this house that introduced British writers like Thomas De Quincey and Tennyson to America, and published native writers like Longfellow and Hawthorne. *The Scarlet Letter* was an immediate sellout, spurred by the denunciations of religious journals and clergymen who called it "a dirty story" belonging in a "Brothel Library." By 1858, Ticknor & Fields was one of the most successful publishing houses in America, whose list included Holmes, Whittier, Thoreau, Emerson, and Mrs. Stowe among the Americans; Browning, Kingsley, Reade, Thackeray, and Dickens among the British. Fields had a special genius for promoting these and other authors. But the firm went into eclipse and died after Fields' retirement in 1871.

Enduring beginnings were made in Boston, however. There was Henry Oscar Houghton, whose character was so strong that he left his mark on the house he founded, Houghton Mifflin, long after he was gone. Before the Civil War, Houghton was one of the finest printers in America, with his Riverside Press; the present house dates its founding to 1865. The other Boston survivor into this century was Little, Brown & Co., whose founders, Charles C. Little and James Brown, were overshadowed by the vivid personalities of Fields and Houghton, but who in a quieter way built a solid house on an early foundation of law books.

In Boston, as elsewhere, excellent publishers rose and fell with alarming frequency, victims of national boom-and-bust or the vicissitudes of the trade. None of the failures was as inexplicable, however, as John P. Jewett, who published *Uncle Tom's Cabin*, the sensation of the era, and two years later another novel, *The Lamplighter*, that was one of the century's best sellers.

Jewett, in common with many other Americans, had begun to follow the tribulations of Uncle Tom when the story ran as a serial in the Washington, D.C., abolitionist paper, the *National Era*. Mrs. Stowe had already taken as much of the manuscript as she had written to the house of Phillips, Sampson, her sister Catherine's publisher, who turned it down. Hearing of this, Jewett made an offer to Mrs. Stowe, giving her a choice of a fifty-fifty split on costs and profits, or a straight 10 per cent royalty. Mrs. Stowe's husband asked the advice of a family friend, Congressman Phillip Greeley, who gave him perhaps the worst advice in publishing history. Take the 10 per cent, he said; don't risk any of your own money on a novel, particularly one by a woman dealing with a subject that was unpopular even in some parts of the North. Consequently the Stowes lost a fortune when they signed an agreement on March 13, 1852, for 10 per cent.

It was Jewett, however, who was soon convinced he had made a great mistake. The story went on and on in the *National Era* and Mrs. Stowe, writing it in bursts of sometimes uncontrollable emotion, seemed unable to end it. Jewett had thought he was going to publish a low-priced, small volume; now he saw himself confronted with a very large novel. If it ran much longer, he wrote to Mrs. Stowe after six months of serialization, he would have to publish the book in two volumes, and that would be too great a risk.

Mrs. Stowe consulted the magazine's editor, Dr. Gamaliel Bailey, and he in turn asked his readers if he should accept Mrs. Stowe's offer to end it as it stood, with Tom's martyrdom and a chapter which would, in the style of the day, simply tell what happened to everyone. The readers were emphatic; they wanted the whole story. Mrs. Stowe went on writing, and Jewett consoled himself with the thought that if the magazine's readers were so demanding the book-buying public would feel the same way. There was already a tremendous excitement about the story in the country; a publisher could ask no better herald of a book's success.

The serial finally ended after twelve months. Two months before it concluded in the magazine, Jewett brought it out on March 20, 1852, in two volumes at $2.50. Its impact was enormous. As Van Wyck Brooks tells us, "If this book was not the cause of the Civil War, as Lincoln said later, it was at least one of the major causes, for it blocked the operation of the Fugitive Slave Law. As a literary event, it was the greatest since Prescott's *Ferdinand and Isabella.* It was a world event, in fact. Macauley, Heine, and George Sand reviewed it. Three Paris newspapers published it at once, and Uncle Tom's Cabins rose all over Europe, as restaurants, creameries, and bazaars. It appeared in thirty-seven languages and three times over in Welsh, into which Scott and Dickens had never been translated; and it sent Heine back to his Bible and made such an impression on Tolstoy in Russia that when he came to write *What Is Art?,* he took it as an example of the highest type, with Dostoievsky's *House of the Dead,* and much of Victor Hugo. In all the history of the printed book, the Bible alone had appeared in so many versions."

For Jewett, it was an unimaginable windfall. His printer kept eight presses running night and day and still could not keep up with the demand. The first printing of 10,000 copies was sold out in a few days. In three weeks, it had sold 20,000; in three months, 75,000; in a year, 305,000.

No book had ever got the kind of advertising Jewett gave *Uncle Tom.* Anticipating modern practice, he ran a series of advertisements informing the public of the book's continuing phenomenal sale. He took copies down to Washington and, with the open approval of Seward and Sumner, touted it to leaders in Congress and the administration. He even published Mrs. Stowe's *Key to Uncle Tom's Cabin,* as though it were *Finnegans Wake* and required further explanation. After the first 100,000 copies were sold, Jewett brought the book out in a one-volume edition at thirty-seven and a half cents, and it roared into the mass market. For the Christmas trade, he had a profusely illustrated edition ready. By the time the Panic of 1857 severely limited every book's sale, it had reached 500,000 and was still selling about 1000 copies a week. It has since sold more than 3 million copies in the United States, and is still selling. The world distribution has been conservatively estimated at more than 6.5 million.

Certainly no book except the Bible has had such a varied career. Its

appearance in hundreds of illustrated editions, its numerous abridg-
ments and adaptations, its appearance in songs, card games, puzzles,
comic strips, and its long life in the theater constitute an extraordinary history. Traveling "Tom Shows" became an American institution,
and in one dramatic form or another the story was played on virtually
every stage in America and many in Europe, where in London alone
there were six productions in 1852, running simultaneously. Some of
the finest actors played the show in America—Joseph Jefferson, Mrs.
Fiske, Maude Adams, Fay Templeton, among others. The Players
Club revived it in New York in 1933, with Otis Skinner and Fay Bain-
ter, and sophisticated theatergoers went out into the night with tears
on their cheeks.

No other book has had such an impact on American culture, and it
is only partly explained by the fact that it provided a focal point for
national emotions over the most emotional issue that has ever confronted the American people. That accounted for its immediate success, but its durability can be ascribed to its unique combination of
best-seller ingredients: its deeply felt religious motif, a chase
sequence that is one of the most celebrated in literature, a titillating
touch of miscegenation, sadism in the whipping scene, other kinds of
violence, the character of Topsy, who was an ideal stereotypical
figure for a predominantly white readership, the uncomplicated moral
conflict between right and wrong, good and evil—these, among others.

In the astounding success of *Uncle Tom's Cabin* could be seen
implicitly the status book publishing had achieved among the media
before the war, and at least a suggestion of what it would be in the
future. From its earlier status as a purveyor of information and entertainment to a relatively small elite, it had become a medium capable
of reaching the mass public, playing a political role and offering itself
as another free forum for ideas, and a unique one because its distribution was not like that of either books or magazines. The figures
Uncle Tom and the sentimental fiction of the fifties achieved demonstrated, further, that book publishing could command audiences far
larger than the other media, and that would be true for the remainder
of the century.

As the result of that fact, the book publisher emerged by the end of
the Civil War as the chief purveyor of ideas in America, and the published book itself as the conveyor of the most varied social and political ideas extant. Advertising had not yet exerted its influence on magazines, and newspapers were hampered by their essentially local
character. The book, however, transported by every conceivable

means, covered the nation, bringing culture, enlightenment, information, and entertainment to every literate person, at prices that only the very poor could not afford. The publishing house had by that time fully demonstrated itself as a civilizing influence as it followed the frontier from coast to coast. Its importance in the life of the people had become plain in the Civil War years, when the South, deprived of the Northern book industry it depended on, was virtually compelled to devise one of its own, despite every difficulty and in the midst of tragedy, simply because people could not do without it.

At the close of the war, publishing had taken on the general aspects it bears today, with some exceptions. The structure of the general publishing house had been established, and the specialty houses were developing rapidly. Authors still had few rights in relation to the publishers, and no copyright protection except domestically, where the law was inadequate. Although publishing was already considered "an occupation for gentlemen"—and in fact the gentlemen in it were a different breed from those who clustered under the buttonwood tree— there was nonetheless a great deal of sharp practice and a kind of competitiveness indistinguishable from any other business.

As the war ended, the book-publishing industry was ready for great progress which would carry it to the First World War, a period in which its organization would be consolidated, its authors given different treatment, and its distribution methods placed on a somewhat sounder basis. It would be a period, too, in which book publishing, as a medium, was finally separated from the magazine and the newspaper and firmly defined as the distinct and unique means of communication it remains today.

8

The Newspaper
as Dissenter

SOCIAL AND POLITICAL DISSENT in the media were dividing them
sharply long before the Civil War. From the first, newspapers had
been the chief defenders of the social status quo, accepting whatever
was ordained as the prevailing view of public morality (meaning
WASP moral standards) as the criterion of what could be printed. So
firmly was this tradition entrenched, with a few conspicuous exceptions, that it was 1931 before the New York *Daily News*, a tabloid not
noted for its reticence, became the first American newspaper to use
the word "syphilis" and in 1934 earned the further distinction of
being the first, perhaps the first in the world, to print "son of a bitch."

Even today, in a period when magazines and books employ language with an unprecedented freedom, newspapers continue to self-
censor themselves in America, in sharp contrast with their British
counterparts, where the language is much more frank. While it will
not use any four-letter words, the New York *Times*, for example, will
use an equivalent if it is justified by direct quotation in the context of
news, as when John W. Dean III disclosed in 1973 that the White
House had proposed ways and means to "screw" its enemies. This was
a large concession in a newspaper which only twenty-five years or so
earlier refused to take an advertisement for Dr. Kinsey's first scientific
study of human sexual behavior, and did not review it for a year.
Most newspapers still use the cliché "a family newspaper" to describe
themselves, although the kind of family to which they are presumably
dedicated disappeared during the sixties, except at certain levels.

Broadcasting shares this dedication, with a scant few breaks in the dike. In both media, "family" applied to "newspaper" or "entertainment" means "no sex."

Magazines in the nineteenth century shared this self-censorship, and for the same reasons, but in our own time have broken away completely in some categories and have softened their traditional stand substantially in others.

Only book publishing, in its broad diversity, before the Civil War was inclined to at least some measure of freedom in recognizing that sex existed, and so elicited a response from the authorities that made these publishers the first articulate dissenters from establishment morality among the media. While there had been successful censorship by the government and a pietistic self-censorship of books in colonial America, it was not until 1821 that a book was brought into court on obscenity charges, and 1842 before Congress made the first of its ineffectual attempts to define obscenity legally.

The obscenity case of 1821 took place in Massachusetts, and the volume involved was that original "obscene" novel, John Cleland's *Fanny Hill* (or, more properly, *Memoirs of a Woman of Pleasure*), which Isaiah Thomas had once sold from under the counter. It had been banned in England for many years, but was published openly there in the seventeen-forties and surreptitiously in America, beginning with several issues put out by Thomas between 1786 and 1814. *Fanny* did not appear in court earlier only because there were no specific obscenity statutes; it had simply been assumed that no one in WASP America would dare to publish anything of the kind. But the 1821 case stirred the moralists to bring pressure on Congress for the passage of an obscenity law, which the legislators obligingly produced in 1842. It was directed at imports rather than native efforts, and confined itself to pictures. There was no reference in it to books, pamphlets, or magazines.

The reason for this specificity was the invention of photography. No sooner was the camera invented than it was used for erotic purposes which became the basis for crude productions that would have been termed "pornographic" in the context of the times. The law Congress passed did not stifle this growing by-product of the media; it only made it illegal.

Literature was brought into public question by the moralists in 1852, when Hawthorne's *The Scarlet Letter* was the subject of a savage attack. The kind of rhetoric employed has a familiar, dismal sound today. The Reverend A. C. Coxe, for example, proclaimed that he was against "any toleration to a popular and gifted writer when he perpetrates bad morals—let his brokerage of lust be put down at the very beginning." (They were still trying to put it down in 1925, when the silent-film version of the book violated Hawthorne's text and produced a marriage for Hester Prynne, at the insistence of the Board of Censorship.)

Walt Whitman was also an early victim of censorship. Although Emerson wrote to the New York *Times* heralding *Leaves of Grass* as "the most extraordinary piece of wit and wisdom that America has yet contributed," the Library Company of Philadelphia was the only library in America recorded as having bought a copy after it was published. It was effectively censored in every other library by the refusal to buy it, although it was not made the subject of a court case until 1881.

In spite of a continuing self-censorship on the part of publishers and the constant efforts of the moralists to keep anything they considered offensive out of the bookstalls, erotic books were being published in the United States before the war, although most of them were undoubtedly sold surreptitiously. The Americana section of the library of the Institute for Sex Research, at Indiana University, the largest collection of erotic literature in the world, contains no fewer than forty-six items published in America between 1800 and 1865. Many of these books were anonymously written and published.

Some of the volumes were shields for bigotry, a common occurrence in this genre. Other erotic books pretended to be guides for the newly married or the not yet married—lascivious copies of the moralistic guides which began to appear before the war. There were also books about the notorious foreign ladies who had the good luck to be notable political figures, like Ninon de Lenclos, whose adventures, real and imaginary, were related in more than one volume.

Another erotic delight was those books which actually were, or pretended to be, accounts of sensational trials. When a bishop of New York was had up for rape and seduction in 1845, even so respectable a house as Appleton printed a carefully edited transcript of the proceedings in 1845.

By 1844, the moralists were attacking masturbation in full force in books like *Important Facts for Young Men*, "showing destructive effects of masturbation, and the frequency of hernia and rupture," published in West Brookfield, Massachusetts. It was acknowledged by 1848 that girls were also victims, in Dr. Jean Dubois's book, *The Secret Habits of the Female Sex; Letters Addressed to a Mother on the Evils of Solitude*, published in New York anonymously.

The erotic classics arrived in 1862 with the publication of Ovid's *The Art of Love*, published in New York by Calvin Blanchard in an illustrated edition. The war years also produced the native erotic novel, which an anonymous press in New Orleans found time to turn out in 1863, despite its difficulties. This anonymous novel is titled *The Libertine Enchantress; or, the Adventures of Lucinda Hartley*. The title page discloses that writers in the genre must have been prolific, since the author lists himself as having written *Confessions of a Washington Belle*; *Beautiful Creole of Havana*; *Adventures of Anna P., or the Belle of New York*; *Child of Passion, or The Amorous Foundling*, "etc. etc. etc." *The Libertine Enchantress* was "beautifully illustrated with designs expressly for this work," the crowded title page continues. Inside, the contents were crudely done but the intent was clear.

There was nothing like this in the magazines, nor in the newspapers, but in the columns where sex was noticeable by its absence, violence, in the true American tradition, was prevalent and unrestrained, not only in descriptions of violence, but in the use of language where politics was concerned, as we have seen in the earlier history of newspapers.

With the new century, however, the newspaper began to emerge as a political dissenter in a somewhat different light. In the years when the political parties controlled the newspapers, or earlier when they were in the hands of revolutionary propagandists, they were primarily organs of dissent. In the relatively calm period that followed Jefferson's departure, however, the large-city papers, at least, began to pay more attention to the news, the parties lost their control of the press, and real editors began to emerge.

In this changed situation, dissent took on a different meaning. It was not so much one party attacking the other, although that continued, of course, but a newspaper operated by a private citizen expressing dissent against the government and the ruling party on behalf of other citizens like himself, who might be in the minority. A modern parallel would be the few large, influential newspapers that opposed the war in Vietnam when it was not popular to do so, or the liberal Southern editors and publishers who fought editorially for civil rights against prevailing political and social attitudes.

The first large-scale expression of the dichotomy came with the War of 1812, which Samuel Eliot Morison has called "the most unpopular war that this country has ever waged, not even excepting the Vietnam conflict." Congress passed the bill declaring it by only 79 to 49 in the House, and 19 to 13 in the Senate. It was a regional approval: eight of ten New England senators voted against it, and eleven of fourteen New York representatives. Enthusiasm for the war centered where it has always centered—in the West and the South—but so little of it existed even so that the War Department could get only 10,000 of the 50,000 one-year volunteers it was authorized to enlist, and was unable to build the regular Army to half its authorized strength.

Federalists in the East opposed the war, but there were others and some were eminent men, like Chief Justice Marshall, Harrison Gray Otis and Timothy Pickering. Even many of the Southern Federalists joined the Northerners in opposition. In Massachusetts, there was open defiance from the state government itself. An address to the people was issued by the lower house of the General Court, advising them to "organize a *peace party* throughout your Country, and let all other party distinctions vanish." Taking a firm pro-British stand, Governor Caleb Strong then proclaimed a public fast to atone for a declaration of war "against the nation from which we are descended, and which for many generations has been the bulwark of the religion we profess."

To shipowners as well as Federalists, the government's war slogan, "Free Trade and Sailors' Rights," was, in the words of Professor Morison, "mere hokum." The owners were getting rich out of neutral trade, and the impressment of American seamen, which American children are still taught was the prime cause of the war, was negligible. Beyond that, the Federalists thought it was wrong to attack England, which represented the "world's last hope" against Napoleon's tyranny.

The oldest, richest, and most respected families in Massachusetts were against the war, but a few supported it. The academic community, especially Harvard, was against it, and the government of the state supported it only as far as federal law compelled. Other New England governments, with the exception of New Hampshire, joined in this resistance. Everywhere in the region there was talk of the "little man in the Palace," meaning President Madison—a forerunner of "that man in the White House" in the years before the Second World War.

As the war went on, and it appeared that the British might win, Governor Strong called the General Court into special session on October 5, 1813, and opened it with a pessimistic speech, which was considered by a committee under Otis' chairmanship. The committee called upon citizens to repel the invaders, but at the same time it deplored the government's war policies, which it said had led to a state of "humiliation, of danger, and distress." Otis proposed that the New England states meet in convention at Hartford to consider what the region ought to do, and after a hot debate the Otis Report was passed, and letters of invitation to other state governors were sent out. Rhode Island and Connecticut accepted at once.

The idea of the convention, as expressed officially, was to draft some constitutional amendments designed to protect the interests of New England, and to permit the states to conduct their own defense. But the Republicans were certain that it was a plot whose aim was secession and a separate peace with England. As Morison points out, there was no truth in this accusation. On the contrary, the Massachusetts leaders and others were earnestly opposed to secession. There was no doubt, however, that they were antiwar, reflecting the strong sentiment of New Englanders generally, who yelled insults when congressmen who had voted for the war appeared on the street in Boston and Plymouth; they behaved much like the anti-Vietnam demonstrators of our own time. Governor Strong, meanwhile, was secretly conducting a personal essay in diplomacy, seeking to establish the groundwork for a cease-fire or a separate peace, and there were even influential men who were earnestly trying to launch a movement for a new union comprised only of the original thirteen states.

The leader of this movement was John "Jack" Lowell, a Federalist leader who came from an old and respected Boston family, and from whom Amy Lowell and McGeorge Bundy are descended, among other eminent people. The Boston Jeffersonians knew John Lowell as "Crazy Jack," or sometimes "the Boston Rebel."

Lowell, a conservative man in every respect except the political, understood media power better than some of his contemporaries. Through print, he spread his plan for a new constitution which would, in effect, eliminate the West from the Union—as Morison says, a proposal "so idiotic that it would hardly be worth serious consideration had it not been seriously promoted in the Federalist press. It amounted to a pistol-point reorganization of the Union." He outlined this plan in an 1813 pamphlet which he signed "A Massachusetts Farmer." It followed on the heels of two strong anti-administration pamphlets, *Mr. Madison's War* and *Perpetual War, the Policy of Mr. Madison*, in which he accused the President of refusing any reasonable peace settlement. Again, the parallel with President Nixon and Vietnam is obvious.

Idiotic it may have been, but Lowell's plan was received enthusiastically by men like Senator Timothy Pickering, Gouverneur Morris, of New York, and Charles Carroll, of Maryland. Pickering pointed out that if Andrew Jackson were defeated in the approaching Battle of New Orleans, the Union would be "severed," with the West accepting British sovereignty in order to get a Mississippi outlet for its trade (something it had frequently threatened), and the other states would have no choice but to join New England if they wanted to be free of British rule.

At this point the dissenting Federalist press became a prime mover in promoting Lowell's idea. With one exception, the Boston papers talked of the plan as a platform for the Hartford Convention, and the Boston *Gazette* predicted that if Madison was not out of office by July 4, 1815, "a new form of government will be in operation in the eastern section of the Union."

The *Columbian Centinal* lent its prestige to promoting Lowell's scheme, as the oldest and most respected of Boston's Federalist papers, advocating the new union in a series of articles whose violent tone recalled the earlier excesses of the party press. Announcing Connecticut's and Rhode Island's acceptances to the Hartford Convention, the *Centinal* employed a graphics device it had used earlier to announce successive state ratifications of the Constitution. The two states, said the text, were the second and third pillars of a "New Federal Edifice Raised," and the accompanying picture showed three columns in place for the edifice, with places for two more. A Republican paper, the *Yankee*, observed that the pillars looked more like snuff bottles in an apothecary's window, giving rise to that party's derisive description of the Hartford meeting as the "Snuff Bottle Convention."

The *Centinal*'s continuing ardent advocacy of the convention brought support from other Federalist papers. In Georgetown, D.C., the *Federal Republican* in an open letter to the President advised Madison to do "immediate justice to all the reasonable claims of New England," and to "withdraw . . . your disgraced and incompetent generals."

After all this furor, of course, the convention produced no radical sundering of the Union. The moderate men appointed by the state legislators as delegates issued a moderate report which rejected any violent action. In an embarrassing (to the Federalists) anticlimax, a committee appointed by Governor Strong to go to Washington and demand federal money for the defense of the state arrived there simultaneously with news of the Peace of Ghent and Jackson's victory at New Orleans.

This mission, as Morison reminds us, created a myth perpetuated by anti-New England regions of America, particularly the South, that its real purpose was to promote the secession of New England. President Lyndon B. Johnson, no doubt drawing on what he had learned from his Texas schoolbooks, as Morison speculates, used the story at his press conference of November 17, 1967, for his own purposes. "There has always been confusion, frustration, and differences of opinion when there is a war going on," he said. "That was true when all of New England came down to secede in Madison's administration in the War of 1812, and stopped in Baltimore. They didn't quite make it because Andrew Jackson's results in New Orleans came in. The next morning they came and told the President they wanted to congratulate him—that they thought he was right all along, although they had come from Boston to Baltimore in a secessionist mood."

Preposterous history, and wishful thinking. No General Jackson emerged to produce a great victory for this president, and no one came to tell him he was right all along, as no one did with Madison.

If President Johnson had known that the myth was originated by the media for which he had so little regard, he might have seen the truth in a different light. The newspapers supporting Madison were assiduous in spreading the story that a secession plot had been cut off only by Jackson's victory and the timely news of the Ghent signing. Thus they successfully distracted public attention from the real story, which was Madison's mismanagement of the war. Americans even believed that Jackson had won the war for them, although the truth was that the Treaty of Ghent ended it at a time when the British expeditionary force opposing Jackson had been recalled without any knowledge in London of whether it had won or lost. The two nations were so anxious to end a war which was unpopular in both countries that the treaty they signed did not even mention the issues over which it had supposedly been fought.

In the controversy over New England's stand against the war, President Madison was not nearly so concerned over what the Boston papers were saying as he was about the Federalist organ on his doorstep, in Georgetown, the *Federal Republican*, whose publishers, Jacob Wagner and Alexander Hanson, were responsible for the "open letter" quoted earlier. Their assault, in this letter and other editorials and news stories, raised for the first time since the Revolution the troublesome question which is still with us today: How far should press criticism go when the country's security is threatened by an enemy?

The parallel with Vietnam is not exact. In our time, "security" has come to mean whatever the president decides it is, whether the country is at war or not, and extending far beyond military operations. "Security" now is synonymous with covering up the mistakes and incompetence of government. In Madison's presidency, it was a far more serious matter. Wrong as the War of 1812 may have been, the nation was in it and its survival was threatened, both militarily and politically. At a time when it appeared that the British might win in the field, and the New Englanders and their Federalist allies elsewhere were talking about making a separate peace with England, and the most radical were discussing pulling out of the Union, here was the *Republican* appearing every day on the desk of the president, who was responsible for conducting the war and constitutionally sworn to protect and preserve the Union.

It would have been completely out of character for Madison even to think of imposing a censorship on the press. This was the man who had fought for the Bill of Rights, with its First Amendment, and who had condemned the Sedition Act as an assault on press freedom. In the tradition of his party's great leader, Jefferson, he was bound to uphold that freedom, on the basis of personal conviction and his party's declared principles.

To Madison's dismay and shock, a reaction shared generally by more responsible citizens, the lawless mob took charge of this situation, as it had been doing since before the Revolution. Although he certainly never authorized them, the President's supporters destroyed the *Republican*'s buildings and presses. The editors saved their lives only because of a timely warning by their friend John Howard Payne, then far away from his "Home, Sweet Home" in Easthampton, Long Island.

Wagner and Hanson had courage, if not good judgment or reasonable restraint. Equipped with another press, they resumed publication in a second building, and thoughtfully provided themselves with food and water behind stout barricades in case they were besieged.

The first issue they put out from this fortress was calculated to infuriate the mob all over again. What they called the President was exceeded only by what the Baltimore fanatics called them when they read it. The common epithet of the Republican mob was "traitor," the code word for political intolerance and bigotry in America. It was a word that seemed at least ungrateful to two members of the *Republican*'s staff, James Lingan and "Light Horse Harry" Lee, who had been generals and heroes only a generation before in the Revolution.

When the mob came again, there was a short, furious battle which threatened to end in a bloodbath after the besiegers brought up a cannon. Those who could still think prevailed at this critical point and a truce was arranged, by which the paper's entire staff was given safe conduct to a jail. It was not enough to satisfy the mob. They destroyed building and press once more, and then assaulted the jail. This time there were no restraints. A few staff members escaped, but nine others were savagely beaten by the mob. Lingan was killed; Lee was maimed for life. It is hard to place the blame accurately for this affair, whether on the vicious stupidity of the rabble or on the intransigent foolhardiness of the editors who had provoked it.

Intransigence was characteristic of the Federalist press. Reading their papers, it could scarcely be told whether the President or the British were the enemy, just as the McCormick-Patterson axis confused Franklin Roosevelt and the Nazis before Pearl Harbor. There was more than a little intransigence on the other side as well in the War of 1812. Even Madison called the *Columbian Centinal* and its firebrand publisher, Major Benjamin Russell, treasonous, but there was some basis for that accusation. It was fortunate, on the whole, that the war ended when it did, or the country might have been torn apart irretrievably, the British would have accomplished what they so nearly achieved in any case, and everything that had gone before would have been nullified. Once more, as in the Revolution itself, the nation and its leaders had been saved not so much by good management as by the incompetence of the British field commanders, who could not take victory when it was easily in their grasp.

Major Russell gave the period that followed Madison's administration a name, "the era of good feelings," which has proved a useful label ever since, but hardly more accurate than a good many of the major's other political analyses. In reality, it was a time when the old disputes were merely being supplanted by others. The Federalist-Republican quarrel was nearly dead at last, but far worse antagonisms were stirring beneath the surface in the slowly developing controversy between North and South. Meanwhile, the grass-roots democratic revolt was brewing that would send General Andrew Jackson to the White House.

James Monroe was a quiet man who ran a quiet ship through his administration, and the Washington *National Intelligencer*, his party's newspaper, which had soothed Jefferson, was equally soothing to him. "Mr. Silky-Milky Smith" had retired as publisher in 1810, succeeded by his two partners, Joseph Gales, Jr., and William W. Seaton, who worked as congressional reporters, dividing Senate and House between them and taking down the proceedings in the new labor-saving device, shorthand. They had converted the paper from a tri-weekly to a daily by this time, and it was making money. It was quiet, steady, and conscientious—the New York *Times* of its period.

There was only an occasional echo of former days. Duane, still editor of the *Aurora*, petitioned Monroe for a special favor. During the War of 1812, he had been a quartermaster in the Army and found himself short in his accounts at the conclusion of the conflict. Seeking a new start, he had used his senatorial friends to try to get him an appointment as an American agent to Venezuela. But Monroe had a good memory, and he had no sympathy for Duane, whom he described as the editor for twenty-five years of "the most slanderous newspaper in the United States. He is now poor, and growing old, and his present proposal is substantially to sell his silence." The President would have none of it.

There was close liaison between the *Intelligencer* and the White House, but it was never the administration's paper, body and soul, as newspapers had been owned by political parties before. The press as a whole, however, was still almost entirely political, as a cynical but substantially accurate analysis by John Quincy Adams in his diary demonstrates. Referring to how some papers were pushing the candidacy of William H. Crawford, the Georgia Senator, for the Democratic nomination in 1824, Adams noted caustically:

> Among the most powerful of his agents have been the editors of the leading newspapers. The *National Intelligencer* is secured to him by the belief of the editors that he will be the successful candidate, and by their dependence upon the printing of Congress; the Richmond *Enquirer*, because he is a Virginian and a slave-holder; the *National Advocate* of New York, through Van Buren; the Boston *Statesman* and Portland *Argus*, through William King; the *Democratic Press*, of Philadelphia, because I transferred the printing of the laws from that paper to the *Franklin Gazette*; and several other presses in various parts of the Union upon principles alike selfish and sordid.

Of the subsequent newspaper war between Crawford and Calhoun, Adams wrote:

> This day the *City Gazette* has three columns of brevier type of the foulest abuse upon McKenney, and upon Mr. Calhoun personally. . . . The *Republican* replies this evening with firmness and moderation to the *National Advocate* and Boston *Statesman*, and reviews its own progress hitherto. If this press is not soon put down, Mr. Crawford has

an ordeal to pass through before he reaches the Presidency which will test his merit and pretensions as well as the character of the nation.

In the end, after this imaginary crisis had passed, Adams found himself in the White House, rather than either Crawford or Calhoun. Adams was, if nothing else, a pragmatic man. He had used the *Intelligencer* as a willing mouthpiece when he was secretary of state, but the paper had supported Crawford, and as soon as he was safely installed, the new President turned to a new Washington paper, the *National Journal*, as his chief support. Its editor and publisher, Peter Force, who also was mayor of Washington during his career, was the President's friend, but Adams' relationship with the *Journal* was never particularly close.

The long, comparative peace in the partisan press came abruptly to an end with the campaign of 1828. The papers supporting Adams and Jackson appeared to be in a competition to see who could make the most scandalous charges. Jackson's papers declared that Adams, when he was minister to Russia, "attempted to make use of a beautiful girl to seduce the passions of the Emperor Alexander and sway him to political purposes." Adams' editors replied with the charge that Jackson's mother was a mulatto. The opposition answered by asserting that Adams' wife was English, not American.

In the spring before the election, Adams had a more immediate, if minor, crisis thrust upon him when his son and secretary, also John Adams, was assaulted in the rotunda of the House en route to the Senate, on an official errand. The assailant was Russell Jarvis, formerly of the *United States Telegraph*, an opposition paper, but now one of the printers of the Senate, who had learned that young Adams, after seeing Jarvis in a White House "drawing room," had remarked that if "Jarvis had the feelings of a gentleman he would not show himself here."

This was the language the President himself used in a special message about the incident which he sent to Congress, asking it to consider "whether any further laws or regulations are necessary to insure security in the official intercourse between the President and Congress, and to prevent disorders within the Capitol itself." Adams was convinced that Jarvis had been brought by his opposition "for the purpose of assassination." No new laws resulted, however.

Adams cooled himself off from these and other tribulations by swimming in the Potomac, a recreation to which he was as ardently devoted as Chairman Mao. The press left him alone on these expeditions, but his friends were constantly worried that he would drown in the treacherous river, and sometimes he was, in fact, in real danger. Disappointing though it may be to feminists, there is no truth to the myth that Anne Royall, the eccentric publisher of two small newspapers, *Paul Pry* and the *Huntress*, once sat on his clothes while he was in the water until he gave her a story. Mrs. Royall was not even in Washington for much of the time between 1824 and 1831, and her papers were not begun until after Adams had left the White House. She would not have been incapable of grasping the opportunity, however. In 1829, she was arrested, tried, and convicted in Washington under the old colonial law governing "common scolds."

Mrs. Royall was the first woman to edit a newspaper of any consequence, and her personal, insistent method of attacking her Washington enemies and her view of life in the capital, recall in some respects the redoubtable Cissie Patterson and the Washington *Times-Herald* of the nineteen-forties. Adams took a chauvinist view of her, which was no doubt accurate. After she had visited him in Quincy, Massachusetts, where he was trying to take a holiday, he wrote, "She continues to make herself noxious to many persons; tolerated by some and feared by others, by her deportment and her books; treating all with a familiarity which often passes for impudence, insulting those who treat her with incivility, and then lampooning them in her books. Stripped of all her sex's delicacy, but unable to forfeit its privilege of gentle treatment from the other, she goes about like a virago-errant in enchanted armor, and redeems herself from the cravings of indigence by the notoriety of her eccentricities and the forced currency they give to her publications."

Such a woman was far more at home in the Jackson administration, which swept in from the West in 1832. The shade of Andrew Jackson is frequently invoked by Democrats today, at their Jackson Day dinners and other fund-raising affairs, as the first great Populist president, a grass-roots leader in the party tradition. He has also been treated admiringly by some eminent historians. But in the light of present-day values, it is difficult to find much to admire. Where the Indians were concerned, he was unquestionably a racist; his attitudes toward them and his treatment of them were alike contemptible. He was a president who believed in violence and force rather than in diplomacy. Philosophically, he was virtually illiterate, and in general qualified as one of the chief proponents of anti-intellectualism in American life. "The context of the times," so often cited in his defense, does not mitigate his attitudes and conduct, much of which today would be considered at the far right of the political spectrum.

In terms of media history, Jackson was unique in several ways. For one, he was the first president to demonstrate how to manipulate and manage the press for partisan purposes. For another, he was the only president to have his own personal newspaper, using it as a direct propaganda arm of the presidency.

He came to power on a wave of campaign controversy in the papers which had not been equaled for virulence since the days of Washington, Adams, and Jefferson. It was typical of him that he was not disturbed when he was accused in the press, accurately, of ordering six militiamen executed after they had been convicted by a court-martial, or having ordered the execution of two Seminole chiefs and their English ally, or killing an opponent in a duel. He was angered, rather, by the widely circulated story that he had lived adulterously with his wife before her divorce was legally valid. These and many other facts attest to the primitive state of Jackson's morality.

His chief newspaper allies were men who were as profoundly wrong about public matters as he was. Francis Preston Blair, a native Virginian, tubercular, fanaticism burning in his eyes, came to public attention in Kentucky, where, during what came to be called the "Relief War," he fought for a moratorium for debtors and the institution of state banks with power to print their own money. It hardly mattered to him that the Supreme Court of Kentucky ruled such laws unconstitutional; his answer was to insist that a new court replace the old one, and that campaign was successful, with a resulting wild inflation that ruined friend and enemy alike. As a reward, he was appointed to be clerk of the new court, and simultaneously (no conflict-of-interest laws existed) president of one of the newly created banks. Then he took on a third job, writing for the *Argus of Western America*, of Frankfort, Kentucky, a paper edited by Amos Kendall.

Kendall also had serious respiratory problems—students of psychosomatic medicine, including those who think there is no other kind, may draw their own conclusions from his and Blair's afflictions—and he had emigrated to Kentucky from Massachusetts in the westward movement of 1814. As a Dartmouth man, he found employment as tutor of Henry Clay's children, at the Clay home in Lexington. It is an index to Kendall's personality that he felt no particular gratitude to Mrs. Clay, who went out of her way to teach him some social graces and also nursed him through a serious illness. These kindnesses and those of his employer scarcely deterred Kendall from writing scurrilous things about Clay after he joined the Jackson forces. He had come to the *Argus* by way of the law, a postmastership in a small town, and editing two failing newspapers. He bought his interest in the paper on credit, and conducted it in such a way that he had to go about armed.

It was the *Argus*, violent and radical in its tone, that was the principal newspaper voice in Jackson's campaign, and when the newly elected President went to Washington, Kendall went with him. The new populist era, ushered in with an inauguration distinguished by the unruly mob that trampled the White House lawn, broke its glassware, stood on its satin chairs, and bellowed for more liquor and food, began with one of the most blatant dispensations of patronage ever seen in Washington. Although he had an understandable bias, Adams was not far wrong when he complained bitterly that "the appointments, almost without exception, are conferred upon the vilest purveyors of slander during the late electioneering campaign, and an excessive disproportion of places is given to editors of the foulest presses. . . . The appointments are exclusively of violent partisans; and every editor of a scurrilous and slanderous newspaper is provided for."

That was Jackson's intention—to reward the editors who had helped him and, if possible, punish those who had opposed. Daniel Webster worked hard in the Senate to save the country, as he put it, from the "typographical corps." Through his influence, the Senate threw out Jackson's nomination of Isaac Hill, editor of the *New-Hampshire Patriot*, to a job in the Treasury Department (he was later elected to the Senate), and also refused to confirm Major Mordecai M. Noah, of the New York *Enquirer*. When Kendall's name came up for confirmation as fourth auditor of the Treasury Department, the Senate vote was a tie, but Vice-President Calhoun cast the deciding vote that confirmed him.

Kendall was made postmaster general in 1835, but his real job was to be Jackson's confidential adviser, in substantially the same relationship as Colonel House to Wilson, Harry Hopkins to Franklin Roosevelt, Sherman Adams to Eisenhower, and Ehrlichman and Haldeman to Nixon. There was something of this last relationship, especially, in the reason Kendall gave in his autobiography for the decision by the administration to start its own newspaper. "It originated," Kendall wrote, "with those friends of General Jackson who regarded measures more than men, and desired his reelection for another four years, not so much for his own sake as to effect reforms in the government which no other man was capable of bringing about."

To edit the *Globe*, as the new organ was named, Blair was brought in from the *Argus*. Jackson had never seen him before, and the spectacle might have unnerved a different man. He was described only half facetiously by his partner, John C. Rives, himself a giant, shaggy Kentuckian, as "about five feet ten inches high, and would be full six feet if his brain were on the top of his head, instead of being in a *poll* behind it. He looks like a skeleton, lacks but little of being one, and weighed last spring, when dressed in thick winter clothing, one hundred and seven pounds, all told ... flesh he has none. His face is narrow, and of the hatchet kind, according with his meat-ax disposition when writing about his enemies. His complexion is fair, his hair sandy, and his eyes blue—his countenance remarkably mild."

Kendall was an even stranger sight, Rives wrote, "bent, nearsighted, badly dressed, with premature white hair, sallow complexion, and a hacking asthmatic cough." He appeared in his white broadcloth greatcoat, buttoned to the throat, even on the hottest days, and because he was subject to migraine headaches, he sometimes had a white handkerchief tied around his head. This apparition was remarked on the floor of the House, where a wondering congressman remarked: "Poor wretch, as he rode his Rosinante down Pennsylvania Avenue, he looked like death on the pale horse."

Rives himself came on the scene later to manage the business affairs of the *Globe*, and with Blair and Kendall became the President's cronies, in what is known as Jackson's "Kitchen Cabinet." The most important policy decisions were made by these strangely assorted men, all of them fanatically loyal to Jackson and quite capable of taking any sort of action to protect him and reelect him.

The *Globe* was started without plant, facilities, or subscription list, but the latter deficiency was quickly remedied with a semisecret and wholly improper pressure applied to federal officers with salaries of $1000 or more. Subscribe, they were told in effect, if you want to keep your job. Kendall also passed the word around that the President wanted departmental printing shifted to the new paper, and in case there was any doubt in the minds of department heads about what they were expected to do, Jackson issued an executive order requiring all Cabinet members to make monthly reports to him on how much money had been spent for printing, and who had been given the jobs. Favors were expected to be given, however, and not returned. When a Jackson man with his own private interests to pursue offered Blair a $100 contribution, the editor sent it back.

In a year, the *Globe* had 4000 subscribers and congressional and departmental printing amounting to about $50,000 annually. The *Tel-*

egraph, leading opposition newspaper in Washington, could not survive the loss of its governmental job printing, and had to suspend. The *Globe* stood virtually alone. It has been described as "a radical paper. It was dogmatic, bold and defiant. At times the editor hesitated when it was political to do so. His gift for satire played to his advantage and to the great discomfiture of the enemy. Blair's sarcasm bit like vipers, and friends and foes alike came to dread his editorial attacks."

Because of its peculiar and particular relationship to the President, the *Globe* was read more carefully abroad than any other American newspaper, as other governments searched in it for clues to what Jackson might be contemplating. The Russians complained about some items in the *Globe* they considered unfavorable to them, and when the American minister, James Buchanan, assured them it was not under the control of the government, they did not believe it, any more than anyone in Washington would have believed this diplomatic fiction.

Highly pleased with what the editors he had appointed to government jobs had done for him, Jackson rewarded more of them when he was reelected in 1836, which brought a sense of disquiet even to some pro-Jackson editors whose consciences were uneasy about this intimate relationship between the presidency and the press. The Richmond *Enquirer*, a Jackson supporter, complained:

> We wish the Executive would let the Press alone. We cannot any more approve of the appointment of so many of its conductors to office, although they may be required to give up their papers, than we approved of the great pains which were taken by Mr. Clay to turn obnoxious Editors out . . . and to put in his devoted Partizans.—We know that General Jackson solemnly disclaims all intentions to *reward* his supporters or to bribe the Press to support his measures. And we believe him—we know also, the reasons by which he justifies these appointments. . . . But we are better satisfied with his *motives* than his *reasons*—with the integrity than with the expediency of the appointment.

If the *Enquirer* had been less partisan, it would have had ample reason to suspect Jackson's motives as well as his reasons. Historians may argue about what was in the President's mind, and quote documents selectively to prove it one way or the other, but there is no question that the effect of what he did was to reward his supporters and to bribe the press to support his measures. Moreover, the reasons he gave for his actions, in a letter to John Randolph in 1831, are so specious that they can be regarded only as the self-serving statements of a politician.

"I was never sensible," he wrote, "of the justness of the exceptions stated to the employment of Printers in the public service. The press is the Palladium of our liberties. Disfranchise those who conduct it: or what is the same thing make the calling of an editor a qualification for the possession of those rewards which are calculated to enlarge the sphere of talent and merit, and which are accessible to other callings in life, and you necessarily degrade it. . . . I refused to consider the editorial calling as unfit to offer a candidate for office; and accordingly appointed them on a few occasions when they were deemed honest and capable." And, he might have added, when they were ardently pro-Jackson and did what they were told.

Like Nixon, Jackson measured people, including editors, by their personal loyalty, in his case perhaps reflecting his military background. He was well aware that two thirds of the newspapers had been against him in his first campaign, and he had no compunction about putting papers like the *Telegraph* out of business if he could. It and other opposition papers, it appeared, were not a part of the "Palladium of our liberties."

As for the *Globe*, it had prospered so in the first two years of its existence that Blair and Rives began another enterprise, the *Congressional Globe*, financed in part by a government subsidy, which offered a full stenographic report of the debates in Congress. It, too, proved to be a gold mine. Kendall shared in the general prosperity. Although he was postmaster general, he was also on the *Globe*'s payroll at $800 a year.

A relationship as close as Blair's with Jackson meant, however, that the *Globe* stood on shaky ground, dependent on the President entirely, its editor traveling with him, eating and drinking with him often, and sometimes appearing at the White House for consultation before the President had breakfast.

It was not surprising, then, that when Jackson went out of office, the whole unique and elaborate structure fell apart. Van Buren was urged by some Jacksonian supporters to drop Blair as editor, but he did not. Blair survived through that president and his successor, William Henry Harrison, as the editor of what was still the administration organ. But James K. Polk, although Blair had supported him, was under too much party pressure to get rid of the editor, who had made powerful enemies, and forced him to sell the paper to Thomas Ritchie, editor of the Richmond *Enquirer,* who changed its name to the *Union.* Polk also deprived the *Globe* of its government job-printing monopoly.

Blair lived to be old, as well as rich, in spite of his frail constitution. His Jacksonianism gave him a natural affinity for Lincoln, and he became one of the President's trusted advisers, although far from enjoying the old "Kitchen Cabinet" status. It was Blair who, on Lincoln's authority, offered the command of the Armies of the Union to Robert E. Lee before the war. He died in 1876 at eighty-five, frail as ever but having outlived most of his friends and enemies. Blair House, the government's official guest residence in Washington, perpetuates today the name of its owner.

Kendall lost his job as postmaster general when Van Buren lost the presidency in 1840, even though he had done much to improve the mail service, performing the additional miracle of making it pay. Blair and Rives helped him find the money to start a fortnightly paper called *Kendall's Expositor,* but Kendall, who was now a poor man, resented Blair's affluence and began to work behind the scenes in an effort to get some of the government printing that the *Argus* jealously hoarded as long as it could. The two old friends quarreled bitterly in their letters, Blair cold and even brutal, Kendall frustrated and nearly hysterical. They broke completely in 1845 after Rives's brother-in-law killed Kendall's son William. A year earlier, Kendall had abandoned journalism and become Samuel F. B. Morse's paid lobbyist to get government aid for the telegraph. As Morse's agent, Kendall made a fortune as the invention made one for his employer. After he retired in 1860, he went back to writing and spent the remainder of his life attacking Lincoln as an incompetent. He died in 1869.

The *Globe* in its brief career demonstrated how an incumbent president could use the press as a personal propaganda weapon, but no chief executive has since tried to emulate Jackson. It also showed how far dissent could be carried by an incumbent president who had the same tool in his hands as his adversaries.

With Jackson's departure, a long era ended in media history. Beginning with Benjamin Harris, the press had won its freedom from government license, and then had sold itself utterly and voluntarily to its former masters. From its use as a revolutionary propaganda machine to its hardly concealed official position as the private organ of a president, it had encompassed the range of partisan expression at the expense of truth and responsibility. As a tool of party and politicians, it had not attained any particular distinction except in the excellence of writing which the best politicians and editors brought to it.

At the close of the Jackson administration, the newspaper in America was not yet a *news*paper in the sense we know it today, but a new era was about to begin.

9

The Great Magazine
Explosion

IN BOTH EUROPE AND AMERICA, the year 1825 was a turning point. Abroad there was a rising wave of revolutionary movement in many countries, and a strong tide of reform was running. Change was the order of the day. Jackson's accession three years later was more than a Populist triumph. It was the beginning of a new era in American politics, with large and far-reaching consequences. The nation had asserted itself as a nation for the first time, and there was a suddenly awakened public consciousness of the continent as the Erie Canal and the Baltimore & Ohio Railroad stretched symbolically westward.

Out of this ferment—and particularly the rapid spread of education, the reduction of illiteracy, the improvements in printing machinery, and the rise of the cities—came the nearly incredible expansion of the magazine business from its modest beginnings to mass-market size, surpassing the simultaneous expansion of the newspaper.

Observing the phenomenon, the *New-York Mirror* wrote in November 1828: "These United States are fertile in most things, but in periodicals they are extremely luxuriant. They spring up as fast as mushrooms, in every corner, and like all rapid vegetation, bear the seeds of early decay within them. . . . They put forth their young green leaves in the shape of promises and prospectuses—blossom through a few numbers—and then comes a 'frost, a killing frost,' in the form of bills due and debts unpaid. This is the fate of hundreds, but hundreds more are found to supply their place, to tread in their steps, and share their destiny. The average age of periodicals in this country is found to be six months."

While the *Mirror* may have underrated the general durability of the new magazines, it did not exaggerate the state of their proliferation. Figures for the period are as incomplete as they are unreliable, but there were about six hundred periodicals existing in 1850 where fewer than a hundred had been published in 1825, and in that quarter century it seems probable that somewhere between four and five thousand were published. Nothing like this astonishing wave of publication has been seen since.

Perhaps the most important part of the phenomenon was the dramatic rise of the general monthly magazines. They had existed before, but now they were about to climb to a peak undreamed of by the earlier publishers.

One of the first ventures in the field proved to be one of the most eventful. It began with the founding in 1826 of *The Casket: Flowers of Literature, Wit and Sentiment* by Samuel C. Atkinson and Charles Alexander, publishers of the *Saturday Evening Post*. (*"Casket,"* it may be added, was a favorite name for magazines. The word was used in the sense of being a repository, with no somber connotations of funerals unless one considered that "literature, wit and sentiment," or whatever else editors had to offer, was "laid out" in these repositories.) As a sister publication of the *Post*, the *Casket* continued for a dozen years, with frequent interchanges of material between the two publications, until 1839, when Atkinson, who had remained as publisher after Alexander left the partnership, decided to sell it to a hustling young man named George R. Graham.

Graham altered the *Casket*'s character by changing it from a rather cheap-looking miscellany to a well-printed, entertaining magazine. Then, in another year, he bought *Gentleman's* magazine, which had been edited as an offstage amusement by the noted actor William E. Burton, who now needed the money for his real career. Combining the two, Graham in 1840 began issuing his new periodical, which he forthrightly if immodestly called *Graham's Magazine*. Almost immediately it became one of the three or four most important magazines in the United States and, as Dr. Mott says, "in the five years 1841–45, displayed a brilliance which has seldom been matched in American magazine history."

Another important innovation was embodied in a New York periodical called the *Knickerbocker* magazine, edited after 1834 by Lewis Gaylord Clark, who became known to generations of New Yorkers as "Old Knick." Drawing on the rich pool of talent then in the city—writers like Irving, Cooper, Bryant, Halleck, Paulding, and Nathaniel P. Willis—Clark added to these such notable New England names as

Longfellow, Hawthorne, Whittier, and Holmes until he was producing a magazine difficult to surpass. The innovation was his section
titled "Editor's Table," in which he talked in a light fashion about
topics of the day, and especially happenings in New York City. This
department was the ancestor of the present-day *New Yorker* magazine's opening "Notes and Comment" section, and, in a more general
way, of the "Editor's Easy Chair" department in *Harper's* magazine
and similar sections in many other periodicals. It gave the magazine a
more personal voice, besides providing the editor with a platform for
his views and observations about contemporary life.

Another development in this new golden age of magazines was the
rapid rise of periodicals for women. Earlier attempts to reach this
audience were dwarfed by the giants which now arose, challenging
the general magazines and arousing not only their competitive antagonism but also the ire of those who thought it preposterous to serve
women with magazines at all. Charles A. Dana, soon to be one of the
most famous of newspaper publishers, deplored in the *Harbinger* for
August 8, 1846, the assumption these magazines "constantly put forth
of being designed for *ladies*, and of representing in some way the
women of the country. . . . Heaven protect us from such literature!"

While feminists today would agree with Dana, the women for
whom the new magazines were intended disagreed. Some of the
material offered them was appallingly bad, but there was plenty of
good reading, too, and they were delighted with the idea of large,
well-printed magazines directed especially at them.

After a few tentative starts, the first really successful periodical in
this field was produced in Boston, in 1828, by Sarah Josepha Hale, a
formidable woman who left an imprint in more ways than one on
national life. She looked like everybody's mother—an ample, full-bo-
somed, pleasant lady who yet had a no-nonsense air of efficiency
about her. She called her new publication *Ladies' Magazine*. It was
meant not only to entertain but to promote Mrs. Hale's deeper interests, which lay in the direction of "female education." Perhaps that
was why her publishing efforts sometimes met with such savage
attacks. In an era when men did not regard women as having any
legitimate interest in life other than keeping house and raising children, Mrs. Hale wanted them to be trained as teachers, and to educate them in "female seminaries." Other magazines had been sickly
and sentimental and domestic. *Ladies' Magazine* boldly campaigned
for women's rights.

After nine annual volumes but only an indifferent financial success,

Mrs. Hale merged her magazine with its chief rival, *Godey's Lady's Book*, going along with it as editor. It was a fortuitous merger. Louis Godey's excellent periodical was certainly the best of the women's magazines before the Civil War. Its contributors numbered the finest writers in the country, and it did what other magazines had not done, except for *Graham's*, by paying them liberally. By 1850 it was selling 40,000 a month—the highest any magazine had yet achieved.

The influence of *Godey's Lady's Book* on other magazines was substantial. Publishers and editors were made to realize that the female market was more important than they had realized and that reaching this market would substantially increase the circulation of any magazine, particularly the general monthlies. Consequently the astute Graham, for one, changed the content of his magazine until half of it, or more, was intended for women. Others did likewise, and went even further by copying *Godey's* directly, to the annoyance of its proprietor. It was even imitated as far away as London.

In sheer numbers, however, the literary weeklies outnumbered the women's magazines and the general monthlies. They were cheap, and most of them soon died. One that survived was the *New-York Mirror*, begun in 1823. Before it expired in 1846, it presented to its readers a fascinating running commentary on the morals and manners of the times, done with wit, grace, and style. Anne Royall's *Paul Pry*, in Washington, was significant too in forecasting the gossip columns and society columns of newspapers in our time, as well as magazines like *Confidential* and *Whisper*.

Still another new category of periodical was the so-called knowledge magazine, offering all kinds of factual information. They emerged in a profusion of "family" and "penny" periodicals with titles often containing the phrase *"Cabinet of Instruction."* How well they instructed was doubted by their contemporaries. Summarizing them in 1835, *Family* magazine deplored these "cheap publications," and continued: "In the zeal of competition ... many stale and useless works were imprudently admitted into some of the publications, and the smallness of the type and bad quality of the paper rendered many of them unsatisfactory and almost worthless. Many of the cheap magazines, also, became satisfied with making up their pages with fragments of ephemeral news, rather than with substantial knowledge, alleviating their dullness by introducing here and there a worthless tale, and only taking care to impose the trash upon the world with the catch-penny glare of engravings."

Meanwhile, the quarterlies continued on their majestic literary way, particularly the *North American Review*, which in this period when it was suffering from indifferent editorship was equaled by magazines like the *New York Review*. The most famous of the quarterlies, aside from the *North American Review*, was Margaret Fuller's journal of transcendental opinion and writing, the *Dial*, which she began to publish in July 1840. Emerson edited it during the second part of its four-year existence. It was not a magazine for the general public. As Dr. Mott puts it, it was "a mystification to the uninitiated, caviar to the general, and a butt of ridicule for the irreverent." Nonetheless, it contained work by some of the best minds in New England, much of which later emerged in book form.

Specialization in the quarterlies was proliferating rapidly, but the most successful were the religious periodicals. More and more, as churches discovered what an ideal platform magazines could be for dissemination of the faith, they turned to this medium as a primary outlet, while also starting their own book publishing houses. Thus the religious press became one of the most rapidly growing and active in the entire publishing business. The Congregationalists alone had at least 25 periodicals, and the Catholics as many as 40 or 50. The *Biblical Repository* asserted in January 1840 that "of all the reading of the people three-fourths is purely religious ... of all the issues of the press three-fourths are theological, ethical and devotional." Eight years later, New York City could boast 52 religious magazines, and according to the census of 1850, there were 191 religious publications in the United States, about half of them newspapers.

The use of magazines as a platform for theological argument led to their use as platforms for secular interests. It was in magazines that the great issues of the day were debated before the Civil War engulfed the nation. The issue of slavery, of course, accelerated slowly to become the leading topic, but it was not the only one by any means. Tariffs were always good for columns of argument, and for many the Oregon question was of more moment than abolition. Some even favored fighting England for the territory, if it proved necessary, while others were inclined to agree with a Boston magazine's verdict, "The territory of Oregon is not worth much. ...." Many of the periodicals that held this view, however, changed their minds after gold was discovered in California in 1848.

Articles by the hundreds concerned the physical problem of getting westward, as the frenzy to extend the rail lines reached a peak in the eighteen-forties, with nearly three thousand miles of new track being laid every year. "Even if the art of flying should be invented," exclaimed the *Illinois Monthly* in 1830, "who would endure the trouble of wearing a pair of wings and the labor of flapping them, when every gentlemen may keep his own 'locomotive' and travel from the Mississippi to the Atlantic with no other expenditure than a teakettle of water and a basket of chips!" The railroads soon had their own periodicals. Four of them were founded before 1850, and half a dozen others had emerged by 1865.

Once slavery, politics, and transportation were disposed of, the magazines before 1850 gave rather short shrift to such other problems of the day as immigration, poverty, and labor conditions. A few writers were becoming concerned about the social problems of the new society being created, but there were few who shared the *Democratic Review*'s alarm in 1849 over the fact that "fortunes of $1,000,000 are now not rare, and some reach $20,000,000, while thousands of starving beggars throng the streets and crown the public charities." There were many more editors who preferred to cite the favorable situation of American labor as compared with the lot of workingmen in Europe. The French Socialists were quoted and written about, but infrequently read with any ardor. Nevertheless, there were those who could not look upon the thriving New England factories without fear of what they might be doing to the structure of society.

There was a good deal of trivia in the magazines, too—endless prose dealing with the fads and fancies of the day, as well as with the innumerable attempts at "reform." It sometimes appeared that the entire American society was split into groups intent on improving the morals and manners of every other group. Temperance at times excited as much passion as slavery; there were nearly a hundred temperance societies by 1828. Smoking was also debated, pro and con, but it was easier to argue the merits of chewing, where feelings on both sides were stronger. Nevertheless, there was a continuing agitation in the magazines concerning tobacco, and in 1851 Boston, at least, made it an offense to smoke on the streets and specified a fine for violators. The mayor, however, a smoker himself, made an exception of Boston Common and provided a circle of seats there in a special corner where tobacco lovers could puff away in peace.

In rapidly growing New York, magazines like the *Mirror* and the *Knickerbocker* were complaining about obscene pictures, the rudeness of omnibus riders, wandering pigs in the streets, and traffic. Most of all—a familiar cry echoing down the centuries—they were perennially upset about the continuous destruction and rebuilding of the city, making it, as one complained, "a city of ruins," as it remains today, when the language is different but the criticism remains as it was more than a century ago.

Still another issue discussed in the magazines has a familiar ring today. The subject was hair—beards, to be specific. Before the early eighteen-forties they had been absent for a long time, almost a hundred years, but suddenly they revived and became a fad. The Secretary of the Navy eventually had to take notice of it, and issued his celebrated "Whisker Order," defining the limits of hair on the face and thereby nearly precipitating a mutiny.

One of the specializations beginning to develop in the periodical press was the sports magazine. The *Turf Register* appeared in Baltimore in September 1829, reflecting an American interest in racing that dated from colonial times. It had been brought over from England, where it was as passionately followed in the seventeenth century as it is today.

A sporting paper of more dubious reputation, although it survived into our own time, was the *National Police Gazette*, begun in 1845 in New York. Its specialty at the beginning was not sport but crime, promising "a most interesting record of horrid murders, outrageous robberies, bold forgeries, astounding burglaries, hideous rapes, vulgar seductions, and recent exploits of pickpockets and hotel thieves." Along with these juicy attractions, the *Gazette* also printed some sporting news, but its readers, which included criminals and those in the city government who protected them, were often outraged, and not infrequently wrecked its offices. Later the *Gazette* was bought by a former police chief, and as the decades went on, it passed through various metamorphoses, although always retaining its special fragrant blend of sex, scandal, and sports. A staple of barberships at the turn of this century, it lost ground steadily as periodicals appeared that made it look like a Sunday-school journal.

Of all the reformers, major and minor, who argued and fought in the magazines before the Civil War, probably those who were for or against women's rights were the most vociferous. Women were breaking out of domestic slavery, a deliverance that appears to be reenacted today. They were in the thick of the abolitionist battle; they were writing for the magazines, and contributing many of the hugely popular novels of the day; and they were struggling, openly, in and out of the magazines, for some kind of parity with men. The first Woman's Rights Convention took place in 1848, at Seneca Falls, New York.

The parallels between the rhetoric of the time and the women's liberation movement today are often striking. In 1841, when women abolitionists had been refused admittance to the World's Antislavery Convention in London, Sophia Ripley summarized the conflict in the *Dial*: "There have been no topics for the last two years more generally talked of than women, and 'the sphere of women.' In society, everywhere, we hear the same oft-repeated things said upon them by those who have little perception of the difficulties of the subject; and even the clergy have frequently flattered 'the feebler sex' by proclaiming to them from the pulpit what lovely beings they may become if they will only be good, quiet and gentle, and attend exclusively to their domestic duties, and the cultivation of religious feelings, which the other sex kindly relinquish to them as their inheritance. Such preaching is very popular."

Betty Friedan or Gloria Steinem could not have said it better.

Mostly the struggle centered on votes for women. Typical of the opposition to this elemental right in the magazines was the protest of the *New-York Mirror*: "The eternal wrangling of discordant opinions about men and offices, and the petty details of elections and caucuses can have little charm for the refined taste or polished judgment, and lend no charm to the intercourse of the domestic circle. . . . No, there can be no excuse for a female deserting her allotted privacy and volunteering to encounter gladiators in the political arena." Most of the women's magazines, it may be added, were opposed to suffrage for the sex they existed, presumably, to serve.

Women who stayed at home with the children, willingly or not, found that the mania for starting magazines had extended to periodicals designed for the young, and while many of these journals were dreary moralizers, the new trend toward entertainment that had already begun in books was also evident in the periodicals, particularly the *Youth's Companion*, begun in Boston in 1827 by the indefatigable Nathaniel Willis, and *Parley's Magazine*, started in 1833 by that mountain of energy, Samuel G. Goodrich. He had to sell it a year later, but under his pseudonym, "Peter Parley," he continued to delight generations of children with the books he wrote and published for them, and with another magazine, *Merry's Museum for Boys and Girls*, which eventually merged with *Parley's*.

All this remarkable expansion of magazines created, or at least began to create, a corps of professional magazine writers, who were known then as "magazinists." Willis was the leader, the first successful professional freelance writer. He wrote for both *Graham's* and *Godey's*, and for a good many other magazines. He had the essential characteristics of a good freelance writer today: he was an excellent reporter, able to work in a variety of fields, and the possessor of a light, smooth, readable style that was a refreshing contrast to the pretentious prose of the day. He wrote both prose and poetry, fiction and nonfiction; it seemed there was nothing he could not make at least a creditable attempt to do.

Few writers of Willis' day would have had the brash confidence to begin a story: "I have a passion for fat women. If there is anything I hate in life, it is what dainty people call a *spirituelle*. Motion—rapid motion—a smart, quick, squirrel-like step, a pert, voluble tone—in short, a lively girl—is my exquisite horror! I would as lief have a *diable petit* dancing his infernal hornpipe on my cerebellum as to be in the room with one. . . ." Willis then goes on to describe in detail the heroine of his story, a fat girl whose name is, appropriately, Albina McLush.

A magazinist of far greater ability and much less income was Edgar Allan Poe, who contributed to more than thirty magazines and served on the editorial staffs of five of them during his tortured lifetime. His magazine life was, unfortunately, as melancholy as his stories and poems. For the contributions he made, some of which were enduring portions of American literature, he got as little money as the pay scales of the time allowed. For his work as editor, he was among the lowest paid. True, he was much less editor than writer, but even so, his genius placed him far above the general run of men who sat in the editorial chairs.

Other exceptional early magazinists would have to include Park Benjamin, one of the originators of the paperback revolution, who was always busy as writer, editor, or both, and T. S. Arthur, of Philadelphia, best known as the author of *Ten Nights in a Bar-Room*, his most successful book. Arthur left a hundred books behind him, many of them filled with his numerous magazine pieces. William Gilmore Simms, better remembered now as a poet, was the leading magazinist in the South, but he was so prolific that his work appeared in many of the Northern periodicals, too.

The most indefatigable of the magazinists, like Arthur, were inclined to be book writers, and there was now, indeed, a natural flow between the magazine and book business—magazine contributions became books, books were excerpted or printed whole in magazines, just as they are today. No one was more deeply involved in this traffic than Mrs. Lydia H. Sigourney, who wrote steadily for fifty years, a tidal output of prose and poetry appearing in more than three hundred magazines, and resulting in fifty-six books. By her own count, Mrs. Sigourney contributed a minimum of two thousand articles to the periodicals. There was, in fact, a whole "writing tribe" of women who wrote for the magazines, but none of them approached Mrs. Sigourney in productivity.

A great many of the magazinists devoted their work to encouraging the arts in one way or another, with the result that there was far too much indiscriminate praise. It was difficult for an American book to get a bad review in an American magazine, although the British press more than made up for this deficiency. Moreover, the reviews themselves were often badly written, superficial, given to generalities, lush language, and padded out with long extracts from the book under review. Critics were often given complimentary copies of a book (standard practice now, but new then) and this appeared to dull their critical faculties. Sometimes the critic had to review the work of a friend or another writer for the same journal, and that also discouraged real criticism. Other critics, it appeared, were afraid of venturing unpopular opinions; and some were simply lazy.

Criticism was also far too often the product of regional as well as individual prejudices. Political and religious feelings helped make much criticism more diatribe than analysis. Nevertheless, there were good critics in the magazines, and they wrote well. Poe's own brilliance offset much of the inferior work he so disdained, and there were other distinguished names among the critics—Lowell, Prescott, Simms, Richard Henry Dana, Margaret Fuller, Emerson, Longfellow, Motley.

If criticism was a major subject of artistic controversy in the magazines, poetry was only slightly less so. There were those who scorned it as trivial when it was not pretentious, while others thought what was being written in America exceeded the best of English poetry, with the exception of Byron's. Certainly the scorners were on solid ground when they talked about the sentimental claptrap that filled so much of the ladies' magazines and the smaller literary weeklies. Much of the poetry, indifferent and otherwise, that appeared in the magazines later reappeared in books, and formed a not insignificant part of the rapidly increasing number of new American books.

Readers were not nearly so addicted to poetry, however, as they were to novels, and fiction in book form was rising to new levels of mass popularity. The magazines took little notice of this development except to deplore it. They were highly critical of novels and novel reading, even though many of them carried such works as serials. These were mostly British, French, and German in origin. American novels were likely to be historical romance, celebrating the remembered glory of the American past, once so close and now receding into the distance. Cooper was chief in this genre. But magazines continued to deprecate novel reading, possibly because people who were reading them were not reading magazines.

In the furor over novels, the growing development of the short story as an art form was largely overlooked, probably because critics hardly knew how to treat it or even what to call it. The magazines were blind to the virtues of American writers who were right under their noses—masters of the short-story form like Poe, Hawthorne, and Irving. Of these, only Hawthorne was given much recognition for short-story writing.

Rivaling fiction and poetry for interest among magazine readers, as well as book lovers, was biography, and the magazines had much of it to draw on to satisfy their audiences. Many of the most noted writers turned their hands to the biographical form—Cooper's "Lives of the Naval Commanders," in *Graham's*, Irving's *Columbus*, and Jared Sparks's excursions into the lives of eminent Americans, among others. Virtually every magazine carried some biographical writing, and a few, like the *North American Review*, made it one of their hallmarks.

History was a natural companion to the interest in biography. With the work of historians like John G. Palfrey, Prescott, Motley, and George Bancroft available to them, magazine editors could make some significant contributions to national culture in this field, and the best of them did so.

Another kind of writing began to attain a prominence in the golden age that it had never enjoyed before. Humor, always so much a part of American life, had been given little notice in the magazines, which, in earlier days, had seemed to think it beneath them. Lewis Gaylord Clark, who was editing the *Knickerbocker* with his twin brother, Willis Gaylord, in 1846, was convinced that "the present age is emphatically the Age of Fun. Everybody deals in jokes, and all wisdom is inculcated in a paraphrase of humor."

A distinctive kind of American humor had begun to appear based on the "tall tale" and the stereotype, both of which persisted well into this century. In a remarkably perceptive analysis of this development, the *Democratic Review* said: "The sources of American humor are various and novel, the scheming Yankee, the wild Kentuckian, the generous Virginian, the aristocratic Carolina planters, the camp meeting, the negro music, the auctioneers and orators, the fashionable clergy, life on the Mississippi and the Lakes, the history of every man's life, his shifts and expedients, and change of pursuits, newspaper controversies, fashions in dress, militia training, public lectures, newspaper advertisements, placards, signs, names of children, man-worship, razor-strop men."

Where the performing arts were concerned, the magazines did not yet serve them well. New York, by this time the national theatrical center, had only a few magazines that were devoted to the drama, and other areas had even fewer. There was some drama criticism in the general periodicals, more in the newspapers. Music did a little better, for, as John Sullivan Dwight, the leading critic in that field, remarked in the *Harbinger* in 1845, "Our people are trying to become musical. There is a musical movement in this country."

Americans were discovering they had a native music, and although the Northerners took a plantation owner's view of them, Negro songs were hailed as indigenous, and delighted everyone. There was little to bolster black self-pride in such songs as "Old Zip Coon" and "Jump Jim Crow" and "Dandy Jim"—the work songs, the blues, the prison songs were not likely to be white popular music—but there was some truth in the *Knickerbocker*'s characterization of them as an "American national opera."

Notwithstanding a widespread interest in music, the founding of orchestras like the Philharmonic Society in New York, and the visits of renowned European virtuosos like the violinist Ole Bull, there were not many music magazines published, and those that were had little to recommend them. The best music critics appeared in the general magazines. There was even less art criticism and fewer art magazines, despite the tradition of American art that had been established in the eighteenth century. There were only occasional articles about art, or criticism of it, in the magazines.

If the arts had not yet inspired many periodicals to support them, the sciences did better. Several agricultural and medical journals had survived from earlier periods, and now more of these and other specialized journals were appearing. Philadelphia was the center for medical publishing, both books and magazines, but other such work was being turned out in Louisville, New York, and Boston. Popular health magazines had begun to appear, full of sententious advice, most of it wrong. On the wilder shores, there were magazines devoted to the healing properties of water, and to phrenology, a fad that surpassed the water cure in popularity. Serious, talented writers and editors inexplicably believed in phrenology, and many of the best magazines devoted space to it. Park Benjamin and Poe were among the believers, and there were only a few skeptics like the *Mirror*, which satirized it unmercifully, or the *Knickerbocker*, which printed this couplet in 1850:

> Thou hast a noble cranium; what remains
> To make thee a great genius? Only brains.

As the magazinist began to come into his own professionally, so did the magazine editor. He was still inclined to vacillate between writing and editing, and the concept of his job as generating and carrying out ideas was not yet developed. But the basic job of planning the magazine and working with writers was established, and so was the task of dealing with business problems.

The leader among the new breed of editors was George Graham, who had been only twenty-six when he started his highly successful periodical. He was destined to be an editor, and began to be one as soon as possible. Graham was endlessly inventive and innovative. If he did not originate the idea, he successfully promoted the practice of listing all his famous contributors on the cover and title page of his magazine, a practice that became, years later, the primary merchandising tool of Hearst's *Cosmopolitan*, and still later common practice on many magazines. Graham was not content to make impressions from steel and copper plates already used elsewhere, as was the custom on the other monthlies; he insisted on new plates, engraved particularly for *Graham's*, a move that astonished and impressed some of his contemporaries.

In shaping his magazine, Graham proved to be not so much a literary figure, advancing the arts, as the kind of publisher familiar to us today. He was aware of the value of big names, and knew he must pay to get them. His offer of higher rates to authors was the act of a publisher buying talent, not an editor rewarding merit. Yet as editor, a post in which he functioned tirelessly, he had the valuable attributes of the best—a genial personality which attracted and held people and allowed him to iron out personal differences. Writers were loyal to him. He shared his success with them, as well as enjoying it himself. Graham lived in a fine house on Philadelphia's Arch Street, driving his bays down the street in a splendid carriage, entertaining the leading literary figures nearly every day in his home.

Graham's generous nature led to his ultimate collapse. With the leading magazine in the country and the largest circulation in the world, he made a common mistake and embarked on an unwarranted and unnecessary expansion, buying two newspapers. Although he had no precedent to guide him, it is historically true that newspaper publishers who buy magazines, and vice versa, are seldom successful, even though notable exceptions like Hearst come to mind. Millions of dollars have been lost in the unsuccessful attempt to be two kinds of publisher. In Graham's case, his merged Philadelphia papers were a disaster, and he compounded the folly by financing a third paper. All the ventures were steady money losers.

These, plus unwise investments in mining stocks, were the reason Graham had to sell his magazine, although he himself believed it was because he had personally written a bad review of *Uncle Tom's Cabin* in the magazine, at a time when Mrs. Stowe was a national heroine. A short time after it appeared, the magazine was sold. He worked on newspapers for a time, nearly lost his sight, and had to retire on a pension provided, ironically, by George W. Childs, the eminent Philadelphia publisher, a man who had once looked up from sweeping the street before his employer's shop to watch, with awe and admiration, as Graham swept down the avenue behind his trotters. Graham died in 1894; his magazine lost its identity in 1858, and became a short-lived ladies' monthly.

The publisher and editor of the magazine that ranked in importance with *Graham's* was a sharp contrast. Louis A. Godey was a man whose sexuality it would be hard to define in the absence of the kind of observations that would have been possible only a few decades later. We do know he was the kind of man who was at home in any domestic gathering of women of his time, talking to them in what he presumed was their own language. He was simple, chubby, benign in appearance, and his attitude toward women was in the best tradition of gallantry. He spoke of his audience as "fair Ladies" or "fair readers," and talked to them as one good friend to another in the pages of his *Lady's Book.* He always capitalized both "Lady" and "Love."

Aside from that aspect of his personality, Godey was an excellent businessman who ran up the circulation of his magazine to a record 150,000 before the outbreak of the Civil War, and left more than a million dollars behind when he died. When he wrote, "Nothing having the slightest appearance of indelicacy, shall ever be admitted to the *Lady's Book*," he was stoutly affirming the incredibly mawkish morality of an era in which the breast of a turkey could only be referred to as its bosom, and the legs of a grand piano at a concert had to be adorned with pants (or "inexpressibles," as they would have had to be called) lest the word "leg" be suggested to the minds of delicate females in the audience.

Astute as he was and in complete tune with his readers, Godey nevertheless acquired a decided asset in 1837 when Mrs. Hale brought her magazine into his fold. He could have had no better assistant than the woman of whom it was said, "Her whole life was a tribute to the respectabilities, decorums, and moralities of life." Not only did she carry on her crusade for "female education" in *Godey's*, but she found time to toss off such pieces of literary immortality as "Mary Had a Little Lamb," and to persuade President Lincoln to adopt her idea of declaring Thanksgiving a national holiday.

Unfortunately, these latter accomplishments have overshadowed her real significance as the pioneer and prime force in getting women into the teaching and medical professions, although that did not dissuade her from compiling a good and popular cookbook among the other volumes she either wrote or edited. She reluctantly gave up her editorial duties in 1877, at the age of eighty-nine. Godey died the following year, and his sons took charge of the magazine, which declined and lost its identity completely when Frank Munsey bought it in 1898.

These were the foremost of the editors responsible for the Golden Age. From them emerge the broad outlines of the magazine editor as a type—an individual of strong personality and many talents, blessed with ideas, armed with determination, and much involved in the society he lived in. Like the men who were founding the great newspapers at the same time, they were powerful and sometimes eccentric people. The giants of the newspaper world may have been more powerful and more eccentric, but the magazine editors were joining them as prime influencers of American culture, and as interpreters of the American scene to a mass audience.

10

Private Enterprise
in Newspapers

ON THE MAY MORNING IN 1835 when the New York *Herald* first appeared on the streets, a line was crossed in media history, sharply dividing the past from the present. Modern newspaper history begins with James Gordon Bennett's paper, and in the next fifteen years the foundations were laid for what has been called the era of personal journalism.

It was more than that, however. The establishment of three great metropolitan dailies in New York—the *Herald*, Horace Greeley's *Tribune*, and Henry Raymond's *Times*—marked a far more radical change in media structure and influence than anything that had happened before, or has occurred since. Between 1835 and the end of the century, the newspaper was established as a capitalist institution, placed firmly in private hands, and freed of both government control and political parties. It was no less politically committed, but now the commitment came from private entrepreneurs who owed their power —and it was the kind of power the press had never enjoyed before—to unprecedented circulations and the force of their own personalities, and that of the men and women who wrote for them.

The most prominent of the new publishers, who were also editors, were eccentric in varying degrees. They were restless, pushing men, for the most part, egocentric and combative, possessed of a certain cynicism and devoted to the making of newspapers, although Greeley and Raymond were politically ambitious as well. By today's standards, truth and responsibility were not always their hallmarks, but in comparison with what had gone before, these ethical ideas were now beginning to blossom where nothing had grown before. The editors might be as partisan as their predecessors in some respects, but what they did was done in their own right, not as party minions. That was true even of Greeley and Raymond, who were practicing politicians.

While the newspapers they produced were sometimes guilty of excesses reminiscent of the past, the competition of these strong-minded men for readers produced a constantly refined conception of news which made the papers entirely different from anything that had gone before. News—distorted on occasion, perhaps, but news—was the criterion by which they lived. With the development of the cylinder press, they were now speaking to mass audiences.

In overcrowded, rowdy, pushing New York City, where the Irish and German immigrant masses were manipulated shamelessly by politicians, the new generation of personal journalist publishers was soon an important factor, but the newspapers they made were read far beyond the borders of the city or state. Greeley's *Tribune*, in fact, was read and heeded nearly everywhere in the country, and for the first time that much-abused phrase "the power of the press" began to take on a new and different meaning.

Bennett was the man who almost singlehandedly changed the course of journalism history, and he would have been the first to admit it, if charged. The eccentric father of an even more eccentric son, he brought to the making of newspapers an entirely fresh concept. Scottish-born, emigrating to Halifax in 1819, he had been desperately poor there and in Boston, had worked at badly paid publishing jobs in New York and Charleston, and then had gotten his first newspaper job on the New York *Courier*, a Sunday paper, where the series he wrote exposing sharp practices in the city's business world made him perhaps the first real investigative reporter in America.

When the associate editor of the New York *Enquirer* was killed in a duel, Bennett got the job if not the title and was soon the paper's correspondent in Washington, where he produced some penetrating articles about politicians, which would now be called profiles. James Watson Webb, the editor of the *Courier*, bought the *Enquirer* and merged the papers, making Bennett the editor.

It was a brief and uneasy alliance. Webb was a flamboyant, swashbuckling opportunist who still wanted to be called "Major," even though he had been compelled to leave the Army after he had fought several duels. He was a violent, arrogant man with no visible principles, and when he suddenly switched from Jackson to the Whig camp, it was to much for young Bennett, whose long years of poverty had made him an ardent populist and Jackson supporter. He resigned.

Broke and out of a job, he tried unsuccessfully to join a new paper that was reaching out for the first time to New York's masses, Ben Day's *Sun*, the first successful penny paper in the nation after three abortive failures. The other papers were selling for six cents. Day was a New Englander who had learned his craft on the excellent newspaper in Springfield, Massachusetts, the *Republican*, operated by Samuel Bowles. He had come down to New York as a compositor, but in the depression of 1833, which was casting a premonitory shadow toward the crash three years later, he started the *Sun* as a desperate gamble, reasoning that a penny paper would prove popular in hard times, and that a substantial market existed, untapped, in the immigrant masses who could not afford six cents. He was right, and the paper was an instantaneous success, hawked in the streets by newsboys, the first of their kind in America. In six months, the *Sun* had a circulation of 8000.

Turned down by Day when he asked for a job (the *Sun's* editor, out of necessity, did all the work himself), Bennett decided to try the same gamble. His total assets were $500, but that was enough to rent quarters in a Wall Street basement and set up an ailing press, supplied with barely enough type, and a desk made of a wide plank laid across two flour barrels. The paper that this press cranked out was unimpressive to look at, a four-page double sheet, ten and a half inches wide and fourteen inches long. The only thing in it that foreshadowed the future was the prospectus on the second page, quintessentially Bennett. It read:

> Our only guide shall be good sound practical common sense, applicable to the business and bosoms of men engaged in everyday life. We shall support no party, be the organ of no faction or coterie, and care nothing for any election or any candidate from President down to constable. We shall endeavor to record facts, on every public and proper subject, stripped of verbiage and coloring, with comments suitable, just, independent, fearless and goodtempered. . . .
> There are in this city at least 150,000 persons who glance over one or more newspapers every day and only 42,000 daily sheets are issued to supply them. We have plenty of room, therefore, without jostling neighbors, rivals or friends, to pick up at least 20,000 or 30,000 for the *Herald*, and leave something for those who come after us.

It was one of the few times in his life that Bennett could be

accused of modesty. In only fifteen months, the *Herald* boasted 40,-
000 circulation, and it was climbing every day. To separate it from
the competition of the other penny dailies which were now becoming
numerous, he raised the price to two cents.

By far the most significant part of his opening statement was its
declaration of independence from political parties and candidates,
and its announced determination to "record facts, on every public and
proper subject, stripped of verbiage and coloring. . . ." No other editor
before Bennett had ever made such a promise, and fact could hardly
be separated from fancy and propaganda in the news columns of previous papers. Bennett, of course, proved to be far from objective, but
he was the first to declare an intention to try to present the news as
fairly and accurately as possible.

The news he gave his readers was primarily local news, at first, of
an unvarnished kind—the kind that mass-circulation tabloids were
purveying so successfully in the nineteen-twenties. In a raw, expanding city, Bennett reported the news of sin and corruption in a blunt,
accurate style, far different from the wordy, mock-elegant manner
which had become standard. His editorials, too, were totally unlike
the pontifications which were the stock-in-trade of other editors. He
slashed away in his half-mocking, populist manner at churchmen, politicians, businessmen, and other establishment figures. He spared no
one and respected no one, which was exactly what delighted his readers, who had the only half-concealed contempt for constituted authority so characteristic of the mass mind. In New York, as elsewhere,
the war between the haves and the have-nots had begun, and Bennett, whose early poverty and frustration had left him with an almost
Marxist hatred of the business world, was the friend of the have-nots.

It was difficult to separate Bennett's overwhelming personality from
the hard, brilliant work he did in the newsroom, but it was there that
he made his lasting contribution. What he did was to organize the
business of news gathering and editing in the pattern which prevails
today. He set up a city staff of reporters who went out on more or less
regular beats, as well as handling spot news. Bennett himself covered
Wall Street and business news with a thoroughness never seen before,
and frequently with savage criticism of the moneychangers. In 1838,
he went to Europe and there organized a six-man staff to cover the
Continent—the first foreign correspondents. At home he extended the
Herald's national coverage with correspondents in strategic cities, and
made a particular effort to get the news from the South, utilizing
Samuel Morse's new telegraph as soon as it was invented. In Wash-

ington he organized the first bureau to cover the capital, and got its members admitted to sessions of Congress.

The effect of these innovations was to revolutionize newspapers. Competing publishers hurried to emulate him, and for the first time, getting and printing the news became the chief object of newspapers. Bennett spared nothing to get the news first, establishing another journalistic criterion. His fast packets cruised off Sandy Hook, intercepting ships bringing dispatches from Europe and getting them into his paper hours before the steamers could dock. Once he met a ship bearing important European news at Halifax and carried the dispatch cases himself by hired locomotive through Boston, Worcester, and New London, then by ferry to Long Island, where another locomotive whisked him to New York. The opposition despaired of beating the *Herald*.

Balanced against this extraordinary enterprise, which was making him richer by the day, was the exhibitionism which distressed his friends and made him more enemies than any other man in town had. His former employer, Major Webb, had become his chief enemy, and the two engaged in an unseemly scuffle when they met on Wall Street one day. Reporting this incident, Bennett concluded: "As to intimidating me or changing my course, the thing cannot be done. Neither Webb nor any other man shall, or can, intimidate me. I tell the honest truth in my paper, and leave the consequences to God. Could I leave them in better hands? I may be attacked, I may be assailed, I may be killed, I may be murdered, but I never will succumb. I never will abandon the cause of truth, morals, and virtue."

Nearly everything in the *Herald* was likely to offend someone. "All we Catholics are devilish holy," Bennett would remark in one of his ambivalent statements about the church in whose faith he had been reared. The death of a beloved brother under the rigors of one of the harsher priestly orders had left him with a bitterness toward the church that he scarcely bothered to suppress.

Bennett could demolish with a stroke. "Ground was broken for the Erie Railroad yesterday," he wrote prophetically; "we hope it breaks nothing else." Sometimes it was no more than a pithy filler: "Great excitement among the Presbyterians just now. The question in dispute is, whether or not a man can do anything towards saving his own soul." Often he boasted of his paper: "Nothing can prevent its success but God Almighty, and he happens to be entirely on my side."

Always he fought the conventional morality of his day, ordering his reporters to write "leg" instead of "limb," except when he himself

satirically referred to the "branches" of dancers. Similarly, the *Herald*
used "shirts" for "linen" and "pantaloons" for what was usually
termed "inexpressibles." One he lashed out: "Petticoats—petticoats—
petticoats—petticoats—there—you fastidious fools, vent your mawkish-
ness on that!"

There were those, particularly his fellow publishers, the clergy, and
the upper classes, who did not think the *Herald* was amusing. This
irritation resulted in what came to be called the "Great Moral War"
against the publisher and his paper. His enemies attacked through
press and pulpit with invective reminiscent of an earlier day: "Stigma
on the city ... vice and vulgar licentiousness ... hypocrisy, ignorance
and bloated conceit ... double apostate and traitor in politics ...
half-crazy, uneducated wretch ... immoral and blasphemous mon-
strosity ... pest ... villain ... forger."

The climax came on June 1, 1840, when Bennett announced his
approaching marriage on the front page of the *Herald* in headlines
and story that seemed incredible even to his friends. He had met a
pretty Irish girl, Henrietta Agnes Crean, at a party, and pursued her
with his characteristic arrogance, which may well have frightened her
into consent. He would have been a hard man for any girl to resist—
six feet tall, somewhat florid, with an intensity in his eyes and voice
that nearly everyone thought compelling. Henrietta was compelled,
and found herself celebrated with this glaring headline:

TO THE READERS OF THE HERALD—DECLARATION OF LOVE—CAUGHT AT
LAST—GOING TO BE MARRIED—NEW MOVEMENT IN CIVILIZATION.

The story that followed began:

> I am going to be married in a few days. The weather is so beauti-
> ful; times are getting so good; the prospects of political and moral
> reform so auspicious, that I cannot resist the divine instinct of honest
> nature any longer; so I am going to be married to one of the most
> splendid women in intellect, in heart, in soul, in property, in person,
> in manner, that I have yet seen in the course of my interesting pil-
> grimage through human life. . . . I cannot stop in my career. I must
> fulfill that awful destiny which the Almighty Father has written
> against my name, in the broad letters of life, against the wall of
> heaven. I must give the world a pattern of happy wedded life, with
> all the charities that spring from a nuptial love. . . .

And it ended:

> My ardent desire has been through life to reach the highest order of

human intelligence, by the shortest possible cut. Association, night and day, in sickness and in health, in war and in peace, with a woman of the highest order of excellence, must produce some curious results in my heart and feelings, and these results the future will develop in due time in the columns of the *Herald*.

While his readers were still recovering from this proclamation, Bennett and his Henrietta were married and took an entirely conventional honeymoon trip to Niagara Falls, an excursion which the bridegroom improved by sending back daily dispatches on the state of the American countryside. On their return to New York, Bennett intended to install his bride in the Astor House until the home he was building for her was completed, but he discovered that his enemies had gone so far as to persuade the courtly proprietor of the Astor House, Charles Stetson (whose more enduring fame rested on the hat named for him), to refuse him the hospitality of the hotel.

Bennett's reaction was typical. "These blockheads are determined to make me the greatest man of the age," he wrote. "Newspaper abuse made Mr. Van Buren chief magistrate of this republic—and newspaper abuse will make me the chief editor of this country. Well —so be it, I can't help it."

In spite of the *Herald*'s and Bennett's success, however, it was not an influential newspaper, although many believed it to be. It was, in fact, the first large daily to demonstrate that even though a paper dominates its circulation field and apparently has a loyal readership, it does not follow necessarily that these readers will accept its politics. The *Herald*'s readers liked its news coverage, and were entertained by Bennett's eccentricity, but they often voted contrary to what Bennett advised them. The power of the press, it appeared, was not necessarily political. Bennett did not succeed in changing the morality of his day, either on Wall Street or in the living room, any more than he succeeded in influencing local or national politics in a significant way. The power to inform that the *Herald* created with its national and international news coverage was far more lasting.

Another New York eccentric, however, and Bennett's chief rival as time went on, demonstrated that it was possible for a newspaper to influence not only its own locality but the nation as a whole. The unlikely vehicle for this demonstration was Horace Greeley, who founded his New York *Tribune* in 1841.

To most Americans today the name of Greeley is remembered, if at all, for a passing remark taken out of context: "Go West, young man." He was an eccentric, like Bennett, but it was a different kind of

deviation. Where Bennett was intensely egocentric, Greeley was a liberal reformer whose dreams were for humanity. He was so widely
known everywhere in the country that he became a popular legend in
his own time, much as William Randolph Hearst was in ours. His
restless, crusading spirit dominated the American journalistic scene
from 1830 to 1870, and although other editors and literary figures
viewed him with some contempt (William Cullen Bryant, the elegant
editor of the *Post*, would not even speak to him), his was the only
journalistic voice heard from New York to California. There were a
good many people in the country who refused to believe anything in
the papers was so unless "Uncle Horace," as he was affectionately
known, confirmed it in the *Tribune*.

A master showman, an amiable medicine man, he was known to
everyone, as a present-day biographer describes him, by his "moon-
faced stare, his flopping trousers, his squeaky slang, his sputtering
profanities, his unpredictable oddities, and his general air of an
owlish, rustic sage. . . ." Vernon Parrington writes of his "round
moon-face, eyes blinking through spectacles, and a fringe of whiskers
that invited the pencil of the cartoonist." In his frock coat and white
hat, he could be seen talking endlessly to people, in New York and
elsewhere.

Those who thought Bennett might have more than a touch of para-
noia were certain Greeley was out of his mind, but they could not be
outraged, or hurt, or angry about him, as they were about the *Herald's* publisher. Instead, they told stories of Greeley's eccentricities,
adding steadily to the legend.

They recalled, for example, how Greeley, an ardent vegetarian,
once absentmindedly ate a large steak under the impression it was
graham bread. They repeated with delight the incident of the visitor
who poured out a tirade in Greeley's office, and when the editor
seemed to be paying no attention, exclaimed, "I've treated you like a
gentleman, which obviously you're not." To which Uncle Horace
responded mildly, "Who in hell ever said I was?" He was a strong-
minded man who kept a goat in the back yard behind his house on
East Nineteenth Street, and who, when his fellow Union League
Club members censured him for befriending Jefferson Davis after the
Civil War, called them "narrow-minded blockheads" and dared them
to throw him out of the club.

In the *Tribune*, Greeley created a newspaper as legendary as he
was, a training ground for other editors, and a forum for every liberal
idea directed to the betterment of humanity, without regard for its

real merits, since Greeley's agile mind leaped from idea to idea, like Eliza among the ice floes, and he was likely to go whooping off after another before his readers had fully absorbed one.

Like Bennett, Greeley had come out of poverty, in his case a New Hampshire farm, from which his father went to debtor's prison. He got his education from the Bible and from working as a printer's apprentice, arriving in New York in 1831, looking the prototype of the Alger hero, with everything he owned in the world slung over his shoulder in a bandanna, and his total wealth, ten dollars, in his pocket.

After a discouraging start on the first penny paper in New York, the *Morning Post*, which died within three weeks, Greeley started his own Whig weekly, the *New-Yorker*, on the proverbial shoestring. Its editorial page spoke with so much vigor and obvious talent that Thurlow Weed, the political boss of New York State, was attracted and hired young Greeley to edit some campaign papers for him. Out of his savings from this successful venture, Greeley launched the *Tribune* on April 10, 1841, when he was only thirty. He supplemented the thousand dollars he had saved with another thousand dollars borrowed; half the total went for printing equipment.

Bennett had a six-year start, but Greeley's editorial genius, expressed in a different way, enabled him to achieve the same immediate success. The *Tribune* reached 11,000 circulation in just seven weeks, although it never matched the *Herald* or its other competitors in readers. Often it was behind with the news, and sometimes it was unpopular politically. But no paper could equal its national influence. That was because the whole staff, from Greeley on down, believed that the "New Morning Journal of Politics, Literature and General Intelligence," as Greeley called the *Tribune* in its first issue, really meant it when the publisher promised it would "advance the interests of the people, and promote their Moral, Political and Social Well-being."

Greeley's editorials were the heart of the paper, the reason for its remarkable influence, but his news staff was the ablest in America, operating under the direction of Charles Anderson Dana, who would soon, after the war, create his own distinctive newspaper from the remnants of Ben Day's *Sun*. Greeley was publisher, Dana was editor, and Uncle Horace's old friend from Brook Farm days, Margaret Fuller, was literary editor for some time. Bayard Taylor wrote travel sketches and the editorials Greeley didn't write. Since the *Tribune* directed a large part of its appeal to farmers, it also had an agricultural editor, Solon Robinson. For a time, Karl Marx was London correspondent, but he quit when Greeley wanted to cut his ten-dollars-a-week salary to five.

By 1854, the *Tribune* had ten associate editors and fourteen reporters, with an outside staff of thirty-eight regular correspondents. Its weekly edition, condensing what had been printed in the daily, went to the remotest corners of the United States and was passed from family to family. As Taylor remarked, "The *Tribune* comes next to the Bible all through the West." In the later words of the historian James Ford Rhodes, it was "a power never before or since known in this country."

When Greeley summed up his philosophy in 1850 under the title "Hints Toward Reforms," it was easy to see why the *Tribune* was known far and wide as the "Great Moral Organ." He believed, said Uncle Horace, that "the avocations of Life, and the usages and structure of Society, the relations of Power to Humanity, of Wealth to Poverty, of master to servant, must all be fused in the crucible of Human Brotherhood, and whatever abides not the test rejected."

Greeley lived in an America that was in transition from an agricultural to an industrial society, a highly painful process full of dislocations, maladjustments, indignities, oppressions, and injustices, along with the normal complement of evil and stupidity. To a man like Greeley, with a highly developed but largely unfocused moral sense, many of these things were intolerable, to be fought with whatever weapon lay at hand. That was why he preached thrift although he never practiced it himself: it was good for humanity. He could ally himself with the conservative Whigs because they were fighting slavery, but he also horrified them because he thought of himself as a philosophical socialist.

Greeley fought hard for his beliefs, with a splendid disregard for consistency. When the Republican Party was founded, he helped to establish it and was at home within its inner circle, but when it failed to live up to his standards, he did not hesitate to run against it for the presidency, with the help of the Democrats. He was for labor unions and free homesteading but he was also for vegetarianism and spiritualism. One of his most ardent crusades was to lift the laboring class "out of ignorance, inefficiency, dependence and want," and for five years or so he preached an imported French brand of socialism known as Fourierism, which advocated cooperative ownership of lands and homes. When he finally lost interest in this idea, he never mentioned it again.

Not all of his crusades were ineffective, by any means. As a printer himself and an advocate of unionism, he organized the New York Printers' Union and became its first president. As a teetotaler, he used the influence of his paper to get state prohibition laws passed. As a humanitarian, he was against capital punishment and succeeded in persuading several states to repeal their laws permitting death by hanging. After a two-hour interview with Brigham Young in Salt Lake City in the summer of 1859, he found himself opposed to Young's views on polygamy, not for the usual moral reasons but because he considered this practice an infringement on the natural rights of women. Through his paper he brought so much pressure to bear on Congress from his aroused readers, who were concerned for more customary reasons, that polygamy was outlawed three years later.

Occasionally he supported the right things for what some considered the wrong reasons. As a Whig, for example, he came out strongly in favor of protective tariffs, not because he wanted to protect the nation's industrialists but because he thought the high standards of labor would be protected by them. His fellow Whigs, during their uneasy alliance, were confused when they read editorials arguing for protectionism and socialism in the same issue of the *Tribune*. The Whigs had something to thank him for, however. Greeley almost singlehandedly sold the idea of high tariffs to the nation's farmers, with whom his paper had its greatest influence. He sold it so well that it is still an article of faith in most parts of the rural community, and in conjunction with the various restrictive tariffs that Congress passed later in the century, has probably caused more economic damage to the country than any other political idea.

Many of Greeley's crusades stemmed from his passion to make the country strong internally. His "Go West, young man, and grow up with the country," was part of the *Tribune*'s westward expansion campaign, in which Greeley constantly urged the federal government to aid the young men who took his advice by passing a federal homestead law, and helping to build railroads and telegraph lines—all propositions which horrified his Whig friends and their Republican successors.

If he were alive today, Greeley would probably be just as unclassifiable as he was in his own time. He was for what the Republicans would now call "creeping socialism," but he was also an isolationist in today's terms, and would be in sympathy with the Republican right wing. He believed that laissez-faire was suicidal, leading to the "anarchy of individualism," yet he preached the rights of the individual. He put his ultimate trust in the fundamental goodness of humanity, a romantic view which accurately forecast his total failure in politics.

James Parton placed his finger squarely on the reason for the *Herald*'s failure to achieve the influence of Greeley's *Tribune* despite its larger circulation when he wrote, "Influence over opinion no paper can have which has itself no opinion, and cares for none." Yet, in the crisis of dissent produced by the Mexican War of 1846, it was demonstrated that the new power of the press was not enough to change the course of national events when a determined president was directing them.

The modern parallel, again, is obvious, and certainly the similarities between the "little wars" of Mexico and Vietnam are striking. Each was an attack on a smaller, weaker nation by the United States, and while the former was at least sanctioned by Congress, the sanctioning itself was of a highly dubious nature. Both were unpopular wars, carried on by presidents who were profoundly wrong and incapable of admitting it. In both, too, dissent was equated with treason, whether it came from the press or elsewhere.

The war with Mexico is a melancholy story of one of the democratic process's more sordid failures, and although it has been explored and analyzed by many historians, it has somehow failed to linger in the American consciousness. It began on the morning of May 11, 1846, when President Polk sent a special message to Congress declaring that America had been invaded by Mexico, that American blood had been shed, and that "War exists, and, notwithstanding all our efforts to avoid it, exists by the act of Mexico herself." As President Lyndon Johnson did, in effect, when he asked Congress to give him the Tonkin Gulf Resolution for the purpose of sanctioning a war that had been in progress for some time, Polk wanted Congress to declare a war that was already under way.

Whether the Mexicans had actually invaded was a question. They had crossed the Rio Grande, but whether that was the boundary with Texas, annexed only five months before, had been a matter of dispute. There was more to the dispute than the boundary, however. Polk was under pressure from businessmen who had suffered losses in Mexico as the result of revolutions. Although $8.5 million had been claimed, a mixed commission had determined in 1840 that only about a quarter of this amount was valid; the rest of the claims were either fraudulent or padded. The Mexican government had defaulted on payment of the valid claims after three installments, leaving $3.25 million yet to be paid. American corporations and states were at the time in default to the British for more than $200 million, but nothing was said about that.

These and other grievances had led Polk to set General Zachary Taylor in motion toward the Rio Grande, with a resulting skirmish between a cavalry force and a reconnoitering party. That was the war the President asked his Congress to declare after it was begun. There was an uproar on the Hill, particularly when members read a House bill, accompanying the message, which authorized the President to accept volunteers and militia. Its hawkish preamble stated blandly, "Whereas, by the act of . . . Mexico, a state of war exists between that government and the United States," the President was authorized to exert his powers as commander in chief. In brief, Polk was calling it a defensive war when the opposite was obviously true.

The Whigs were not in the majority in the Congress, a fact which the administration forces took advantage of at once. They limited the debate to two hours, and then stifled it by a parliamentary maneuver, on the ground that haste was needed to save Taylor's army from possible further casualties and even destruction.

Two hours after the House got the bill, it was passed, 174 to 14, stampeded through over the protests of dissenters like John Quincy Adams and other eminent Whigs. Then it went to the Senate, where next day the same tactics were employed. A single day was allowed for debate, and over the protests of the Whigs, the bill passed 40 to 2. Two Whigs had the courage to oppose it; Calhoun refused to vote, and asserted later that he believed the bill would not have gotten the vote of 10 per cent of Congress if the members had had the time to read the documents accompanying it.

Press dissent centered in Boston, the Whig capital, but Greeley was outspoken and sarcastic in the *Tribune*. "Grant the Father of Lies his premises," he wrote, "and he will prove himself a truth-teller and a saint by faultless logic. Shut your eyes to the whole course of events through the last twelve years . . . and it will become easy to prove that we are a meek, unoffending, ill used people, and that Mexico had kicked, cuffed and grossly imposed upon us. Only assume premises enough, as Polk does, and you may prove it is New Orleans which has just been threatened with a cannonade instead of Matamoras, and that is it the Mississippi which has been formally blockaded by a stranger fleet and army instead of the Rio del Norte."

But the war went on, and it divided the country. In Washington, the Whigs, both North and South, opposed it, and the Democrats supported it, although there were also divisions in the parties, precipitated by the slavery question. There were those who thought the administration wanted to take Mexico and extend slavery there and through Central America, and Southern Whigs who opposed the war were hardly aghast at this idea. Those who embraced the idea of Manifest Destiny, just like those who tried to sanctify the war in Vietnam, did so by depicting the United States as the defender of liberty in the world, even though every country in Southeast Asia that the Americans touched lost what civil liberties it possessed and became a military dictatorship. In Polk's day, those who believed in Manifest Destiny were more frank about it: they were unabashed in proclaiming their desire to absorb all of Mexico, and they had no strong objections to extending slavery. The antislavery people termed them "doughfaces."

Why was it so easy to pass a declaration of war with such divisions in the country and in Congress? asks the historian Frederick Merk. Because, as he says, Polk took sharp advantage of a momentary wave of hysteria in the country—"our boys are being attacked and slaughtered by the Mexicans"—and engineered the stampede. Greeley was blunt about it. He saw the vote as all that could be expected from an attack on the flag, and published an editorial expounding this view, entitled "Our Country, Right or Wrong!" He wrote:

> This is the spirit in which a portion of the Press, which admits that our treatment of Mexico has been ruffianly and piratical, and that the invasion of her territory by Gen. Taylor is a flagrant outrage, now exhorts our People to rally in all their strength, to lavish their blood and treasure in the vindictive prosecution of War on Mexico. We protest against such counsel. . . .
>
> We can easily defeat the armies of Mexico, slaughter them by thousands, and pursue them perhaps to their capital; we can conquer and "annex" their territory; but what then? Have the histories of the ruin of Greek and Roman liberty consequent on such extensions of empire by the sword no lesson for us? Who believes that a score of victories over Mexico, the "annexation" of half her provinces, will give us more Liberty, a purer Morality, a more prosperous Industry, than we now have? . . . Is not Life miserable enough, comes not Death soon enough, without resort to the hideous enginery of War?
>
> People of the United States! Your Rulers are precipitating you into a fathomless abyss of crime and calamity! Why sleep you thoughtless on its verge, as though this was not your business, or Murder could be hid from the sight of God by a few flimsy rags called banners? Awake

and arrest the work of butchery ere it shall be too late to preserve
your souls from the guilt of wholesale slaughter!

As Merk points out, the minorities in both parties failed because
the Whigs were afraid they would be destroyed if they opposed the
war, as the Federalists had been in opposing the War of 1812, while
the Democrats had a guilty conscience because it was the joint resolution they had sponsored annexing Texas which had been so vague
about boundaries that it could be said to have caused the war.

As the bloody conflict went on, the Whigs denounced it as unconstitutional, but they continued voting supplies for it because they did
not want to be accused of depriving troops in the field. By praising
the troops and exalting the generals, especially if they were Whigs,
they were able to marshal so much popular sentiment against the
unpopular war that they got control of the House, and consequently
of the budget, which was a humiliating setback for the administration. But Polk went on defending the war, insisting that the Mexicans
had invaded the country and attacking the Whigs who claimed the
opposite, charging them with giving "aid and comfort to the enemy."
The Whigs called this presidential attack "an artful perversion of the
truth . . . to make the people believe a lie." That cry, too, was taken
up in the press. In the Boston *Whig*, Charles Francis Adams wrote a
biting editorial about Polk, referring to this president "who feels very
sure that he is right, and also that the justice of his policy is understood by 'the great body of the people.'"

Thus the Silent Majority and Vietnam in 1846.

Opposition to the war was increasingly bitter, yet it went on with
military victories until the All Mexico and Manifest Destiny movements could almost taste the ultimate triumph. Their strength centered in the urban masses, who were stimulated by the penny press of
New York, Philadelphia, Baltimore, and Boston.

In the end, the opposition press won a victory of sorts. It had not
been able to stop the war, although it had amply exposed its perfidy,
but it helped to get the treaty ending it adopted in a form Polk would
have preferred not to accept, by capitalizing on the country's great
desire for peace, and by constantly reminding the voters that the war
was draining the nation of resources which were needed to meet its
urgent domestic needs. Merk and other authorities believe the treaty
would have been even harsher than it was, and much more of Mexico
taken, if it had not been for the dissent which found its focus in the
press.

It was, on the whole, a rather hollow victory. If the editor of the most influential paper in the country, Greeley and his *Tribune*, could do no more about the war than to get the treaty modified, then the press could be said to have lost power, compared with the pressures the partisan papers had been able to bring on government in earlier days. Still, it had shown itself able to rally opinion and, perhaps even more important, had provided an outlet for dissent which the other media could hardly satisfy as well, in the circumstances.

By virtually defying the press, and calling it traitorous, Polk had merely carried a step further the stiffening resistance by presidents to pressures from the media. When Bennett had established his Washington bureau under Polk's predecessor, John Tyler, the administration's supporters in Congress had been so upset by the zeal of the *Herald* reporters on Capitol Hill that they had invoked an old Senate rule limiting the privilege of the floor to two men from each paper in Washington, thus cutting off Bennett's men. The rule was invoked only against the *Herald*, and in spite of Bennett's protests to Clay and the President himself, the issue was deftly buried in committee. The *Herald* offended Polk even more by continuing to print matters concerning the conduct of the war that he was trying to keep secret, and by refusing to tell him its sources. Polk did not trust even the newspapers that were friendly to him.

Whether they were justified or not, politicians all the way from mayors to the president himself were fearful of press power, particularly of its most influential voices, like Bennett and Greeley. When he came into office, James Buchanan was at pains to write a conciliatory note to Bennett, whom he had known earlier, attempting to patch up the differences between them, although he neither liked nor trusted the editor. A few weeks after his inauguration, he wrote quite frankly to Mrs. Bennett, acknowledging her congratulations, and saying:

> ... I am glad to learn that Mr. Bennett has promised you "to stick by my administration through thick and thin." Thus far he has given it a powerful support with occasional aberrations, for which I am always prepared and do not complain. He is an independent man and will do just what he pleases—though I know there is an undercurrent of good will towards me in his nature and he is disposed to treat me fairly. The *Herald* in his hands is a powerful instrument and it would be vain for me to deny that I desire its music should be encouraging and not hostile. Mr. B. makes his mark when he strikes and his blows fall so fast and heavy it is difficult to sustain them. . . . It is my desire as well as my interest to be on the best of terms with him. . . .

It would be difficult to imagine such a letter being written by any president in this century.

To all politicians in those contentious times before the Civil War, when passion was increasingly the watchword of the hour, the arrival of the New York *Times* and its young publisher, Henry Jarvis Raymond, must have come as a considerable relief. Some portions of the public may have welcomed him too—those who were tired of Bennett's sensationalism and cynical views, or equally weary of Greeley's liberal high-mindedness.

Raymond was neither eccentric nor populist in his opinions. The son of a well-to-do upper New York State farmer, he had a degree from the University of Vermont, where he had studied so hard that his health was impaired. At Vermont, he had begun contributing to Greeley's *New-Yorker*, so it was quite natural that after his graduation he came to ask the editor for a job on his new *Tribune*. He was no raw recruit from the country. Money had given him the opportunity to travel in Europe, to know some of the influential men of his time, and he was worldly by comparison with most of his contemporaries in the business. Greeley astutely made him his chief assistant, at eight dollars a week.

There is no other figure like Raymond in media history, just as there is no other paper like the *Times*. A born nonpartisan in a journalistic sense, at the same time he was paradoxically in love with politics. In the back of his mind stirred that worm of ambition which has made and ruined so many careers, the urge to rise and rise in public office until—until—the White House itself! From the beginning Raymond was fatally afflicted with that disease which, as Bernard Baruch often observed, would impel a man to get up from his deathbed and start walking toward Washington.

As Greeley's assistant, Raymond applied the sound principles of newspaper management which seemed to come naturally to him, and saved the *Tribune* from disaster during its first few struggling months. He had the help of a friend in the business office, a Vermonter named George Jones, and in their spare time these two men planned their own newspaper.

The venture had to be postponed for lack of capital. Jones went to work for a bank in Albany, and after two years with Greeley, Raymond quit and moved to the *Courier and Enquirer*, where he soon got himself so deeply involved in Whig politics that newspapering was almost a sideline. He was elected to the State Assembly in 1849, and after his reelection to a second term, became speaker in 1851. His alliance with the Free Soilers cost him his job with Major Webb, and after a brief tour of duty as editor of *Harper's New Monthly Magazine*, he and Jones, with whom he had been corresponding, contrived to accumulate the astonishing capital sum of $100,000 and with it they established the *Times* in 1851. Only ten years before, Greeley had started the *Tribune* with $2000, and sixteen years previously Bennett had done it with $500.

In the usual declaration of principles, appearing in the inaugural edition, Raymond set the tone for his paper in words which have been its guidelines for more than a century: "We do not mean to write as if we were in a passion—unless that shall really be the case; and we shall make it a point to get into a passion as rarely as possible."

Coming as they did at a time when the country was beginning to be torn apart, these words were greeted with utter disbelief by old hands in politics and newspaper making. But Raymond meant them, and he carried out his policy successfully. He made the *Times* the kind of newspaper it remains today—balanced, accurate, written and edited on the highest level. Its rational fairness, free of abuse and passion, was at once in striking contrast to nearly every other newspaper in the country. Notwithstanding, there were those who attacked it then in almost the same terms that are used today, and for the same reasons.

So the newspapers stood on the eve of the Civil War. They were now organized to get the news, which would be highly important to their readers. They were independent of government and party, but many of them were as violently partisan as ever, and that too would have an effect on the war. In the dark years ahead, it was not only the Union that was to be tested, but the media themselves, and most particularly the newspapers. It was, in brief, to be the greatest test of the First Amendment, and all it implied.

11

The Media
and the Civil War

A DARKNESS FELL on the land in 1861. Four years later, when it lifted, the nation was not the same, nor would it ever be again. The Union was saved, the slaves were freed, but the United States had gone through an emotional experience so profound that the fabric of national life was altered in fundamental ways. The wounds that were opened have never been healed, the basic questions raised never really answered.

Magazines were among the foremost recorders of the struggle, playing a different role than either newspapers or books. That they were able to do so was a miracle in itself, since they were hit much worse by the emergencies of the war than newspapers. Moreover, many of them were still trying to recover from the bad times of the Panic of 1857 when the war came. The Panic had ended the careers of prominent periodicals like *Graham's*, the *Democratic Review*, and the *New-York Mirror*. The survivors had no more than recovered when the war came, bringing with it soaring costs, manpower problems, and the severe disruption of distribution.

For Northern magazines, the last difficulty was the worst. Virtually overnight, in common with the book publishers, they lost their Southern market, and that was particularly disastrous to magazines like *Harper's* and *Godey's Lady's Book*. Some periodicals were able to survive because they were popular with soldiers, who also read the Civil War equivalent of World War II's *Yank*, called the *Soldier's Casket*—gruesome unless one recalls the contemporary meaning of the word "casket" as applied to magazines.

For magazines in the South, the war meant absolute disaster. Most of their supplies—ink, paper, and machinery—came from the North, and although their circulations were much more local, they soon did not have the physical means to carry on business in many cases, nor did they have the manpower as the war dragged on. Others could not afford the ruinous postage rates imposed by the Confederate government. In spite of these enormous difficulties, both magazines and book publishing survived, and there were some periodicals that managed to get through the war, missing issues only rarely. Astonishingly, there were even a few starts, although none survived long.

Newspapers prospered where magazines could not during the war, because the papers were selling a commodity, news, that was in great demand. Several of the magazines also offered news of the war, and people were eager to read their accounts of events and personalities, and to study eagerly the illustrative woodcuts they carried. But for immediate news, they turned to the newspapers to learn the outcome of battles, to scan with anxious fear the daily casualty lists. Both media gained in circulation during the war, but newspapers did better.

Magazines and newspapers alike were helped in their survival by the increasing flow of advertising into their pages. There was enough of it now to justify the existence of the first magazine devoted to the advertising business, *Pettingill's Reporter*, started in 1850 as the house organ of the ad agency bearing the Pettingill name. Advertising already had its critics, who were saying much the same things about it that are said today. *Vanity Fair*, a magazine of social and political comment, reported satirically in 1860: "A model Advertisement-Writer in the *Herald* calls the sewing machine 'a swift-fingered sister of love and charity.' Let us hereafter speak of the Cooking-Range as the warm-hearted minister to appetite and contentment; of the Daguerreotype Apparatus as the bright-faced reflector of beauty and worth; and, among other ingenious contrivances, of the Model Advertisement-Writer as the soft-headed distributor of mellifluous soap."

During the war, the tone of the magazines was quite different, naturally, from what it had been before the conflict. Then the debate over slavery and states' rights had risen to a furious tempo, and magazines were more political than they had ever been. William Lloyd Garrison's *Liberator*, founded in 1831, was the most eloquent of the abolitionist organs, as the voice of the New England Anti-Slavery Society. Other abolitionist organizations had their magazines or newspapers, but none had Garrison's fiery pen to command. Few periodicals have ever been so ardently loved or hated as the *Liberator*.

In spite of those who despised it, the *Liberator* was safe enough in Boston at first. The abolitionist journals nearer the South, in the border states, were not so fortunate. The office of the Cincinnati *Philanthropist* was raided twice by a mob in 1837, and again four years later. Its editor, Dr. Gamaliel Bailey, started another abolition paper in Washington in 1847, the *National Era,* and this magazine soon gained a wide reputation for itself, first because of the literary work it carried by Nathaniel Hawthorne, including "The Great Stone Face," and then for its serialization of *Uncle Tom's Cabin.*

Some magazines, like Bailey's and Garrison's, were devoted to the slavery question. Others, both the general and the specialized, discussed it more and more, especially the religious reviews and weeklies. They were far from uniformly abolitionist, of course. The debate was dividing the churches, North and South, as it was the rest of the nation. The Presbyterian *Biblical Repository,* for example, quoted the Scriptures to attack the abolitionists and defend the institution of slavery, even after the war began. On the other hand, the *North American Review,* which ordinarily spoke in a calm and reasoned voice, printed in capitals the Jacksonian battle cry: THE FEDERAL UNION—IT MUST BE PRESERVED. That was as early as January 1833, during the argument over South Carolina's nullification action.

As the debate grew more strident on the eve of the war, there were mass meetings in New York and Boston to protest what was regarded by many as unwarranted revolutionary provocation by the *Liberator.* The result of a tumultuous meeting in Boston was mob violence against Garrison and the destruction of his press, while in Charleston another mob rifled the mailbags and burned the Northern antislavery papers they found there.

At least some of the magazine press believed that the newspapers, reflecting the interests of the businessmen who were generally in favor of the *status quo,* were inciting the mobs. After the sacking of the *Liberator,* the great Methodist organ, *Zion's Herald,* a newspaper itself, came to Garrison's defense with an angry cry: "And this is the land of LIBERTY! Our soul is sick at such hypocrisy! ... Who are the authors of this riot? The daily press of this city...."

Oddly enough, there was less passion in the articles supporting slavery that appeared in such Southern magazines as the *Southern Quarterly* and *Southern Literary Messenger,* which felt they could hardly avoid the question but did not often raise their voices when they were discussing it. Their reserve began to wear thinner, however, after 1850, as the number of abolitionist journals continued to climb in the North, although most of the leading magazines there still opposed abolition, and prominent editors refused to believe that the question would not be resolved peacefully.

With the coming of the war, there was a sudden increase in both magazines and newspapers, as the disputants sought to find new voices for themselves. By contrast, some magazines before the war were convinced it was their duty to rule out political argument; consequently the great issues of the day did not appear in *Graham's* or many of the ladies' magazines. By the time the campaign of 1860 brought emotions to the boiling point, however, even the general magazines engaged in the battle swirling around Lincoln. The Eastern magazines were generally disappointed in Lincoln's nomination, and some of them joined the newspapers in ridiculing him unmercifully. He was, said *Vanity Fair*, "a longitudinal person with a shambling gait . . . slabsided. . . . He has a thin, almost nasal voice, and his grammar is not so far above suspicion as Caesar's wife is reported to have been."

The debate over slavery itself was virulent and exhausting. Among those exhausted was Charles Francis Adams, who wrote in a new magazine, the *Atlantic Monthly*, "What is coarsely but expressively described in the political slang of this country as '*The Everlasting Nigger-Question*' might perhaps be considered as exhausted as a topic of discussion if ever a topic was." That was written in April 1861, and the "*Question*" was on the eve of a bloody answer.

There were ponderous debates on the descent of man, and where blacks came into it. The Bible was invoked or rejected, depending on the magazine, to justify slavery or to condemn it, and the Southern periodicals talked of how much worse it was to enslave labor by means of money than by the beneficent system of the South. Slavery was even defended by some journals in the far West. There was a veritable rash of antislavery sentiment in many of the North's church periodicals, led by the *Liberator* and the *National Era*. Two black magazines also joined the attack: *Frederick Douglass' Paper* and the *Anglo-African Magazine*.

Black writers and editors had been issuing their work sporadically in the North since Phillis Wheatley's poetry in 1770, but the first black periodical was not issued until 1827, when Samuel Cornish and John B. Russwurm issued *Freedom's Journal*. Black historians believe that it was easier to launch a magazine or newspaper at that time than it was later in 1861, when repression more than balanced the agonizingly slow rise of literacy and education among the black population.

Russwurm was the leading spirit of *Freedom's Journal,* which was begun to counteract the attacks of a New York paper devoted to hate-mongering against Afro-Americans. He was the first black college graduate in America, taking his degree from Bowdoin in 1828. There were not enough black people who could afford to buy the *Journal,* even with the additional support of white abolitionists, after its name was changed to the *Rights of All,* and it was quietly suspended in 1830. Russwurm went on to teach school in Liberia, where he published the *Liberia Herald* and eventually became governor of Maryland at Cape Palmas.

No black publication, however, had such an impact on the public as a pamphlet written by a *Journal* contributor, David Walker, titled "Appeal, in four articles; together with a Preamble to the Coloured Citizens of the World, but in particular and very expressly, to those of the United States of America." Walker was a freeman from North Carolina who opened a secondhand clothing store in Boston in 1827 and began to hold meetings designed to lay plans for a slave insurrection. With only a little education, he was nevertheless an able writer, and his fiery pamphlet was like a slap in the face to the South. In Louisiana and elsewhere, men who were found to have it in their possession were thrown into jail, whether white or black. The mayor of Savannah wrote to the mayor of Boston and demanded that Walker be punished, but although the Bostonian expressed his own disapproval, he made no move against Walker. In Virginia, the legislature, stirred to a towering passion by the pamphlet, nearly succeeded in passing a bill that would not only have prohibited such "seditious" literature, but would have ended the education of free black people.

There were other individual blacks in the North who wrote books, articles, pamphlets, and poetry, but probably the most compelling writing to appear were the stories of the escaped slaves, including such well-known figures as Sojourner Truth, Douglass, and Josiah Henson, whose story is said to have been the inspiration for *Uncle Tom.* Mrs. Stowe met him in Boston.

Altogether, there were twenty-four magazines issued by blacks before the Civil War began, most appearing seldom or irregularly, and many indistinguishable from pamphlets because they were published with a minumum of materials and money. Their names reflect pride and purpose: *Mirror of Liberty,* the *Elevator,* the *Clarion,* the *Genius of Freedom,* the *Alienated American,* the *Ram's Horn,* the *Colored American.* They were published primarily in New York City and elsewhere in that state, but there were others in Pittsburgh,

Cleveland, Cincinnati, and San Francisco. In the pages of these periodicals there was little else but the overwhelming preoccupation of
the men who made them—antislavery agitation.

Probably the most important and effective of black publications
was Douglass' *North Star,* which he established soon after he
returned to the United States in 1847 from the two years in Great
Britain and Ireland which were the turning point in his life. Before
then, he had thought of emancipation as simply physical freedom;
after being treated as a man and an equal abroad, he began to think
of it as social equality and economic freedom. Having come home
and bought his liberty over the objections of white radicals who
thought he was condoning slavery, he established the *North Star* and
it became his organ, and the organ of the movement for seventeen
years. It was a weekly, printed on a large sheet, costing eighty dollars
a week to produce, and sent to about 3000 subscribers. The proprietor
changed the name to *Frederick Douglass' Paper,* he said, to distinguish it from other papers which had "*Star*" in their titles, but no
doubt he was also aware of the selling value of his name.

To those who argued with him about establishing the paper (so
many other black periodicals had failed, they said, and he had no
training for such an enterprise), Douglass replied, as he relates in his
autobiography: "I told them that perhaps the greatest hindrance to
abolition principles by the people of the United States was the low
estimate ... placed upon the negro as a man, that because of his
assumed natural inferiority, people reconciled themselves to his
enslavement and oppression, as being inevitable if not desirable. ...
In my judgment a tolerably well conducted press in the hands of persons of the despised race, would, by calling out and making them
acquainted with their own latent powers, by enkindling their hope of
a future, and developing their moral force, prove a most powerful
means of removing prejudice and awakening an interest in them."

The bigots of Rochester did not get this message. They burned
Douglass' house, including twelve volumes of his paper. Bennett's
New York *Herald* suggested that Douglass should be exiled to
Canada and his presses thrown into the lake. But the black editor had
white friends, "nonvoting abolitionists," as they were called, men like
Chief Justice Chase, Horace Mann, Joshua Giddings, Charles Sumner,
and W. H. Seward, who held festivals and fairs to raise money for his
paper until Douglass could become a "voting abolitionist." One special friend, Mrs. Julia Griffiths Crofts, came to his rescue when Douglass had mortgaged his house to pay current expenses, and the paper

was heavily in debt. In a year of her efficient management, she enabled him to increase circulation from 2000 to 4000 copies, pay off debts and lift the mortgage.

Only one antebellum black periodical survived into the twentieth century. The *Christian Recorder* was less a propaganda organ than a church news magazine and discussion forum for its founder, the African Methodist Church, which had been organized in 1816 and within two years had begun a publishing department. There was little market at first. Most potential readers lived in slave states, where they could not get an education, and consequently were unable to read. By 1841, however, there were enough literate blacks in the North to encourage the New York Conference in establishing a periodical, intended to be a monthly magazine but issued quarterly for lack of funds. It brought conference news to church members for seven years, then changed to a weekly and in 1848 became the *Christian Herald,* later the *Christian Recorder,* in 1852.

This magazine was regarded by Southern slaveholders and Northern sympathizers as an extremely dangerous publication. It was forbidden circulation in the slave states, but with the help of the Christian Commission, it reached Southern freedmen, soldiers in the Army and black people in hospitals.

As a matter of rather strange principle, antislavery whites in the North did not want their publications to go to slaves, but abolitionist literature did get into the hands of those who could read and write, and when it did, they read accounts of revolutionary ideas in France, of the deeds of Toussaint L'Ouverture and other black leaders elsewhere in the world, and were heartened in their cause.

When war finally came, magazines plunged into the conflict with the remainder of the press. Every issue of the general magazines had material of some kind about the war. A few became violently partisan. Astonishingly, the *Knickerbocker* changed from a gently satiric review of New York life to a rabid Copperhead journal. Even periodicals devoted mostly to literature, like the *Southern Literary Messenger,* followed the progress of the war closely.

Probably because they were more in competition with the newspapers, the weeklies made an effort to cover the war in depth. *Harper's Weekly* was especially outstanding. Its correspondents and artists, writing and sketching directly from the battlefields, produced war reporting that ranked with the best in the newspapers, and the woodcuts reproduced from the artists' sketches provided a valuable pictorial record of the war, supplementing the even more important photographic record being compiled by Mathew Brady and others. *Frank Leslie's Illustrated Newspaper* was not far behind *Harper's* in picture-text coverage.

The more virulent of the magazines on both sides hesitated at nothing to keep hatred of the enemy alive during the war. In the North, *Continental Magazine* printed a poem celebrating the widely believed myth that Southern ladies used the bones of dead Yankees to decorate their homes. In the South, the *Southern Monthly* declared, speaking of the Yankees: "They are a race too loathsome, too hateful, for us ever, under any circumstances, to be identified with them as one people."

Abolitionist magazines, like the newspapers, kept up a steady pressure on the President to emancipate the slaves. The *Liberator* quoted an ecclesiastical exhortation in Roxbury, Massachusetts, which advanced the idea that "God has become an abolitionist!" Still, the Copperhead press, opposing both the war and abolition, went on publishing in the midst of the conflict.

In the South, the magazines were inclined to take a grand, dramatic, even romantic view of the great conflict. In one of them, *De Bow's Review*, appeared these incredible words in January 1861: "With all its attendant evils—with all its tragic horrors—with all its mighty retinue of sorrow, sufferings, and disasters—war—civil war—war of kindred races—is not the greatest calamity that can befall a people. . . . There is in war a sublime and awful beauty—a fearful and terrible loveliness. . . ."

Charles D. B. De Bow, the publisher who wrote these words, had a vision of a New South developed through exploitation of the region's industrial resources. Educated in Charleston College, De Bow had begun his career as a lawyer and was regarded as an enlightened Southern leader, yet he came out strongly for reopening the African slave trade, which is now estimated to have killed 20 million people, and in fact was elected president of an organization called the African Labor Supply Association. He was the Confederacy's cotton-buying agent during the war, and operated his magazine from business headquarters in Richmond, until he had to suspend in August 1862. He revived it briefly for a year in Nashville, where he had gone to live after the war.

For magazines, the war years were the last in which they flourished as regional publications. Afterward, they became far more national in character, and those that were rooted nationally before the conflict began were the leaders of the modern era in magazine publishing. Sectionalism and localism survived only in the smaller periodicals.

In the book-publishing business, the war meant far different things to North and South. In the North, those publishers who lost their Southern markets, and that meant particularly the textbook publishers, had to rebuild their businesses in order to survive, and some failed to do so. But publishing was a recognized industry in America by the time the war came, and most of it, which was in the North, held solid. By the time the conflict ended, the earlier mixtures of printing, bookselling, and publishing were dissolving rapidly into separate entities. The industry had been revolutionized technologically, the major problems of the trade more or less defined, and the paramount one, distribution, identified.

In spite of all the usual wartime difficulties, book publishing in the North during the conflict was not unprofitable, and in fact there were huge successes with individual books, especially novels, as readers sought relief from horror and bloodshed. The publishers, too, were still enjoying whatever benefits of the great fifties boom they had been able to salvage from the Panic of 1857. Publishers remembered with nostalgia the sales figures of the Fantastic Fifties, when American book publishing reached the climax of its initial thrust into the mass market in a boom never approached before. More best sellers had been published in that time than in any previous decade. *Harper's Monthly* recalled in 1857 that in the previous seven golden years, "every book of every publisher was in the twenty-sixth thousand, and the unparalleled demand was increasing at an unprecedented rate; ... presses were working night and day...."

This boom, which died down necessarily during the war years but resumed when it was over, celebrated what would today be called the virtues of Middle America. Many of the biggest best sellers followed what Dr. Mott calls the "Home-and-Jesus formula," in which the kind of family life that would later be delineated in radio soap operas was the basis of the plot, mixed in with admonitions to youth. The solutions to all problems were religious ones, demonstrating the direct line of descent in this genre from the behavior books of the eighteenth century. The war did not greatly change the formula. It flourished again in the seventies and eighties.

The outstanding publishing event of the war years was the simultaneous publication in April 1862 of *Les Misérables*. Translated into nine languages before publication, it appeared on the same day in eight of the world's great cities: Paris, London, Berlin, New York, Madrid, Brussels, St. Petersburg, and Turin. It could hardly have appeared at a worse time in America—only three days before Shiloh, one of the worst hours of the war for the Union cause. It was also a risky publishing venture, since it was so long it had to be published in five volumes. Yet it sold 50,000 before the war ended, and in its first half century in America recorded a sale of at least a million.

Les Misérables was published in the South by the leading publisher, West & Johnston, of Richmond, in 1864. They had gone to extraordinary lengths to do it, paying a blockade runner to smuggle a copy into the Confederacy. The only translator they could obtain was a "vagrant captain," according to *Lippincott's Magazine*, who demanded to be paid in advance, in gold, a fee of $30, or about $1200 in Confederate money. Johnston paid the money and the captain disappeared with it, not to be seen again. The publishers then somehow obtained a copy of a reprint edition published in New York and set to work on it with editing pencil and scissors, expunging anything that might offend Southern sensibilities. The result, printed on a paper of ghastly green manufactured from raw cotton, was a version Victor Hugo would scarcely have recognized—a fact duly noted in the North, where the edition became known as *"Lee's Miserables."*

It was a miracle that it was produced at all. Publishing in the South during the war was conducted under incredible difficulties, and yet remarkable things were accomplished. Before the war began, there had been an increasing interest in literature in this region, largely because of the reputations of writers like Poe and William Gilmore Simms. The demand, as the booksellers were quick to say in their advertisements, made it possible to bring down prices so that books could be sold almost as cheaply in the South as in the large cities of the North. Yet there were only a few publishers in the South when the war broke out. Many starts were made between 1861 and 1865, as the Southerners strove desperately to supply themselves with books, but most were destroyed in the conflict.

A publishing industry, if it could be called that, had to be virtually created from scratch in 1860, since the region had been almost totally dependent on the North and on England for books. Only three houses of consequence existed in 1860: Randolph & English and West & Johnston, both in Richmond; and Sigismund H. Goetzel, in Mobile. Richmond, Charleston, and New Orleans were the literary centers.

Once Northern and foreign manufacturing were cut off, a new production pattern had to be established, but again, many of these new industries joined the old ones in oblivion as a result of the war's devastation and the collapse of the Confederacy. Of the 555 paper factories in the United States reported by the census of 1860, only 24 were in the South. The same census reported 151 book, job, and newspaper establishments in eleven Southern states. There was no stereotyping or electrotyping; in fact, only three states possessed such equipment in 1860. Nor were there any typefounding plants in the South, although elsewhere in America there were 32 of them, and 53 lithography plants as well. The South did have 17 bookbinding and blankbook shops.

By the time the war was over, a trade-periodical survey reported book manufacturers in only four of the states in the Confederacy, a loss of 14 in the decade. Only one Southern typefoundry remained (in Virginia) and only 15 bookbinding plants. Nevertheless, the war gave a surprising impetus to Southern book publishing, as many printers and booksellers turned to publishing in an effort to take up the slack. Their difficulties were formidable. When the supply of rags ran out, the paper mills had to turn to raw cotton and other fibers; consequently the quality of paper declined sharply as the war went on. At the most acute stage, some newspapers were printing on wallpaper and a few books were bound in this material. Even so, there was simply not enough paper of any kind to go around, and many newspapers and periodicals had to suspend publication.

Notable among the books published in the Confederacy were textbooks and children's books. It is worth noting that in spite of the white-hot passion of the war, especially in the South, Confederate textbooks were not propaganda instruments, with some exceptions which have distorted the total output. All told, the Confederate publishers had issued 127 textbook titles by the end of the war, in editions of from 10,000 to 30,000, many going through several editions.

There was a considerable amount of religious publishing during the war, directed toward both soldiers and civilians, and concentrated chiefly on keeping everyone supplied with Bibles, since the supply from outside, normally the American Bible Society, was cut off. The Bible societies in the Confederate states, at a convention in Augusta in 1862, organized the Bible Society of the Confederate States of America to further encourage the printing and publishing of Bibles. As a result of its efforts, 33,559 Testaments and 28,201 Testaments and Psalms had been published by April 1863, with 12,000 more on the press. Many thousands more were published before the war was over, but it was never enough to keep up with the demand. The war itself was a religion in the South, and those who fought it were more religiously minded than any army since Cromwell's, in the opinion of some scholars. Consequently, the outpouring of religious works, especially tracts, was tremendous, within the limitations of the publishers.

The General Tract Agency, of Raleigh, alone published 21,892 pages of tracts in the eighteen months after it began operations on June 1, 1861.

Music was also a major activity of Confederate publishing, because the soldiers transferred their cultural patterns of home entertainment to the battlefields and camps, as far as they were able.

Otherwise, Confederate publishers' lists during the war included what their Northern brethren were issuing—peacetime items like almanacs, maps, broadsides, laws, governmental reports and the documents of both religious and secular organizations. Not surprisingly, nothing that emerged from the Southern publishers was of lasting merit. The circumstances encouraged them to publish only whatever they could get that would be useful to the Cause in some way. If literary creativity was stifled, it was because writers were caught up in the struggle and almost universally dedicated to it. Within these limitations, the performance of the Confederate publishers was extraordinary.

Nothing that occurred in book and magazine publishing during the war, however, could match what was happening in the newspaper portion of the media, where government and press were locked in a war within a war, with Lincoln as its central figure. The President followed the newspapers closely and depended on them for news. Time and again he sought out correspondents just returned from the front who could give him fresh information. He sent for Henry Villard, the *Tribune's* tall young correspondent, on the morning after the battle of Fredericksburg, telling him, "We are very anxious and have heard very little." Villard had seen it all, hurried back to the capital, and telegraphed a report to his paper so gloomy that Greeley would not print it until it could be confirmed. Villard repeated what he knew to Lincoln, who spent a half hour asking him detailed questions.

Lincoln was well aware that his nomination had been achieved only with the help of the press, specifically the Chicago *Tribune*, whose editors, Joseph Medill and Charles Ray, had manipulated the convention and gotten their Illinois man nominated by giving away important posts in the new administration, without the candidate's knowledge, in return for swinging state delegations to the Lincoln nomination. Medill and Ray had kept their man carefully sequestered in his rooms in the Iroquois Hotel, seeing carefully selected visitors, until the nomination was achieved, when he was told how it had been accomplished. "You didn't leave much for me, boys, did you?" Lincoln observed wryly. Later, he repudiated these promises, in whose making he had had no part, and this had not pleased Medill, who was strong for the Union but lukewarm about Lincoln. Medill, in fact, organized a stop-Lincoln movement in 1864, but until then the President found the *Tribune* useful in fighting Wilbur Storey's Chicago *Times*, a violently Copperhead organ—the two papers were once armed and barricaded against an expected assault by the other—and in combating Bennett's assaults on the President.

Something of the *Tribune*'s temper can be gleaned from its editorial advice to the *Herald* when Bennett was booming Grant as "the People's Candidate" in 1864. Medill advised him that his paper would not be "allowed to paw and slobber over our Illinois General, and if it has any regard for its 'throat' or its 'fifth rib,' it will take warning and govern itself accordingly." For the *Herald* to advocate Grant was "a gross libel on him and an insult to his friends," the *Tribune* cried. "Unless it keeps its unclean and treacherous hands off of him, it may expect to get 'tomahawked.'" Bennett replied that the *Tribune* was "the sewer into which goes everything too dirty for its New York namesake to print."

It was easy enough for Mr. Lincoln to identify his enemies in the press. They were editors like Manton Marble, of the New York *World*; Storey and his Chicago *Times*; Samuel Medary and the Columbus *Crisis*; Benjamin Wood and the New York *Daily News*; Charles H. Lamphier and the *Daily Illinois State Register*, in Springfield; and Marcus Mills "Brick" Pomeroy, of the La Crosse (Wisconsin) *Democrat*.

No president since Washington, and none afterward, endured so much from the press as Lincoln. He was accused of all kinds of misconduct—drawing his salary in gold bars, drunkenness, granting pardons to get votes, needless slaughter of men for the sake of victories, even treason. This assault remains one of the darkest, most shocking chapters in media history.

In the Copperhead papers, and some others, the President was referred to by such epithets as "a slang-whanging stump speaker," "half-witted usurper," "mole-eyed," "the present turtle at the head of government," "the head ghoul at Washington," and other epithets even less complimentary. There was not a major paper Lincoln could depend on, except the New York *Times* and Samuel Bowles's Springfield *Republican*, in Massachusetts. The Springfield (Illinois) *Daily State Journal* was the only newspaper in the country that never wavered in its admiration for the President.

Nothing was too much for the Copperhead press. It was not above forging state papers, disseminating vicious libels, and even encouraging rebellion. One of the prime centers of dissent was New York City, where the war was highly unpopular. It was opposed not only by businessmen but by the Irish and German laboring masses, who did not understand and were not interested in the ideology of the conflict and could foresee only fighting and perhaps dying for a remote cause, or else enduring the rigors of wartime living and probably losing jobs to liberated slaves drifting up from the South and flooding the labor market. Their normal bigotries were highly sharpened where blacks were concerned.

Mayor Fernando Wood was an outspoken foe of the President and the war. He declared that New York ought to establish itself as a free city and separate itself from the Union, becoming sovereign, like the South. In that way, he said, it could hold its trade and still keep its connections with the remainder of the country. Mayor Wood, whose administration was one of the most corrupt in the city's history, had a brother, Benjamin, who was a successful businessman at forty. With the help of Fernando, Benjamin bought a thriving morning newspaper, the *Daily News* (not related to the present paper of the same name), and quickly made it one of the leading Copperhead dailies of the country, openly advocating the Confederate cause and urging the city to secede. At almost the same time, in 1861, he was elected to Congress.

The attacks of the *Daily News* on the administration finally reached such a point that the government could not ignore them. The New York postmaster was ordered to refuse the paper for mailing. Ben resorted to Railway Express, but the government put a stop to that by planting detectives on every express train leaving the city. When they spotted bundles of the *Daily News*, the papers were seized. Ben could do little but suspend publication; an important part of the paper's revenue came from out-of-state circulation.

When publication was resumed nearly eighteen months later, a switch had been made from morning to evening but the paper was more virulent than before. The private war between Ben Wood and his brother against Lincoln and the Union came to a climax in 1863, when an editorial in the *News*, published just before the Battle of Gettysburg, helped to precipitate the mass insanity of the draft riots. Vicious mobs of mostly Irish workingmen gathered in Central Park and marched on the city, fighting with police in the streets, burning a black orphan asylum, lynching unfortunate black citizens who came in their path, and eventually succumbing only to federal troops hastily brought in from the battlefields of Pennsylvania. In those five days of terror, more than two thousand men and women were killed, and eight thousand more were injured; the property damage was estimated at more than $5 million.

Wood's violent attacks kept him and the paper in constant trouble. At the time it was suspended, the *News* had been named in a grand jury presentment, with three other papers, charging disloyal conduct. Then, in 1864, Congress itself moved against its disloyal member. Formal charges were brought against Wood in the House for disloyal statements he had made on the floor. The charges were referred to the Judiciary Committee, and never were heard of again. As for the *News*, until the last gun was fired, it continued to insist that Union victories were frauds, and that the Southerners would never be defeated. "You may conquer, but you can never subdue them," Ben wrote.

The New York draft riots were not unique, although they were by far the most severe. In 1863, the draft quotas were arousing widespread protest in the cities, and in Chicago, Medill headed a committee of three to come to Washington and make a personal protest to Lincoln over the call levied on that city, which had already sent 22,000 men and had endured heavy casualties among them.

Lincoln heard the committee out quietly, and then, as Medill recalled later, said quietly: "Gentlemen, after Boston, Chicago has been the chief instrument in bringing this war on the country. The Northwest has opposed the South as the Northeast has opposed the South. You called for war until we had it. You called for emancipation and I have given it to you. Whatever you have asked for you have had. Now you come here begging to be left off from the call for men which I have made to carry out the war which you have demanded. You ought to be ashamed of yourselves. I have a right to expect better things of you. Go home and raise your six thousand extra men. And you, Medill, are acting like a coward. You and your *Tribune* have had more influence than any paper in the Northwest in making this war. You can influence great masses, and yet you cry to be spared at a moment when your cause is suffering. Go home and send us those men."

It may have been the only time in his life that Medill was abashed, and he had grace enough to admit it. "I couldn't say anything," he wrote later. "It was the first time I was ever whipped, and I didn't have an answer. We all got up and went out, and when the door closed, one of my colleagues said, "Well, gentlemen, the old man is

right. We ought to be ashamed of ourselves. Let us never say anything about this, but go home and raise the men.' And we did, six
thousand men, making twenty-eight thousand in the war from a city
of a hundred and fifty-six thousand."

As for New York, it had a Copperhead mayor, a leading Copperhead newspaper whose publisher was openly charged with disloyalty
in the Congress, a laboring mass whose sympathies were pro-South-
ern, and a segment of businessmen who were against the war because
it hurt their enterprises. Nonetheless, the majority of its citizens, particularly the middle class, were abolitionist and pro-Lincoln.

No one was made to realize that more acutely than Greeley, unless
it was Bennett. At the beginning, Bennett had his own unique solution for the quarrel. Let the seceding states go, he said in the *Herald*,
and then reorganize the Republic under the South's new constitution,
leaving out the New England states. It is doubtful whether Bennett
really believed in this harebrained idea, but the paper's readers took
him seriously and a mob of several thousand gathered outside the
Herald's new building, with the intention of burning it down.

Narrowly saved from this disaster, Bennett thought better of his
policies after Fort Sumter was fired on. Overnight he switched party
lines, turned in his yacht to the Union, and offered his son as a sacrifi-
cial lamb, ordering him to enlist in the Navy. After completing these
rituals, he supported Lincoln, although in a lukewarm way, except
when it pleased him to do otherwise.

As for Greeley, he had been a moving force in the abolitionist
cause, and for a time Lincoln valued his cooperation so much that he
gave him preferential treatment in the White House. But then Greeley began to deviate, in his own peculiar way, and soon it appeared
that he had taken over the conduct of the war himself. As the most
influential editor, his support was considered important, both in
Washington and New York, where the *Tribune*, the *Times*, and the
Herald were the only three of the city's seventeen daily newspapers
to support the President and the war in any degree. Nine were
defenders of slavery, and five others were definitely Southern sympathizers.

Greeley's enemies remarked skeptically that the editor might not
have been so ardent an abolitionist if he had ever visited the South,
since he was inclined to change his mind after firsthand examination.
The South was the one section of America that Uncle Horace had
never visited, and his understanding of it was limited. But he knew

that slavery was wrong, and he believed devoutly that secession would be fatal to the American idea. Southern travel would certainly never have converted him from these beliefs.

When it came down to the nub of the day's issues, however, these beliefs collided head on with Greeley's natural pacifism. He could not accept the idea of war. He was ready, at first, to let the Southern states go, as Bennett was, if that was the only way, and in this his managing editor, Dana, agreed with him. Dana, who had been as much of an idealist as Greeley, was becoming increasingly cynical about the world, but he still found himself in agreement with his employer on most large questions—except labor unions, which he abhorred. Fort Sumter severed their relationship and changed their lives, as it did so many thousands of others. Greeley was totally against the war in the beginning, and Dana was for it, so Uncle Horace asked for his friend's resignation and got it. Thus the newspaper which had done more than any other to oppose the spread of slavery seemingly refused to take the final step.

Before he left, Dana had committed the *Tribune* to the war in Greeley's temporary absence and given the Union forces a headline which became a ringing battle cry, "Forward to Richmond!" Lincoln and his cabinet were so pleased with this kind of support from an important paper that when Secretary of War Stanton heard about Dana's resignation, he offered the editor a job in the War Department, and there Dana began a new and even more distinguished career. As for Greeley, he continued to give the President an uncertain support; Lincoln could not always be certain which side he was on.

But if there was one item of faith about which no one was permitted to have any doubt, it was Greeley's fervent opposition to slavery, and that was enough to alienate him from the New York mobs who gathered for the draft riots of 1863; consequently the *Herald* and Greeley were on their list of prominent targets. These mindless men began with the destruction of the Enrollment Office, draft headquarters, at Third Avenue and Forty-Sixth Street, then rolled across the city, looting, burning, and killing.

Sidney Gay, the *Tribune's* managing editor, a former Underground Railway agent, watched the mob's progress with apprehension. He saw the crude banners—NO DRAFT! KILL THE NIGGERS!—and heard their shouts: "To the *Tribune*! We'll hang old Greeley to a sour apple tree." Gay warned Greeley and told him he ought to prepare to defend the building against the mob, but Greeley observed calmly, "It's just what I expected, and I have no doubt they will hang me. But I want no arms brought into the building."

Then the mob flowed into Printing House Square, and its raucous yells reached to the men inside: "Down with the *Tribune*! Down with the old white coat that thinks a nigger is as good as an Irishman!"

Accounts vary as to what happened next. Some contemporary narratives say Greeley went out of the building by a back door, hurried down an alley and into a nearby tavern, Windust's restaurant, where he often ate, and hid out under a table until the mob, giving up, went on to other mischief. A more heroic version, and one that seems more characteristic, says that he announced in his squeaky voice, "If I can't eat my dinner when I'm hungry, my life isn't worth anything to me," and, clapping on his floppy hat, he took a friend's arm (possibly Gay's) and strode through the mob unafraid to his dinner. In any case, he and the *Tribune* escaped damage, except for a few stones thrown at the windows, but only because that most unmilitant of men, Henry J. Raymond, came to his paper's rescue.

From his *Times* office across the square, Raymond had watched the mob's threatening actions against the *Tribune* building, and remarked calmly that what the men required was "grape, and plenty of it." He organized a *Times* expeditionary force to go to the *Tribune*'s rescue. It was armed principally with two mitrialleuses—a new invention, a breech-loading machine gun with several barrels. Raymond gave one to a *Times* stockholder who happened to be there—it was Winston Churchill's grandfather, Leonard Walter Jerome—and took the other himself. Minié rifles were handed out to the reporters and printers.

With the aplomb of a general on the battlefield, Raymond sent sixteen *Times* men around the back way to the relief of the besieged *Tribune* men. Meanwhile, two hundred policemen, gathered from various parts of the city, poured into the square, pistols at the ready and nightsticks flying. When they were finished, more than fifty rioters were lying dead or injured.

When Greeley came back to work next day, the square resembled a battlefield, littered with debris, barricades overturned, smoke still rising from fires. In the *Tribune* office, he found Gay in charge of a veritable fortress, including a howitzer and several bombs. He ordered them taken away, but the rioters were once more gathering outside, and Greeley fearlessly walked out among them again, so the story goes, to hear Governor Horatio Seymour address the crowd and plead for order. Back in the office again, Greeley sat moodily in the newsroom with the reporters rather than be near the arsenal outside his office. When he was through work for the day, he would have gone home on the horsecar, as he usually did, but Gay persuaded him to go instead in a private carriage.

After soldiers from thirteen regiments had arrived in the city, order was restored and vigilantes who called themselves Volunteer Specials helped patrol the streets, taking more credit than they deserved, some thought. One of them enraged the remnants of the mob anew by remarking that "the Irish cattle" had had "impressed on them a respect for order." Greeley apologized sardonically in the *Tribune*: "The Irish in the police department have won the respect of good citizens. They nobly shot down their fellow countrymen and women."

Greeley did not appreciate Raymond's armed intervention on his behalf. They were political enemies because both wanted to be "king." It was sad that these two men who had so much to give to journalism should have ruined their lives for politics, a field in which they were supremely unqualified. Raymond was good at the practical side of politics—that is, getting elected—but once in office, he was not politician enough to succeed. Greeley, on the other hand, might have done well in office, but in spite of his remarkable influence with the voters, he could not get himself elected.

Aside from the politics of the war, the newspapers gave an outstanding example of what they could do, in this first major conflict they had an opportunity to cover. No war had ever been reported so freely and completely, and Bennett's genius made the *Herald* stand out above all the others—audacious as always, amazingly complete, and nearly always accurate. War coverage cost Bennett more than a half million dollars, but the effort brought him to the peak of his success: one issue alone in 1864 sold 132,000 copies, unprecedented for those days. The *Tribune* was its most serious competition, but Bennett had the satisfaction of knowing that Lincoln himself read the *Herald* above all others.

War correspondents were known as "specials," and Bennett had forty of them in the field, including Henry Villard, the young Bavarian immigrant who was considered the best. Good as they were, however, Villard and his colleagues found themselves matched on occasion by some unlikely "specials" from other papers. One was an unknown young reporter from the Cincinnati *Gazette*, Whitelaw Reid, who would one day carry on the *Tribune* from where Greeley left it. Reid's account of the Battle of Shiloh was the talk of the business, and his story of Gettysburg, from the vantage point of Cemetery Hill, the most exposed point, was considered a classic.

An unknown reporter sometimes found himself in the distinguished company of no less a correspondent than the publisher of the New York *Times*. Raymond assigned himself to the field, where his speed and accuracy were soon legendary, and his stories of Bull Run were acclaimed as masterpieces.

Dana saw as much of the war as any correspondent, but from a unique vantage point. Invited to Washington by Stanton after his resignation from the *Tribune*, he was assigned, in reality, to spy on Grant. Ostensibly his mission was to examine the pay service, but secretly he was ordered to join Grant at headquarters and provide Stanton with daily reports which would enable the Secretary to estimate what Grant was doing, and was capable of doing.

It was a superb piece of reporting, in which Dana used the talents that had made him a great managing editor on the *Tribune*. Sifting and analyzing thousands of facts, he made it clear at last in his reports what a commander the Union possessed in Grant, and ultimately resolved Lincoln's command problem. As a reward, after Vicksburg, the President appointed Dana assistant secretary of war. He was immediately assigned to do the same kind of reporting on General Rosecrans, and on the basis of these reports, Rosecrans was removed from his command. Afterward, as the administration's personal reporter, so to speak, Dana traveled with Grant and Sherman through Chattanooga, Missionary Ridge, Lookout Mountain, and other campaigns.

The correspondents, in general, enjoyed a freedom in their coverage they do not have even today. It was in keeping with the nearly complete freedom the press now enjoyed in its new prosperous, independent, and aggressive state. Every faction tried to use its own newspaper supporters to influence public opinion, in the classic manner, and sometimes they were so successful as to influence actual military decisions. Politicians and generals sometimes found themselves in an undignified scramble for press support, and those who ignored or resisted newspaper power, like General McClellan, might find themselves removed.

Inevitably large questions were raised about the relation of press to government, questions which had not been debated since the War of 1812. There were pro- and antiwar papers, all of them hotly partisan except for the New York *Times*, and the perennial problem which has never been solved plagued both Washington and the editors: how to balance national security and the public's right to know.

In this struggle the press was in a different position than it had been before. Thanks to Bennett and the other New York giants, it was much more powerful, and its ability to gather and disseminate news had been enormously enhanced by the coming of the telegraph and the railway post. Balanced against these factors was the nearly total ignorance of the military commands, both North and South, on the subject of censorship, with which none of them had had the advantage of experience. There were, in addition, the overwhelming tides of hate and bigotry, washing over and nearly obliterating the national idealism which had prevailed since the Revolution.

The President exhibited the greatest patience and leniency in this conflict of interests; his enemies mistook it for weakness. Frequently he used the papers as a sounding board, particularly through the New York Associated Press, which he relied upon as unbiased. He often spoke openly to reporters covering the White House, besides consulting them directly when they had firsthand information to give him which he could not get elsewhere, and thus in a sense he inaugurated the modern presidential press conference, although it was not a formal procedure.

In the field, it was a different matter. When the editorial directors of the papers back home or their reporters were in conflict with military commanders, the commanders were likely to take punitive action against the correspondents.

Censorship was firmly imposed in the field after Bull Run. McClellan, who understood the situation better than most of the other commanders, called the correspondents together in 1861 and offered them a plan of voluntary censorship, much like the one that prevailed in the Second World War, but like most voluntary plans this one did not work because there was no unanimity among the participants. Some papers were conscientious about it; some were not; some virtually ignored it. To further confound the issue, the direction of censorship became an internal struggle between the State and War departments. The voluntary system, rendered virtually useless by these handicaps, lasted three months, after which Congress took away the control from State and gave it to War, where Stanton, just coming into office, succeeded in improving matters.

After his order of 1862, requiring correspondents to submit their copy to provost marshals, who were instructed to delete only military information, the sole difficulty remaining lay in the administration of the order, which was interpreted variously by generals and their provosts, some of whom were concerned more with public relations than with the problem of censorship.

General Sherman was the worst of the government's field problems. While it was true that there were correspondents who gave him more than enough provocation to be angry and arbitrary in his treatment of them, particularly when they wrote stories disclosing military information in a most dangerous way, Sherman was also the kind of commander who did not hesitate on occasion to attribute his own failures to information leaks in the papers. His attitudes toward the press were often much like those of General Patton in World War II—that is, he never missed an opportunity to excoriate a correspondent or a newspaper, nor a chance to use one if he could be useful. The press at one point circulated a story that he was insane, and no doubt he was, in the nonclinical sense that applies to military men (and others) whose egocentricity pushes them beyond the limits of rationality.

When one of Greeley's reporters filed a story which was a clear violation of censorship, Sherman had him arrested as a spy, and would have had him shot if Lincoln had not intervened. This incident was serious enough to bring about a logical reform. Correspondents were thereafter accredited, as they are today, and had to be acceptable to field commanders in order to gain accreditation. Another step was to exclude British correspondents, who had been a difficult problem on the Union side because of Britain's sympathy with the Confederate cause. (A half century later, American correspondents were excluded briefly by Britain and the other allies in the beginning of the First World War because of American sympathies with Germany.)

In the end, these changes and a more relaxed attitude on both sides, government and press, led to such cooperation that Sherman was able to make his march to the sea without disclosure of his plans in the newspapers at any stage. It is interesting to speculate what might have happened if the march *had* been reported fully. Would an outraged public opinion in a war-weary North have revolted against this unnecessary piece of savagery, or would the home-front Vietnam morality prevail and the public turn away from what it did not want to think about?

By comparison with what had gone before, the press was infinitely more responsible in its coverage of the Civil War than it had been in its previous history. For the first time, there was a great deal of factual, relatively unbiased news from the battlefields at a time of the most intense partisanship, and that was a long step forward. In the editorial columns, however, there was the same kind of irresponsibility that had always existed, and the treatment of Lincoln was inexcusable on any grounds. Until matters improved in the field, and correspondents and commanders both got a better understanding of their responsibilities, there was some irresponsible reporting, too, where purely military matters were concerned.

This irresponsibility, at home and in the field, brought the press into direct conflict with the government and produced the most serious threat to its freedom it had known since the days of royal licensing. Some historians justify what the Lincoln administration did on the ground that it was a question of the Union's survival, but that leads us to the familiar contemporary ground of ends justifying means. How often have we heard the cry, here and elsewhere in the world, that it is necessary to defend representative government by suspending the liberties of the people it is supposed to represent?

Lincoln was a liberal by nature, far more so than most of the other men in his party, but in his overwhelming zeal to save the Union he permitted his government to employ high-handed infringements of fundamental freedoms. Writs of habeas corpus were suspended. There was widespread suppression and censorship. Secretary Stanton declared that "no news gatherer, nor any other person, for sordid or treasonable purposes can be suffered to intrude upon" national agents "to procure news by threats, or spy out official acts which the safety of the nation requires not to be disclosed." Under this doctrine, Stanton, and Seward as well, had some Copperhead editors thrown into Fort Lafayette or the "Old Capitol" as prisoners, with no formal charges ever filed against them, and where civil-court remedies were unavailable to get them out.

Suppression began with the outbreak of war. Postmaster General Montgomery Blair used his power to deny the mails to newspapers he considered subversive, and he would not permit post offices to relay messages to enemy areas. Telegrams between North and South were seized in the constant search for traitors. Stanton and General Scott compelled the telegraph companies, illegally to be sure, to stop sending any information of a military nature, which naturally affected the work of the correspondents. Congress redressed this summary repression by transferring such authority to Lincoln in 1862. Still, the government made it clear that those who abused it might find themselves subject to arrest, and dissent was more often than not interpreted as disloyalty. The generals themselves sometimes became instruments of suppression. In the Northwest, Burnside arbitrarily seized and suppressed newspapers he thought were treasonous.

By contrast, the South was a model of conduct, but that was because there was virtually no dissent; all were united in the Great Cause. Nevertheless, the Press Association of the Confederate States of America—"PA," in its familiar logotype—was one of the marvels of the war. All of the South's forty-three wartime dailies were members of it. Its news of the conflict was a model of objectivity, for the most part, and was sometimes more reliable than Northern reporting of the same events.

It may be added that the unity of the South was not only the result of common feeling, but a purging or silencing of dissenters. Consequently, freedom of the press existed only within narrow limits. The papers might attack or question individuals, or the government (if they didn't go too far), but they were not permitted even to question the validity of slavery, or the Cause itself.

In the North, particularly, the war considerably advanced newspaper technology. In using the telegraph as the chief transmitter of news, correspondents learned to write more concisely, since this transmission was expensive. There was much less florid writing and rambling opinion than before the war, although the stories still were considerably short of modern style. But they were more readable, and that meant a great deal to postwar mass journalism.

The telegraph also produced the invention of the summary lead— that is, the first paragraph containing the who, what, when, where, and why of a story, still a standard form. It came about because correspondents could not always be sure their entire dispatch would find its way through the precarious telegraph system, and so they tried to make sure that the essential facts would arrive if the rest of the story were cut off.

In the composing room, the invention by William Bullock in 1863 of the web perfecting press, which printed both sides of a continuous roll of paper on the rotary press, guaranteed that the new market created by the war could be supplied in quantity. This press, of course, was the prototype of the kind in common use today.

The Civil War did not really come to a close until that April night in 1865 when Lawrence Gobright, the Associated Press's man in Washington, flashed the fateful first bulletin: "The President was shot in a theater tonight, and perhaps mortally wounded." When the news reached the streets, there was a final outpouring of venom and hatred which had characterized the relationship between public and press from the beginning. Mobs swarmed into the offices of several Copperhead papers and destroyed presses and types, tarring and feathering or threatening to lynch the proprietors if they could catch them.

Plainly, if the war had established the newspapers as a valuable and more responsible medium, it had not diminished their role in American life as the purveyors of a kind of freedom which the people it was intended to benefit were not sure they wanted.

Part Three

The Media and the Rise of a Technological Society

12

The Newspaper
as Investigator

As THE ROLLING TIDE of industrialization engulfed America in the last half of the nineteenth century, there was a growing division between the haves and the have-nots, precipitating the social and political struggles which have reached a new climax today. In this economic and cultural upheaval, the media played diverse roles of extraordinary significance which have never been given their proper due in general historical writing.

In the closing decades, for examples, magazines such as those issued by major book-publishing houses (Harper's, Scribner's, Lippincott's, Peterson's) were the primary keepers and dictators of upper-class culture, just as the *North American Review* was the bellwether of the intellectuals. They did not neglect social issues, but such concerns were viewed more as interesting phenomena than as matters of vital interest. More important were the flamboyant new picture magazines, like *Frank Leslie's Illustrated Weekly*, which foreshadowed the later muckraking era, with its investigative reporting, and placed themselves in direct competition with the crusading role assumed by some newspapers. At the same time, women's magazines and the general periodical were revitalized and given new direction by the first of a generation of great editors.

Book publishing became the comprehensive open forum it is today, in which all the social issues of the times, as well as mass entertainment and culture, were discussed and purveyed. A second paperback revolution in the seventies and eighties broadened the mass market again, while the effects of that market could be seen clearly in another way, with the unprecedented (and unequaled since) craze for reading, and for particular authors, like Kipling, Du Maurier, and Browning, who attained the status that rock stars enjoy now.

While all the media exploited the mass market in their individual ways, the newspapers were perhaps in the best position to do it. The powerful entrepreneurs of the press, rich and secure after the Civil War, built up mass readership to unheard-of circulations. Sometimes this exploitation was utterly cynical, sometimes it was reasonably honest. By contrast, in the Midwest and the South there was growing up a new and more enduring concept of the newspaper's role in society. The Midwestern editors thought of their papers as organs devoted to community service, and that idea also comprehended crusading against local crime and corruption. These papers were oriented more toward their local communities than toward the great cities of the East. In the South, the best editors were influential in preventing Reconstruction from becoming a worse shambles than it was, and in the West, a flamboyant kind of newspapering developed that was typical of the last frontier.

In the decade after Lincoln's assassination, the country seemed to change almost intangibly before the eyes, and as it changed, the first generation of newspaper giants died with the old era. Henry Raymond, called upon to guide President Johnson's Reconstruction policies, failed to do so successfully and allowed himself to be outmaneuvered by the President's enemy, Thaddeus Stevens. He died suddenly in 1869, only forty-nine, of a cerebral hemorrhage while he lay in the arms of his actress friend Rose Eytinge in her house on Ninth Street. Greeley wrote an obituary editorial that was a flat contradiction of nearly everything the *Tribune*'s editor had said about Raymond while he was living.

Uncle Horace himself was not far from the end. He had broken his heart trying to hurry social evolution and bring about the reforms he so ardently wanted for humanity. Now, in his old age, he pulled himself together for a last fight to attain the greatest prize he had wanted from the beginning. Running against Grant for the presidency in 1872, he placed his faith in the farmers of America, who had always been his close allies. With their help, he thought, he would be elected and could then put into practice those true Republican principles he had so long fought for, on one side or another. But these people in whom he had believed, the farmers and those others he referred to grandly as "humanity" (meaning the Silent Majority), betrayed him.

They elected Grant by more than 750,000 votes—an added humiliation.

A few days before the election Greeley's wife Mary had died, and five days after his defeat a distraught Uncle Horace wrote, "I am not dead, but I wish I were. My house is desolate, my future dark, my heart a stone. . . ." In the house of a friend on Fifty-Seventh Street he lay ill, in a physical and mental decline, while his associates on the *Tribune* fought for control of the paper. Removed to a private mental hospital in Pleasantville, he sank into a coma and died on November 28, 1872.

He had wanted a simple burial. "Plant me in my favorite pumpkin arbor," he had written, "with a gooseberry bush for a footstone." Instead he got a Fifth Avenue church funeral, complete with three ministers and a solemn procession of prominent pallbearers and mourners, including Grant, the man he hated and who had defeated him. Following Grant were the men who had been struggling ruthlessly for control of his paper as he lay dying. He might have been consoled, however, by the thousands of plain people who lined the avenue and wept unashamedly as the funeral cortège rolled by. They were Uncle Horace's people, who loved him in their way, and knew instinctively that they were seeing the passing of a great editor, perhaps the greatest American journalism had known.

The only individual who would have disputed that estimate was James Gordon Bennett, who had no doubt about the identity of the greatest journalist. He was at his peak as the war ended. Rich and successful, no longer the scourge of Wall Street but the defender of privilege, this strong-willed man had outlasted his enemies, and if he had few friends, at least there were fewer people—as he would have put it—who might betray him. He had no wish to serve anyone. When Lincoln offered to make him minister to France, he declined. There was nothing left for him to fight for, and so in 1867 he turned the *Herald* over to his son and retired.

When he died in 1872, only a few months before Greeley, a good many of his enemies were among the pallbearers, including Uncle Horace. Bennett had always sneered at Greeley and his concern for humanity, of whom he had once said: "The great mass of mankind, living in civilized society, are happy. The suffering and misery are only exceptions to the general condition. The world is an excellent world. It is a happy world. . . ."

If Bennett did not attain his fondest ambition, it was because it was impossible. "My ambition," he once wrote, "is to make the newspaper

Press the great organ and pivot of government, society, commerce, finance, religion, and all human civilization. I want to leave behind me no castles, no granite hotels, no monuments of marble, no statues of bronze, no pyramids of brick—simply a name. The name of James Gordon Bennett, as one of the benefactors of the human race, will satisfy every desire and every hope."

It would hardly have satisfied a man of Bennett's clinical egocentricity, but he did revolutionize newspapers and set an enduring pattern for the medium. Only by divorcing his personality from his accomplishments, however, can we measure his real stature.

He left behind him an equally unusual son, fully as mad, if not more so, and yet one who was as innovative in his approach to newspapering as his father. James Gordon Bennett, Jr., came into control of the *Herald* in 1867, when he was just twenty-six, his personality deeply scarred by his abnormal childhood. No son growing up with such a father could have escaped unscathed in the best of circumstances, and in Bennett, Jr.'s, case there were other traumas. As a small boy, he saw little of his father, but he felt the effects of the Great Moral War because he and his mother, along with Bennett, Sr., were socially ostracized. If they were recognized in the street, people were likely to call insults after them, or vent their hatred of Bennett on these innocents in other ways.

Such humiliations, and Henrietta's fears of what effects the Moral War might have on a growing boy, led her to take him abroad when he was five, and they spent most of their time in Europe, principally in Paris, until the boy's midadolescence, quite literally refugees from their own country. The experience had a lasting effect on young Bennett. He grew up without a father's influence, under the complete care of his protective, possessive mother, and with a strong feeling of alienation from America and its way of life. He learned to love Paris, and the European way of living in general, and one may assume he was extremely reluctant to come home again just before the war. The final thrust of the knife was his father's insistence that he join the Union Navy. He must have realized that patriotism and principle played no part in the move, that it was only a sop his father was throwing to the abolitionists in the effort to save his paper.

When the war was over, Bennett, Jr., was brought into the *Herald*, given a quick tour of duty ending with the managing editor's desk, and made to understand that he would soon be running the paper. Fortunately, he had inherited his father's keen sense of news, and like Bennett, Sr., he was a natural editor. Outside the office, he was a profligate bachelor-about-town, erratic and impulsive, an easy spender, given to fits of high temper and jealousy.

Assuming control of the *Herald*, he at once gave a demonstration of what his unique contribution to the newspaper business was going to be. The father had shown his rival (and the world) how to get the news; the son proved to be a genius at making it happen. Later, this kind of newsmaking would become the victim of an academic cliché, "pseudo-news," confusing the inspiration for an event with the event itself. Whether Bennett made it happen voluntarily or someone else was the involuntary trigger, the result was the same: something happened.

Bennett, Jr.,'s initial inspiration was to send Henry Morton Stanley, an English journalist, in search of David Livingstone, an explorer-missionary, who had disappeared into the bush of East Africa early in 1866 on a search for the source of the Nile, during which he intended, idealistically, to put a stop to the slave traffic from which the Arab traders were getting rich. Other papers had carried lengthy stories about Livingstone's disappearance; it was Bennett's idea to send a reporter to find him.

The deal was made in a Paris hotel room, with Stanley getting a thousand pounds to begin his search, and the promise of more thousands until he found Livingstone. It was ironic that the man sent to rescue the avowed enemy of the slave trade should write later, about the Civil War, that he "had a secret scorn for people who could kill one another for the sake of African slaves. . . . Why a sooty-faced nigger from a distant land should be an element of disturbance between white brothers was a puzzle to me."

Stanley's stories as he continued his search excited the nation, jumped the *Herald*'s circulation, and produced a dialogue which has achieved immortality:

"Dr. Livingstone, I presume?"

"Yes."

To which Stanley added, "*Finis coronat opus* [The end crowns the work]."

Since Stanley wrote a different version of how he found Livingstone in a travel book he produced later, and since the missionary himself set off immediately on a new expedition into the interior and died there, no one can be sure of how authentic Stanley's stories were. But the assignment had an unexpected result. Convinced of Africa's future by his stay there, Stanley remained on the continent for most of what remained of his working life, sending back stories which are credited with awakening the great powers to the economic possibilities of Africa, and precipitating the scramble to establish colonies. It was not inappropriate that a man who had only contempt for black people should be an inspiration for colonialism.

Having discovered how successful making news could be, Bennett began surrounding himself at home and abroad with investigative reporters, and became a fountainhead of ideas for them to carry out. He made Januarius Aloysius McGahan, an Irish farm boy from Ohio, the first noteworthy foreign correspondent in the American newspaper business by sending him, first, to cover the Franco-Prussian War, then assigning him in pursuit of a Cossack expedition on its way into Central Asia to conquer Turkestan, the only country in the region still resisting Russian expansionism. McGahan's truly spectacular adventures, both real and imaginary, enchanted the *Herald*'s readers and were widely reprinted. Later, McGahan was on the bark *Pandora*, which Bennett had chartered for him so that he might head a *Herald* expedition to find the fabled Northwest Passage. The correspondent barely escaped with his life.

Aside from his genius for making news and raising circulation, Bennett was a contemptible man, an arrogant, half-mad tyrant, a drunkard who needed only two glasses of his favorite champagne to carry his belligerency to insane lengths. He had some of the best reporters and editors of the day working for him, but they did not stay long.

A tall, spare man, with a drooping mustache and a thin, aristocratic, saturnine face, Bennett was reckless of both life and money. He spent nearly $30 million in his lifetime, and it was typical of his insensitivity toward both money and what it would do that his idea of alleviating the misery brought on by the Panic of 1873 was to open a soup kitchen in the slums and dispense from it samples of *haute cuisine* brought down from Delmonico's kitchens.

In the end, his madness alienated him from the friends who still accepted him, who tolerated his gaucheries and arrogance because he was a very rich and influential young man. On New Year's Day 1877, he was making the traditional calls on friends, sipping a drink with each one, coming at last to the home of his fiancée, Caroline May, the daughter of a well-known doctor. As he made his way through the room in a drunken state, horrifying the guests by slapping men on the back and telling crude jokes before the ladies, he was suddenly seized by the urge to relieve himself, and did so nonchalantly in the fireplace.

Next day, at high noon, Caroline's brother Fred confronted Bennett on the steps of the Union Club with a cowhide whip in his hand.

Bennett took the first two lashes stoically, then his natural arrogance asserted itself and he leaped on young May. Fellow members separated them. When he was on his feet again, Bennett challenged the other man to a duel.

It was a harmless affair. May, who was over his anger by this time and ready to see some humor in the incident, fired into the air. Bennett, who had little sense of humor, would have killed his antagonist if he had not been so nervous. The two men shook hands, but Bennett was not ready to forgive. Something had happened to him which changed the course of his life and made him a bitter, disillusioned man who was resolved never to live in New York again. He gave up the old family home in Washington Heights, his villa in Newport, and his townhouse at 37 West Forty-Seventh Street, and lived the rest of his life in Paris, except for infrequent trips back home. When he was not in Paris, he was at his "lodge" in Versailles, or cruising on his yacht, the *Lysistrata*, with its hundred-man crew, or lounging in his villa at Beaulieu.

Wherever he was, he edited the *Herald* by means of a constant flow of cables, letters, and conferences with editors and writers whom he summoned across the Atlantic at the slightest whim. If he loved anything or anyone, it was France, especially Paris, where he established the Paris *Herald* (now the *International Herald Tribune)* in 1887. At home he started an afternoon edition of the *Herald,* the *Evening Telegram,* which was called by Henry Villard "that pink drab of lowest journalism." For years it drained the morning paper's profits, but in the end it was the sole support of the *Herald* in that great paper's declining days.

The stories of Bennett's remote editing of the *Herald* are legendary in the newspaper business. Once an editor cabled Bennett in Paris that a man who had been summoned to the presence could not be spared because he was indispensable, and Bennett, asking for a list of the paper's indispensable men, fired them all when he got it. On an infrequent trip home, he was met in New York harbor by only one *Herald* reporter, whom Bennett in a fit of pique made city editor on the spot because a delegation had not been sent to meet him. He became an international figure known to everyone as the Commodore —a spender, a sportsman, involved in mysterious scandals, frequently drunk. He still had it in him to make one more news sensation in 1879, by financing the expedition of the ship *Jeannette* on a voyage of discovery to the North Pole. It was crushed by the polar ice and sank with all hands.

Yet there were positive things in Bennett's life and work. In 1883, he helped John MacKay establish the Commercial Cable Company, whose interlocking financial arrangements with the *Herald* helped to keep it one jump ahead of its rivals with the news. Later he was the first publisher to take up the causes of the airplane and auto, and his love of yachting made the *Herald* the best maritime paper in the United States for generations. The international outlook he acquired by his absence from the States helped the *Herald* to gain a clear superiority in foreign news.

But these creditable endeavors were overshadowed by Bennett's developing madness as he grew older. For a time, a man from the *Herald* had to follow him around Europe secretly, canceling anti-Catholic cables denouncing the Pope which he was likely to send in his drunken state. Even sober, his instructions to the editors in New York often passed credibility. One of his passions was the owl. On his orders, scarcely an edition of the *Herald* was printed for some time without an owl story in its columns, and eighteen huge bronze replicas of the bird perched atop the façade of the *Herald* building on Park Row. He was also preoccupied with dogs from time to time, and his paper fought the vivisectionists long before Hearst.

His last days were a *tour de force* of irony. In a reversal of everything he had clung to before, he deserted his bachelorhood for marriage with the widow of a French baron, and left the Catholic faith to become an Episcopalian. He heard with apparent indifference the news that his heavy spending had so weakened the *Herald* that it was being kept alive by the *Telegram*. At last, he died of a heart attack at his Beaulieu villa in 1918.

Bennett's chief competition in New York for a long time came from a man whose career had begun when the *Herald's* owner was still a child. Charles Anderson Dana had, as noted before, learned the business from Greeley and did much to establish the *Tribune* on sound economic grounds, which Uncle Horace was incapable of doing for himself. It was this ability to translate the principles of good business management into the operation of a newspaper that Dana contributed to the profession. More than that, he was a hardheaded man who would have done well in any other kind of business, particularly in that era of ruthless, unprincipled practices. In a day when the robber barons, the accumulators, were amassing the great American fortunes, Dana was showing his fellow publishers how to do well, if not necessarily to get rich. Considering the rather haphazard way newspapers had always been conducted, this was a distinct forward step, and was the first move toward the kind of institutionalization that newspapers have experienced in this century.

As any other businessman would have put it, if you have a good product, you can sell it. Dana's *Sun* was a superb editorial product, so well done that its excellence persisted long after his death. As the son of a country storekeeper whose business failed (his mother died when he was nine), Dana was a man who understood poverty and hard work. Fortunately he had the intellectual equipment to make a different kind of life for himself after he was cast into the world, alone and penniless, at eighteen.

Dana's intellect must have been exceptional. He learned Latin and Greek by himself, read his way through the world's literary classics, and got into Harvard without conditions at nineteen. There hard study nearly ruined his eyesight, and he had to leave at the end of his junior year. It was while he was teaching Latin and Greek at the Transcendentalists' Brook Farm that he met Greeley, and eventually came to the *Tribune*.

As the New Year's Day incident, and the subsequent whipping and duel, changed Bennett's life, so did an episode outside the office change Dana's. While he was on the *Tribune*, and still an intensely idealistic young man under Greeley's influence, he made a long European trip, in 1846 and 1847. What he saw completely reshaped his life. It was a time of crisis everywhere on the Continent, when mighty tides of revolution and unrest were changing the fate of nations. Where some might have responded to this with revolutionary fervor, Dana the idealist saw only what seemed to him the appalling results of power politics and political chicanery. He documented much of what he saw in correspondence for the *Tribune*, a model of analytic reporting.

Dana came home from this trip with his idealism lost, and the beginnings of a corrosive cynicism about men and events which deepened as he grew older. Idealism was replaced with the practical principles of nineteenth-century business management. His split with Greeley was inevitable after that journey, even if their immediate quarrel over politics had not occurred.

After his wartime service as Lincoln's White House "spy," Dana spent two years in Chicago editing the *Republican*, but he dreamed of having his own paper in New York. With the help of the influential men he had met during the war years—Roscoe Conkling, Cyrus Field, and Alonzo Cornell, among others—he raised $175,000 and bought the *Sun*.

It had fallen on evil days. Moses Beach and his two sons had taken it over from Ben Day, but they were printers, not editors. When it began to fail, they had sold it in 1860 to a man named Morrison who had been converted in the great revival of 1858, and now wanted a paper to spread the good news. Under his editorship there was an incredible interval when prayer meetings were held in the city room and editorials urged the Union generals not to fight on Sundays. After a year of it, Morrison gave the paper back to Beach, who thought himself lucky to sell it to Dana. At that point, its circulation had fallen to a low of 43,000. In less than three years, Dana brought it back to the top of the New York heap with an average daily circulation of 102,-870, and in six years it had reached a peak of 131,000.

That was accomplished in the face of intense competition from the *Herald*, which until that time had been the leader. The formula behind Dana's success was a simple one. The *Sun*, he promised in his opening announcement, would "study condensation, clearness, point, and will endeavor to present its daily photograph of the whole world's doings in the most luminous and lively manner." In later promotional advertising he declared that the *Sun*'s news was "the freshest, most interesting and sprightliest current, and no expense is spared to make it just what the great mass of the people want."

Better than did the Bennetts, father and son, Dana knew what the mass of his readers wanted. They might enjoy Junior's audacious sensationalism, as they had appreciated his father's ability to bring them the news more quickly and accurately than the others. But Dana added that professional polish which only superior writing and editing can bring. Both papers filled their columns with the hard news of a big city's life—murder, scandal, interviews, corruption, politics—but Dana added two improvements. One was what came to be called the "human interest story," which he virtually invented. The other was a sharpened sense of news value, expressed in the immortal words of his city editor, John B. Bogart, who advised a young reporter, "When a dog bites a man, that's not news; but when a man bites a dog, that's news."

Dana also gave his readers a brisk, well-written editorial page. Bennett, Jr.,'s lack of interest in editorials had made the *Herald*'s page seem perfunctory after Bennett, Sr.,'s grandiloquent pronouncements. The editorials Dana wrote were meant to be read, and no doubt he knew they would make people angry. In them he expressed his perverse view of life, which included a conviction that no confidence could be placed in any man in public office, together with a pervasive skepticism about all human loyalties.

Aside from the editorials, the *Sun* was full of good and even memorable work. For example, one of Dana's editorial writers, Francis P. Church, achieved fame with a single line in one editorial: "Yes, Virginia, there is a Santa Claus." Among the reporters were men like Julian Ralph and David Graham Phillips, the latter one of the best investigators of the century, whose stories of corruption in city, state, and national government made him a celebrated figure. Another remarkable investigative reporter was Jacob Riis, who revealed the horror of slum life to comfortable New Yorkers and other Americans who had never ventured into the Lower East Side. Abroad, Dana boasted the *beau idéal* of foreign correspondents, Richard Harding Davis. In managing this glittering stable, Dana, unlike either Bennett, was an encouraging and helpful boss; he was at home and most human when he was working.

Dana and Bennett, Jr., came into their own in New York at almost the same time, coincidental with General Grant's accession to the White House in 1868. In the subsequent eight years, the nation was given an example of the power the press now possessed—and its limitations. Grant was well aware of what this new breed of editors could do; the lessons of the war had not been lost on him. He was conscious that Thomas Nast's brilliant cartoons in *Harper's Weekly* had been a major factor in getting him elected, and he understood that the seat of press power in New York would influence his administration. In a most unusual story carried in the New York *World* about two months before inauguration, the country got a unique view of how the general viewed his potential friends or enemies.

The *World's* correspondent had obtained, not from Grant but from friends and associates, what he asserted were the President-elect's opinions of prominent men in public life, including the leading editors There is no reason to suppose they were not true, and they were revealing.

Of Greeley, Grant said: "Mr. Greeley has published some unpalatable things about me, but I have no doubt he thought at the time they were true.... The world is better for Greeley having lived in it and erred in it. I like Greeley better than I have any reason to suppose he likes me." Of Dana: "Dana is a man for whom I ought to have a great contempt, but to whom I owe nothing but good will. He came to me a spy upon my conduct. He reported favorably. If it had not been for his favorable report, I should probably have been removed from my command. . . ." Of Bennett, Sr., a fellow Scot: "Bennett, like a true Scotchman, is ever ready to trade upon the misfortunes of his adopted country. He cares not how terrible a time it is for the country, if it is only a good time for newspapers. He made his paper famous by making it infamous. It mattered nothing to him who was harmed, so that he made money. . . ." Of Raymond: "Raymond always reminds me of a jumping-jack. He is heads up or tails up just as Seward or Weed move him. When Raymond goes wrong I always feel like forgiving him, for he knows not what he does. . . ."

As his administration progressed, it was not Grant but the editors who pronounced judgment, as their reporters ferreted out scandal after scandal in a massive corruption that was not seen again in American politics on such a scale until Watergate, which has many parallels with Grant's ordeal. These parallels are obvious, for example, in Vernon Parrington's assessment of Grant:

> Honest himself, he was the source of more dishonesty in others than any other American President. His eight years in the White House marked the lowest depths—in domestic affairs at least—to which any American administration has fallen. . . . Scandal and corruption whispered all about him, the hands of his closest advisers were dirty; yet he stubbornly refused to hear the whispers or see the dirt. In judging men and policies he was no more than a child. He could never distinguish between an honest man and a rascal. He was loyal to his friends and open-handedness he regarded as a mark of friendship. In the end it turned out like the thieves of Jericho his blatant followers despoiled him of nearly everything.

From the beginning, the press was suspicious of Grant. He was no sooner in the White House than his patronage appointments of kinsmen to himself and his wife, perhaps as many as forty-eight, aroused criticism. Then his rich friends, of whom he appeared to have an inordinate number, began to shower him with gifts which he gratefully accepted: three houses, including one in Philadelphia said to be worth $60,000; sixteen horses; a house in New York City, worth $100,000, bought later with money raised by a group of friends.

Grant's sister married Abel S. Corbin, an associate of Jay Gould and Jim Fisk, the most unprincipled men in a Wall Street where principle was always in short supply. Gould and Fisk were soon involved in a conspiracy to rig the gold market, using Corbin's wife to give them access to the White House so that they could make the President an unwitting part of the plot. That plan was exposed by Greeley and the *Tribune*, but under pressure from the paper, demanding that the Treasury begin selling its gold, Grant stood fast as the price went up until at last, when the order to sell was given, the gold market collapsed in a disastrous "Black Friday," in which Fisk himself was a heavy loser.

Grant was adjudged innocent by most of the papers, although it was considered that he was perilously close to involvement. But the whole affair was enough to turn Dana, with his deep distrust of all politicians, completely against the administration. He charged that the President was in the hands of "charlatans and adventurers," and accused him of "frightful blunderings and flounderings." But he was in a dilemma with the campaign of 1872: great as his distaste for the President might be, he could not bring himself to support Greeley.

The other prominent editors of the nation had no such personal feelings. Most of them fought hard against Grant's reelection, and for the first time, when the returns were in, it was clear that the power of the press did not extend to denying public office to a popular man. People were fully informed in their papers about the iniquities already visible in the administration, but they disregarded the facts and the editorials and voted for Grant anyway, blindly, as they have so often done. Similarly, in 1936, 1940, and 1944, the electorate returned Franklin Roosevelt to office in spite of the opposition of two thirds of the nation's press.

In his second inaugural address, Grant took notice of his situation. Declaring that he had never asked anything but to do his duty, he declared: "Notwithstanding this, throughout the war, and from my candidacy for my present office in 1868 to the close of the last presidential campaign, I have been the subject of abuse and slander scarcely ever equaled in political history." But, he concluded with satisfaction, he could disregard opposition "in view of your verdict, which I gratefully accept as my vindication."

It was not long, however, before the unrelenting press began to disclose a depth of corruption in the administration which even a myopic electorate could not ignore. The Crédit Mobilier scandal had already cast its sinister shadow over Grant before his reelection when the *Sun*, on September 4, 1872, first exposed this fraud by which Union Pacific Railway promoters meant to divert to their own pockets, through a dummy company, some of the profits derived from building the line.

Several highly placed Republican politicians, beginning with Vice-President Colfax, were charged with accepting stock in this company in return for what these officials could do for them. As in the Watergate affair, so many of the administration's people were involved in the plot that it was quite possible to believe there were few honest men in or around the White House. Nevertheless, Grant was reelected and, in the end, only two obscure representatives were censured by the House for their conduct.

At the same time that the *Sun* and other newspapers were pursuing this matter, Congress was quietly preparing what came to be known as the Salary Grab, in which the outgoing legislators intended to increase the President's salary and their own.

In foreign affairs, the trouble spot was Cuba, where the long continuing revolt against Spanish rule had generated considerable sympathy in the United States, and some agitation to acquire the island by whatever means were necessary, legal or illegal. Dana was involved in pro-Cuban activities, and so were all the other New York papers except the *World*, but press opinion was more evenly divided elsewhere. There had also been a movement in 1870 to annex Santo Domingo, which proved to be the Grant administration's Bay of Pigs, so ineptly did Grant handle it. Opposed by the Cabinet, the Senate, the Attorney General, and all the New York papers but the *Herald*, the treaty of annexation was finally defeated, at further cost to Grant's stature.

To continue the contemporary parallels, Grant seemed undisturbed by criticism from the press or anyone else, and simply turned his back on it, even when Dana accused him of being drunk, and even when the papers blamed him for the Panic of 1873, which was caused more by unimpeded railroad speculation rather than by any direct act of the President. But it was difficult for Grant to maintain his isolation as the grimy cloud of scandal grew around him. In 1876, the *Herald* charged corruption in the War Department and demanded an investigation. The House obliged and found that Secretary of War William W. Belknap had indeed taken bribes for selling trading posts in Indian Territory. Impeached, he resigned to avoid trial but was acquitted by the Senate, although all but two of those who found him not guilty said they had voted that way because they thought they had no jurisdiction over an official who had resigned. Worse, the President's brother Orvil was involved in this shady business.

That scandal followed closely on the heels of the Whiskey Ring, another fraud, exposed by the St. Louis *Democrat*'s editor, G. W. Fishback. This was a conspiracy of revenue officials (led by a Grant appointee) and distillers to defraud the government of tax money in St. Louis and other cities. The resulting investigation brought the indictment of 238 people, including General O. E. Babcock, Grant's private secretary, who was saved from conviction only by the President's personal intervention.

In the face of all these and other events, the blackest in the nation's history until Watergate, Grant had the effrontery to refer to them in his final message to Congress as "errors of judgment," and to add that it was inevitable that "differences of opinion between the Executive, bound by an oath to the strict performance of his duties, and writers and debaters, must have arisen. It is not necessarily evidence of blunder on the part of the Executive because there are these differences of views. Mistakes have been made, as all can see and I admit, but it seems to me oftener in the selections made of the assistants appointed to aid in carrying out the various duties of administering the Government. . . ." In short, Grant wrapped himself in the presidency and blamed others for the nearly total corruption of the government.

The Grant administration confirmed Dana's most cynical feelings about politicians, and thereafter no president could please him. Having helped to ruin Grant's impossible dream of a third term by coining the famous campaign phrase "Turn the rascals out," he gave only lukewarm support to Greeley, whom he always referred to sarcastically, *à la* H. L. Mencken, as "Dr. Greeley." In the disputed Hayes-Tilden election of 1876, Dana took Tilden's side and refused to recognize Hayes as long as he was in office by any title except "the fraudulent President." To Dana, Garfield in 1880 was little better than a common thief, and his opponent, General Hancock, was described as "a good man, weighing 240 pounds." Dana opposed Cleveland for no better reason than the refusal of a political favor, and he had an even worse opinion of the other party's candidate, Blaine.

When he was not attacking presidential candidates, successful and unsuccessful, Dana wrote biting denunciations of labor unions and strikes, and civil service reform. In New York, he supported some of the most fragrant Tammany candidates. The McKinley Tariff Act, to which he gave his unqualified approval, is now considered one of the most damaging pieces of legislation ever enacted. But one has to admit that Dana's editorials on all these subjects sparkled and demanded to be read, even though they were devoid of any moral content.

There was only one man in New York journalism who approached Dana as a provoker of public opinion. Edwin Lawrence Godkin, who signed himself E. L. Godkin, was the opposite side of the coin in every possible respect. A transplanted Anglo-Irishman, born in England, he was devoted to America and spent his life trying to correct the evils of democracy. He was an idealist, an unabashed and undiscouraged fighter for the rights of man. Naturally, Dana despised him. Godkin fought hard for the masses, but he disdained to mix with them, or even to write for them. His paper, the *Nation*, which he edited brilliantly from 1865 to 1899, was one of the most widely quoted in the country but so unprofitable that it had to be rescued from oblivion by the *Evening Post*; the *Nation* became the *Post*'s weekly edition in 1881.

Godkin's editorials were addressed frankly to intellectuals, which accounted for the paper's small circulation. He even remained aloof from his professional colleagues, and indeed from nearly everyone else. A strange, lonely man, he directed his energies toward liberal, progressive causes, of which he was the best and most effective advocate in America.

The *Nation* never reached a circulation of more than 35,000, and sometimes it fell below 10,000, but its influence was out of all proportion to these figures, and its editorial viewpoints penetrated to the farthest corners of the country, trickling down through exchanges, and through sermons and lectures given by people who would be called in today's jargon "opinion makers."

Godkin was an indifferent editor, but he was an editorial writer of the most exceptional talent, and this instrument, combined with his extraordinary integrity, enabled him to teach the country, as Henry Holt, the book publisher, once said, "more than any other man in it."

In his editorials, Godkin opposed everything Dana stood for, with a moral austerity at the opposite pole from cynicism. He battled for civil service reform and against high tariffs, for sound currency and against corruption in government. Day after day he pursued his adversaries with such cold, witty irony, such penetrating shafts of insight, that it was sometimes too much even for the paper's readers. A story was circulated about the old lady who lived alone in the country, but was not afraid because, as she said, a carrier boy threw her copy of the *Evening Post* on the porch at dusk, and "it just lay there and growled all night."

Godkin was not without his weak points. He never understood the tidal rise of labor unions in the latter part of the century, for instance. But he was nevertheless a powerful, constructive force in the country, in sharp contrast to Dana, who in the end was only a rich man able to vent his prejudices in a daily newspaper—the personification of personal journalism.

The two men died within five years of each other. Oddly enough, it was Dana who made the best use of his later years. Before his death in 1897, he had learned most of the European languages, conducted classes in Dante, raised rare foreign trees, shrubs, and flowers, and regarded himself as a connoisseur of wines. He spent much of his time with musicians, writers, and artists, and in short died quite unlike the way he had lived. His editorial enemies pursued him to the end, but at his death the *Sun* felt it unnecessary to carry an obituary. Everyone in the country knew Dana.

When Godkin died in England in 1902, his health broken, it appeared to some that the great day of the editorial page had died with him. Certainly it never spoke again with the same conviction, strength, and authority as it had when Greeley, Dana, and Godkin were writing it. Of Godkin's editorials it could be said that they had some lasting influence. As Henry Villard, the *Post*'s publisher, observed, "Almost every one of the reforms in government of our day, Godkin championed, and always by going to the root of the thing, by seeking the underlying principle and setting it forth."

For the others, Dana and Greeley, the result was different. Greeley's selling of the high-tariff idea to the farming population was long-lasting but destructive. Dana's editorials annoyed presidents and made some of them fear him, but they did not decisively influence any elections.

The power of the press, then, as it developed in the latter part of the nineteenth century, derived not from its influence on the electorate, but on what it was originally intended to be by those citizens who had demanded the First Amendment to protect themselves from government. The papers' investigative function, standing between the elected rulers and the governed, made them at last the instrument Jefferson had envisioned.

Freed from party control, with their news function developed and their audience vastly increased, the newspapers, beginning with Bennett, Sr., assumed the role in American life they were meant to attain. Not even the eccentricities of the powerful editor-publishers who controlled them before 1900 could alter the significance of that fact.

13

The Second Golden Age
of Magazines

IN THE UPSURGE of magazines after the Civil War, leading to a new "golden age," the business of making periodicals began to take the shape it would have in the next century. While there were failures, they were not as numerous as they had been, and the best of the new ones came to stay. Several great names were established, some whose roots went back to prewar days, others representing new ideas.

One of the old periodicals that came to full flowering was the *North American Review*, forgotten today by everyone except journalistic and literary scholars, but nevertheless perhaps the finest magazine ever published in America. Dr. Mott asserts correctly that its files are "unmatched by that of any other magazine of American thought through nearly a century and a quarter of our national life."

At its peak, during the eighties, even its rivals had to admit its overpowering superiority. One of them, the *Review of Reviews*, said with admirable candor: "It is unquestionably true that the *North American* is regarded by more people, in all parts of the country, as at once the highest and most impartial platform upon which current public issue can be discussed, than is any other magazine or review."

As the oldest magazine of continuous publication in the country, having begun its long life in 1815, the *Review* had gone on for sixty years scarcely changed. It was widely respected, solid, and dull, so that in the post-Civil War era, that explosive period in American life which Howard Mumford Jones calls the Age of Energy, it had declined, in the face of stiff competition, to the point of expiration.

At that juncture Allen Thorndike Rice became its editor and emerged as one of the first to establish the proposition that great editors make great magazines. The idea of the magazine editor as a one-man show, imprinting his image on a publication so that it was identified with him, had begun with Graham, Godey, and Mrs. Hale, but it flowered with Rice and his contemporaries in the business. That conception has not changed until our own time.

How much it has changed is easily established. As late as 1950, editors were closely identified with their magazines, and most people, even some of those outside the media, could name them and knew about them as people. Today it would be hard for anyone not in the magazine business to identify any more than three or four editors, publishers, or editor-publishers.

Rice showed what one man, unhampered by boards of directors, stockholders in publicly held companies, or conglomerate executives, could do when he was able to control a magazine himself. A native Bostonian, barely twenty-three at the time, Rice had plenty of money and needed it, because the magazine for which he had paid only $3000 had a subscription list of 1200 and an inherited annual deficit of alarming proportions.

Going to work busily on a half dozen fronts, Rice made the magazine a bimonthly, moved it from Boston to New York, changed publishers from the book house of James R. Osgood & Co., in Boston, to D. Appleton & Co., in New York, and, most important, opened up the pages of his periodical so that it was no longer a regional intellectual publication but a forum for ideas, of which the United States had a superabundant supply at that moment. Rice told his readers that the *Review* was to be "an arena wherein any man having something valuable to say could be heard."

The result of that policy was to make it an intellectual platform on which the best thinkers and writers of the day could discuss the problems of the new industrial society rising in America. Henry George and David Dudley Field argued the theory of the single tax. Parkman attacked woman suffrage, and Lucy Stone, Julia Ward Howe, and Wendell Phillips, among others, defended it. J. A. Froude and Cardinal Manning debated the role of the Catholic church, while Robert G. Ingersoll aroused a public outcry with his atheistic attack on religion in general. Walt Whitman contributed some essays. Richard Wagner talked about his life and career, and William Gladstone contributed more than a dozen articles about politics. General Pierre G. T. Beauregard reminisced about his Civil War experiences, and General Grant talked about the Nicaragua canal.

With this kind of fare, provoking discussion and quotation, the circulation had climbed to 17,000 when Rice died suddenly in 1889. The magazine was then making an annual profit of $50,000. Under a new editor, Lloyd Bryce, who had been Rice's friend at Oxford, the *Review* continued its climb until in 1891 it reached an all-time circulation peak of 76,000, with subscribers paying five dollars a year. From that high point it began a slow descent that stretched over decades, although it still remained distinguished under the long editorship of Colonel George Harvey, who bought a controlling interest in 1899. Harvey, who had been the *World's* managing editor in its early days and a successful businessman operating electric railways, turned out to be an exceptional man, editing both the *Review* and *Harper's Weekly* simultaneously, besides serving as president of Harper & Brothers, the publishers, after 1900.

The *Review* survived, with dwindling circulation, interest, and capital, until about 1936, when it was bought by an agent of the Japanese government as an American front. (That, oddly enough, was the kind of fate that befell several notable American magazines, including *Scribner's*, which ended its distinguished career as a propaganda organ of the German-American Bund; and the *American Mercury*, which ultimately fell into the hands of an extreme right-wing Texas hate group.)

Another of the old magazines that flowered late was the *Youth's Companion*, founded in 1827 and published continuously until it fell a victim to the Great Adjustment of 1929. In the late nineteenth century, it was one of the most popular magazines in America, and entertained generations of American youth. Again, it was a great editor who made it famous—Daniel Sharp Ford, who became principal owner and editor in 1857 and continued until he died in 1899. Thousands of his readers knew him as "Perry Mason" because he called his organization "Perry Mason & Co." rather than use his own name.

At its peak, the *Companion* was of such high quality that parents as well as their children were reading it. To find names like Gladstone, Lord Bryce, Thomas Hardy, Rudyard Kipling, and those of famous presidents of universities and noted professors was, to say the least, unusual. Jack London first came to public notice in its pages in 1899. Sex, crime, or anything considered immoral was rigidly excluded. The emphasis was on action, adventure, humor, and what young people themselves were doing, along with science, anecdotes, and puzzles.

Magazine history was affected less, however, by the *Companion's* contents than by its circulation methods. It was the first periodical to use effectively the device of giving premiums for annual subscriptions, a practice it began in the late sixties. For more than a half century afterward, it issued every year in late October a "Premium List Number" containing pictures and descriptions of the treasures that might be had for obtaining two or three or whatever number of subscriptions. The list, which covered thirty-six pages of the *Companion* by the eighteen-eighties, included everything from magic lanterns to printing presses, from dolls to Elsie books.

There was no doubt about how well this method worked. Readers waited for the annual issue as eagerly as they awaited Santa Claus, and circulations gained until the *Companion* led all other magazines for a time, with a figure of 400,000 in 1887, and passing half a million in 1898. The subscription rate was not high; it remained at $1.75 from 1870 until nearly fifty years later. But the success of the premium method spread through the magazine business until it raged like a fever, reaching the point of absurdity in many cases and even causing the premature death of some periodicals. At its peak, the method would enable a supersalesman to furnish a small store. Most of those who used it had sense enough to give up the idea when its usefulness was exhausted. Only the *Companion* continued the practice successfully, until late in its career.

In the end, the *Companion*, like so many other old magazines surviving from the nineteenth century, was a victim of changing times in the twenties. It is axiomatic that magazines which find themselves unable to change rapidly enough expire, and sometimes the change must be radical. When the *Companion* died in 1929, merging with the *American Boy*, its circulation down below 300,000, there were nostalgic tears shed by more than one adult who had stopped reading it years ago. It was the young who no longer needed it; they had gone on to other things.

Still another long-lived magazine was the *Scientific American*, begun in 1845 and in better health today than at any other time in its history. From 1846, when it was acquired by Orson Munn and Alfred Beach (son of Moses Y. Beach, once publisher of the *Sun*) for a few hundred dollars, it began to record the scientific progress of the nineteenth century, and to support it against the assaults of quacks and nonprogressives alike. The sons of the two owners carried on their work into this century, and the magazine became a monthly in 1921. Today, under the direction of one of the industry's dynamic publishers, Gerard Piel, the *Scientific American* is probably the most highly regarded magazine of its kind in the world.

But of all the magazines begun in the nineteenth century and surviving to the twentieth, the most prestigious and generally noteworthy were the two started by the Harper brothers, whose book-publishing house, of which the magazines were offshoots, is known today
as Harper & Row. The first of their periodicals, *Harper's Monthly,*
begun in 1850 as *Harper's New Monthly* magazine, is still extant.
Harper's Weekly, established seven years later than the monthly,
came to an end in 1916.

The monthly was begun without apology as an aid to the book-
publishing business of the Harper brothers, who used several pages of
it to advertise forthcoming books. Otherwise, it was to be a survey of
contemporary English literature, as varied as possible, and with many
different departments. Dickens was the centerpiece of the table of
contents. He contributed short stories, and later his novels *Bleak
House* and *Little Dorrit* were serialized. Dickens and other British
writers were pirated at first, but most of them were paid later, including Thackeray, whose *The Newcomes* and *The Virginians* were serialized, and George Eliot, with *Romola.* Its famous department "The
Editor's Easy Chair," still carried today, began in 1851, and its first
occupant was Donald G. Mitchell, whose *Reveries of a Bachelor* was
a best-selling Harper book.

In the eighteen-fifties, *Harper's Monthly* was the most successful
magazine in America, with its combination of English serials, its wide
variety of shorter work, and its many illustrations. The first printing
had been a modest 7500; but by the time the war began, it had
passed 200,000, it was rich, and jealously abused by its fortunate
competitors. *Putnam's,* one of these, conceded resignedly, "Probably
no magazine in the world was ever so popular or so profitable."
Wilkie Collins, Dickens, Trollope, R. D. Blackmore, and Hardy continued to swell its popularity. Americans were not serialized until the
eighteen-eighties, but they appeared often as short-story writers and
came to dominate that form in the magazine.

By the nineties, *Harper's* had reached its peak as a general illustrated literary magazine and, as Dr. Mott observes, it had probably
"attained the very zenith of success among the world's periodicals of
that class. . . ." It was achieving enormous popular successes with
such serials as Du Maurier's *Trilby,* which set off a national craze,
and Mark Twain's *Personal Recollections of Joan of Arc,* published
anonymously. In the stifling, hypocritical morality of the day, reminiscent of the insanity of the eighteen-forties, Henry Mills Alden, the
editor, did not hesitate to edit out of Hardy's *Jude the Obscure* (pub-

lished as *Hearts Insurgent*) bits and pieces he felt could not be "read aloud in the family circle." He even dropped an entire chapter out of Henry James's translation of Daudet's *Tartarin de Tarascon* for that reason.

Although it was not as long-lived, *Harper's Weekly* was as distinguished in its own way, providing a vivid picture-text history of American life from 1857 to 1916, much as *Life* did in this century from 1936 to 1973. Pictorially and textually, it was nearly always interesting and often brilliant. The magazine was Fletcher Harper's "pet enterprise" and he managed it until he retired in 1875.

In format, the *Weekly* was somewhere between a magazine and a newspaper, and in fact called itself a "family newspaper." Its emphasis was on the news. The physical shape was a small folio of sixteen pages at the beginning. Unlike the monthly, it plunged into political discussion wholeheartedly before the Civil War and during it. Its pictorial coverage of the war was superb, particularly the work of the young artist Thomas Nast, which was neither downright realistic illustration nor the satirical cartoon he became famous for later, but rather the kind of mood drawing Bill Mauldin did so successfully during World War II.

The *Weekly's* circulation was a healthy 100,000 through the war. It climbed afterward and reached 160,000 by 1872. Pictures held the most fascination for its readers—illustrations and cartoons of contemporary life, particularly Nast's political cartoons, which reached their climax in the seventies, when he was a prime factor in the exposure of Tammany Hall's iniquities.

After 1884 the *Weekly* began to decline, although it continued to improve in physical appearance and the display of its pictures, and carried the work of many of the best English and American writers of the day. Nevertheless, it continued to slide a little every year toward eventual oblivion.

For a century or more, the *Atlantic Monthly* has been bracketed in the public mind with *Harper's Monthly* as one of the two most distinguished literary periodicals in America. Like its rival, the *Atlantic* also began life as the offspring of a publishing house, Phillips, Sampson & Co., in Boston. Its first editor was James Russell Lowell, who would take the job only if his friend, Oliver Wendell Holmes, would be a contributor. That resulted in the *Atlantic's* publication of *The Autocrat of the Breakfast-Table*.

Sold to another publisher, Ticknor & Fields, in 1859, for a mere $10,000, the magazine emulated *Harper's* by not plunging into the war, although it printed Emerson's essay on the Emancipation Proclamation and devoted considerable space to Reconstruction.

In 1869, while Fields was on a European trip, Mrs. Stowe submitted an article about Byron, intending, as one critic put it, "to arrest Byron's influence upon the young by overwhelming him with moral reprobation; instead of that, she has raised the interest in Byron to sevenfold intensity." By mercilessly exposing the poet's libido, Mrs. Stowe created the greatest magazine sensation since her own *Uncle Tom's Cabin* ran as a serial, and in doing so she cost the *Atlantic* 15,000 shocked subscribers who refused to renew. The Panic of 1873 contributed further to the magazine's slipping circulation; it was down to 12,000 in 1881. By this time the periodical had a new publisher, H. O. Houghton, whose various publishing ventures settled by 1880 into the prestigious Boston firm of Houghton, Mifflin & Co.

In the seventies, the *Atlantic* acquired a new editor, William Dean Howells, the literary arbiter of his day, who broadened its horizons. As he put it later, "Without ceasing to be New England, without ceasing to be Bostonian, at heart, we had become southern, mid-western, and far-western in our sympathies. It seemed to me that the new good things were coming from those regions rather than from our own coasts and hills."

Heresy in Boston! But Howells was correct, and the magazine profited from his insight. He himself contributed both fiction and nonfiction, further increasing the periodical's reputation. The most remarkable contribution, however, was Thomas Bailey Aldrich's *Marjorie Daw*, one of the most formidable popular successes of the day; nothing the magazine ever printed surpassed it in popularity.

In 1881, Howells was succeeded as editor by Aldrich, who was more like Lowell in his tastes, and he in turn was succeeded by Horace E. Scudder, who added more articles on social topics. But the *Atlantic* did not attain its peak until Walter Hines Page became editor in 1896. Aggressive, young, a Southerner, Page was foreign to everything the *Atlantic* had been, but he boosted its prestige and circulation by turning it to some mild muckraking and political controversy. Strange but distinguished names appeared in the magazine: Theodore Roosevelt, Woodrow Wilson, E. L. Godkin, William Allen White, Booker T. Washington, Jacob Riis. Page also secured a big best-selling novel as a serial, Mary Johnston's *To Have and to Hold*, which nearly doubled circulation.

He was succeeded by Bliss Perry, followed by Ellery Sedgwick, who helped organize the Atlantic Monthly Co., which began to publish the magazine in 1909. Sedgwick made it the lively, literary periodical with a world view that it remains today.

More and more editors were putting the stamp of their personalities on the magazines. It was Howells' *Atlantic*, Godkin's *Nation*, and —to complete the leading intellectual triumvirate—Holland's *Scribner's Monthly*. Dr. Josiah G. Holland looked and talked like the popular magazine editor he was. His sympathies were not with the struggling masses of industrial America, as were Godkin's, but with the upper middle class to which he himself belonged. A member of the class of original WASPs who now controlled the country, Holland was able to talk to a large audience in the pages of *Scribner's*, and he knew how to speak to them in their own language, instilling into the magazine's pages the moral, broad-gauged conservatism of his genial personality. That made *Scribner's* the great middle-class magazine of its day, although its literary quality was sometimes high enough to rank it with *Harper's* and the *Atlantic*.

At the opposite end of the spectrum from these respectable gentlemen of intellect was Frank Leslie, whose life could have been one of the lurid tales his magazine published. He was an adventurer, with a quick, lively mind and a driving ambition—perhaps the first editor or publisher to fully comprehend the mass mind.

London-born as Henry Carter, he started life as a wood engraver, and came to America in 1848 at twenty-seven. In his earlier days, he had sent drawings to the London *Illustrated News* under the pseudonym "Frank Leslie," to protect himself from his father's wrath, and it was under this name that he began his career in America. Leslie worked for a time as an engraver, then got into the magazine business with periodicals for women, which did so well they made it possible for him to start *Frank Leslie's Illustrated Newspaper* in December 1855.

In spite of its name, this "newspaper" was actually a weekly magazine of a kind now plentiful all over the world, treating the news of the day with liberal use of pictures and some text. Its pictures were something entirely new in magazine publishing—illustrations of an event no more than two weeks after it took place. Like the news magazines and picture periodicals of our time, it attempted to cover music, drama, fine arts, racing and other sports, and books, all in departments. In addition, it printed popular serial fiction.

To Leslie, news meant sensation. He was not much interested in sober political events. With a true instinct for the mass market, he looked for the war in Nicaragua, the bloody conflict in Kansas, the sensational New York murder. It took nearly six months for this formula to penetrate the market, and during that time Leslie was nearly ready to give up, but then the tide began to change, and in its third year the *Newspaper* could claim 100,000 circulation. The delighted publisher immediately spawned a whole new series of magazines: *Frank Leslie's New Family Magazine,* 1857; *Frank Leslie's Budget of Fun,* a year later; *Frank Leslie's Ladies' Magazine,* 1871.

In the early years of the *Newspaper,* it showed what this kind of periodical could do to influence its audience—an audience able to absorb more from pictures than from words. With considerable courage, Leslie attacked one of the scandals of New York, the distribution of "swill milk." Cows in the dairies supplying the city with milk were fed with distillery refuse, which poisoned them and contaminated their milk, although they continued to produce until they died. Since the dairies and the distilleries were hand in glove with the Tammany political machine, and everybody was making money, all reform attempts had failed until Leslie's attack.

He had the weapon that worked. When his readers saw, in vivid pictures, the incredible filth of the dairies, the grotesque, dying cows, and the milk being carted into New York in open barrels, there was a horrified outcry of public revulsion. The Board of Health tried to gloss over the scandal with a reassuring statement but Leslie rejoined, "Every one of those cows has a vote!" and he sent off detectives in the wake of the milk wagons to record the places where milk was left, a list he published with an accompanying warning to the customers that they were poisoning their children. The politicians he attacked tried to have Leslie indicted for criminal libel, but a grand jury refused.

The end result was a complete victory for the publisher and his paper. The mayor was forced to permit a committee from the New York Academy of Medicine to make its own investigation, which completely confirmed everything *Leslie's* had reported. Two years later the state legislature passed a law ending the "swill milk" disgrace forever, and Leslie was presented with a gold watch and chain by a grateful public.

Leslie's was not always preoccupied with virtue, however. The publisher was not above capitalizing on sensational crime for the sake of circulation, and he gave space to prizefighting, a sport the periodical occasionally deplored. During the war years the magazine produced week after week a priceless history in pictures of the conflict. Its treatment did not have the literary luster of *Harper's,* but it was more enterprising in its coverage of public affairs, and generally livelier as well. At the end of 1864, Leslie wrote: "We have had since the commencement of the present war, over eighty artists engaged in making sketches for our paper, and have published nearly three thousand pictures of battles, sieges, bombardments, and other scenes incidental to the war." The paper also had as many as a dozen correspondents in the field.

After the war the *Newspaper* had its vicissitudes, which were more than matched by a spectacular scandal in Leslie's private life. He was separated but not divorced from his English wife in 1867 when he went on a junket to Paris with his managing editor, Ephraim G. Squier, and Squier's wife, a striking, statuesque redhead who was editing *Ladies' Magazine* at the time. What happened in Paris and subsequently, was told in titillating detail six years later when Mrs. Squier divorced her husband. She married Leslie as soon as it was final.

The two were a handsome couple, whether they were in their grand Saratoga home, touring California in a private railroad car with a retinue of writers and artists, or working together in New York. These extravagances ended with Leslie's bankruptcy in 1877. He continued to edit his properties under an assignee until he died in January 1880, with the *Newspaper* at a low point of 33,000 and half his other properties discontinued.

Mrs. Leslie succeeded her husband and at once demonstrated that she was an even better editor, and a far better business manager. She paid off his debts, regained control of the property and, with sure journalistic instinct, stopped the presses at the moment the news of Garfield's assassination reached her, and remade the pages. The result was a $50,000 profit on a single issue. She improved the paper physically, too, with better paper and a more attractive cover, while she employed her formidable personality to attract new writers. Circulation began to rise again, and Mrs. Leslie became as much of a figure in New York as her late husband had been.

It turned out that she had been divorced one or more times before she left Squier. It was said she had Creole blood, and she herself claimed to be of royal descent, with a right to the title of "Duchesse of Bazus." A contemporary magazine described her at her desk "dressed in a French costume that is stayed and stiffened till it fits without a wrinkle or a crease. Her sleeves are poems, her back is a study, and her waist could be spanned by a necklace. She wears the tiniest of shoes, and carries a painted feather fan."

Mrs. Leslie sold her property in 1889, and although the *Newspaper* continued to be published, the heart had gone out of it. It was more political and sober, less sensational, and as time went on it became an unofficial organ of the Republican Party. However, under John A. Schleicher, who bought it in 1898, it combined politics, social comment, reviews, and artwork so successfully that in the first years of World War I it reached a peak circulation of nearly 400,000. After the war, it declined rapidly in the depression of the early twenties and died in June 1922.

"Never shoot over the heads of the people" had been Frank Leslie's motto, and that was the key to the mass-market journalism being practiced in newspapers and magazines alike during the closing decades of the nineteenth century. The success of both Leslies was duplicated and excelled by other mass-market editors and publishers.

In fact, the magazine business was growing with astonishing speed. There had been only about 7000 periodicals in 1865, but in the next two decades, 8000 or 9000 had been published; and 33,000 were still in existence in 1885. After that the acceleration continued. In 1895, the *Nation* reported the birth of magazines "in numbers to make Malthus stare and gasp," while in 1897, the *National Magazine* complained: "Magazines, magazines, magazines! The news-stands are already groaning under a heavy load, and there are still more coming." There were, in fact, more than 4400 of them by 1890; five years later, about 5100; and at the end of the century, more than 5500. For purposes of quick comparison, there are roughly 18,000 today.

The Chicago *Graphic,* a journal of opinion, remarked in 1892: "The development of the magazine in the last quarter of a century in the United States has been marvelous, and is paralleled by no literary movement in any country or in any time. Every field of human thought has been entered and as the field has broadened new magazines have arisen to occupy the territory, and the magazine has become not only a school of literature but of science, art and politics as well."

In this second golden age, there was an increasing variety of periodicals, and in general a marked improvement on old formulas, along with some more or less new ideas. A few excellent magazines failed to survive—periodicals like the *Galaxy,* New York's answer to the *Atlantic.* This magazine printed Mark Twain for some time, and Henry James, Trollope, Turgeniev in translation, Walt Whitman, Sidney Lanier, Bayard Taylor, Bret Harte, and Joaquin Miller, among others.

It carried such diverse work as William Cullen Bryant's translation of the *Iliad* and General George Custer's *Life on the Plains,* which was still running when the events on the Little Bighorn cut it short. Yet it succumbed in 1878 and had to sell out to its rival, the *Atlantic.* There was then, as there is now, only a limited market for intellectual magazines in America.

Otherwise, the field was broadening and deepening. Fletcher Harper's agile brain conceived *Harper's Bazar* (it did not become *Bazaar* until 1929), with its fashion plates, which for years came directly from the magazine's great Berlin counterpart, *Der Bazar.* Another publishing house joined Harper's and Scribner's with a literary periodical when *Lippincott's* magazine appeared in 1868, conservative in tone but the best printed in its category and consistently high in its quality. It was *Lippincott's* that began the practice of printing complete novels in a single issue—Wilde's *The Picture of Dorian Gray* was one of its major successes—and it also introduced Sherlock Holmes to American audiences. Later, it printed Paul Laurence Dunbar's works, Mary Roberts Rinehart's first novel, and Carolyn Wells's first detective fiction. It disappeared finally in 1914.

Following the Harper-Scribner-Lippincott tradition, *Appleton's Journal* began publishing in 1869 and soon established itself as a magazine of tremendous variety. Its most notable editor, Oliver Bell Bunce, originated in its pages the work that finally appeared in book form as *Picturesque America,* with Bryant's name as editor, although Bunce did the work. The pictures and sketches that made this work so notable as a view of late-nineteenth-century America appeared first in the magazine. *Appleton's* never quite achieved success, despite its enticing variety, and died in 1881.

With the resources of their houses to draw on, these magazines which were products of the great book-publishing firms were able to do remarkable things. *Scribner's,* for example, published in 1873 and 1874 a long series, "The Great South," by Edward King, with many illustrations by J. Wells Champney. It ran for 450 pages in successive issues of the magazine, and employed more than 430 engravings. Author and artist traveled together to get the material, traversing more than 25,000 miles by carriage and stagecoach and in the saddle. The whole project cost the magazine $30,000, which it more than retrieved when the series appeared in book form.

Scribner's enjoyed greater success than any other publishing house venture except *Harper's* until 1881, when the book publishers and the magazine publishers had a falling out. As a result, the magazine split off and changed its name to the *Century Illustrated Monthly*. Holland died that year, to be succeeded by Richard Watson Gilder, one of the most noted literary figures and editors of his day.

The *Century* got off to a spectacular start with a vast series of Civil War articles by the generals who had directed the battles, and by such civilians as Mark Twain. Grant's pieces, four of them, for which the magazine paid him $1000 each, later became the basis for his *Memoirs*, published by Twain's subscription firm in Hartford. Converted into book form, this series became *Battles and Leaders of the Civil War*, a famous set of books which the company published for decades. It earned more than $1 million, and the *Century* followed it with Nicolay and Hay's *Lincoln*, for which it paid $50,000; that, too, became a standard book.

While Gilder remained as editor, and that was twenty-eight years, the *Century* remained one of America's best magazines, but when he died, there were no capable hands to take it up, and it too died at last in 1930, its circulation below 20,000. Scribner's, which had agreed not to start a new magazine in the same field for five years as part of the dissolution agreement, resumed its periodical under the firm name in January 1887, with Edward L. Burlingame as editor. This able man had a formula to meet the competition: deal with popular topics in a literary way, and charge twenty-five cents a copy as against the thirty-five charged by the others. It was a formula so successful that the magazine hit a circulation peak of more than 200,000 between 1910 and 1911, when it was hailed by the *Outlook* as "an important contribution to permanent literature." But it declined from that point on, with the dismal end result noted earlier.

Religious magazines had been a staple of the periodical press from the beginning, but after the Civil War they proliferated until they came to constitute a large class by themselves. Their number doubled between 1865 and 1885, from 350 to more than 650. Not many were of high quality. The monthly and quarterly reviews were ponderous, dull, full of theological scholarship, while the weeklies were lively enough but so full of petty controversy they seemed provincial. Sometimes the weeklies went so far in their denunciations of each other, and of their common enemies, that the ruling bodies of the churches passed motions of censure against religious papers in general.

The religious press—and the general magazines, on occasion—debated such fundamental issues as evolution and the afterlife, especially the possibilities of the existence of hell. They had reason to be concerned, too, with the condition of organized religion itself, which was losing a great deal of its fundamentalist grip on the population. More and more people inside and outside religious faiths were demanding that the churches worry less about which people were going to get into heaven and more about the role churches should be playing in society. These feelings erupted in both the secular and religious press, and even in popular novels.

It was now even possible for the agnostics, the atheists, and the freethinkers of various stripes to be heard. "Bob" Ingersoll was attacked violently in many quarters, but his pleas for atheism were printed in the best magazines and made him famous. There were at least a half dozen avowedly atheistic or agnostic magazines blooming in the latter part of the century.

As the end of the century approached, it was clear that the religious and secular press had been the focus for disclosing a great theological change occurring in American life, brought on by unprecedented criticism of the Bible on historical and literary grounds, the inroads made by scientific thought on lay thinking, the growth of the idea of evolution, and a vast reevaluation of man's moral nature.

In the denominational journals, toward the close of the century, there was less emphasis on more general news and greater attention paid to denominational news, supplemented by other kinds of religious reading. These periodicals, many of which had begun life looking like newspapers, were now uniformly magazines in size as well as in content. They were wise to make the change, and indeed had been forced to do so by the rapid rise of daily newspapers after the war, which made the periodicals seem both imitative and ineffective. The New York *Tribune* observed in 1890: "Religious papers have found a formidable competitor in the secular press, which now treats religious questions and news with an ability and a fullness that no religious paper can hope to excel. This has compelled the religious papers ... to develop new features of their own in which the secular press cannot compete with them."

The net result of this change, however, was the beginning of a decline in the religious press during the nineties, one that is still going on today. The suspensions and consolidations began slowly at first, and then more rapidly in this century. As *Zion's Herald* forecast accurately, as early as 1904, "The old-time religious paper is gone."

That was true, but since there were so many different kinds of religious periodicals extant—at least a dozen categories—there was no danger the religious press would disappear, although it might diminish. Today the emphasis in religious publication has swung from magazines to books. All the major religions are served by their own publishing houses, and some of these have become large organizations in their own right, with retail outlets around the country. Religious book publishing has also become a highly profitable subdivision of large general publishing houses. But the great days of the religious periodicals are gone.

In their period of ascendancy after the Civil War, the religious magazines enjoyed with secular periodicals the benefits of the rapid nationalization that was occurring in the nation. Nationalization meant a greatly increased audience for the magazines. A great homogenization of the American people was beginning, and the periodical press recorded the process, helping the rapid spread of magazines across the country. The centers of publication continued to remain in the East, however, as they do to this day, in New York, Philadelphia, and Boston.

Several cities drew attention to themselves with their magazines. St. Louis, by 1870 the third largest city in the country and the home of what came to be known as "the St. Louis movement," had as its chief ornament the *Journal of Speculative Philosophy,* which a critic in the *Educational Review* declared had "made St. Louis famous throughout the civilized world." Otherwise, the city was the home of a few magazines for women and some specialized journals, particularly in the medical field.

Chicago, however, was the Western city that posed the greatest threat to Eastern superiority. Its astounding growth was the wonder of the nation, but most people thought of it simply as the great commercial center west of the Alleghenies, and they were truly surprised to find by 1870 that it was also the focal point of considerable literary activity. During the sixties and seventies, nearly a hundred magazines with at least some literary flavor were published in the city, and the Lakeside Publishing Company was printing no fewer than nineteen magazines in different fields.

Among the other Midwestern cities, Cincinnati published a good many class (that is, quality) periodicals and story papers, while Toledo was the home of several others, especially the *Blade,* a weekly once edited by the humorist who signed himself "Petroleum V. Nasby."

San Francisco, ebullient, wild, growing, stood alone as the publishing center of the Far West. Its magazines were inclined to have the same characteristics as the city, especially the weekly and monthly miscellanies. The most famous of them was the *Overland Monthly,* made so because of the editorship of Bret Harte—or, more properly, Harte's contributions, since he was no editor. After Harte departed, the magazine was dead within five years.

Another San Francisco periodical to make its mark was the *Argonaut*, founded in 1877 by Frank M. Pixley, a rich California journalist. As with the *Overland*, one writer made it outstanding—Ambrose Bierce, who wrote a scintillating column called "Prattle." In his characteristic style, Bierce began his columnar chores with a solemn statement of intent: "It is my intention to purify journalism in this town by instructing such writers as it is worth while to instruct, and assassinating those that it is not."

In this new national market, there was a natural inspiration to try new ideas. Innovation was in the air as the magazine business gathered force in the latter part of the century. Old patterns still persisted, but there were those who were intent on pushing out the boundaries.

Ebenezer Butterick had produced something new even earlier, in 1863, when he devised in his tailor shop in Fitchburg, Massachusetts, the tissue-paper dress pattern that soon became familiar to millions of American women. So successful were Butterick's patterns that he moved to New York the following year, and in a short time headed a business growing so rapidly that he could hardly control it. One of the offshoots of this enterprise in 1872 was a fashion magazine called the *Delineator*, which had reached a circulation of 200,000 by 1888, and 500,000 in June 1894, running more than 200 pages an issue.

As time went on, the scope of the magazine broadened beyond fashion to include both fiction and articles, although most of it was light reading. Thus the form of the women's magazine was established for decades to come—a mixture of hammock fiction, fashion, and articles and departments covering every home activity. In the trade, this kind of publication came to be known as a "cookie-and-pattern" magazine. It was based on the belief that these were the primary interests of women and that they either could not or did not care to think about anything outside the home. By following this formula, the *Delineator* and other magazines made fortunes for a long period, until changing times and the changing position of women in society caught up with them. That did not happen to the *Delineator* until the nineteen-twenties.

One of the most radical changes in magazines during this time of innovation came with the advent of *St. Nicholas*, the first fresh voice in children's magazines since *Peter Parley*. It was the creation of

Roswell Smith, who had been one of the Scribner's founders, and its first editor was Mrs. Mary Mapes Dodge, whose *Hans Brinker and the Silver Skates* (written entirely from research in the New York Public Library) became a children's classic. Beyond any doubt, *St. Nicholas* was the best magazine for children ever published in America.

Beginning at an inauspicious time, during the Panic of 1873, the magazine was so beautiful physically and so warm and glowing inside that it captured an audience immediately—an audience that grew ever larger and more faithful. Its peak circulation was 70,000, under Mrs. Dodge's editorship. The contributors were the best writers for children available, and readers of that generation never forgot meeting in the pages of *St. Nicholas* such splendid company as *Little Lord Fauntleroy, The Hoosier School Boy,* and the *Recollections of a Drummer Boy*—along with *Two Little Confederates,* just to balance the Civil War scales.

Later on, *Tom Sawyer Abroad* ran serially, and Theodore Roosevelt contributed *Hero Tales from American History.* Kate Douglas Wiggin was a contributor, and so were Rupert Hughes, Brander Matthews, Robert Louis Stevenson, and G. A. Henty. Perhaps the most memorable of all *St. Nicholas's* pages, however, were those that carried Rudyard Kipling's *The Jungle Book.*

With contributors like these, it is easy to see why children who grew up with this magazine found it an experience they treasured all their lives. Like other magazines, however, when its great editor was gone, it began to wither. Mrs. Dodge died in 1905, and a succession of new editors and new owners could never restore the magazine to the glory it had enjoyed for the twenty-five years that she edited it. After so many changes that the original could scarcely be recognized, *St. Nicholas* was suspended in 1940, revived briefly in 1943, then disappeared.

Another fresh new voice in the waning years of the century was that of *Puck,* setting the tone for a kind of golden age of humorous magazines. This grandfather of the *New Yorker* began as a German-language comic magazine in New York, the work of a Viennese artist, Joseph Keppler.

The motto of the magazine, running under the impish figure of Puck himself, was the Shakespearean quotation "What fools these mortals be!" (familiar in our time at the masthead of the Hearst Sunday comics), and the magazine was intended to prove this aphorism. *Puck's* targets were primarily the political villains of the day and the corruption that followed in their wake. While the assault was carried partly in satiric pieces, it was the cartoons that constituted the main battery. "It is not refined humor that makes *Puck* a political power," said the *Critic* magazine, "it is the coarse strength of its cartoons, which thus far have been drawn almost uniformly in the interests of popular morality and political integrity." *Puck* also attacked the abuses of organized religion and the social nonsense of the day, but its general offering was light humor.

In time, as a result of its success, the magazine had rivals which surpassed it. *Judge* appeared for the first time in October 1881, founded by a dissident group of artists from *Puck*. By the time it hit its peak in the nineteen-twenties it was perhaps the best humorous magazine ever published in America. *Judge*'s major rival was *Life*, not the picture magazine of the thirties but the only humor magazine to challenge *Judge* successfully. It followed its rival by two years, and after an extremely discouraging start (nearly all of its third issue came back from the newsstands), it caught on with the public and reached a high point in 1887, when the drawings of Charles Dana Gibson, who was then not yet twenty-one, first appeared. His Gibson Girl became almost a symbol of the nineties—"this serene, self-reliant, beautiful American girl," as Dr. Mott calls her, noting that for nearly twenty years, while she flourished, she was accompanied by the Gibson Man—"square shouldered, firm-jawed, handsome, well groomed, self-possessed." They were unreal as people, but they epitomized the elegance of the Mauve Decade. For women, the Gibson girl was a model, while even the men tried to emulate the Gibson Man by shaving off their mustaches.

There were other significant magazine starts in the closing years of the century. The *Literary Digest* appeared on March 1, 1890, edited by Isaac Kauffman Funk, who had been a Lutheran preacher, a book and magazine publisher, a leader of the Prohibition Party, and a lexicographer of note. In 1888, Peter Fenelon Collier launched his *Collier's Weekly* as *Once a Week;* the name change came in 1895. P. F. Collier, as his firm name was established, made a fortune out of selling "library sets" of standard authors on the installment plan and by mail, disposing of 50 million of these books by such methods in the last three decades of his life. But it was his magazine that made his name known all over the country, beginning with its superb coverage of the Spanish-American War in pictures and text.

In the women's field, the *Woman's Home Companion*, in our time a household word, began to be issued under that title in January 1897, having started as the *Home* in Cleveland, Ohio, early in 1874. The title change reflected the editor's opinion that the word "lady" had been abused and that "the noblest ambition of our end-of-the-century femininity is to be a 'woman.' . . . The use of 'lady' as a synonym for 'woman' is vulgar."

In the same year that the *Companion* was issued under its new name, another appeared under the same circumstances. *McCall's* magazine, like the *Delineator*, began as an outlet for the dressmaking patterns of a Scot named James McCall. The magazine had started life as *The Queen: Illustrating McCall's Bazar Glove-Fitting Patterns*, in 1873.

As the century ended, the first generation of twentieth-century magazines was in existence, with its roots put down more or less solidly and prepared to dominate the scene until new forces rose in publishing to create different ways of interpreting the American scene than had been known before.

14

Book Publishing
and the Mass Market

WHILE THE NEWSPAPERS were investigating politics and the magazines
were expanding their cultural range in every direction, book publishing was finding new ways to reach the mass market, and in doing so
was disclosing for future generations a great deal about nineteenth-
century American life.

Books encompassed everything that was being done in newspapers
and magazines, while adding an extra dimension of their own. They
might feed the magazine business, and sponsor part of it, but they
remained a different kind of enterprise. In a day when gentlemen
crooks like Jim Fisk could become public heroes (to Godkin's disgust), the book publishers were a breed apart. They had their eccentricities but they were not clinically egocentric, like so many of the
newspaper giants. They were idea men, as were the best of the magazine publishers, but they also thought of themselves as keepers of a
literary heritage, as well as educators of the masses.

There was an air of dignity, even of austerity, in their offices. When
fire broke out in the Harper offices one day about lunchtime, the
Harper brother who happened to be at his desk calmly removed, with
no undue haste, all the undeposited cash that happened to be lying
about before he walked out of the building. This had been his first
thought.

Publishers were not unaware of commerce, in short, and struggled
hard against each other for their share of the booming mass market,
but for the most part they did it with a gentlemanly approach that

would have resulted in their early fleecing if they had used such methods in the cutthroat atmosphere of Wall Street, where manipulators like Fisk and Daniel Drew ate such lambs for breakfast. The publishers knew all about piracy, and competition forced them to practice it, but the best of them paid British authors anyway, and agitated for international copyright for more than a half century. Piracy came to an end because the publishers themselves demanded it, and virtually forced a reluctant government to write and enforce international copyright law. No evidence exists that businessmen in any other occupation ever asked the government to regulate them in the name of fairness.

There was a continuity in the publishing business that did not exist in the other media. The great houses that had started before the war —Wiley, Harper, Appleton, Scribner, among others—were being carried on after it by sons and eventually grandsons well into the twentieth century, while newspaper and magazine publishers and editors came and departed. The boom-and-bust character of the American business cycle destroyed many of the lesser publishing houses, but the leaders, although some were shaken, survived. When the unthinkable happened at the end of the century, and the house of Harper not only went bankrupt but fell into the predatory hands of the Morgan interests, it was quickly reorganized, Morgan got out of it, and the house went on to new distinctions.

No better evidence of the unique character of publishing, in this respect, can be found than the fact that more than a hundred houses begun in the nineteenth century have survived into the present, and several of the leaders predate the Civil War. The fact that they have been able to survive while so many of their business practices remain relatively unchanged in a technological society is a tribute to their solidity as institutions, as well as their resistance to change.

The nature of both newspaper and magazine publishing has altered radically in this century. In periodicals, nearly all the mass-market publications are products of enterprises begun in the twenties and thirties. As for newspapers, none of the leaders today bear any resemblance to those of the eighties or nineties.

In the exploitation of the nineteenth-century mass market, a kind of publishing grew up, stemming from the first paperback revolution, that had its own dynamics and exists today in some aspects of paperback publishing. It began as early as 1861 with the publication of Mrs. Henry Wood's *East Lynne* by the New York firm of Dick & Fitzgerald, whose list was otherwise principally occupied with cheap home entertainment books. This sentimental soap opera, set in England and written by a British author, was the forerunner of a phenomenally successful genre. Published first in paperback at seventy-five cents, it was so successful that the Chicago printing firm of M. A. Donohue & Co., founded the same year, turned out more than 400,-000 copies for several publishers. By the time Mrs. Wood died in 1887, at least a million copies had been sold, and it continued to sell into the twenties. Like *Uncle Tom*, it was translated to the theater and played on virtually every stage in America, in tents and in "opera houses," until the announcement "Tomorrow night, East Lynne" became a part of the language.

A year after *East Lynne* came *Lady Audley's Secret*, by Mary Elizabeth Braddon, another English writer, which made so much money for her London publisher that he built a villa with the profits and called it Audley Lodge. In America, the book appeared first in Frank Leslie's *New Family* magazine; then Dick & Fitzgerald brought it out in paper at fifty cents.

More lasting than either of these ladies was the success of the woman who called herself Ouida, a baby-talk contraction of part of her real name, Marie Louise Ramée. Ouida lived in a fantasy world she never outgrew, which may be understandable in view of the fact that her father was a real-life Scarlet Pimpernel, who made mysterious visits to France and eventually died there, it was said, in the street fighting of the Revolution of 1848. His daughter began to call herself Marie Louise de la Ramée when she was still a young girl, and invented a background to go with the name. Of her several books, all of them implausible stories of intrigue and adventure, two of them made her an international figure: *Under Two Flags*, and *A Dog of Flanders*. The former was the first of the Foreign Legion novels. Published in this country by Lippincott in hard covers at two dollars, it ran through any number of paper editions at ten to twenty cents, and finally reappeared as a memorable motion picture with Claudette Colbert and Ronald Colman. *A Dog of Flanders* became a well-loved children's classic, still read today.

Sentiment and romance were the ingredients of all these books. They were escape literature, escape from the realities of industrial America and its pressing social problems, and were not entirely what came to be known as "cheap" publishing, meaning in content as well as price. R. D. Blackmore's *Lorna Doone*, for example, was no literary masterpiece but it was not *Lady Audley's Secret* either. It celebrated old virtues that seemed in danger of disappearance—love of nature, simple narrative, "good" people in rural surroundings. In London, eighteen publishers rejected *Lorna Doone* before it was published in 1869, but by the time Harper's pirated it in 1874, it was on its way to a million-copy sale.

Among the virtues that older people feared were endangered was simple humanity, which seemed lost in the corruption of marketplace and government. That was why Dodd, Mead & Co. had a small gold mine in E. P. Roe's *Barriers Burned Away*, a novel based on the aftermath of the Chicago Fire. Roe, a Presbyterian minister from Highland Falls, New York, rushed to Chicago after the event and was deeply impressed by the way catastrophe brought people together. Topical and badly written it may have been, but although it seems unreadable now, it was still selling in the forties and had reached nearly 5 million.

This kind of publishing reached its logical climax between 1875 and 1893, when the country was inundated with paperbound "libraries," an event often called the Second Paperback Revolution. Here the publishers were exploiting the new mass market in the same way the newspaper and magazine people had done, but with their own kind of product. The result nearly ruined the industry.

The Beadle Dime Novel had set off this second "revolution," but its successes were equaled if not eclipsed by what happened after 1875, the year Donnelley, Lloyd & Co., of Chicago, began to publish their famous Lakeside Library. These were quarto volumes, set double-column, and sold for ten cents. The publishers' prospectus declared: "The great, popular want today is for Cheap, Good Literature. Dime novels are issued by the million, and good books by the thousand, but to the mass of readers the one is as distasteful as the other is inaccessible."

Donnelley made them accessible, first on a semi-monthly basis, then three times a month, and at last once a week. It was publishing on the cheap, since the list was made up of American novels whose copyright had run out, and easily available pirated English novels. Beadle & Adams responded to this challenge with their Fireside Library, and soon there were the People's Library, of Myers, Oakley & Co., with Street & Smith as part owners; Frank Leslie's Home Library, and finally George Munro's Seaside Library. By the fall of 1877, there were at least fourteen of these "libraries" in circulation. Munro was proving the most successful, with titles like *East Lynne*, *John Halifax, Gentleman*, and *Jane Eyre*, and a busy press turning out a novel every day.

Never likely to let a moneymaking opportunity escape them, the Harper brothers took notice of the phenomenon in 1878, issuing the Franklin Square Library at the same ten-cent level as the cheap publishers. Isaac K. Funk, not quite yet the founder of Funk & Wagnalls, tried quality paperback publishing with his Standard Series, while Dodd, Mead began to put out E. P. Roe in twenty- and fifty-cent editions. Henry Holt, who had joined the old-line leaders with his own publishing house, established a Leisure Moment Series in 1883, and before long Houghton Mifflin, Appleton, Scribner's, and other major, established houses were in the business.

While this dignified kind of exploitation was going on, a maverick named John B. Alden, who had been a secondhand book dealer in Chicago, appeared in New York in 1879 and threw the paperback market into an uproar with his Acme Editions, which were cloth-bound books selling for fifty cents. He followed this with a dollar series, the Aldus Editions, distinguished by their better paper and printing. He further alarmed the establishment by putting out what he termed Revolutionary Pamphlets, three-cent editions of Shakespeare plays or Macaulay essays. This became the Elzevir Library in 1883, with slightly higher prices—two to fifteen cents.

The old houses and the booksellers were alarmed by this "Revolution in Books," as Alden grandly advertised his enterprise. He boldly stated his intent to overturn standard book-publishing practices with his cheap editions and his marketing technique, which was designed to undercut the retail bookstores by using department stores and other high-discount outlets. The book trade journals and associations raged at him, predicting that this kind of low-profit publishing would end in bankruptcy. Alden agreed. He thought it would be the bankruptcy of the other publishers—but they were right, and he asked for an assignation in 1881.

Alden had made a lasting impact on the business, however. His smaller and more convenient books ended the quarto craze, and the libraries began to appear in twelvemo editions, which in this century were popularly known as "pocket books," even after the phrase infringed the title of the publishing division which adopted that name.

The paperback "pocket book" was now the new king, and with Alden's failure (he later came back to the business as a cheap-book publisher), an even more flamboyant exploiter took over the mass-market field. He was John Lovell, a Canadian who came to New York in 1875 and began to issue cut-price sets of English books. He followed that in 1882 with Lovell's Library, standard and popular reprints in bright colors for a dime, mixing classics like *Vanity Fair* and the trashiest of sentimental novels with complete indifference. He soon had two new series, one at fifty cents and another at a dollar.

That set off another flood of series imitating Lovell's—a greater inundation of books in the new size than even the quartos had produced in the seventies. When the popularity of these was nearly exhausted, the tide swung to clothbound titles at twenty-five to fifty cents. By 1887, twenty-six libraries were on the market, their prices ranging from a dime to a dollar and their content varying from the cheapest romance to the classics.

The beginnings of the book club were here. It was an idea that had been approached before the Civil War, when the American Tract Society, distributing its millions of publications everywhere a piece of paper could be carried, inaugurated a "Tract of the Month" program. Now Funk & Wagnalls, whose series was called the Standard Library, compiled a subscription list of 16,000 people who agreed to pay four dollars a year for the privilege of getting a book every two weeks.

From the beginning, it had been obvious to old hands in the publishing houses, including those who had been forced by competition or greed to get into the struggle, that this kind of low-profit book selling could only end in disaster. As the eighties closed, these numerous prophecies were being fulfilled. The market was glutted with "libraries," profits were sinking in key with the quality of the product, and the remainder stocks were forming huge piles. In desperation, novels were even being hawked on the streets, like newspapers. Lovell tried to save his skin by an audacious plan to buy up thousands of sets of plates from the other publishers and unite his rivals in what amounted to a trust, the United States Book Company. In the hands of a more competent businessman it might have worked, but Lovell was essentially a snake-oil salesman and his grand scheme failed in 1893. That marked the end of the Second Paperback Revolution, although some of the companies survived it and went on publishing.

While the whole episode had been sordid enough in some respects, considering the pirating, the price cutting, and the pushing on the market of huge quantities of junk, the revolution had also brought many of the classics and a long list of "good books" to the attention of people who had never heard of them before. The horizons of the mass audience had unquestionably been widened, and with that, the way had been opened for the modern bestseller, whose titles were beginning to be listed for the first time about the turn of the century.

Children were also beneficiaries of the new mass-market publishing. They and their parents were reading Mark Twain avidly and, on the other side of the coin, were absorbing the adventures of Horatio Alger, Jr.,'s heroes, who were false models in themselves but managed to convey a great deal of information about the places they lived in. Alger told his readers much more about New York than he did about real people leading real lives. There was even more truth in *Treasure Island*, which appeared for the first time in Boston in 1884. A year later came *A Child's Garden of Verses*, so beloved for generations. At the same time and again in Boston, *Heidi* made her appearance on the scene. Most of the best-loved children's classics appeared within a few years of each other: *Five Little Peppers and How They Grew* and *Uncle Remus*, both 1880; *Black Beauty*, 1890; *Bob, Son of Battle*, 1898; *Beautiful Joe*, 1894; *Age of Fable*, 1882.

The war of ideas going on in the magazines and newspapers during the closing decades of the nineteenth century was not diminished by being placed between book covers. General Lew Wallace, for example, came to write *Ben-Hur* after a train conversation with Robert Ingersoll, in which he found himself arguing the divinity of Christ with the atheist and discovering that he was ill informed. That impelled him to make a study of the life of Christ, and his famous novel was the result. Its long life, tremendous sales (well over 2.5 million), and lasting popularity were due not only to its basic narrative strength but to its elemental theme—the sacred and the profane, religion and sex. It was a theme that would be the key to hundreds of other successes in this century.

Ben-Hur also made publishing history in another way. In 1913, Henry Hoyns, the sales manager of Harper's, sold Sears, Roebuck & Co. a million copies in one order, the largest single order in the history of the business.

An indication that the country was changing was the popularity in the eighties of a pro-Catholic book, Ludovic Halévy's *L'Abbé Constantin*, after many decades during which anti-Catholicism had made bestsellers out of other books. In some respects, however, things remained the same. The huge success of a minor eccentricity like *Mr. Barnes of New York*, by Archibald Clavering Gunter (who published it himself), was based on delight in the fictional depiction of an American cleverly outwitting Europeans. It was another basic formula, so successful that Gunter turned out two novels a year to supply the demand, thirty-nine all told in two decades. The title itself inspired a wave of imitators—"*Mr.*" (and sometimes "*Miss*") of one place or another—until Gunter silenced them with his own parody, *Miss Nobody of Nowhere.*

Some evidence that a large body of readers now existed capable of appreciating good literature was provided by the popularity of Tolstoy in the eighties. *War and Peace* was published in New York in 1886. There were two editions, one in six small volumes at $5.25 in cloth and $3 in paper, the other in three volumes of Harper's Franklin Square Library at twenty cents each. The book had been published in Russia two decades earlier. Thomas Y. Crowell issued *Anna Karenina* in the same year, and it enjoyed a larger success than it might have had because of the attempts of moralists to suppress it.

In fact, good writers—as opposed to those who were turning out the sentimental romances of these years—became so popular in the nineties that they created a phenomenon never seen before or since in America. Writers had fan clubs, so to speak, and were treated as public celebrities in the manner of pop singers today. The clubs were devoted mostly to discussing and reading the work of their favorites, and they were part of the mania for joining organizations that swept America toward the end of the century. The General Federation of Women's Clubs had been organized, and so had the Chautauqua Literary and Scientific Circle. Clubs devoted to Robert Browning and his works were extremely popular, and there were similar circles which met to consider Kipling, Omar Khayyám and the *Rubáiyát*—even Henry George, whose *Progress and Poverty* had appeared, and Francis Bellamy, whose *Looking Backward* was a leading social topic.

The publishing business supplied this public, as it did the mass market for sensation and romance, with books that, still far from being distinguished examples of bookmaking, were increasingly better-appearing, with more and finer illustration. Thus the publishers were penetrating a large part of the population, through newsstands, mail order, subscription, retail selling in bookstores and department stores. Schools, libraries, clubs, and cheap publishing had created a voracious public for books.

Sometimes a single author could make the reputation of a publisher. F. N. Doubleday was the second new major publisher to appear before the century's end (Henry Holt preceded him), and it was Kipling who was a major factor in putting his house on a solid basis. By the time the author died in 1936, Doubleday (George Doran had joined the firm, making it Doubleday, Doran & Co.) was still selling more than 100,000 copies of Kipling's works every year.

Kipling inspired the major "literary fever," as it was called, in the nineties. His popularity reached a peak in 1899 when he lay ill in New York, near death, the busy street roped off outside so traffic would not disturb him, hourly bulletins issued by the doctors. Then he suddenly recovered and went home. As he complained with some bitterness later on, the public apparently never forgave him for not dying in New York. His sales began to fall off immediately afterward.

The major "fever" to compete with Kipling was the one surrounding George Du Maurier and his novel *Trilby*, the story of an Irish girl and her adventures in Paris, where she not only posed in the nude but came under the influence of the evil hypnotist Svengali, whose name soon became a household word. The book appeared first serially in *Harper's Monthly*, where it was bowdlerized by removing references to models posing in what was known as "the altogether" and to people having mistresses, as well as passages which appeared anti-Catholic. When Harper's published the book, the deletions were restored, on the assumption (which has prevailed until recently) that book readers are more tolerant than those who read magazines.

Two years after it was published in 1894, Justin Huntly M'Carthy wrote in the pages of the *Gentleman's Magazine*: "Never in our time has a book been so suddenly exalted into a bible. It flowed in a ceaseless stream over the counters of every bookshop on the American continent. It was discussed in the dialect of every state in the Union. Clergy of all denominations preached upon it from their pulpits. Impassioned admirers, for the most part women, formed societies and debated over the moralities and the possibilities of the altogether. . . . Finally, somebody made a play of it and fanned an adoration that has not yet begun to flag higher and higher above the fever line of the human thermometer. The delight of the Republic became a delirium when *Trilby* took incarnation in the body of Miss Virginia Harned."

Trilby was a national phenomenon like *Uncle Tom*. There were Trilby songs, Trilby parodies (*Drilby*), a burlesque opera (*Thrilby*), and a Trilby circus. A Florida town was named for her, with the names of characters in the book given to the streets. There were, in addition, a Trilby shoe, Trilby hams, Trilby sausages, a Trilby hearth brush. Since Trilby O'Farrell had small feet, "Trilbies" became slang for them. Trilby appeared in advertising, and she was debated up and down the country. This "fever" lasted an incredible ten years, while Harper's, which had paid only $10,000 outright for the book, made so much money that it generously sent Du Maurier a check for $40,000 against royalties in 1895.

It is hard to explain the Trilby craze in terms of the American character, but much easier to understand why Charles M. Sheldon's book *In His Steps*, which first appeared in 1896 as a series in the *Chicago Advance*, a Congregationalist weekly, has since sold more than 2 million copies in America, according to Dr. Mott, who corrected Dr. Sheldon's highly optimistic estimate of 8 million in the United States and 12 million in Great Britain and Europe. Mott estimates total worldwide sales at about 6 million. The reason for the book's success is not difficult to determine. Sheldon, a young Congregationalist minister, was first to raise the question, What would Jesus do if he returned and saw the state of the nation? Readers were thus able to pass judgment vicariously on the world they had made without fear of immediate retribution.

If Americans were religious, or believed they were, they were also lovers of their own humor, and the publishers exploited that vein too, with books recounting Davy Crockett's adventures, the letters of Petroleum V. Nasby, the stories of Artemus Ward, and such regional classics as Edward Eggleston's *The Hoosier School-Master*. More popular than any of these, however, was *David Harum*, by a Syracuse banker named Edward Noyes Westcott, who unfortunately died six months before his homespun novel was published. Issued in 1898 at $1.50, *David Harum* was still selling in the nineteen-forties, when its total sales had reached nearly 2 million.

As always, Americans were fascinated by their own history, and the nineties saw the beginnings of a long period when the romantic historical novel was the most popular reading in the nation, supplanting the sentimental romance. That was a step upward. These books were much better written, for the most part, and although the history was of an extremely dubious accuracy, at least it gave people a sense of their past—something that seemed to be disappearing by the nineteen-sixties.

When the bestseller list first began to appear in 1895, in the pages of a new magazine, the *Bookman*, it was clear that the book-publishing business had supplanted both newspapers and magazines not only as a source of entertainment but as the chief purveyor of information and ideas in America.

15
The Media as Activists: I

Since the days when James Gordon Bennett, Sr., proclaimed himself the people's only defense against the iniquities of the money men in Wall Street, the concept had been growing of the press as a "watchdog" over government and business, on behalf of the public. Today the effort is often made to depict this as a historic role assigned by the First Amendment, but, as we have seen, that was not the case. The potential for the role was always there, and certainly the people who demanded a First Amendment had that idea foremost in mind, but there was no effort to implement it until Bennett arrived.

At the beginning Bennett thought of himself as a public defender, but that concept changed as his wealth and his madness increased, and his son had no regard for the public interest whatever. Greeley was a sincerely dedicated defender, but sadly permitted his personal thirst for the presidency to diffuse his dedication. Dana could have been one of the most potent public defenders on record if he had not lost his early idealism. Henry J. Raymond was even more a victim of political ambition than Greeley, but the paper he created was the first to give evidence, after he had gone, of how powerful a role the newspaper could play in behalf of the public—the role Jefferson had envisioned.

After Raymond's death, the *Times* had been directed for a while by his friend and partner, George Jones, the business manager, who relied for editorial direction on three outstanding editors who succeeded each other: Louis J. Jennings, John Foord, and Charles R.

Miller, Jr. It was Jennings and Jones together who directed the exposure of the Tweed Ring—one of the finest hours in the development of the *Times* and a significant episode in media history.

William Marcy Tweed, the sachem of Tammany Hall, was one of the most accomplished plunderers of a city which, like Boston and Chicago, had suffered from corrupt city governments almost since its founding. Tweed began his remarkable career as a member of the Common Council in 1852, and amassed a fortune through the prevalent mode of streetcar franchises, city land sales and other such devices. In 1868, he and a gamy cast of municipal scoundrels were swept into New York's chief public offices by a Tammany landslide, and the most gigantic frauds in the city's history began.

On July 8, 1871, the *Times* published an exposé of the Tweed regime. Tweed's answer to the charges provided some conception of the formidable task Jones faced. A month after they were made, Tweed held a giant rally in and outside of Tammany Hall to demonstrate solidarity. Governor John T. Hoffman, who was in Tweed's pocket, sat beside the boss, and near him was Samuel J. Tilden, chairman of the Democratic State Committee. Jim Fisk was one of the principal speakers; only a year before, he and Jay Gould had precipitated Black Friday on the stock market.

Not long after the rally, Tweed solemnly called in six eminent citizens to inspect the city's books, and in a few hours they certified the records as correct and well kept—a task that would have taken accountants three months to accomplish. One was John Jacob Astor, the city's chief landlord. Another was Moses Taylor, a banker and railroad investor, who had been Cyrus T. Field's partner in laying the Atlantic Cable; Field's brother, David, was later Tweed's chief lawyer. On the list, too, was Edward Schell, another rich banker, one of whose four brothers, Augustus, later succeeded Tweed as head of Tammany. Ironically, a fourth member was Marshall O. Roberts, one of the *Sun*'s owners, who had profiteered during the Civil War by chartering and selling steamships to the Union.

It was said that this *ad hoc* committee had been advised that they would get tax relief in return for their cooperation. Others asserted that they were threatened with sharp tax increases if they did *not* cooperate. Either way, Tweed controlled them. To underscore the point, he spoke to several of the *Times*'s largest advertisers, who obliged by removing their advertising. At the same time, there were questions raised about whether the paper really held title to the land it stood upon.

Jones persisted. A new article disclosed that Tweed had padded the city payroll with 1300 people who were described as "rowdies, vagabonds, sneak thieves, gamblers and shoulder-hitters." These hoodlums were engaged in such activities as painting park lamps on rainy days, making it necessary to redo them. The response to this revelation came from Jones's fellow editors, rather than from Tweed. The *Sun*, quite naturally, had already excoriated the *Times*, but so had the *World* and other papers. Now Dana himself sneered: "The decline of *The New York Times* in everything that entitled a newspaper to respect and confidence, has been rapid and complete. Its present editor, who was dismissed from the London *Times* for improper conduct and untruthful writing, has sunk into a tedious monotony of slander and disregard of truth, and black-guard vituperation. . . ."

There was no truth in this charge against Jennings. Dana did not like him because he was English, and because he was married to an actress, an occupation still only a step away from whoredom in the public mind.

Tweed was resourceful. He tried to buy control of the *Times* through a deal with Raymond's widow, who held thirty-four shares of the paper's stock, using Gould and Cyrus Field as front men; but Jones saw through that plot easily and declared editorially that *"no money"* would persuade him to sell any of his own stock, which would be necessary for someone else to gain control.

As is so often the case, Tweed was broken by a single disgruntled individual, James O'Brien, who besides being sheriff had been head of the Young Democrats. He was a Tammany insurgent with ambitions to get a larger share of the graft, and he hoped to replace Tweed. O'Brien had a friend and agent whom Tweed had just appointed county auditor, not knowing the connection between the men, and through this channel O'Brien obtained the documentary proof of Tweed's corruption and laid it one night on Jennings' desk. It was material copied straight from the city ledgers.

There was a final desperate move on Tweed's part to get Mrs. Raymond's stock, taking advantage of the fact that she had been separated from her husband, apparently over his affair with Miss Eyting, and needed money. But that failed, too, and the *Times* laid before the public the proof that O'Brien had provided. Editorially, it reminded the other papers of their neglected duties as defenders of the public:

> We apprehend that no one will complain of a lack of facts and specifications in the articles to which we now call the reader's attention; and that not even the *Tribune* or any other of the eighteen dai-

lies and weekly papers that have been gagged by Ring patronage will be able to find an excuse for ignoring the startling record presented here, on the ground that it is not sufficiently definite.

Tweed was now alarmed enough to attempt a truly desperate maneuver. He sent his chief bagman, Controller Richard B. "Slippery Dick" Connolly, to offer Jones a bribe of $5 million if he would pull back and hold off, and drop the case. Jones coldly refused.

Connolly could not understand such honesty. "Why, with that sum you could go to Europe and live like a prince," he exclaimed.

"Yes, but I'd know I was a rascal," Jones said, and later observed wryly, "I don't think the devil will ever make a higher bid for me than that."

Once the lid was off, the revelations followed rapidly, not only in the *Times* but in *Harper's Weekly*, where Thomas Nast's savage cartoons so aroused the public that Tweed tried to buy off the cartoonist with a half-million-dollar bribe.

When the entire fraud was disclosed, it appeared that the Tweed gang had gotten away with a sum estimated at somewhere between $75 million and $200 million, only a fraction of which was restored. Confronted with the disintegration of the structure he had built, Tweed was revealed not only as a criminal but as a savage, contemptible man who could say, and mean it, "If I were twenty or thirty years younger, I would kill George Jones with my own bare hands."

As it was, he had to face arrest and jail. He escaped but was captured in Spain by an official who recognized him from one of Nast's cartoons. Returned to the Ludlow Street jail, he died there. Connolly, however, got away with enough money to spend the rest of his life in luxury in Paris.

Coming as it did at a time when the newspapers were rooting out the corruption in the Grant administration, a cause in which the *Sun* was much more involved than it was aware of the stench under its own nose, the Tweed Ring scandal provided the *Times* opportunity for a remarkable demonstration of courage and defined a role for the media that everyone could understand. Partisans might argue, even in the face of the facts, that the papers were "out to get" Grant, but there was no possible way for anyone, even dedicated Democrats, to defend the Tweed Ring. The *Times* had obviously behaved admirably in the public interest against the most formidable odds.

This had been an honest effort on behalf of the public. There now occurred another demonstration in New York of how newspapers could pretend to play the role of public defender, while the real purpose was to gain circulation in a highly competitive situation. Jones was fighting for survival and for the public good. Joseph Pulitzer and William Randolph Hearst were fighting for circulation and consequently more money. Hearst, who didn't really need the money, was also engaged in the kind of power struggle which was one of the keys to his complex personality.

They were complicated men. Pulitzer's life is still not well understood today, primarily because of the gloss laid over it by the *World*, the great newspaper he founded, and the prizes and the School of Journalism he left behind him. Without question, he did make some substantial contributions to the practice of newspapering, but his personal eccentricities, in the manner of the Bennetts, and his senseless struggle with young Hearst, diluted much of what he might have accomplished in his lifetime. The *World* did not become the superb instrument by which it is remembered until after its founder's death.

Pulitzer professed a great deal more than he fulfilled. It is a melancholy fact that his chief contribution to the business was the invention of the formula that Hearst later took up and made famous—sex on the front page and a kind of spurious morality on the editorial page. Hearst had no discernible public morality in any real sense; his private sense of morality, although not many people believed it, was impeccable only in the area of sexuality, where he was something of a puritan. Pulitzer professed the highest sense of morality in every respect, but where the welfare of his paper was concerned, he appeared ready to make any kind of concession that might prove necessary.

As a young man, he was a strange sight, "about six feet two and a half inches tall, ungainly in appearance, awkward in movement, lacking entirely in the art of human relations." Born in 1847 of a good Jewish-Hungarian family, his early life was bizarre, to say the least. He left his native Mako, Hungary, at seventeen because he could not abide the man his widowed mother, whom he idolized, had married. He had been given a good education by private tutors, but he was not fitted for anything in particular. His ambition was to be a soldier. This "tall, scraggy youth with long, thick black hair, large head, and oversized nose," as one of his biographers has described him, wandered about Europe looking for an army to join. But even in a world torn by wars and revolutions, he could not find a recruiting sergeant who would take him. He was told he had weak eyes and an unpromising physique. He may also have given some indication of the approaching nervous disorder that would eventually make his life a living torture.

After being turned down by the Austrians, the French Foreign Legion, the British Army, and even by the old sea captains in Hamburg, where he tried to ship as a common seaman, Pulitzer would have gone home from the North Sea port except that he fell in with an agent of the Union Army in America, busy hiring promising young men who would get their passage while he pocketed the $500 bounty given for these recruits, who would then be substitutes for men who did not want to be drafted. Pulitzer signed up immediately.

Later he told several stories about his voyage to America. For a man whose watchword on his newspaper was "accuracy, accuracy, accuracy," Pulitzer was extremely vague about the details of his early life. One story, the best, said that he found out about the bounty on the way over, jumped ship in Boston Harbor, and collected the $500 himself. In any case, he enlisted for a year in the First New York (Lincoln) Cavalry, which had been organized by Colonel Carl Schurz.

Pulitzer found army life intolerable once he was in it. His most prominent characteristic was his incessant asking of questions, and he despised anyone who withheld information. These were admirable qualities for journalism, but hardly useful in the military. His skirmishes on the battlefield were far outnumbered by those he fought in the barracks and on the parade ground. Once he was nearly courtmartialed when he struck a noncommissioned officer.

Out of the Army in 1865, he was alone and broke in New York, sitting in City Hall Park with the other unemployed and staring out at the formidable façade of Park Row, where the offices of the *Times*, the *World*, the *Tribune*, the *Herald*, and the *Sun* were clustered. At the moment Pulitzer had no yearning to inhabit them. He only wanted to get a job and learn English. When a man with a crude sense of humor told him the best place to learn the language was in St. Louis, he made his way there—to the city which had the largest concentration of Germans in the country.

At least he could use his native tongue in St. Louis, and he was soon working on the *Westliche Post*, the leading German-language daily. In his first year, he mastered English, obtained a certificate of naturalization, and became the city's leading reporter, whose furious energy made him well known to everyone, particularly to the political leaders at the State House, where he spent a good deal of his time. Impressed with his vivid, knowledgeable reporting, these leaders decided he ought to run for the state House of Representatives.

As a legislator, Pulitzer was the same explosive human being he had been as a reporter. Only a year after he was seated, he shot and wounded a well-known lobbyist, but his numerous friends saved him from serious trouble. From the legislature he became one of St. Louis' three police commissioners, worked hard for the Liberal Republicans, and helped nominate Greeley in 1872. Pulitzer was one of those several newspapermen who had backed Greeley and were deeply disappointed by Uncle Horace's failure. He turned to the Democrats and became a lifelong member of the party.

Now he began a series of intricate movements in the newspaper business, during which he acquired a part interest in the *Post*, sold it at a profit, bought the bankrupt *Staats-Zeitung* for next to nothing, and sold its AP franchise to the *Daily Globe* for a substantial profit. With this money he studied law, was admitted to the bar, married a distant cousin of Jefferson Davis, and in 1878 stood at a crossroads in his career. He could have gone on to become a successful politician; and other roads were open to him. Instead, he chose journalism, and bought the St. Louis *Dispatch* for $2500. He had enough additional resources, $2700, to operate the paper for seventeen weeks, he estimated. Merging it with his first love, the *Post*, to form the *Post-Dispatch*, he was making $45,000 annually with it after the first three years.

From its first day, the *Post-Dispatch* attacked corruption, inspired by Pulitzer's slogan, "Never drop a big thing until you have gone to the bottom of it." Thus he joined the ranks of the crusaders, to become the most vociferous of the public defenders. It has always been dangerous for the media to defend the public. In Pulitzer's case, he was in trouble when a prominent lawyer whose activities had been attacked came in person to call the paper's chief editorial writer to account, in the old manner, and was killed in the resulting quarrel. But in spite of this and other episodes less sensational, the *Post-Dispatch* won public acceptance and respect as a fearless newspaper of unblemished integrity; and so it has remained to this day, still in the Pulitzer family and carrying on the crusading tradition he established.

Pulitzer was soon a rich man, ready to conquer New York if the opportunity offered. On his way to Europe in May 1883, seeking escape from his growing nervous restlessness, he stopped off in New York, where Jay Gould's representatives sold him the New York *World* for $346,000. Gould thought he had concluded a shrewd deal, since the paper had been struggling for life ever since its founding as a penny religious daily. He knew Pulitzer could afford it. The *Post-*

Dispatch was netting its publisher $85,000 a year by this time, and the *World* purchase was to be paid in installments.

Pulitzer believed he knew what to do with his acquisition. On the first day of publication under its new owner, the *World* printed something more than the usual grandiloquent statement of purpose. It was perhaps the finest expression of journalistic idealism ever written, and it is still carried today on the editorial page of the *Post-Dispatch*. The statement declared the purpose of a newspaper to be as follows:

> An institution that should always fight for progress and reform, never tolerate injustice or corruption, always fight demagogues of all parties, never belong to any party, always oppose privileged classes and public plunderers, never lack sympathy with the poor, always remain devoted to the public welfare, never be satisfied with merely printing news, always be drastically independent, never be afraid to attack wrong, whether by predatory plutocracy or predatory poverty.

The *World* also announced a ten-point platform. It was for the taxing of luxuries, inheritances, large incomes, and monopolies. It advocated abolishing all special privileges possessed by corporations. It demanded tariffs for revenue only, civil service reform, severe punishment for corrupt officials, and punishment for employers who tried to coerce employees in elections.

It would have been difficult to find a better definition of the newspaper as public defender—against all other institutions including poverty, which had not yet been institutionalized. What Pulitzer really meant by "predatory poverty" is still a mystery. It may have been no more than rhetoric.

There is little doubt about what the rest of the platform meant. Like the early Bennett, Pulitzer meant to attack privilege and corrupt government, and there was a great deal to attack. But there was something puzzling in the way he went about it. On the front page of the *World* the mixture was as before, brewed by the elder Bennett and improved upon by Dana—a blend of sex, scandal, and corruption. On the editorial page were well-written expressions of Pulitzer's intellectual idealism. In short, a front page for the workingman and an editorial page for intellectuals of Pulitzer's stripe. The result did not wholly please either class. The workers didn't know what Pulitzer was talking about on the editorial page, and the intellectuals deplored the *World*'s sensationalism.

It is fascinating to speculate what might have happened if William Randolph Hearst had never come to town. Pulitzer might have dropped, or at least toned down, the sensationalism and wound up as a competitor of the New York *Times* instead of the *Journal*. There was no pretense about his editorial page; he meant what he said. But he also understood that sex and crime sold newspapers, and it was necessary to meet Dana's *Sun* on those grounds if he expected to survive among the leaders. Dana's passing, so near Hearst's arrival, might have led to an alteration of a formula for which Pulitzer did not have much heart. His mind was on honest politics and the betterment of the human condition.

Hearst's mind was on making money. Among all the media entrepreneurs of the century, he was the only one who had been born rich, the son of Senator George Hearst, of California, who had made a fortune out of Nevada silver. His life had been shaped by his beautiful, artistic, cultured mother—a sharp contrast to her rough and ready husband—who took Willie to Europe when he was only nine and gave him the grand tour. Young Hearst grew up with a knowledge of art and culture gained from his mother, but he had inherited from his father a ruthless, driving ambition for power and achievement.

It was the kind of drive that made him drop out of Harvard at the end of his sophomore year, where he had lived luxuriously, learned nothing, and made contemptuous fun of the faculty, which included men of the stature of George Santayana and William James. While he was in Harvard, and on his frequent trips to New York, Hearst came to know and admire the *World*, particularly its front page. The editorial page left him indifferent; Hearst was no intellectual. He believed that Pulitzer had the right idea about making newspapers, and he conceived a passion to imitate him and, if possible, surpass him. Persuading his father to give him the San Francisco *Examiner*, which the Senator had acquired in settlement of a political debt, he took over the paper at twenty-four and began his legendary career.

Hearst made the *Examiner* a more flamboyant and sensational *World*, without the New York paper's editorial idealism. Since he could afford to hire anyone he liked, he surrounded himself with a brilliant staff of editors and writers who doubled the paper's circulation in the first year. By 1893 it was up to 60,000 and he passed the rival *Chronicle*. The kind of paper Hearst created was perhaps best expressed by Arthur McEwen, its city editor, who said that when he looked at the *Examiner*'s front page, he said, "Gee, whiz!" When he looked at the second page, it elicited an astonished "Holy Moses!" and the third page produced a bellowing "God Almighty!"

The ideas Hearst used were not particularly original. Essentially they were extensions and elaborations of what Bennett, Sr., had done in the *Herald* and Pulitzer in the *World*. The emphasis was always on mass appeal, on the sensational and the so-called human interest story. These were methods employed at the time on many American newspapers, but Hearst improved on them. The essence of the improvement was to get the best writers and reporters money could buy, and to add the new dimension of photography, done in the same sensational manner.

As a public defender, Hearst projected himself then and later as a man beyond the appeal of party politics, although he supported nearly all the parties at one time or another—a St. George in search of dragons intent on devouring honest citizens and middle-class taxpayers. It was easy for Hearst to go beyond party politics, because he had no real political convictions of his own. Nonetheless, his crusades were among the most formidable in an era of crusading.

This was the kind of man who came to New York in 1896, leaving the *Examiner* in competent hands, and started a new morning paper he called the *Journal*, with which he meant to repeat his San Francisco success—as he had intended from the beginning. The West Coast was meant to be his schooling, the East Coast his graduation present.

Having only recently conquered Dana, Pulitzer understood that he must fight the front-page battle of sex-and-crime all over again, and he had little heart for the task. A general physical failure, perhaps induced by the long struggle with Dana, had compelled him to retire from on-the-spot management of his paper in 1887. Worse, he was going blind, and his nervous affliction had half crippled him by this time. The worst manifestation was an extreme sensitivity to noise. He had made his apartment soundproof, and found he could edit his paper from there in relative comfort, unless some thoughtless editor consulting him should drop something, or crumble a piece of copy paper in his hand. That was enough to send Pulitzer into a pitiful attack of nervous frenzy.

As the disease developed, the restlessness it produced in him kept him traveling constantly. Like Bennett, Jr., he became a voluntary exile, moving about constantly for nearly twenty years, editing the *World* from wherever he happened to be. If he stopped at a hotel, he had to rent the rooms above and below and on both sides to ensure the quiet which was essential. Sometimes he crossed and recrossed the ocean without stopping. In spite of it all, he continued to edit the *World* closely, with incredible tenacity and intelligence. His curiosity never wavered.

Facing Hearst, he fought back, ill as he was, with courage but with
the mistaken idea that he could beat the young man at his own game.
He had established the *Evening World* in 1887, and the revenue from
this extra edition helped in the morning battle, but the profits which
Pulitzer had been able to build up through sound management could
scarcely match the millions in family fortune which were Hearst's
resources. Pulitzer dropped the price of the morning *World* to a
penny, so that he would at least be fighting on even terms in that
respect. The difference, however, was not only a financial one. It lay
in Hearst's genius for mass journalism, and Pulitzer's mistaken determination to hold that market no matter what it cost.

The Hearst formula was simple. He adopted Pulitzer's ideas wholesale, having admired them from the beginning, and then carried them
a step farther in extravagance and boldness. It was possible for him to
do this successfully because of his virtually unlimited resources and
because he had a better sense of the mass mind than Pulitzer,
although there was nothing in his background or his personality to
account for it. It was sheer instinct.

Pulitzer watched in frustration as Hearst hired away some of the
best men on his staff, and it was small consolation that he raided the
other papers as well. There were even literary figures like Julian
Hawthorne and Stephen Crane in the Hearst ménage. The *Journal*
excelled particularly in its art department, where Hearst, drawing on
his memories of the German comic cartoons he had seen while he was
with his mother in Europe, directed the creation of comic strips.
Richard Outcault drew the first of them, inventing a stick-figure character known as the "Yellow Kid" because the *Journal* used color, for
the first time in a newspaper, on the Kid's costume. The phrase
"yellow journalism," which came into popular use when Hearst fell
into public disrepute and later was applied indiscriminately to all
sensational journalism, was derived from the blameless "Yellow Kid,"
who had been designed only to entertain.

After Outcault came Rudy and Gus Dirks, with their "Katzenjam-
mer Kids"; Jimmy Swinnerton; and the creators of "Foxy Grandpa,"
"Happy Hooligan," "Alphonse and Gaston," and a dozen others. The
art department also employed a young artist named John Barrymore,
who frequently had to be rescued from neighboring bars.

The use of color was only one of the innovative procedures which
emerged from the *Journal*'s mechanical department, which was in the
charge of Hearst's close friend George Pancoast, a mechanical wizard
imported from the San Francisco *Examiner*. Pancoast set up the first
press capable of printing four to sixteen color pages, and it turned out

the first Sunday comic section in color, a revolutionary development which had lasting effects on American popular culture. The *Sunday Journal* was also the first to use halftone photographs printed on newsprint.

On the front page of the daily edition, whose makeup was much like the *World*'s, the *Journal* carried on crusades that Pulitzer and his staff had completely overlooked. In doing so, it foreshadowed the muckraking magazines of the early twentieth century, attacking the "criminal corporations" in a manner that would have given Hearst readers fatal convulsions at a later date. Hearst even hired Ella Reeve "Mother" Bloor, later a Communist Party heroine, to expose the evils of the packing industry, in the style of Upton Sinclair's *The Jungle*.

When it came to the editorial page, Hearst made no attempt to imitate Pulitzer's intellectual, high-minded appeal. He developed, instead, what he believed was a much more direct route to the masses. The editorials, most of which he wrote himself in the beginning, were done in his deliberate, distinctive style—short paragraphs, short sentences, simple words. Their content represented what Hearst professed to believe at the moment, ideas that he thought would move his audience: the eight-hour day, the direct election of United States senators, woman suffrage, federal income taxes (they were considered a blow aimed at the rich in those days), the rights of labor, and municipal ownership of public services. It was, in essence, a socialist platform designed to mobilize opinion and to portray Hearst as the champion of the downtrodden masses instead of as their exploiter.

One who was not fooled by what Hearst was doing was Godkin, who growled disdainfully on the editorial page of the *Post*: "A yellow journal office is probably the nearest approach, in atmosphere, to hell existing in any Christian state, for in gambling houses, brothels, and even in brigands' caves there is a constant exhibition of fear of the police, which is in itself a sort of homage to morality or acknowledgement of its existence."

It is difficult to understand today why it was that a circulation war in New York between two strong-minded newspaper publishers should have an effect on national opinion. That effect has been exaggerated by newspaper historians and underestimated by the academic historians, but there is no doubt that it existed. What Pulitzer and Hearst said and advocated was reprinted and discussed in other newspapers across the country, in pulpits, and from other public platforms. It was mistakenly believed by politicians that large blocs of votes could be swung by such strident appeals to the masses, and they respected the supposed power of this new mass medium. Their respect no doubt diminished when Hearst ran for mayor of New York and was soundly defeated, and declined further after he was later elected to the House of Representatives, where his influence proved to be near zero, not solely because he so seldom appeared in Washington.

But the crucial test of the new mass-media power, particularly as it applied to Pulitzer and Hearst, came when their struggle coincided with the Spanish-American War. It is still widely believed that Hearst started the war, and as proof there is cited the famous telegram, of dubious authenticity, from Hearst to the noted artist Frederic Remington, who had asked to be relieved of his Cuban assignment because nothing much was happening. "Please remain," Hearst is said to have cabled. "You furnish the pictures and I'll furnish the war." Later, Hearst was charged with having conspired to blow up the battleship *Maine* in Havana Harbor so as to implement his promise, an act so utterly out of character that no one with the slightest knowledge of Hearst would believe it.

In reality, Hearst's name is scarcely mentioned in present-day histories of the United States, and if it appears at all in specific studies of the Spanish-American War, it is usually no more than a footnote. The reason is that the war and the role of the media in it was a far more complicated matter than the flamboyant participation of Hearst and Pulitzer.

As the historian Frank Freidel points out, the possibility of war with Spain had existed since the Spanish authorities and the Cuban revolutionaries first began their lengthy and bloody struggle in 1868. The first phase ended ten years later, and an uneasy truce prevailed until the struggle resumed with even greater fervor in 1895. Pulitzer hired young Winston Churchill to report what was going on in Cuba, and he contributed some perceptive dispatches to the *World*. "My general conclusion," he wrote in one of them, "is that European methods of warfare are almost out of the question in a wild countryside," a hard truth the British regulars had learned more than a century before from the embattled farmers.

Other correspondents were less perceptive as the war dragged on into 1898, and there was a good deal of inaccurate reporting, exaggerating the condition of the ravaged island beset by hunger and disease. The situation seemed intolerable to many Americans, and public pressure began to build up on President McKinley and the Congress. Part of this pressure came from the press, whose most influential members had been skeptical about the revolution only three years before. "The most alarming Cuban revolutions have occurred in New York for many years—in speeches," the New York *Times* had advised, and the *Tribune* added, "It is doubtful whether any real attempt has been made to raise the standard of revolt in any quarter of the island. Revolutionists are most numerous and demonstrative in the cigar factories of New York or the cafes of Key West." The *Evening Post* and the *Herald* were equally uncommitted.

These comments had come in February 1895. By March the road to war had been opened with the kind of headline that inevitably precedes it: "OUR FLAG FIRED ON." A steamer had arrived in New York with the report that it had been fired on in the Windward Passage by a Spanish gunboat. In fact, the shots had been blank and the intent was to search the ship for contraband, but the jingo machine had been set in motion. "The next Spanish gunboat that molests an American vessel," said the *Sun*, "ought to be pursued and blown out of the water."

That crisis died down, but both the magazines and the newspapers were now openly debating the possibility of war with Spain. The *Literary Digest* asked, "Are Americans spoiling for war?" and concluded that they were, citing Manifest Destiny, a popular sympathy for revolutions in behalf of freedom, and the commercial possibilities for munitions makers. Opposition to intervention came largely from Democratic papers, particularly the Louisville *Courier-Journal*, whose noted editor, "Marse Henry" Watterson, deplored "counterfeit patriotism" and attributed war enthusiasm to those who could expect to profit from conflict.

The nature of the press in America in 1895 gave newspapers a predominant role in the national debate that was now beginning. The wave of popular ten-cent magazines like *McClure's* and *Munsey's* had only just begun, and they had not assumed the national importance they would have after the turn of the century. Only 30 per cent of the population lived in urban areas, and the bulk of the people, in rural areas and small towns, depended heavily on newspapers for information and entertainment, which were supplied by the 14,000 weeklies and 1900 dailies then extant. The national literacy rate was 88 per cent, possibly more, and newspaper readership had never been higher, equaling 25 per cent of the population that was ten years old or older. New York's numerous papers drew a combined circulation of 2 million from a total population of nearly 3 million, and the competition there and in every city was intense. New York had no fewer than fifteen dailies and more than twice as many weeklies, but even in a town as small as Emporia, Kansas, there were two dailies.

At the beginning of the agitation for war, it appeared that a cautious President and a somewhat less cautious Congress were the victims of hysterical jingoism on the part of the *Journal* and other Democratic papers, with the *World* and less committed newspapers joining in for the sake of circulation, while the Republican press stood more or less solidly behind the President and his party. But then, as the pressure built up, more and more of the conservative papers joined in the cry for intervention, until even the religious journals were proclaiming a "holy war." It is doubtful whether much of this clamor had any direct effect on the White House, but the effect on public opinion was unmistakable, and the groundswell favoring war that rose in the nation began to affect both Congress and the President.

The preceding administration of Benjamin Harrison had been accused by the "yellow" press of carrying on a pro-Spanish policy, and so the outcry that arose from these papers when it appeared that McKinley had no intention of changing course was understandable. But it went further than a simple difference of opinion. Again, there was the spectacle of an administration that was not ready to tolerate dissent from its policies, and was quite prepared to throw out the First Amendment if thought necessary. The line runs clear and true from the War of 1812 to Vietnam and Watergate.

In the case of McKinley, the administration made no outward show of resistance to criticism at first, but the time came when the President's Cabinet discussed the possibility of having the editors of the New York *Evening Post* and the Springfield *Republican* indicted for treason. It was becoming clear, however, that no matter what the pressure from newspapers and magazines might be, the jingoists in the Senate were more vociferous and more powerful. The Senate was seriously discussing finding the means to force McKinley's hand and make him declare war.

The newspapers had been struggling toward the achievement of some standard of fairness and accuracy in the news columns, retreating slowly from the bad old days, but now, in the heat of the interventionist debate, they began to show the old reckless disregard for truth they had exhibited in the days of the political, partisan press. It was a kind of last hurrah for the old days of journalism. The era of the lurid headline was far from over, of course, with the end of the

war, but in the twenties and afterward it was confined to a few sensational tabloids dealing with sex and scandal, or else to papers of the
far right or far left. Never again after the affair in Cuba was over,
even in the hysteria of the First World War, would newspapers headline a story with such an imaginative opening as: "The War Ship
Maine was Split in Two by an Enemy's Secret Infernal Machine."
That was in the *Journal*, but the *World* was just as fanciful in its desperate struggle against Hearst. No wonder Godkin wrote in disgust,
"Nothing so disgraceful as the behavior of these two newspapers ...
has ever been known in the history of journalism." While this was
patently untrue, the papers' conduct *was* a retreat to the past, and it
was shared by some organs in other parts of the country.

If the administration had no hesitation in finding treason among
respectable dissenting editors, many of these editors had no hesitation
in attacking such venerated figures as the Pope, who tried to inter-
vene in the cause of peace and was forthwith denounced for "Papal
meddling."

In the face of the attacks on him as weak and vacillating, McKinley
tried to draw the cloak of his office around him, resisting the pressure
to make him declare war in almost the same way that Presidents
Johnson and Nixon resisted pressure to stop warmaking. McKinley's
faithful secretary, George Cortelyou, wrote:

> The vile slanders uttered against him . . . have only tended to
> endear him to those of us who see him as he works here in the Execu-
> tive Mansion, early and late. . . . The sensational newspapers publish
> daily accounts of conferences that never take place, of influences that
> are never felt, of purposes that are nothing but the products of the
> degenerate minds that spread them before a too-easily-led public.
>
> One of the most absurd lies that have found currency is the one to
> the effect that the President sees only the favorable side of the corre-
> spondence which comes to the Executive Mansion. . . . The President
> sees everything, whether in the shape of mail, telegrams, or newspa-
> pers, that can indicate the drift of public sentiment. . . . The ranters in
> Congress, the blatherskites who do the talking upon the street-corners
> and at public meetings, and the scavengers of the sensational press
> misrepresent public opinion when they assert that this country is for
> war except as a necessity and for the upholding of the national honor.

While much of this defense was self-serving and some of it absurd,
on the other hand a majority of the American press, in attempting to
influence the nation's foreign policy, did concoct a series of news stories, editorials, pictures, and headlines which constituted the most

depressing display of unabashed jingoism in the history of American journalism. It shot the circulations of the *Journal* and the *World* well past the million mark, and it helped to stir the people into an emotional response which pushed the reluctant McKinley into a war that should never have occurred. The part the media played in this propaganda is not one of which they can be proud.

Once the war started, both the *Journal* and the *World* spared no expense to cover it. The cost of the entire circulation struggle between Hearst and Pulitzer has been estimated at figures varying from a half million to $8 million. It is certainly higher than the lowest figure, because Hearst spent that much on his own account.

Although its resources were considerably less, the *World* was not without distinguished coverage. To match Hearst's famous war correspondent, Richard Harding Davis, who became the prototype of the modern version and something of a national hero in his own right, Pulitzer sent Stephen Crane, whose *Red Badge of Courage* had appeared in 1895, as a correspondent. Crane, who had been living from hand to mouth doing pieces for the *Tribune* and the *Herald*, responded by filing some of the war's best stories. They were not tales of battle, for the most part, but of soldiers and soldiering—the kind of reporting Ernie Pyle was to do in the Second World War. He could cover the hard news just as capably, however, and proved it in his stories from Guantánamo Bay in June 1898, when the first American casualties were recorded: his detailed, informative story appeared on the *World's* front page. He was cited later for his bravery under fire.

Later, he made the mistake of describing too accurately the behavior of New York's Seventy-First Regiment in the charge up San Juan Hill, which brought down the patriotic wrath of Hearst, who charged that Pulitzer was slandering the heroism of New York's own sons. Colonel Theodore Roosevelt did not forgive Pulitzer for printing the story, and later, when he was president, his active animosity led to one of the more sordid presidential violations of the First Amendment. As for Crane, his cool disregard for his own safety in the field was, apparently, not only the result of personal courage but a feeling that his life was running out in any event. Soon after San Juan, he came home, broken in health; he had only two years to live.

Hearst's coverage of the war was accomplished in his usual magnificent style. He chartered a tramp steamer with a printing press and a small composing room in its hold, big enough to print an edition of the *Journal,* and set sail for Cuba himself with a crew of reporters and photographers.

The *Journal's* men not only covered the war, they fought in it on occasion. Early in the conflict a Hearst reporter named Karl Decker rescued the beautiful Evangelina Cisneros, daughter of an insurgent leader, from a Havana prison in an incident straight out of a bad movie. Hearst inflated this incredible episode to the proportions of an international incident, and it did much to arouse emotions at home and thus push McKinley further toward war. At the battle of Guantánamo Bay, Hearst himself headed a foray in a steam launch, in which he landed on the beach and captured twenty-six frightened Spanish sailors stranded there, delivering them as prisoners of war.

As a climax of the *Journal's* personal war effort, James Creelman, the paper's dignified chief correspondent, who was always "Mr. Creelman" even to the other reporters, personally led an infantry charge at the battle of El Caney, during which he was wounded. Creelman wrote about what followed in his book, *On the Great Highway*:

> Someone knelt on the grass beside me and put his hand on my fevered head. Opening my eyes, I saw Mr. Hearst, the proprietor of the New York *Journal*, a straw hat with a bright ribbon on his head, a revolver at his belt, and a pencil and notebook in his hand. The man who had provoked the war had come to see the result with his own eyes, and finding one of the correspondents prostrate, was doing the work himself. Slowly he took down my story of the fight. Again and again the tinging of Mauser bullets interrupted. But he seemed unmoved. That battle had to be reported somehow.
>
> "I'm sorry you're hurt, but"—and his face was radiant with enthusiasm—"wasn't it a splendid fight? We must beat every paper in the world."

Governor Sadler of Missouri half seriously proposed that Hearst send down five thousand of his reporters to free Cuba. If he had thought of it in time, no doubt the publisher would have done it.

The cost of the war was more than financial for Pulitzer, although that was serious in itself, since he had been compelled to reach deeply into his reserves. But his precarious health was worse than ever, and he had seen his newspaper so lowered in public esteem during the battle with Hearst that it had been banned, along with the *Journal*, from a good many homes, clubs, and libraries. Taking on two such opponents as Dana and Hearst in succession had nearly wrecked both Pulitzer and the *World*. In the years remaining to him, he tried to mend the damage, and succeeded with his paper; his health was beyond repair.

In Cuba, the small armies of Hearst and Pulitzer could charge about the landscape relatively unimpeded, participating in battles, suffering few conflicts with the military. In the Philippines, where there was so much more to be ashamed of, the administration dealt severely with the correspondents as part of a general effort to stifle dissent at home and to keep what it was doing under a Vietnam-Cambodia-Laos kind of secrecy. To draw the parallel once again, it was the conviction of the imperialists in the government and their commanders in the field that the insurrectionists would not be able to function if it were not for the encouragement they were getting from those in America who opposed the war. To that, the anti-imperialists replied with the charge, which was true, that the commanders in the Philippines and the government at home were censoring any news which reflected badly on either the military or the administration. In a magazine called *The Verdict*, George Luks, later a noted figure in the Ashcan School of painting in America, drew a cartoon captioned "The Way We Get the War News," showing a correspondent trying to wrote his copy while two generals with drawn swords surround him and a third holds him by the arms.

The fighting in the Philippines was much as it would be later in Vietnam, over much the same kind of terrain. There were atrocities on both sides, but the Americans went somewhat further. They took no prisoners, laid waste to villages, and shot down men, women, and children indiscriminately, in the fashion of Mylai. As Freidel has written: "On one notorious occasion, they shot up a wedding party. To elicit information from reluctant villagers they resorted to such Spanish techniques as the 'water cure.' ... Others were hanged briefly to refresh their memories."

When all this began to emerge from soldiers' letters home, even though some of the stories were repudiated and the American command went to extraordinary lengths to persuade some of the writers to repudiate themselves, there was a cry of outrage from the anti-McKinley portion of the press. But a stony apathy on the part of the public demonstrated once more that mass bigotries and obsessions are hardly affected by anything the media may say. The electorate sent McKinley back to the White House, and the anti-imperialists were thoroughly defeated, just as the horrors and immorality of Vietnam, both public and private, failed to prevent Nixon's election in 1972.

When the Philippine Insurrection finally ended, more Americans had been killed in it than in the Spanish-American War, and an estimated 200,000 Filipinos had perished. Hearings were held on the Army's brutality, and convicted officers got off with perfunctory reprimands. The dissenters, including the press, had failed to do any more than stir briefly the uneasy conscience of the American people.

One of the chief dissenters was Mark Twain, who declared angrily in a speech at the Lotos Club, in New York, that the American flag ought to be altered to have "the white stripes painted black and the stars replaced by the skull and crossbones. . . . It would be an entirely different question if the country's life was in danger, its existence at stake; then . . . we would all come forward and stand by the flag, and stop thinking about whether the nation was right or wrong; but when there is no question that the nation is in any way in danger, but only some little war away off, then it may be that on the question of politics the nation is divided, half-patriot and half-traitors, and no man can tell which from which."

Twain's assertion, so aptly descriptive of the American state of mind in 1973 (after nearly a half century in which nothing whatever has been learned by men in power), was somberly confirmed by the wave of public indignation against the newspapers that swept the country after McKinley was assassinated. The papers that had been printing the truth, or as much as they could get of it after censorship, about what had been going on in the Philippines, were condemned by a public that was quite as unable to face reality then as it is now. Hearst, who had handled the facts in the most sensational way, was particularly blamed, and because his *Journal* had been the most violent and contemptuous of McKinley's critics, there were those who charged it with responsibility for the President's death. They saw no mitigation in the fact that the paper, in the usual hypocritical Hearstian way, had now become one of McKinley's principal eulogizers.

It was recalled that seven months before the President's assassination, Governor Goebel of Kentucky had similarly been shot down, and Ambrose Bierce, who was then writing for Hearst, had written a quatrain:

> The bullet that pierced Goebel's breast
> Can not be found in all the West;
> Good reason, it is speeding here
> To stretch McKinley on his bier.

Two months later, the *Journal* had declared editorially: "If bad institutions and bad men can be got rid of only by killing, then the killing must be done." Both that statement and the quatrain could be explained in rational terms. Bierce was not a clairvoyant, nor an accessory of assassins; his poetry only meant to convey that the kind of political violence that could kill Goebel might easily kill McKinley, as in fact it did. The *Journal's* bloodthirsty editorial was no more than its usual overheated rhetoric; it is impossible to believe that Hearst or anyone else on the paper plotted to kill McKinley or encouraged anyone to do it.

The assassination of McKinley was the act of one deranged man, acting alone, as in the case of Oswald and President Kennedy, but in both instances the true believers of conspiracy theory would have none of it. The least of the claims in the *Journal's* case was that Hearst's inflammatory editorials had inspired the assassin. Many thought that the publisher was part of a plot, and those who hated other publishers linked them with the plot too. In short, the event made it possible for those who did not like the media to show their anger, as they had done from the beginnings of a free press. Once they had burned down the print shops and destroyed the type and done violence to the proprietors. Now they banned the *Journal* and sometimes the *World*, along with a few other offenders, from their clubs and libraries. Progress had been made.

The papers that had not attacked McKinley joined in the condemnation of the others, thus putting themselves squarely on the side of virtue, but it was not enough to prevent a demand in some quarters for laws to limit press freedom where the President was involved. It took a magazine, the *Bookman*, to point out that the "respectable" papers had made violent attacks against the President too, and that no president had ever been killed because of newspaper influence, and that no connection existed between the assassination of McKinley and the attacks on him.

In their raucous defense of the public interest, which was largely synthetic except for Pulitzer's basic idealism, the role of the newspapers in the Spanish-American War, the Philippine Insurrection, and in the McKinley administration generally overshadowed some of their real contributions to national life. Hearst had given pop culture the comic strip, with whatever its future implications might be. He and Pulitzer had also led the way in showing how newspapers could now cover a war and bring information to the public in a way that had not been possible before. Unfortunately, there was considerably less truth in the coverage of this war than there had been in the Civil War. Some correspondents were instructed by Hearst and Pulitzer to show how cruel and inhuman the Spaniards were, and they faithfully obliged. That, of course, would not be difficult in any war; cruelty and inhumanity are the hallmarks of armed conflict between nations.

If there was a large element of irresponsibility in the war coverage, there was also a great financial drain, which took away whatever profits might have been achieved from high circulations. If the war had lasted two more years, Arthur Brisbane wrote later, every New York paper would have been bankrupt. There may have been nearly five hundred correspondents covering the struggle, some of them operating from whole fleets of press boats; the *Journal* eventually had ten of these boats, and the *Herald* and the Associated Press five each. Sampson's fleet barely outnumbered the newspaper boats.

Most of these reporters had never covered a war, unlike their European counterparts, but they did well. Richard Harding Davis, the most noted of them, pointed out that "they had been trained in a school of journalism which teaches self-reliance and, above all other things, readiness of resource. In consequence, they met the new conditions without anxiety, and by using the same methods they had formerly employed in reporting a horse show or a fire, they succeeded in satisfactorily describing the operations of our army."

It may have been satisfactory from some standpoints, but the net result was no great credit to journalism. Professor Charles H. Brown observes in *The Correspondents' War* (the best account of the media's role in this struggle):

> Correspondents could have alerted the nation about the bungling of the War Department if they had told the truth about conditions at Tampa. They showed a reckless disregard for national security by writing about ship and troop movements early in the war and by their diatribes about the helplessness of the American army at Santiago during the truce negotiations. They puffed up minor naval and land engagements into stupendous feats of martial achievement. They were mixed up in their feelings about their role as reporters and patriots, interfering with military operations at times and leading or taking part in fighting that should have been left to the soldiers. But as Davis also wrote: "They kept the American people informed of what their countrymen—their brothers, fathers, and friends—were doing at the front. They cared for the soldiers when they were wounded, and, as Americans, helped Americans against a common enemy by reconnoitering, scouting, and fighting. They had no uniform to protect them; they were under sentence to be shot as spies if captured by the Spaniards; and they were bound, not by an oath as were the soldiers, but merely by a sense of duty to a newspaper, and by a natural desire to be of service to their countrymen in any way that offered."

If it demonstrated anything, the role of the media in the Spanish-American War was further proof that the press had the power to influence the masses on a large scale only if the masses were ready to be influenced. In 1898 they were ready.

16
The Media as Activists: II

WHILE PULITZER AND HEARST were casting themselves in the role of public watchdogs, the idea of the media as activist defenders of the people's interests was taking root in a different place. It became the primary function of a new kind of periodical, the ten-cent magazine, which was perhaps the most remarkable phenomenon in the years just before and after the turn of the century. The idea of pricing magazines at ten cents or lower was certainly not new, but the tremendous success of the ten-cent categories for a time dwarfed everything else that was happening in the magazine business.

The emergence of the ten-cent periodical as a powerful social force began with the founding of *McClure's* in June 1893, forcing its already established rivals, *Munsey's* and *Cosmopolitan*, to lower their prices to ten cents. *Peterson's* and *Godey's* also went down to a dime. There followed a flood of ten-cent periodicals, until Frank Munsey estimated in 1903 that they comprised about 85 per cent of the total circulation of magazines in America. Besides his own (*Munsey's*, naturally), Munsey guessed correctly that the biggest moneymakers were *Argosy*, *Cosmopolitan*, and *McClure's*. Other magazines tried a five-cent price, and some even went down to one or two cents, but only the *Saturday Evening Post* did really well at a nickel.

The basis of the ten-cent magazine's popular appeal was its liveliness and variety, its many and well-printed illustrations, its coverage of world events and progress at home—and most of all, its head-on confrontation with contemporary social problems.

The rise of the ten-cent magazine made the older and more expensive periodicals feel threatened. "The Revolution in the art of engraving, not to say its destruction, is threatening a change in the conduct of magazines," said the *Independent*. "What will be the effect on the high-priced illustrated magazines, like *Harper's*, the *Century*, and *Scribner's*, it may not be easy to foresee; but it seems probable that they will not find it wise to reduce their price to a like figure. . . . The reason is that they will wish to maintain that higher, purer literary standard which succeeds in securing the best but not the most numerous readers. . . . The fit audience in an educated country like ours is not few, but it is not yet unlimited; nevertheless, it is the only audience worth addressing, for it contains the thinking people. The rest may or may not be sturdy citizens, may count in the militia and the population and the lower schools; but they are not the ones who delight to seek the instruction they need most."

As Sam McClure pointed out in rebutting this elitist view, it would be hard to find a magazine with higher literary standards than his own. *McClure's* contributors included Stevenson, Kipling, Howells, Gladstone, Conan Doyle, Edward Everett Hale, and others of the same caliber.

Above everything else, the ten-cent magazine was creating a huge new mass market for general magazines, particularly the monthlies. In 1885 there had been only four of these monthlies able to boast a circulation of 100,000 or more; their price ranged from twenty-five to thirty-five cents. In just two decades their number had grown to twenty, with a total circulation of more than 5.5 million. Nearly all were priced at ten or fifteen cents. They were in more or less direct competition with that spreading phenomenon of the newspaper business, the Sunday paper, which Pulitzer and Hearst had by this time established solidly. The *Saturday Evening Post* saw little difference between the two media. "A good magazine is a good newspaper in a dress suit," it asserted.

There were four leaders in the ten-cent-magazine field, and the personalities of the men who originated them could hardly have been more different. First to arrive was the *Argosy*, another offspring of Frank Munsey's fertile imagination. In the newspaper business, Munsey was known as the "Grand High Executioner of Journalism," because he bought and merged old and honorable papers ruthlessly, without regard for tradition or ideals or even the needs of the community. Munsey was first and always the businessman, with the morals of the countinghouse, as his biography, *Forty Years—Forty Millions*, makes clear. When it came to magazines, he was a resourceful innovator.

Beginning his improbable career as a lonely boy in charge of the telegraph office in Augusta, Maine, home of the mail-order periodical, he used his superb talents as a salesman to get to New York with borrowed money, and then to persuade a magazine publisher, E. G. Rideout, to set him up in business on December 2, 1882, with the *Golden Argosy, Freighted with Treasures for Boys and Girls*. Improving on this start, Munsey cleverly juggled his financing in a way that would have made him seem insane to sober businessmen until he had established a new adult magazine, *Munsey's Weekly*, in 1889, which soon became simply *Munsey's*. In 1888, the *Argosy* for children became an *Argosy* for adults.

The adult *Argosy* was printed on the kind of rough paper called pulp, giving a name to a whole category of cheap magazines that thrived through the twenties and early thirties. Its stories had little love interest; they were adventure and mystery tales, aimed at men and boys, by popular authors of outdoor stories like Albert Payson Terhune, William McLeod Raine, and Louis Joseph Vance. But *Argosy* also carried the work of James Branch Cabell, Sidney Porter (he was not yet using "O. Henry"), Susan Glaspell, and Mary Roberts Rinehart. One of the serial writers was young Upton Sinclair.

Munsey's was not as immediately successful. It did not catch on until the publisher brought it out as a ten-cent periodical in 1893. Its first issue at this price sold 20,000 copies; four years later, it was selling 700,000 a month. Given Munsey's views on business, it is not surprising that his magazine was not among the muckrakers. "*Munsey's* Magazine has never been committed to the muck-raking theory, and never will be. Muck-raking is one thing, and progress is another," the publisher said.

The magazine did sell sex, however; Munsey was not above that. There were legitimate nudes displayed in the department titled "Artists and Their Work," which led the magazine every month, and less cultured undraped female figures appeared in departments titled "The Stage" and "Types of Fair Women." Other magazines might be annoyed by Munsey's half-dressed women and undressed statuary, but the proprietor did not temper the wind to these shorn lambs until his circulation was secure at over half a million. Otherwise, the magazine purveyed fiction, both serials and short stories. Hall Caine's famous novel *The Christian* gave it a good start in that division in 1896, and it was followed by serials from H. Rider Haggard, F. Marion Crawford, and Anthony Hope.

In between the debuts of Munsey's two magazines came *Cosmopolitan*, which began life in Rochester, New York, as a home monthly published by a firm of printers and office-supply manufacturers. After various changes of ownership, it fell into the hands of John Brisben Walker, a remarkable man, then forty-one, who had made successive fortunes in iron manufacturing and real estate, and had been a successful newspaperman as well. As one critic put it, Walker "introduced the newspaper ideas of timeliness and dignified sensationalism into periodical literature."

Beginning in 1892 with the acquisition of William Dean Howells as co-editor, Walker put together a notable staff. The co-editorship lasted only four months, however. Walker could not have worked with anyone else because he was cast in the mold of all the great magazine editors: he was the czar, the man who made all the decisions, and the magazine was to be whatever he made it. Because of his efforts, by the end of 1892 *Cosmopolitan* was among the best-illustrated magazines in the country, with more emphasis on public affairs than on fiction; it boasted a circulation of 300,000 by 1898. As one of the most important magazines dealing with domestic and foreign affairs, its coverage of the Spanish-American War ranked with the best magazine efforts, and its reports from abroad were often extraordinary.

Walker was well ahead of his time. As early as 1902, he proposed a world congress of nations, and in 1897 he was hard at work trying to revise what he termed the "frozen curricula" of universities. It was Walker, too, who foresaw the eventual decline of the great American railways, and urged the government to nationalize them. Beginning in 1892, Walker also began pushing the idea of "aerial navigation"; *Cosmopolitan* was far ahead of every other magazine in its acceptance and sponsorship of air transportation. Similarly, Walker did everything he could to advance the cause of the horseless carriage as soon as it appeared.

As an editor, Walker was as ruthless and arbitrary as any of his nineteenth-century predecessors. When Tolstoy's *Resurrection* began to run in *Cosmopolitan* in 1899, he thought some of the sexual descriptions were offensive, and deleted them. As the serial went on, he decided it would be impossible to make the book chaste enough for his pages and simply discontinued it. He much preferred writers like H. G. Wells, in any case, and was the first to print *War of the Worlds* and *The First Man on the Moon*. He was also one of the first editors to recognize Jack London as a major writer.

Cosmopolitan did not get into the muckraking business until 1905, when Hearst acquired it for $400,000. To him, a magazine was only an extension of the Sunday newspaper, except that more time could be spent on it to make it readable and "dressy." Under his direction, *Cosmopolitan* became more sensational, like the Hearst papers, and passed easily, although rather late in the day, into muckraking.

The last of the four ten-cent leaders to start was *McClure's*, and it proved to be the most sensational in many ways. No doubt that was inevitable, considering the personality of its founder, Samuel Sidney McClure—S. S. McClure, as he was known—who was one of the great showmen of his time. Like so many other nineteenth-century publishing figures, McClure came from a background of poverty, and clawed his way to the top. Irish-born, he came to this country, got an education at Knox College, and afterward went into the business of syndicating fiction and other feature material to newspapers. His partner was John Sanburn Phillips, a Midwesterner who had gone to school at Harvard and Leipzig.

When they decided to start a magazine in 1893, Phillips had $4500, McClure only $2800. But Sam McClure had something else more valuable, a natural flair for magazine making and the kind of personality that virtually ensures success.

However, it took a writer and a subject, as so often happens, to bring the magazine to public attention. The writer in this case was Ida M. Tarbell, soon to be the queen of the muckrakers, and her subject was "Napoleon," illustrated with pictures from the Hubbard collection. This serial more than doubled *McClure's* circulation, which had been a limping 40,000.

Hiring Miss Tarbell as a staff writer, McClure put her to work immediately on a new project out of his active brain. Lincoln had been dead thirty years, but Sam's editorial instincts told him that people would never get tired of reading about him, particularly in a time when his honesty was in such contrast to the prevailing moral climate. At the moment, too, there were many people living who could talk about him from personal knowledge. "Look, see, report," McClure instructed his new writer. The result was Miss Tarbell's *Early Life of Lincoln*, begun in 1895 in the magazine; it meant the addition of 75,000 new readers. The series was full of unpublished material, and it was illustrated with many Lincoln portraits never in print before.

McClure backed up this kind of enterprise with fiction by Stevenson and Anthony Hope, and Kipling's *Captains Courageous* and *Stalky & Co.* His short-story contributors included Thomas Hardy, Conan Doyle, Stephen Crane, and Joel Chandler Harris. Kipling's *Jungle Tales* also ran in *McClure's* as a series of short stories. McClure provided his readers with a good deal about scientific discoveries of the day, railroads, wild animals, exploration, and public personalities.

It was the plunge into muckraking in 1902, however, that finally made *McClure's* preeminent. In its January 1903 issue, the magazine declared: "We did not plan it so, it is a coincidence that this number contains three arraignments of American character such as should make every one of us stop and think. 'The Shame of Minneapolis'—the current chapter of the history of Standard Oil by Miss Tarbell, Mr. Ray Stannard Baker's 'The Right to Work'—they might all have been called 'The American Contempt of Law.' Capitalists, workingmen, politicians, citizens—all breaking the law or letting it be broken. Who is there left to uphold it? . . . There is no one left—none but all of us."

The stories mentioned in this editorial note were landmarks in the turbulent history of muckraking. The Minneapolis article was one in a celebrated series by Lincoln Steffens called *The Shame of the Cities.* Baker's assault on the leaders of labor unions was his opening gun; he went on to attack the misconduct of the railroads. These series attracted so much public attention that by the time the Panic of 1907 occurred, *McClure's* was approaching half a million.

"Muckraking" is a word that has lost its original meaning since Sam McClure's day. It has fallen into disrepute as signifying a somehow dishonorable exploration of shady practices that ought better to be left uncovered, as some people regard the Watergate exposures. It carries today the connotation of political attack. But in McClure's day it was the "New Journalism," hailed and discussed in much the same terms as today. Professor Louis Filler, whose study of this period, *The Muckrakers,* is as sound as it was thirty-five years ago, called muckraking in the early nineteen-hundreds "a new, moral, radical type of writing by men and women who yesterday had been entirely unknown or had written less disturbingly. These writers savagely exposed grafting politicians, criminal police, tenement eyesores. They openly attacked the Church. They defended labor in disputes which in no way concerned them personally, decried child exploitation, wrote pro-suffragist articles, and described great businesses as soulless and anti-social."

In brief, this was activist writing of the same stripe as the "New Journalism" of today. The difference in impact on the readers was not the same, however. In those days of American innocence, most citizens were not aware of the evils of the industrial society accumulating under their noses. Since they were predominantly rural and small-town people, without the instant communication of radio and television, they knew that the city was evil (the "big, wicked city" was a cliché), but they knew it mostly by hearsay. Insulated from the realities of big business, they were ignorant of the uncontrolled monster that industrialization had created. Brought up on simple articles of faith, many of them entirely mythical, they believed themselves to be living in a natural, ordained order of things, in which the American way of life was one of the supreme blessings of the universe.

But now, in the pages of the new ten-cent magazines, these people who were accustomed to reading their magazines for entertainment and genteel information were told that the institutions which made up their way of life were rotten with corruption of every kind. People who had never been interested in business and politics suddenly found that reading about them could be as exciting as the pages of fiction.

Predictably, the reaction from conservative quarters was one of indignation—not at what was being revealed but at those who were doing the revealing. They were destroying magazine standards and ruining literary style, it was said. As the "New Journalism" provides a handy label today, the critics of the muckrakers called what was being written the "literature of exposure," and it was meant to be a term of derogation, linked with "yellow journalism." Professor Filler tells us: "Some blamed the new President, Theodore Roosevelt, for the advent of these magazine reformers, holding that he was a radical and an encourager of radicalism. Another theory was that this sensationalism was a craze, an accident, a natural offshoot of Socialist theory and Democratic practice." Whatever the cause, it was clear even to the critics that the mass audience wanted to read these revelations, and believed most of them, particularly when indictments and convictions followed in their wake.

Today, by contrast, the new literature of exposure has to fight a vast public apathy, an unwillingness even to think about anything unpleasant, especially when establishment values are attacked. Few want anything to interfere with either the pursuit of money or pleasure. The newspapers whose enterprise makes them the bearers of bad news are attacked and, ironically, the magazine and book writers whose fact is often fiction are more believed. Television commentators who are prime and trusted sources of news are disbelieved when they say something viewers don't want to hear.

The catalogue of social ills uncovered by the muckrakers is an impressive one—matching those of our own time and often depressingly similar—beginning with what was probably the first muckraking article, *The World of Graft*, by Josiah Flynt, published in *McClure's* in 1901. By the following year, the magazine was in full cry with Lincoln Steffens' *Tweed Days in St. Louis*, and Miss Tarbell's first installment of *The History of the Standard Oil Company*, the first step toward the dissolution nine years later by the Supreme Court of this first giant monopoly. That year, 1902, also saw the publication of James Howard Bridge's *The Inside History of the Carnegie Steel Company*.

By 1903, the newspapers had joined the muckrakers. The solid investigative reporting in the magazines was having a dramatic effect on the kind of exposure the papers had been carrying on since Bennett's day. In the past, with some exceptions like the *Times's* uncovering of the Tweed frauds, reporting had tended more to the sensational than to the factual, designed more to startle and sell papers than to inform. Often, too, it had been used as a political club to beat an opposition party. Now, inspired by the kind of hard digging which produced the work of Steffens and Tarbell, the newspapers adopted the new style of investigation. The symptoms of change could be seen in the treatment of a scandal in the United States Post Office, broken by the papers in March 1903, and pursued assiduously by the press.

McClure's continued to carry most of the new writing, but other magazines were joining it by 1904. Edward Bok, who was making the *Ladies' Home Journal* into a mass magazine, attacked the patent-medicine fraud, and the *Arena* launched a crusade against the trusts with *Twenty-five Years of Bribery and Corrupt Practices; or, The Railroads, the Lawmakers, the People*. In *Everybody's*, a maverick financier, Thomas W. Lawson, began his personal campaign against organized finance with *The Story of Amalgamated*. Ellery Sedgwick, the editor of *Leslie's*, cited America as the "Land of Disasters" in calling for a fight against railroad accidents. Later in 1904, another explosion occurred when the *Era* began to attack the manner in which the great insurance companies were being operated, while Lawson, in *Everybody's*, focused on the evils of a single organization, the New York Life Assurance Company.

During the following year, Charles Edward Russell exposed the Beef Trust in *Everybody's*, Burton J. Hendrick started a long exploration of insurance in *McClure's*, Samuel Hopkins Adams wrote *The Great American Fraud* for *Collier's*, an all-out assault on the patent-medicine industry, and Baker put "The Railroads on Trial" in *McClure's*.

By 1906, these articles were overflowing into books, and some writers chose that medium for their exposés, particularly Upton Sinclair, whose revelations about the meat-packing industry in *The Jungle* shocked the country.

Cosmopolitan, late in joining the muckrakers, produced one of the most important of the investigations with David Graham Phillips' "The Treason of the Senate," which disclosed in nauseating detail the corruption of the Senate by big business, particularly Standard Oil. Nonprofessional writers were joining in, as *McClure's* printed a sordid story of corruption in Silverbow County, Montana, by C. P. Connolly, who had been a district attorney there. At the same time, Edwin Markham appeared in *Cosmopolitan* with a series on child labor. The promise of further revelations came in October when a group of the most prominent muckrakers, including Steffens, Tarbell, Baker, Peter Finley Dunne, and William Allen White took over *American* magazine. In another unique development, *Success* inaugurated what it called the People's Lobby, with Mark Sullivan as president.

That was the high point of the muckraking era. A slow decline began, but there were milestones: Charles Edward Russell's attack on the finances of Trinity Church, in *Hampton's*, one of several assaults on organized religion's financial status; William English Walling's "Race War in the North," in the *Independent*, an article that led to the founding of the NAACP in 1908; an attack on maladministration in the Department of the Interior by *Collier's*, *Hampton's*, and others, in 1909.

The reform movement which the muckrakers spearheaded had its casualties. The Los Angeles *Times* building was dynamited and destroyed by two crooked officers of the Structural Iron Workers' Union, with a loss of fifteen lives; and in January 1911, David Graham Phillips was assassinated in New York City. There was, by this time, a general movement to end muckraking. There was a great deal more muck to be raked, but the public was unable to face any more bad news and wanted to hear good news again. The muckrakers themselves were turning to other kinds of writing, and some of the magazines they had worked for, like the *American, McClure's,* and *Collier's,* were being transformed into innocuous formats; a few lesser publications had failed.

There had been some famous victories as the result of public pressure generated by muckraking. The Federal Reclamation Act of 1902 put a brake, although not a very substantial one, on the exploitation of natural resources. The Supreme Court dissolved the Northern Securities Company in 1904, and in the same year the man who had prosecuted the "boodlers" Steffens had exposed in St. Louis was elected governor of Missouri. In 1905, the leaders of the Beef Trust were indicted for conspiracy to restrain trade, and convicted and sentenced (only to see the conviction reversed). Insurance companies were regulated for the first time, and the fight for railroad regulation had some successes. The meat inspection bill was passed by Congress after Sinclair's exposé, and public indignation compelled the passage of a Pure Food Bill. Municipal corruption in San Francisco was ended, temporarily at least, and the Mann Act was passed—another futile gesture toward curbing prostitution. And as a kind of climax, the Standard Oil Company was ordered dissolved by the Supreme Court on May 15, 1911.

These were some of the reform successes that muckraking could take much of the credit for bringing about. Sadly, at the end, the muckrakers retreated in the face of organized counterattacks by business. Advertising was becoming too important for the magazines to continue their activist role. But, as Professor Filler points out, the muckrakers did unite the country and bring it a painful step closer to maturity, and they "ushered in modern times."

What are we exposing, nearly three quarters of a century later? Why, corruption in government and business, misfeasance and malfeasance in office at every level, the evils of great corporations and great labor unions—the mixture as before. The exposures are being answered, too, in the same terms as before, and public apathy, complacency, and willful ignorance threaten to end them in favor of business as usual. More and more, the dictum of Walt Kelly's comic-strip character, Pogo, "We have met the enemy and he is us," appears to be more historically appropriate as a national motto than "In God we trust." It is no accident that the cynical addendum to the latter, "All others pay cash," is one of the oldest clichés in the language.

Temporarily, muckraking made magazines the most important

medium in the country, but in following the trend, the newspapers were brought into opposition to federal power in a way that had not been seen since the Civil War.

President Theodore Roosevelt's relations with the press remain an intriguing puzzle, never adequately explored. A writer himself, familiar with the operations of the media, and on the whole well disposed toward them, Roosevelt nevertheless displayed on occasion a myopia toward the press that brought him into sharp conflict with it. No doubt the reason was his towering ego, and a self-confidence bordering on simple arrogance, which resented criticism or any implication that he was anything less than he considered himself to be.

The New York Assemblyman Roosevelt who declared boldly, "I think that if there is one thing we ought to be careful about it is in regard to interfering with the liberty of the press," was the same man who, as president, argued with equal sincerity that a newspaper correspondent whose editor changed his political views so that he opposed what he might have favored previously should resign at once, otherwise it would be understood "that his honor was for sale." He would have been astounded and angry if anyone had pointed out the absurdity of that statement.

Yet Roosevelt had a fondness for working newspapermen. Steffens, for example, saw him every day during the hour he submitted himself to the barber, and for a time appeared to have the freedom of the executive offices. The President often tried out ideas on him. Similarly, Isaac Marcosson, a noted interviewer who had been the first reporter to be granted an interview by John Archbold, the remote president of Standard Oil, had easy access to Roosevelt. Other newspapermen were similarly favored.

In the light of these facts, it is hard to understand why the President, who had made a great deal of political capital out of his role as trustbuster, was the man who coined the word "muckraking" as a derogatory description and led the fight to end it—aided by some of his admirers in the newspaper press itself, which had seen its efforts diminished by the magazines.

According to Major Archie Butt, the military aide who was also the President's confidant, Roosevelt had decided tastes among the newspapers. He read regularly only the New York *Herald* and *Tribune* because, as Butt wrote, "he knows he will not find anything in them to upset his digestion." Butt goes on to quote the President as saying, "I could not stand the *Evening Post* or the *Sun* after a hearty meal." Roosevelt did not take press criticism easily, even though Butt pointed out to him that for every newspaper critic there were fifty others who were ready to defend him. The press was, on the whole, his friend.

All except for one of its leaders—the *World* and Pulitzer. The paper had recovered from the excesses of the Spanish-American War, and it was still the largest in America, with a full-time staff in 1897 of 1300 men and women, and an annual budget of $2 million. It sold a million copies a day, morning and evening, and on Sundays it expanded from a twenty-four-page to a seventy-two-page maximum, about half of it advertising. It was considered, conservatively, to be worth $10 million, and to be making a 10 per cent profit. Only thirty-four years later, it was sold for $5 million and disappeared soon after.

It was undergoing a renaissance in the muckraking years, the result of an extraordinary new editor, Frank I. Cobb, who had been chief editorial writer for the Detroit *Free Press*. Pulitzer had scoured the country, sending out a posse of personal emissaries, to find a man to whom he could give full control of the editorial page, with the understanding that he would be editor when the publisher died.

Almost at once, Cobb helped initiate the most famous of the *World's* muckraking efforts. Picking up leads opened by the magazines, Cobb directed an investigation into the affairs of the Equitable Life Assurance Society, disclosing that some of its officers were using company money for their own investments. As the inquiry broadened, the New York Life was also involved. The resulting investigation by a legislative committee not only substantiated everything the *World* had charged, but brought to full public attention the committee's counsel, a young attorney named Charles Evans Hughes, who vaulted to the governorship in 1906.

Cobb's enterprise soon involved the paper in a public quarrel with Roosevelt, in which the issue of press freedom was argued once more. The issue rose from the *World's* determination to find out what had happened to the $40 million paid by the United States for the rights of the defunct French company which built the Panama Canal. Cobb suspected that some, at least, of this money had gone to government insiders, particularly to William Nelson Cromwell, a promoter, attorney, and mystery man of the Roosevelt administration.

As the 1908 campaign neared its end, the *World* charged that blackmailers were trying to get a part of the Panama millions out of Cromwell and his friends. On the eve of the election, the Indianapolis *News* published an editorial which strongly denounced the whole deal and demanded to know the whereabouts of the money. The editorial was based on the *World*'s story. When it was brought to the President's attention, he replied with a letter released to the press which attacked Delavan Smith, publisher of the *News*, and William M. Laffan, the New York *Sun*'s publisher. He did not mention Pulitzer or the *World*.

Cobb's editorial on the following day, titled "The Panama Scandal —Let Congress Investigate," was perhaps the strongest editorial attack on a president since Lincoln's day. It accused Roosevelt of "deliberate misstatements of facts in his scandalous personal attack" on Smith. It called on Congress to make "a full and impartial investigation of the entire Panama Canal scandal." In effect, it charged the President with lying, in four separate statements, and added that Roosevelt must have known these statements were "untrue when he made them." Again the paper raised the cry: "Who got the money?" and ended: "The inquiry was originally the *World*'s, and the *World* accepts Mr. Roosevelt's challenge."

Confronted with this earlier version of Watergate, the President reacted characteristically. Unlike the Nixonian strategy of withdrawal and denial, Roosevelt struck back angrily at a paper he had loathed since Crane's story of San Juan Hill, which had cast a hateful shadow on his image of himself. He sent a special message to Congress, denying any wrongdoing and calling the stories "scurrilous and libelous in character and false in every essential particular." Of Pulitzer, he said:

> It is idle to say that the known character of Mr. Pulitzer and his newspaper are such that the statements in that paper will be believed by nobody; unfortunately, thousands of persons are ill informed in this respect and believe the statements they see in print, even though they appear in a newspaper published by Mr. Pulitzer. . . . While the criminal offence of which Mr. Pulitzer has been guilty is to form a libel upon individuals, the great injury done is in blackening the good name of the American people. It should not be left to a private citizen to sue Mr. Pulitzer for libel. He should be prosecuted for libel by the governmental authorities.

It was more a tirade than a message, and it raised substantially, for the first time since the administration of John Adams, the question of how far a newspaper could go in criticizing a president. The result was a governmental criminal libel suit filed in District of Columbia Criminal Court. Indictments on five counts were returned against Pulitzer, his managing and night editors, and the Press Publishing Company. A seven-count indictment was returned against Delavan

Smith and his associate, Charles R. Williams. The law on which the indictments were based had been written in the time of Charles II.

No legal justification existed for the bench warrants which went out immediately for the defendants, since their implementation would have resulted in taking the men out of their own jurisdictions to Washington for trial. Pulitzer avoided the confrontation by staying offshore on his yacht, aptly named the *Liberty*. The others stood their ground.

A federal judge in Indianapolis dismissed the case against Smith and Williams, soon after the United States district attorney resigned rather than be a party to the action. The federal court declared: "If the history of liberty means anything—if constitutional guarantees are worth anything—this proceeding must fail." In Washington, the Attorney General agreed; he had the indictment against Pulitzer and the others dismissed.

That was not the end of the action, however. Roosevelt had written to Henry L. Stimson, then federal district attorney for southern New York, saying, "I do not know anything about the law of criminal libel, but I should dearly like to invoke it against Pulitzer, of the *World.*" Stimson invoked it, on the technical ground that twenty-nine copies of the *World* had been circulated at West Point, a federal reservation, thus violating a law intended to protect harbor defenses from malicious injury "and for other purposes." Pulitzer was not indicted, but the *World* and its managing editor were. This specious piece of legal humbug was rightly dismissed by the court on the ground of jurisdiction, and the *World* was upheld unanimously by the Supreme Court, on appeal.

From the beginning, the affair had been one of the President's worst misjudgments, among many, and there was little that could be said for it of a tolerant nature. The decision's practical effect was to establish that the federal government could not sue newspapers for criminal libel in its courts. Cobb called it "the most sweeping victory for freedom of speech and of the press in this country since the American people destroyed the Federalist party more than a century ago for enacting the infamous Sedition Law." Nevertheless, for the first time in this century a president of the United States had attempted to assert the doctrine that the rights of the chief executive were of a higher order than the First Amendment, or any other law that happened to be inconvenient in asserting presidential authority.

William Howard Taft, who succeeded Roosevelt, did not have his predecessor's sublime arrogance, but he exhibited even less understanding of the press. Archie Butt disclosed this amusingly, if unwittingly. He wrote:

> Last night after dinner, when he asked if the New York papers had come, Mrs. Taft handed him the New York *World.*
> "I don't want the *World,*" he said. "I have stopped reading it. It only makes me angry."
> "But you used to like it very much," said Mrs. Taft.
> "That was when it agreed with me, but it abuses me now, and so I don't want it."
> "You will never know what the other side is doing if you only read the *Sun* and *Tribune,*" said this wise woman.
> "I don't care what the other side is doing," he answered with some irritation.

More like a petulant child than a president of the United States, and a revealing symptom of Taft's inadequacy.

With President Wilson and the Democrats back in the White House in 1912, the newspapers believed themselves in better odor in Washington, on the strength of the new President's assurance that he was in favor of "pitiless publicity" for public business. He backed this conviction by instituting the first formal, regular White House press conferences. But Wilson had only the academician's belief in the theory of press freedom. When it came to the realities of public office, he proved to have little confidence in newspaper publishers, and not much more in reporters. A shy and sensitive man, he could not tolerate the idea of personal publicity for himself and his family. The inevitable collisions occurred, and it was not long before Mr. Wilson was writing to a friend:

"Do not believe anything you read in the newspapers. If you read the papers I see, they are utterly untrustworthy. They represent the obstacles as existing which they wish to have exist, whether they are actual or not. Read the editorial page and you know what you will find in the news columns. For unless they are grossly careless the two always support one another. The lying is shameless and colossal."

Taft believed Wilson was a better manager of the news than most people imagined. Eight months after he retired as president, Taft wrote to Elihu Root: "The use of the Washington correspondents by this administration has been masterly and ... moves me to say that Theodore is not the only pebble on the beach in the use of the press. It shows a keenness of the use of political instruments and an ability in this direction that rouses my very great admiration, however much it may break the idea that so many people have formed of Woodrow's character."

In his naïve way, Taft in this letter exposed the fact that a new presidential conception of the press had come into use with the new century. The press was now to be "used" as a "political instrument." It was an idea that would be considerably more effective later, in adept hands.

President Wilson did not, in general, do battle with individual publishers or newspapers, as other presidents had done before him. His quarrel was a broader one: he disapproved of the way newspapers operated, and he never understood their practices. Yet no other president was ever given such power over newspapers as he enjoyed through the wartime acts governing censorship, espionage, and sedition. The government's censorship power was exercised long before American entry into the First World War, when a censor was installed at Vera Cruz to monitor what the correspondents were sending back about the second armed interference by the United States in Mexican affairs, this time in an effort to ensure a government that would be properly grateful to American oil and other interests that were doing business in Mexico, and which, it was feared, would be expropriated if the revolutionary movement was successful.,

While this sordid affair was going on, war had broken out in Europe. At the beginning, the Allies found little sympathy for their cause in America. The press in the United States was so pro-German that at first correspondents could not get accreditation from the Allies, who did not trust them, and had to cover the war from Berlin. Mary Roberts Rinehart, the mystery-story writer, was the first to see the war from the other side when, as a *Saturday Evening Post* correspondent, she succeeded in enlisting herself with the Belgian Red Cross and went to the front. The Hearst papers were so antiwar that when the hysteria for American entry began to build up, it was widely believed by superpatriots that the publisher was a German spy who was flashing messages from his Riverside Drive apartment to submarines lying below the surface in the Hudson River.

When war actually came, freedom in America was the first casualty. State and federal laws and city ordinances together deprived the willing citizens of constitutional liberties, including the protection of the First Amendment, which suffered most. Totally unmindful of the monstrous evil embodied in the first Sedition Act, which had been held up for more than a century as one of the worst failures of American democracy, Congress passed early in 1918 a second Sedition Act, supplementing the repressive Espionage Act already in force. Under this act, offenses included the willful writing, utterance, or publication of any "disloyal, profane, scurrilous, or abusive language about the form of government of the United States, or the Constitution of the United States, or the military or naval forces of the United States, or the flag of the United States, or the uniform of the army or navy of the United States, or any language intended to bring the form of government of the United States, or the uniform of the army or navy of the United States into contempt, scorn, contumely, or disrepute." At the same time, the Postmaster General was given further power to end whatever privacy still existed in the mails after the Espionage Act.

It was argued, of course, that these measures, which were directly antithetical to the entire theory of government upon which the nation rested, were essential because the United States was fighting for its life. But in England, where the citizens were in considerably more danger of losing their country, the censorship laws were far less severe. The eagerness with which press and public accepted these restrictions in America testified not only to the emotional binge of patriotism they were undergoing but to their willingness to suppress dissent, to forgo in the heat of the moment every victory for liberty that had been achieved since the first Sedition Act had been repealed.

Every part of the media was censored during the war, including the burgeoning motion-picture business. There was little resistance and, in reality, it was dangerous to resist. People not only had the government to fear but their fellow citizens as well. Hundreds of thousands of people, acting either as individuals or as members of patriotic societies, were ready to inform against anyone they thought might be writing, printing, or filming anything subversive. The atmosphere was like that of any totalitarian state, whether right or left, but it was all done in the name of liberty and freedom.

The question remained: Would this atmosphere be carried on to any extent when the war was over? At the time, it would have been considered an absurd idea, but as events have proved, the end of wartime controls did not mean the end of the idea of censorship as a political weapon. Instead, it went underground, so to speak. In government at every level, and among social, political, and economic organizations, censorship continued under various disguises, as a means of protecting entrenched institutions and what is always described as the "American way of life."

The freedom that was enjoyed before the First World War has never fully returned, and in fact has been steadily eroded in the United States as it has continued to disappear all over the world. In the continuing power struggle between freedom and authority, it is abundantly clear now that only those who truly desire and understand freedom will have it. In the First World War, the American people demonstrated that where the First Amendment was concerned —a freedom on which all the others rest—they were ready to give it up any time that emotion prevailed over reason.

17

The Idea of Community
Service

WHILE THE MEDIA of the East were struggling against each other and the government, fighting the battles of press freedom and circulation, another kind of concept was growing up elsewhere. It was the idea of community service, whether the community was a small town or a city as large as Kansas City or Chicago.

Few of the newspapers outside New York considered themselves leaders of national thought. Their interests were local or regional; their mission as they conceived it was to be a bulletin board for the community, and activist only where local politics were concerned. While this idea did much for the community, it led to the kind of parochialism expressed in the often quoted remark by a Rocky Mountain editor that a dog fight in the streets of Denver was worth more space than a war in Europe. Time has not diluted that notion in many places today.

Other factors were at work in this situation. The emphasis was beginning to shift from circulation to advertising as the lifeblood of the newspapers, and while they were still free to attack the advertisers, the interests of businessmen and publishers, once poles apart, were approaching each other. The distribution of goods had moved out of local scope into regional and national patterns, brand names were proliferating, competition was keener, and there was an obvious demand for better merchandising methods. One of the best methods available was newspaper advertising, which could now be national and regional as well as local. Thus an important new source of advertising revenue, deriving from the growth of national big business organizations, was opening up to the publishers.

The cities were undergoing an explosive population expansion, which was being served by a growing number of retail outlets for goods and services—most of them advertisers, actual or potential. In the old days, the amount of local retail advertising had been helpful to a newspaper's income but not critical. In the new order, it would soon mark the difference between success and failure for some newspapers, no matter what they might do editorially.

All these complicated economic factors worked together like an intricate machine. Population growth stimulated business growth, which created a need for better merchandising, which stimulated the rise of advertising, which became increasingly important to the life of newspapers, which were able to meet the advertising needs of business because their circulations were growing with the population and they were reaching the people the advertisers wanted to reach. This is such a commonplace fact of life today that it scarcely seems possible its real development began less than a hundred years ago.

From the publishers' standpoint, the rise of advertising could not have taken place at a better time. It was becoming more and more expensive to produce newspapers in the latter part of the century. The only way these costs could be met was through larger circulation and expanded advertising volume based on increased readership. Intense competition began to develop in both areas, and the papers which exhibited superior business talents were the survivors. In the end, as costs and competition mounted, a newspaper could not exist without efficient business management, and so in some respects newspapers began to resemble other businesses.

In this shifting of newspaper publishing patterns, personal ownership became more and more the property of the small daily and weekly, while the big-city papers were increasingly corporate enterprises. Business, however, was good everywhere. Publishing opportunities bloomed in cities and villages, regardless of size.

Everything contributed to the growth of the mass media. The constant expansion of education and the consequent rise in literacy created more potential newspaper readers every year. The interests of Americans were being continually broadened and their cultural desires stimulated by the steady development of bookstores, libraries, art galleries, theaters, and opera houses. These interests found their most popular expression in newspapers and magazines through reviews and articles, supplementing the constant cultural flow from the book publishers.

Newspapers were now heavily concentrated on hard news, which was written in the clearer style first developed by the correspondents in the Civil War and the Spanish-American War. They were aggressive, as they had always been; institutionalized blandness had not yet set in. On the editorial page there was as much diversity of opinion as ever; editors had not yet developed the predominant business-oriented viewpoint which has come to characterize the editorial page of the late twentieth century.

More than any other development, however, it was the community service idea that dominated newspapers outside the area blanketed by the New York giants. The leader was clearly Joseph Medill's Chicago *Tribune*, which may well have been the first to introduce this concept as we know it today.

Medill was, in many respects, the James Gordon Bennett, Sr., of the Middle West. He had come to the *Tribune* in 1855 at the age of thirty-two, and for the next forty-four years he was its life. He was managing editor during the first eight years, and editor in chief from 1863 to 1866, after which he made a brief excursion into public life as a member of the Illinois Constitutional Convention, of the Civil Service Commission, and eventually as mayor of Chicago. Returning to the *Tribune* in 1874, he took over complete editorial and business control of the paper, retaining it until he died in 1899.

If anything, Medill's *Tribune* was more uninhibited than Bennett's *Herald*. As an editor, Medill was more of a public figure than Bennett; he did not have nor need the New Yorker's infinite capacity for self-aggrandizement. Medill had his eccentricities too, but they were milder. He was, essentially, a fighter and a leader, and he unquestionably led Midwestern journalism during his lifetime. No one could doubt that the *Tribune* was one of the most personal of personal journals. Like the *Herald* and other papers of its stripe, the *Tribune's* language was frequently from the gutter. It was a paper which dealt in extremes, stopping at nothing either to attack an enemy or to promote a cause.

Medill professed the usual lofty ideals common to the publishers of his day. A newspaper, he asserted, ought to be "the organ of no man, however high, no clique or ring, however influential, no faction, however fanatical or demonstrative, and in all things to follow the line of common sense." Medill's common sense had something of the same quality as Bennett's, who, it will be remembered, expressed the same pious thought in almost identical language.

The *Tribune* grew up with Chicago, and it was the city's favorite paper. After the great fire of 1871, it was the *Tribune* which appeared with its famous editorial, "Cheer Up!" containing the slogan which became at once the whole city's battle cry: "Chicago shall rise again!" Running on a "Fireproof Ticket" the following year, Medill was easily elected mayor.

After he returned to the editor's chair, he applied new vigor to his job, doubled the paper's circulation in a decade, and made it one of the best newspapers in the country, in the professional sense. In other respects, it was characterized by Medill's dogged opposition to every humanitarian or reform measure extant. In the bloody Chicago labor wars, Medill was for stringing up the leaders. His recipe for dealing with the unemployed, whom he equated with strikers, was set forth in an unbelievable editorial of 1884 in which the *Tribune* declared that "the simplest plan," provided "one is not a member of the Humane Society, is to put arsenic in the supplies of food furnished the unemployed or the tramp. This produces death in a short time and is a warning to other tramps to keep out of the neighborhood."

Medill had the confidence of ignorance, not only about the great forces which were shaping America but about a good many other things as well. Sometimes it was hard to separate the ignorance from simple eccentricity. His passion for simplified spelling—"telegrafed," "infinit," and similar barbarisms—remains in somewhat modified form in the *Tribune* of today. Other fancies were transitory, as for example his conviction that most malfunctions of human affairs were caused by sunspots, until he became equally convinced that microbes were at fault. A reporter who had not heard about the change wrote a piece attributing the plague in Egypt to sunspots. Medill solemnly went through his copy and changed all the "sunspots" to "microbes."

Medill was an opportunist and an apologist for privilege and all its abuses. He made the *Tribune* a vituperative defender of big business, but he also made it a well-written, well-edited newspaper which was highly successful long after the time when its influence had declined to no more than the reinforcement of the convictions of a hard-core element in the Republican Party's right wing. It was not only the *Tribune*'s professional excellence in departments other than the political, but its devotion to the interests of Chicago which accounted for its success.

A similar devotion was expressed in Kansas City, where William Rockhill Nelson became the apotheosis of the public-service publisher. Nelson had made and lost a considerable amount of money in the business world before he founded the *Evening Star* on September 18, 1880. He had been attracted to the newspaper business through his interest in politics. As a result of managing Tilden's campaign in Indiana, he learned about the power of newspapers, bought an interest in the Fort Wayne *Sentinel*, and in two years had decided to devote his career to publishing.

The *Star* announced itself as "independent but never neutral," which no one believed, the public having become cynical about the public pronouncements of publishers. Nelson meant it, however, and proved it in the following years by pursuing an entirely independent political course, backing men and issues as he saw them, without regard for party.

It was not its independence that made the *Star* successful, however, although that sturdy quality was not unappreciated by its readers. "Community service," the phrase Nelson used to express his philosophy, was the solid foundation. To him the words meant that in its news columns the *Star* would be predominantly local, a family newspaper for Kansas City families. Where the giants in New York, and even Medill to some extent, had considered the editorial page the hard core of the newspaper, Nelson had little regard for it. He thought reporters were the most valuable men on the paper, and the use he intended to make of them was to investigate the deplorable condition of Kansas City and, if possible, to bring some order into its lawless, violent atmosphere. It was a sprawling, reckless town, notorious for its corruption, at the mercy of unprincipled men.

The *Star* dug in. It attacked the fraudulent elections, the well-protected gambling and vice rings, the scandalous condition of public transportation, and the unpaved, muddy, shabby physical condition of the place, which looked more like a freshly settled frontier community than an important Midwestern crossroads. "Let's pull Kansas City out of the mud!" Nelson proclaimed as the *Star*'s slogan, and he did.

Naturally, not even a man of his energy, equipped with a paper as fearless and able as the *Star*, could hope to bring about complete reform. Kansas City corruption has remained a fact of life into our own time, although its shame has been no worse than that of other American cities, and not nearly so bad as some. But Nelson's campaigning made a substantial dent in the sorry conditions of his time by marshaling every last bit of good will and civic pride among the citizens. Corruption was brought under control, if not eliminated; and best of all, perhaps, the *Star*'s program of physical rehabilitation made Kansas City the splendid place of parks and boulevards it is today. Nelson was something new in publishers: a man who stayed out of politics, remained independent of party, and devoted himself to his paper. Before he died in 1915, he had the satisfaction of seeing Kansas City emerge as substantially the kind of metropolis he had envisioned.

It was significant of the kind of journalism Nelson represented that not only did his paper accomplish much for the community, but it did not falter without him to guide it. In later years, the *Star* continued to be one of the best papers in the nation, a training ground for eminent reporters, editors, novelists, playwrights, and radio and television personalities. It continued to call itself independent, a fiction difficult to maintain when it was widely recognized as the authentic voice of Middle Western Republicanism.

Still another kind of service was embodied in Victor Fremont Lawson, Nelson's counterpart in Chicago as an advocate of community service. Lawson's role in media history was a double one. He founded the Chicago *Daily News*, one of the nation's best papers for many years, and he made the Associated Press a great news-gathering organization. Born in Chicago of Norwegian parents, he began his career by inheriting his father's Norwegian-language newspaper, *Skandinaven*; but he soon took over the *Daily News* from an old school friend, Melville Stone, who was in trouble because he was a splendid editor but not a good manager. With Stone in the editor's chair and Lawson as publisher, one of the most potent partnerships in the business was formed.

In acquiring the paper, Lawson was not simply gratifying personal ambition. His family immigrant background had given him a strong sense of duty to America; he intended to repay the nation, and Chicago especially, for what it had done for him. Looking at his native city, he saw what Nelson had seen in Kansas City—a shambles of crime and corruption, only on a larger scale. The moral and political climate of Chicago had resisted improvement since the city first rose on the Lake Michigan mud flats, but Lawson, an idealist, intended to try. He was not the first, and the last has not been seen. Chicago appears to be relatively impervious to reform.

Lawson declared that the *Daily News* would be:

> Candid—That its utterances shall at all times be the exact truth. It is independent but never indifferent;
> Comprehensive—That it shall contain all the news;
> Concise—The *Daily News* is very carefully edited, to the end that the valuable time of its patrons shall not be wasted in reading of mere trifles;

Clean—That its columns shall never be tainted by vulgarity or obscenity;

Cheap—That its price shall be put within the reach of all.

Stone and Lawson between them carried out these high-minded principles with astonishing fidelity, and they made a profound impression on the crowded Chicago newspaper scene, where the papers were devoted largely to character assassination, of political figures and each other. Nor did their newspaper have the *Tribune's* provincial air, which led Medill to carry on a running warfare with the Eastern papers and everything they represented. The *Daily News* was local in a different way, devoted to reforming Chicago, if that were possible, without the flamboyant tactics Medill and the others used to sell newspapers. The method was much like Nelson's and the result was in part the same—that is, the newspaper quickly numbered itself among the nation's best, although Lawson never succeeded in making the impression on Chicago's corruption that Nelson did on Kansas City's. The job was too much for mortal man.

As for the Associated Press, it was Lawson who saved it from disaster. At the beginning, it had functioned as two separate agencies, the New York Associated Press and the Western Associated Press, but in 1882 the divisions had come under the direction of a Joint Executive Committee, consisting of three New York men and two representing the West. Eight years later, Lawson became aware that the New York wire, carrying the day's quotation from the New York Stock Exchange, was being manipulated to the greater profit of financiers in New York and the ruination of small investors. In the rigged wire reports, quotations might be delayed until the close of the Chicago exchange, when it would be too late for investors outside New York to react to closing prices. Sometimes, too, the financial news was specially phrased to convey particular meanings to those in the inner circles.

Appointed by the Western AP as chairman of a three-man committee to investigate the charge that the United Press was either stealing or otherwise illegally acquiring AP news, Lawson spent three months as an investigative reporter. When some Eastern members of the AP tried to discredit and even abolish his committee, Lawson was convinced, as a man brought up on Chicago corruption, that the evil went right to the top.

At the meeting of the Western AP in Detroit the following year, 1891, Lawson was able to unfold the whole sordid story. The nation's wire services, AP and UP alike, were actually in the hands of a three-man trust, consisting of Walter Phillips, director of the United Press; William Laffan, business manager of the New York *Sun*; and a financier named John Walsh. These men were the principal owners of the UP, but they had been able to gain control of AP news as well by means of a secret deal, negotiated through private gifts of valuable stock, with five of the AP's executives and members.

The assembled Western AP publishers could scarcely believe it when Lawson told them who these men were. The list began with no other than Charles Anderson Dana himself, who at the moment was chairman of the Joint Committee as well as the *Sun*'s publisher. Another was Whitelaw Reid, then the highly respected head of the *Tribune*, and the New York AP's representative on the committee. There were also two prominent Western publishers, W. H. Haldeman and Richard Smith, both representatives on the Western AP committee, and William Henry Smith, the combined AP's general manager.

What this highly placed combine had been able to do was shocking. It had, first of all, been giving the UP most of the AP's news without charge, thus reducing the UP's operation costs to a minimum. The resulting inflated profits were divided among the five. The agency's financial news report had been tampered with in several ways, as Lawson had surmised, which further increased the income of the conspirators. After disclosing other unsavory details, Lawson produced the key document which completed his exposé, a formal contract among the five men legalizing their arrangement. It had been executed in 1888, because the fraud had grown so large and profitable that the partners no longer trusted each other.

If anyone expected the conspirators to wither and retreat in the glare of exposure, he overestimated the character of men like Dana. He and his fellow cabalists meant to wreck the Western AP, if possible, and secure their news-gathering monopoly. The Western publishers had broken away from the New York AP and named a new Executive Committee, with Lawson as chairman, and so it became a clear issue. If the Western AP members could not present a united front and preserve their organization, it quite obviously meant that the trust would control all wire news and sell it purely for profit. In that case business interests would always come before the integrity of the report, and the idea on which the AP was based would be lost.

To help him form a united front, Lawson persuaded Melville Stone to be general manager of a reorganized AP. Stone led the battle with the UP for clients—so successfully that the leading papers in the Midwest had switched from UP to AP by 1894, and two years later the *Sun* and the *Journal* were the only UP clients in New York.

In the end, Dana had to file a bankruptcy petition for the UP and the battle was over, at a nearly ruinous cost to the AP of $1 million. There were some publishers who refused to join the AP, and these men organized the Publishers' Press, which eventually merged with the Scripps-McRae service to form the United Press Associations— now United Press International (UPI), since the acquisition of Hearst's International News Service.

Through all this, Lawson did not neglect community service. His paper fought hard for a system of postal savings banks, and could take some credit for the 1910 federal act establishing them. In Chicago itself, the *Daily News* was in the van of every civic reform movement, and Lawson himself gave a great deal of his own time and money to various city organizations.

The monumental integrity and devotion to constructive reform which Lawson brought to the newspaper business contrasted sharply with most of what had gone before in the history of American newspapers. He and Nelson were the first major figures in the business to demonstrate that a newspaper need be neither a propaganda organ nor a personal weapon, that it had even more power when it was used for unselfish ends. The press was developing what it had never before possessed: a sense of responsibility. That had been the missing ingredient in its progress, and the addition changed the character of the business. Questions about the nature of freedom and responsibility were yet to come.

That this was not solely a Midwestern phenomenon could be seen in the South, where two fine newspapers were created by men of high idealism. One was Henry W. Grady, a statesman who might have done as well in Congress as in the newspaper business. As a young editor, Grady emerged from the misery and confusion of Reconstruction to help provide a solid answer to the question: What next? He knew his people and he understood that it was not political guidance they were seeking so much as a philosophy, a direction to take, a constellation of ideas around which they could reshape their future.

Growing up in his native Athens, Georgia, Grady was a quintessential Southerner who started out to be a lawyer but then found himself attracted to journalism and worked for several Southern papers, as well as serving as Bennett, Jr.,'s Atlanta correspondent, before he bought a quarter interest in the Atlanta *Constitution* with the help of a $20,000 loan from Cyrus W. Field.

In a series of editorials and articles, he gave his fellow Southerners an answer to their question of what next. They needed to diversify their crops and break the habits of the past, he said. They should take an inventory of their local resources and find out the best means to develop them. Over and over he insisted that the South must attract and build industry to survive; it could no longer exist on agriculture alone. With a daring uncommon for the time, he told them bluntly that the Negro stood in a new relationship to them, whether they liked it or not, and somehow black and white must learn to live together. These ideas gave him a national prominence. In the South, he was hailed by some as a man who was turning the eyes of Southerners away from the lost past toward a hopeful future. In the North, his editorials were reprinted everywhere, welcomed by people who were weary of hatred and eager to make the Union stronger. When Grady made a speech, "The New South," at a meeting of the New England Club in New York in 1886, it was considered to be one of the finest speeches ever made from an American platform.

Grady died three years later, of pneumonia, after making a similar speech in Boston, but the *Constitution* was carried on in his image by two brilliant colleagues, Clark Howell and Joel Chandler Harris, who was a great newspaperman as well as the creator of Uncle Remus.

If Grady had not died so young, he might well have become an even larger figure in journalism and the nation's political life. As it was, he left the stage to the South's only other commanding figure on the newspaper scene, Henry Watterson; and "Marse Henry," as he was known, carried on in his own way Grady's effort to convert the Old Confederacy into the New South.

Watterson was another kind of man. By Southern standards, he was barely Southern, having been born in Washington, D.C., and brought up there and in the Tennessee home of his congressman father. Moreover, his newspaper, the Louisville *Courier-Journal*, was in the border state of Kentucky, and its office today is in fact no more than four blocks south of the Mason-Dixon Line. Yet it would have been difficult to find a more thoroughgoing Southerner than Watterson. He was an impressive man, the like of whose shaggy eyebrows were not seen again until the days of John L. Lewis, and the later days of Senator Sam Ervin. They overshadowed the one eye he had lost when growing up, and the bright-blue right eye, which had a peculiarly penetrating power. His mustache and goatee, along with his string tie and frock coat, made him look like the incarnation of a Kentucky colonel, and his high, clear voice could fill a large hall. As Henry Villard wrote: "Whenever he appeared on a Southern platform, men and women beheld the 'Lost Cause.' . . ."

He was not, however, a professional Southerner. Booker T. Washington, who knew him well, could testify to that. "If there is anywhere a man who has broader or more liberal ideas concerning the Negro, or any underdeveloped, I have not met him," Washington said. Watterson hated the cartoonists who depicted him as a stereotyped Southern colonel, mint julep in hand, lounging picturesquely amid the magnolias and white columns. It was true that he presided in patriarchal glory over a splendid Southern mansion, Mansfield, whose verandahs and green lawns made it the "Tara" of the border states, but Watterson hated to be called "colonel" and he drank champagne, still wine, and beer, preferring them in that order.

Watterson became editor of the *Courier-Journal* on November 8, 1868, and occupied that position with increasing distinction for the next fifty years. Grady was only eighteen at that time, and Watterson anticipated him with an editorial campaign to regenerate the South and heal the breach with the North. But where Grady argued for social and economic ideas, Watterson proposed a practical deal: in return for some of the rights and privileges it had lost to the victorious North, the South would guarantee civil and legal rights to the Negroes.

It was the kind of proposition not likely to satisfy anyone. Northern liberals like Greeley and Carl Schurz backed him, but other liberals argued that the Constitution already guaranteed Negro rights and it was the duty of the federal government to enforce them. Abolitionists of the more extreme sort asserted that it would be a mockery to restore anything to the beaten rebels. On the Southern side, most unreconstructed rebels wanted no deals at all with the North, particularly if it meant granting more than the irreducible minimum of freedom to the Negroes.

Watterson worked hard through the established political system to promote his plan, but after Tilden was defeated in the disputed election of 1876, he abandoned party politics, declared himself independent, and never again found an occupant of the White House with whom he could agree for an entire term. His feud with President Roosevelt attracted national attention and, by a curious coincidence, duplicated the attacks on a later Roosevelt by other strong-minded editors. There was a prophecy of things to come in Watterson's declaration that Roosevelt was a paranoiac who intended to be dictator of the country; he urged other members of the family to put this psychopath away.

When war broke out in 1914, Watterson was perhaps the first American editor to exclaim, "To hell with the Hohenzollerns and the Hapsburgs!" He urged United States entry from the beginning, and his editorials on the subject won him the Pulitzer Prize in 1917. A year later, he retired and went to Florida, where he wrote his two-volume autobiography, *Marse Henry*. He died in 1921.

Watterson was a personality, and unfortunately he was more and more aware of it as he grew older. If he had been less of a personality he might have been more effective as a crusading editor, but even so the thousands of words he poured into his editorials did much to further the ideas about the South that he and Grady both believed in. The *Courier-Journal* was a one-man show while he edited it, and because of the force of that personality it was a constantly entertaining and politically significant show. When he was gone, it went on being a distinguished newspaper, one of the top half dozen in the nation.

Together, Watterson and Grady exemplified a liberal, progressive element in Southern journalism which persists today in the cities where they established great newspapers. It is to be found, too, in a few other Southern cities, in a region where the general character of the press is still by and large provincial. If one were listing a dozen of the best metropolitan newspapers in the United States, four of them would be Southern. Another four or five in smaller communities are not only well edited and progressive, but courageous in the face of bigotry and extreme social pressures.

Community service in the South was regional rather than local, as it was in the Middle West. In the Far West, it was again local, but distinguished by a flavor consistent with the wide-open character of the region itself. The West of common usage in the latter half of the nineteenth century, it must be remembered, was not always what we think of today as the Far West. By "West" people often meant the broad spread from Ohio to the Pacific. Thus the Western Associated Press was made up of what would now be considered Midwestern newspapers. But Cincinnati, Chicago, Denver, and San Francisco had one thing in common: they were inhabited by people much closer to the frontier than those in the settled cities of the East, and they liked their journalism raw. A few good, responsible newspapers did well, but most of them were as flamboyant as a saloon dance hall on a Saturday night.

There was, for example, Wilbur F. Storey's Chicago *Times*, a herald of the "jazz journalism" of the twenties. "Old Storey" was yet another eccentric, a dissipated tyrant who had the acute news sense characteristic of all the foremost nineteenth-century editors. With his wild white hair and beard, he was a familiar figure in Chicago, particularly in the courts, where he once had twenty-four libel suits pending against him at the same time. His paper was most noted, and quoted, for its headlines, in which alliteration and puns were combined with unabashed editorializing. "DEATH'S DEBAUCH," read the headline over a railroad wreck story; "THE HOUSE THAT VANDERBILT" heralded a piece on a Vanderbilt will. Storey loved to collect short, scandalous pieces from the wire copy and run them under such blanket heads as "SEXUAL SKULDUGGERY," or "FRAIL FEMALES."

For some macabre reason, Storey and his chief headline writer, Horatio W. Seymour, the telegraph editor, were especially fond of stories about hangings. One was headlined "FEET FIRST," with the next deck reading, "That's the Way They Shoved Bill Green Down Among the Fireworks." On another the head was "A DROP TOO MUCH." But the *Times* surpassed itself with the one it used on a hanging in which four repentant murderers were executed following last-minute prayers. "JERKED TO JESUS," shocked Chicagoans read.

In his later years, Storey exhibited so many aberrations in his personal life, as in the *Times*, that it was no surprise when he was adjudged insane, and he died soon after in 1884.

Nothing that happened in Chicago or elsewhere, however, could match the fantastic medicine show put on in Denver by Frederick Gilmer Bonfils and Harry Heye Tammen, or the struggle for dominance in violent San Francisco between men like the young Hearst and Fremont Older. This was journalism which bridged the centuries not only chronologically, but in the mixture of old and new ways of making newspapers. It was personal journalism of the Bennett variety, carried well into the new century in which the business institutionalizing of the press was steadily going forward elsewhere.

Only a small taste of the strong brew provided by Bonfils and Tammen in Denver can be provided here. The whole gamy mess has been preserved with wit and affection by Gene Fowler in his classic *Timber Line*, which records the happenings in Denver in detail.

Frederick Bonfils, the real entrepreneur of the partnership, was born in Missouri, dropped out of West Point, sold insurance and real estate, and under numerous aliases operated the Little Louisiana Lottery in Kansas City. He was caught up in the *Star's* reform wave and was escorted by the police to the city line, from which he migrated to Denver, where in 1895 he met Harry Tammen, currently serving at the long mirrored bar in the Windsor Hotel. Tammen was four years older, from Baltimore, and had begun as a pinboy in a bowling alley, but at an early age discovered the occupation for which he was best qualified—bartending.

Both men were ideally cast. Dark, trim, and handsome with a neat black mustache, the confidence man Bonfils was Clark Gable playing a Mississippi River gambler. Tammen looked like the character of Joe the Bartender created by Jackie Gleason, chubby and good-natured, the kind of man to whom strangers found themselves giving confidences.

Bonfils had never met a confidence man abler than himself until the day he encountered Tammen, who talked him into investing $12,500 of his Kansas City money in a nearly extinct afternoon paper, the Denver *Evening Post*, established three years before. Bonfils and Tammen took it over on October 28, 1895, dropped "*Evening*" from the title, and began what was to be the strangest career in newspaper publishing.

The partners knew nothing about journalism, but they knew a great deal about human nature and they understood the free-wheeling nature of Denver. They had two policies. One was to proclaim as loudly and as often as possible that everything the *Post* did was for the Denver public's good. The *Post* cuddled up to its readers with slogans like "Your big brother," "The paper with a heart and soul," and "So the people may know."

The *Post's* second policy was to attack everything in sight with the biggest headline type and reddest ink in the shop, and with whatever other devices came readily to hand. The two publishers began by exposing lotteries, a subject on which Bonfils was an authority. It was not a random choice. Bonfils had been in Kansas City long enough to see how successful Nelson was by concentrating on local news and crusading for the public welfare. Perversely adopting the ideas of his onetime enemy, Bonfils announced that the *Post* would operate on the principle, mentioned earlier, that "a dog fight in a Denver street is more important than a war in Europe."

In carrying out this policy, the partners divided their talents. Tammen was the promoter who thought up outrageous stunts to keep the paper under the public's nose. Bonfils, the shrewd gambler, was in charge of the money drawer and editorial policy. When the paper was financially secure, he moved it into one of the best locations in town, where he indulged his peculiar passion for red, which he had been able to express before only in the *Post*'s screaming banner headlines. He caused the walls of his and Tammen's office to be painted a flashing red. They called it the Red Room, but Denverites had another name for it—"the Bucket of Blood."

Bonfils and Tammen also moved the *Post* into high gear, now that they could afford to defend libel suits. No one in the city or the state was safe. The suits were not long in coming, but the partners took them in easy stride and went on to new outrages. Sometimes the victims, in the manner of the early days, came into the office to fight a few rounds with the owners.

On one occasion, during a violent strike against the Denver transit system, the *Post* had been presumed, as a friend of the people, to be on labor's side, but it proved instead to be advocating the management cause. A mob of strikers, sensing an inconsistency in the paper's attitude, swarmed into the *Post* building and began taking it carefully apart until they were restrained. They did not stop to read the pious motto over the entrance: "O Justice, when expelled from other habitations, make this thy dwelling place."

Sometimes, when it suited the proprietors, the *Post* did give shelter to justice. It fought for reforms in the child-labor practices of the times, and in the management of prisons. It was always alert to the straying fingers of public officials. But it surpassed itself one winter when the cost of coal had reached what Bonfils deemed an unreasonable level. The *Post* would keep its readers warm and happy, he declared, and promptly leased some mines, out of which he trucked coal around town and sold it to *Post* customers at considerably lower rates.

On two occasions the proprietors of the *Post* took on the United States government. In 1914, they were under the scrutiny of the Interstate Commerce Commission when an ICC hearing disclosed that the Rock Island Railroad had paid $60,000 to the *Post* for a purpose which it quaintly listed as "editorial advertising." Since the railroad was regulated by the government and the *Post* enjoyed—indeed, luxuriated in—freedom of the press, nothing came of it.

In 1924, however, a far more disturbing incident occurred. Bonfils was called before the Senate committee investigating the Teapot Dome scandal, which succeeded in extracting from him the information that the *Post* had been attacking Harry F. Sinclair, chief figure in the scandal, not out of an excess of virtue but through connivance with a man who had brought suit against Sinclair—whose payoff of a million dollars had stopped the suit and the *Post*'s attacks simultaneously. The American Society of Newspaper Editors was sufficiently aroused by this episode to recommend through its Committee on Ethics that Bonfils be expelled from the organization, but he escaped on a technicality. Three years later, having saved face, he resigned.

Tammen died while this affair was going on, and Bonfils was left alone to carry on a battle of a different kind, which he regarded as much more serious. Even with $1 million a year profit and a circulation of 150,000 daily and twice that on Sunday, he was not wholly prepared to take on a bustling publisher named Roy Howard, whose Scripps-Howard League had just bought the *Rocky Mountain News*. Howard was a personal journalist with an unerring news sense, but he was also one of the new century's ablest managers of newspaper properties.

For two years these men fought it out in an expensive, fantastic conflict which had the people of Denver bemused. At one point the papers were locked in a contest in which they offered free gasoline in varying amounts up to five gallons for every customer who inserted a want ad in the Sunday editions. While it lasted, every Sunday was a Roman holiday in Denver as the citizenry went joyriding and the newsboys staggered under the weight of Sunday editions of more than a hundred pages, predominantly classified ads.

Bonfils was a fighter right up to the end. In 1932, when he was seventy-two, he filed a $200,000 libel suit against the *News* for publishing a story quoting a speech at a political convention by the publisher of the Grand Junction *Sentinel*, Walter Walker, who had said of Bonfils: "The day will come when some persecuted man will treat that rattlesnake as rattlesnakes should be treated, and there will be general rejoicing. . . . Bonfils is a public enemy and has left the trail of a slimy serpent across Colorado for thirty years."

Before the case could be tried, Bonfils died, leaving behind him a bookful of legends and $8 million. Tammen had left $2 million. In their wills both men bequeathed much of their fortunes to good works of various kinds. These bequests must have been the result of conscience; they could hardly have resulted from a lack of imagination.

Something of the newspaper climate in Denver could be observed on a larger scale in San Francisco, where the bohemian, cosmopolitan atmosphere was even more friendly to journalistic mayhem. As in the case of both Chicago and Denver, the story of San Francisco newspapermaking, in and out of community service, can hardly be encompassed in a few pages. Its full flavor can only be suggested.

For years after the Civil War, the Golden Gate scene had been dominated by one paper, the *Chronicle*, which had begun as a free theater program sheet of four pages called the *Dramatic Chronicle*. It evolved into a regular newspaper, enterprising enough to be the only paper in town to get out extras on Lincoln's assassination. It was a newspaper on the lines laid down by Nelson and Lawson, a community-service paper which fought civic corruption, campaigned for community improvements, and extended its horizons to boost California. In fighting to reform the state constitution, and to struggle against land monopoly and the machinations of the powerful railroad barons who were building the Southern Pacific empire, the paper inevitably made enemies. Charles De Young, who with his brother Michael had founded the *Chronicle*, was shot and killed in 1880 as a result of the paper's battle against the Workingmen's Party. Earlier, De Young had shot and wounded the party's mayoral candidate—whose son was the editor's assassin.

Taking over from his brother, Michael gave the paper a more conservative cast as the state's chief journalistic upholder of Republican principles. De Young was also a member of the Republican National Committee for eight years. Active in civic and national affairs, he nevertheless kept a tight hand on the *Chronicle* until he died in 1925.

It was this paper that young Hearst challenged with his *Examiner*, as related earlier. Hearst not only printed the news first if he could possibly get it, but he was first in everything else he could think of. Writers like Ouida, Anna Katherine Green, and Gertrude Atherton appeared on newspaper pages for the first time in the *Examiner*. The first music ever printed by a daily paper in the West appeared in the paper. Hearst even went up in a balloon, accompanied by a flight of homing pigeons and a photographer, and while he stared down the sunburned gullets of his fellow natives, he sent the birds fluttering back to the *Examiner* office with exclusive descriptive stories and pictures of how the city looked from the air.

If it seemed impossible to compete with a paper possessing the resources and staff of Hearst's creation, the prospect did not dismay a man who was at the opposite pole from Hearst. He was Fremont Older, a Wisconsin farm boy who came to California after a restless period in which he sought to find a place for himself in a hostile world—a tall, awkward youth moving from job to job, from one temporary home to another, after his divorced mother married again and moved to California.

After several California newspaper jobs, he was hired to be managing editor of the *Bulletin*, a rapidly failing property. This position crystallized Older's tremendous energy and talent and released these qualities. He was determined now to be a success, and, as he wrote later in his autobiography, he meant to be ruthless about it, not caring whether his sensational stories and headlines "might make people suffer, might wound or utterly ruin someone."

Such a drive was certain to produce results, given Older's undoubted abilities, and it did. He was a born crusader. In the beginning, his *Bulletin* crusades did not stem from his convictions but solely from his purpose to increase the paper's circulation and thus help his personal fortunes. He decided to engage in combat the Southern Pacific Railroad, which virtually owned California through a system of widespread and utterly shameless bribery. Legislators, officials, and many of the state's newspapers were on its payoff list— including the *Bulletin* itself, Older discovered, which was down for $125 a month to guarantee its good will.

Moving against this giant network of corruption, Older first got his friend James D. Phelan elected mayor of San Francisco. The intention was to set up a reform government in the city that could serve as an opening wedge to fight the railroad's political machine. Watching Phelan, a completely fearless and honest man, carry out his part of the bargain converted Older from simple opportunism. As he wrote later, he acquired his "first social sense."

Phelan's major battle was the obtaining of a new city charter, which meant exposing and checking the corruption of the city's public utilities. These had been returning regular subsidies to the papers, including the *Bulletin*, and W. A. Crothers, the publisher, was reluctant to give up his share. Older found himself opposing his boss as well as the machine.

In the subsequent conflict, Older was kidnaped by a gunman who lost his nerve before he could kill the editor. In turn, Older kidnaped a Chinese confederate of Abraham Ruef, the city's political boss. Eventually, the editor was victorious. Ruef went to prison for extortion in 1908, at the end of a trial in which the prosecutor was shot dead in the courtroom. A young lawyer politician, Hiram W. Johnson, succeeded him.

As soon as Ruef was in jail, Older began to have second thoughts. He decided it was the system and not the man that was to blame, and he began another crusade to get the boss out of jail, a move far more difficult than to get him in. Older was so obsessed with the idea of penal reform that he did not care whether people thought he was crazy or had "gone soft." He arranged the release of a San Quentin convict, printed his story of prison life in the *Bulletin*, then set him up as head of a bureau to help ex-convicts get a new start. He also fought capital punishment and, in an ever-broadening scope, a good many other social evils. His crusading for the rights of labor leaders and their unions led him to embrace the extreme left wing of the movement, which brought down the fire of the conservative element. All these crusades produced circulation, however, and Crothers continued to let him use the *Bulletin* as a platform.

Older's *cause célèbre* was the Preparedness Day parade bombing in San Francisco on July 22, 1916. In the face of the prevailing fanaticism, Older declared his belief that Thomas J. Mooney and Warren K. Billings, the men convicted of the crime, had been framed. Their conviction, he said, was a monumental injustice, a mockery of the judicial process; and he kept up a steady fire of protest. A year after the bombing he was printing letters which charged perjury in the trial. This was too much for some of the paper's conservative advertisers, who complained to the publisher. Older was asked to resign.

It was logical at the time for Hearst, who had opposed most of Older's crusades, to offer him the editorship of the *Call*, which the publisher had bought as an evening companion for the *Examiner*. Hearst told him to "bring the Mooney case with me," Older recalled later. For Hearst it was a splendid deal. He acquired a first-class news executive, experienced in the crusading which was also a characteristic of Hearst papers in their constant push for circulation, and he assumed that a certain amount of Older's reputation would be reflected, thus adding to the Hearst public image as a friend of the masses. As a final touch of irony for Older, Hearst bought the *Bulletin* in 1928, and made him president and editor of the combined *Call-Bulletin*.

Hearst made the complete circle of political beliefs, or pretended beliefs, in his lifetime, and Older did much the same thing. He had started crusading in the persuasion that it was good for his paper's circulation and his career, but little else. Then he acquired the strong moral convictions which led him into prison reform and the Mooney case. Under Hearst, he returned, as may have been natural, to his original conclusion. Crusades were good circulation builders, he said; they would never reform the social system.

The only crusade he maintained was the one for Hearst himself,

who had won his unwavering admiration by taking him in with the
Mooney case when he could have been shouldered out of San Francisco journalism. The years on the *Call-Bulletin*, where Hearst gave
him free rein, were the happiest of his life. He became W. R.'s most
vociferously loyal employee, even helping his second wife, Cora, to
write an authorized biography of the publisher. Older died suddenly
of a heart attack in 1935, after a pleasant afternoon spent writing an
editorial about Montaigne's essay on death.

In his career, Older had combined both activism and community
service in San Francisco, but the activist side predominated. His
dynamism, and that of the other giants of metropolitan journalism,
tended to obscure what was happening to the community-service idea
on a lower level, that of the country newspapers, where the circulation figures were lower but the quality often as high. The chief preoccupation of country editors was to provide the local voice for which
no imported paper could ever be a satisfactory substitute.

Country newspapers, of course, had existed from the beginning,
but with the exception of a few isolated figures like Joseph Dennie in
his Walpole, New Hampshire, days, they did not reach their full
effectiveness until the community-service idea was placed in the
hands of exceptional editors. Meanwhile, weekly journalism grew rapidly.

Weeklies had a high mortality rate because so many of them were
used for special purposes and were dropped when the purpose was
satisfied. They advanced the shifting fortunes of political groups,
promoted the settlement and sale of lands, served as organs for mis-
sionaries, and enlivened Army posts. The editors seldom showed
enough enterprise to fill the whole paper with local news; two thirds
or more of the space was likely to be filled with "literary" material—
essays, poems, sketches. Their circulations seldom passed 1000 and
their advertising columns, aside from what retail linage could be
obtained, consisted of legal and patent-medicine ads. Almost every
village as large as a thousand inhabitants had at least two papers,
usually representing opposite political faiths.

But in spite of the transitory character of much of the country
press, thousands of papers were well established and prosperous.
Their editors were personal journalists in the truest sense of the term.
They were also important people in their small towns—more important than the entrepreneurs of New York and Chicago, who had to
compete with one another for attention. A circulation of 1500 or so
was enough to sustain the average country weekly, and a modicum of
legal and retail advertising would put it well into the black.

Country journalism had reached a peak in America by 1914. There were 14,500 weeklies, and their service was something the communities involved could hardly do without. Not only did they bring local merchants and consumers together through advertising, but they recorded births, deaths, and marriages, social events, and the happenings of everyday life in the town and in the surrounding countryside. They faithfully reflected the existence around them in its exterior aspects, but the private lives of citizens and the interior life of the town did not appear in print unless the circumstances made it unavoidable. Not even the coming of rural free delivery in 1897, bringing city dailies into farm mailboxes, shook their position. They were more prosperous than they had ever been, as national advertising began to add to income and both advertising and subscription rates increased.

The preoccupation with local news meant that the editors were prominent in local affairs, particularly in politics, and so the country press tended to be more partisan at a time when the city press was becoming less personal with the decline of the one-man show. National politicians tried to exploit the country press by distributing propaganda in plate and ready-print form, and they succeeded on occasion, but country editors were inclined to be independent as well as partisan and made their own choices.

Two small-town editors succeeded in making themselves national figures. One was Edgar Watson Howe, known to the nation as Ed Howe, the "Sage of Potato Hill," publisher of the Atchison (Kansas) *Globe* for thirty-six years. The *Globe* was a daily, but Atchison was a typical small town, and its paper was the authentic independent voice of the small-town editor, raised to a higher level in this case by Howe's writing ability and iconoclastic mind. He differed from most of his fellows by his willingness to shock and offend his readers, not excluding the advertisers.

Howe began publishing the *Globe* in 1875, at twenty-one, with a backlog of $200 and the help of his brother Jim. What separated it at once from other papers of its size was the editor's particular genius for writing and editing. His work was so individual and outstanding that within a month the paper was operating in the black, and in a few years the two competing papers had to quit.

Howe's impact on the town of Atchison is unmatched in the history of American newspapers, and even now it is hard to believe. In this small town in the heart of the God-fearing Midwest, he began an extraordinary personal campaign against women, religion, and the churches. At first the citizens were incredulous. Then came the inevitable counterattack. There were advertising boycotts, canceled subscriptions, and rival newspapers founded, all of which failed. Through it all Howe roamed the village streets and the surrounding countryside serenely, gathering news, and he prevailed. The reason was simply stated, with a pardonable pride, by his newspaper publisher son, Gene, who wrote later: "He was the greatest reporter in America; he was so regarded by many leading newspapermen. The *Globe* vibrated with his sparkle and humor, and it became the most quoted daily in the United States. Opposition could not stand against it; Atchison people simply could not resist reading his paper."

Still, it is hard to understand, in retrospect, how he was able to survive and even become a national figure when his attacks on both religion and women verged on the incredible. "Never have I known a sincere religious man or woman," Howe wrote. He told his readers that men and women were natural enemies, that civilization itself was threatened because women had become spoiled and extravagant, and urged an actual revolt of the nation's men against women. In his opinion, a woman ought to be her husband's chattel, without rights or privileges. Naturally, his own marriage was wretched and had ended in divorce by 1901.

In spite of it all, Howe became a Kansas institution. Those who were offended by his views learned to overlook them; others were amused by what he wrote. Much of this tolerance may have derived from the fact that Howe put Atchison on the map. The *Globe* was quoted by newspapers everywhere, particularly Howe's "paragraphs," as he called them—sharp, sometimes witty aphorisms. One issue of the Boston *Globe* carried fifty-eight of these "paragraphs," which were useful as fillers. Atchison became known as "Ed Howe's Town," and Howe himself the most famous country editor in America. He added to his reputation by publishing in 1882 an excellent novel, *The Story of a Country Town*, and his autobiography, *Plain People*, published in 1929, remains one of the best written by an American. He died in 1937, at eighty-four, consistent to the last in his views.

William Allen White, a fellow Kansan who succeeded Howe as the best-known country editor in America, thought Ed was a "lovable, kindly old grouch," in spite of the overwhelming evidence that Howe was neither lovable nor kindly. White himself was the antithesis, and much more typical of his breed. He was as uncompromisingly blunt in his beliefs as Howe, but he was blunt on the side of humanity and ideals; consequently he was more admired by his fellow Americans, who wanted most to hear the good news, not the bad.

White was born in February 1868, in Emporia, Kansas, the town in which he was to do his life's work. His training was on the Kansas City *Star* under Nelson, during which he absorbed the publisher's community-service idea, carrying it back to Emporia in 1895, where he bought the town's five-year-old *Gazette* for $5000 and published it until his death.

His special talent was editorial writing, and he was the best since Godkin, although he spoke in a different language—the language of the people in small cities and towns everywhere in America. Intellectuals on city papers sometimes sneered at his folksy approach, but they underestimated him, because he could be biting and even cruel when he chose. He came to national prominence a year after he took over the *Gazette* with a single editorial, "What's the Matter with Kansas?" In one stroke, it elevated White to be one of the Republican Party's chief spokesmen. In later, less partisan years, he called this famous essay "conservatism in its full and perfect flower."

But the editorial was a fair sample of the kind that flowed from White's typewriter in an unending, accomplished stream. Such talent made him so valuable to the politicians that in 1912 he was a Progressive Party national committeeman, in a brief flight from Republicanism; and later he was one of the chief movers behind the scenes to get Herbert Hoover into the White House, a careful undercover campaign which went on for years. When it ended in success, White found himself disillusioned, a liberal Republican unable to go along with the President's conservatism.

White was a fearless editor who spoke out boldly no matter who might be offended. He attacked the Ku Klux Klan when it was not only unpopular but dangerous to do so, setting a courageous example for the small-town and small-city editors of our own time in the South and elsewhere who have attacked racism and bigotry at considerable risk to their lives and property. Until the end of his life, on January 29, 1944, White battled for what he believed was honest and right. He even criticized his fellow publishers in terms which would have been resented far more had they come from anyone else.

By the time White died, the country press had changed dramatically from what it was when he began. Where once it had been lively, independent, and politically diversified, the trend was to a gray conformity of conservative Republicanism everywhere in the nation except the South, where there was an even more conservative viewpoint representing the Southern Democrats. Metropolitan dailies had become big business; small-town papers had become small business. In both cases, the viewpoint was the same.

Today, the old-style publisher-editor has been replaced by the small daily or weekly operator who runs his paper on business rather than editorial principles, often as part of a chain, and who shuns anything which might irritate his readers and advertisers. Now and then a striking exception occurs, but mostly the small-town paper has the same political coloration as its big neighbors. It functions, as it always has, primarily as a community bulletin board, and it does the job better than it did even twenty-five years ago, as the result of improved mechanical equipment, greater use of pictures, the application of modern management principles, and a more professional approach to the news. Beset by expanding big-city circulation zones and the competition of radio and television, it has concentrated on the one thing it does which cannot be duplicated: the coverage of purely local news.

More recently, the decentralization of great urban centers into smaller, suburban towns, grouped around their own subdivisions and shopping centers, has inspired the growth of new suburban weeklies, triweeklies, and small dailies. Most of these papers are successful and smart-looking; some are small gold mines, fat with advertising. But color and individuality have virtually disappeared from country journalism, with a few scattered exceptions. Now these papers are plastic reflections of a plastic society.

Part Four
The Media in the Twentieth Century

18

The Great Transformation: I

Two MAJOR DEVELOPMENTS, neither of which could have been foreseen by the framers of the First Amendment, have transformed the media in the twentieth century. One is the triumph of the technological society and the resulting institutionalizing of the means of communication. The other is the rapid rise of radio and television to a position of dominance over the other media. These facts have confronted us with so many entirely new problems that there has been a tendency to isolate the media from their historical past and treat them as children of this century. On the contrary, the line runs clear and true from the beginning.

The transition from the old order to the new was well under way by 1914 in the newspaper business. Arthur Brisbane, who as Hearst's right hand was in a position to know, had observed gloomily in 1904: "Journalistic success brings money. The editor has become a money man. 'Where your treasure is, there will your heart be also.'" There was nothing new in the fulfillment of this prophecy. The lives of Bennett, Sr., and Dana were witnesses to the fact that journalistic success, like success in any other business, could change crusaders for the poor to defenders of the rich and privileged. In the twentieth century, however, this fact took on new meanings.

As the institutionalizing of the newspaper proceeded, the few publishers and editors who were highly individualistic, in the nineteenth-century manner, stood out as anachronisms and sometimes became unjustly celebrated. Such an editor was the *World*'s Charles E.

Chapin, a sadistic psychopath who gloried in his reputation as the toughest man who ever sat at the city editor's desk. Of the many stories told about him, a large share of them apocryphal, the enduring one is his command to a reporter who had been beaten up and kicked out by a reluctant news source: "You go back and tell that sonofabitch he can't intimidate *me*."

The late Stanley Walker, noted city editor of the New York *Herald Tribune,* called Chapin "the ablest city editor who ever lived," but that was only professional glorification of a cliché, that the city editor must be rough and tough to be successful. In practice, Chapin was a contemptible man. When the excursion steamer *Slocum* sank with an appalling loss of life, he "capered about the city room," as Allen Churchill tells us, "with every trace of enjoyment, to make him seem a figure of jerking, hysterical life in a ballet with a background of morbid death. He would run up and down peering over shoulders to read the nauseating details of the tragedy as they were typed out. Then, standing erect, he would shout, 'Women and children jumping overboard with clothing afire! Water full of charred bodies!' and between these jackal outcries, he would strut exultantly up and down, humming a simpering, happy, tuneless tune."

Of this iron-handed despot, his star reporter, Irvin S. Cobb, coined the memorable phrase, often quoted and misattributed, on hearing Chapin was ill: "Let's hope it's nothing trivial."

Churchill described him: "He was granitefaced, and under a close-clipped military-type mustache, his mouth seemed a tight, straight slash. On the bridge of his thin nose perched a tortoise-shell pince-nez, anchored to his buttonhole by a dignified black ribbon. . . ." And a contemporary wrote of him: "His face was a graying paving block, with jaws as square as a lynx's jaws, and as tight. His snake eyes were dull and empty. The shallow light from those eyes never seemed to come from within but from without. His voice seemed to match the rest of him. Big game hunters say that a hostile leopard has a voice like that."

Chapin had the consummate bad taste to be proud of his loathsome personality. He wrote: "In twenty years, I never saw or spoke to a member of the staff outside the office or talked to them in the office about anything except the business of the moment. I gave no confidences, I invited none. I was myself a machine, and the men I worked with were cogs. The human element never entered into the scheme of getting out the paper. It was my way of doing things."

In the end, Chapin's megalomania led him to frantic speculation in the stock market and ultimate financial collapse. In a suicide pact with his wife, Nellie, he shot and killed her but failed to turn the gun on himself, and after some unsavory plea bargaining enhanced by the political influence he still enjoyed as a result of the *World*'s power, he pleaded guilty to second-degree murder charges and was given a twenty-years-to-life sentence in Sing Sing. There he was amazingly rehabilitated, with the help of Warden Lewis E. Lawes. He edited a prison paper so successfully that it had to be taken away from him as a threat to the authorities; then he carried on a strange love affair by correspondence with a young girl from Cleveland, who aspired to be a writer, and their letters were published in book form. They met at the prison, and she appeared to be, inexplicably, in love with him. His personality changed completely as a result. He raised roses and built a splendid prison garden. When he died in 1930 it was, in effect, from a broken heart over the destruction of his garden to make room for prison expansion.

Chapin gave to the business a stereotype so indelibly imprinted on the public mind that it still thrives today in the image of the irascible, demanding, tough city editors who inhabit motion pictures and television plays about newspapers. This conception has its roots in Chapin, but enjoyed its flowering in the Hearst brand of journalism, where city rooms were frequently burdened with sadists somewhat less accomplished than Chapin who felt themselves compelled to fulfill the stereotype. Ben Hecht and Charles MacArthur immortalized this kind of news executive, who was particularly prevalent in the twenties, in *The Front Page*. When it is revived today, there are no doubt many theatergoers who see it less as a museum piece than as a faithful reflection of how newspapers were operated in the twenties and, for all they know, may still be operated today.

In fact, even in Chapin's time this kind of newspapering was passé, an anachronistic holdover from the more primitive days of journalism. The excuse for the city editor's legendary toughness was the pressure of competition, and indeed a man at that desk in a town with several newspapers had to have a high degree of professional competence to survive. But most city editors got the news without sadism or self-dramatization. The *World*, in fact, was not celebrated for the news Chapin obtained. His specialties were sex, crime, and disaster—run-of-the-mill spot news. He had no sense of humor, nor the slightest understanding of human beings; and for a man to whom news was life, he had little respect for the facts if the facts were inconvenient.

The *World*, then, as a prophet of the new order, derived its reputation as the best newspaper in America far more from Frank Cobb, its brilliant editor, than from Chapin's city-room antics. Then, when Cobb was gone, Walter Lippmann succeeded him as editor and carried on in his style, although in a somewhat more subdued way. These editors, who pounded away with attacks on privilege and corruption, were backed by a stable of first-class reporters and writers, men like Irvin S. Cobb, Heywood Broun, and Franklin P. Adams, and by such cartoonists as Rollin Kirby, all working under a managing editor, Herbert Bayard Swope, who had his own peculiarities but was nevertheless the best man in his position with the exception of Carr Van Anda, of the *Times*.

In spite of its reputation and unexampled quality, the *World* failed because Pulitzer's two sons, Ralph and Herbert, were not able to guide it through the rapidly changing conditions that were transforming the press. They mistakenly raised the price of the paper to three cents in 1925, while the competing papers remained at two cents. The new tabloids were also cutting into circulation, and costs were rising. In spite of frantic efforts to save it, the *World* disappeared in 1930 when Roy Howard bought it, suspending the morning and Sunday editions, and merging the *Evening World* with his *Telegram* to form the *World-Telegram*, which ultimately absorbed the *Sun* as well.

The *World*'s passing, mourned by people in and out of the newspaper business, was symptomatic of what was happening to newspapers. Mergers were the order of the day—many of them carried out by Frank Munsey, the telegraph boy from Augusta, Maine, who had been so successful with *Argosy* and *Munsey's* in the magazine business. His most significant acquisition as a newspaper entrepreneur was the *Sun*, which he bought in 1916 for $2.5 million. At this stage, the paper was distinguished by its managing editor, Keats Speed, and its excellent reporting staff, led by Frank Ward O'Malley, whose talents as a feature writer were so much admired that the phrase "O'Malley of the *Sun*" became a part of the New York mythology.

The *Sun* lost so much money covering the First World War that Munsey looked around in 1920 for papers he could merge with it. There were fourteen of them in New York at the time, not including the foreign-language press; only three survive today. In a series of coolly calculated strokes, Munsey bought the *Herald*, the *Telegram*, and the Paris *Herald* for $4 million from the Bennett estate, merged the morning *Sun* with the *Herald*, and passed on its name to the evening edition, which he operated in competition with his own *Telegram*.

He made other minor deals, but the climax of his operations came with his attempt to acquire the *Tribune*, which he meant to merge with his *Herald*. Here, however, he encountered the determined opposition of the *Tribune*'s owners, Ogden Mills Reid and his talented wife, Helen Rogers Reid. When they refused to sell, Munsey offered to sell them the *Herald* and its Paris offspring for $5 million. That transaction enabled the new *Herald Tribune* to pursue its editorially successful but often financially rocky course until it was sold in 1958 to John Hay Whitney; it went under a few years later, while it was still one of the best newspapers in the world.

Although Munsey was blamed for the shrinkage of the New York newspaper field, he only hastened a process which was, in any case, inevitable, and would be repeated in Chicago and other large cities as time went on. He was a businessman who had an unsentimental attitude toward the newspaper business, which profoundly irritated those who loved it and considered it a profession, or at least a calling. Their opinion was expressed by William Allen White's famous obituary in the Emporia *Gazette*: "Frank A. Munsey contributed to the journalism of his day the talent of a meat-packer, the morals of a money-changer and the manners of an undertaker. He and his kind have about succeeded in transforming a once-noble profession into an 80 per cent security. May he rest in trust!"

This kind of honesty about the deceased, it may be added, is another quality that has disappeared from the newspaper scene. Today there is something good to be said about the worst scoundrels, and those who were rightly condemned one day are piously enshrined the next, when they are no longer there to be gratified by it.

The decline experienced by the dailies in New York had been a commonplace of Philadelphia journalism even before Munsey. There were thirteen dailies in that city in 1895, and only eight in 1913. Cyrus H. K. Curtis, who had shown himself a genius in making magazines, tried to duplicate his success with a newspaper, the *Public Ledger*; but although it ranked with the New York *Times* and the Chicago *Daily News* in its foreign coverage and had numerous other virtues, it failed to survive Curtis' death in 1933, when the small newspaper empire the publisher had built fell apart. Only one of his seven papers remained.

In Chicago, there were eight newspapers in 1904, but by the time the consolidators were through in our own time, there were only four, under two ownerships.

Everywhere in the nation, the story was the same, particularly in

the morning field, which was being hit hard by the developing prefer-
ence of readers and advertisers for afternoon papers. The number of
morning dailies dropped from 500 to 388 between 1910 and 1930. By
1933, there were forty cities in the nation with populations of more
than 100,000 which boasted only one morning daily. The growth of
the two largest chains, Hearst and Scripps-Howard, was also hasten-
ing the consolidation process. Sixteen papers succumbed to the
Hearst ax between 1918 and 1928, while the Scripps-Howard interests
accounted for fifteen more between 1923 and 1934.

Not all the victims deserved to live, judged on their merits, but it
was sad to see such traditional papers of real excellence as the Boston
Evening Transcript go under. Those who wrote of its passing recalled
its elegant days, when a Beacon Hill butler reported to his master,
"Sir, there are two reporters and a gentleman from the *Transcript*
waiting to see you." In Boston, the eleven major newspapers of 1900,
under seven ownerships, were reduced to eight newspapers under five
ownerships three decades later. The story was the same in Baltimore,
Milwaukee, Detroit, San Francisco, Los Angeles, and other cities.

Chain journalism and the trend to consolidation was clearly a major
media phenomenon of the century, and one of its most significant
developments. Edward Wyllis Scripps, better known as E. W. and
self-styled as a "damned old crank," did not invent the chain idea, but
he was the first American publisher to make it work. He made it work
so well that he left behind him one of the richest legacies in journalism: the Booth Newspapers of Michigan, the Scripps League of
Newspapers in the Northwest, the John P. Scripps papers on the
Pacific Coast, and the Scripps-Howard chain, with its allied United
Press International, United Press Feature Service, and two other syn-
dicates.

Born in 1858, Scripps was a man in the tradition of the nineteenth-
century publishers. Building his empire from bases in Cincinnati,
Detroit, Cleveland, and St. Louis, he retired in 1890 at thirty-six,
driven to it, as his granddaughter's husband, Charles R. McCabe,
wrote, by "a combination of misanthropy, raw nerves and family
exacerbations," which "drove him as far away from his kind as was
possible without loss of nationality." He moved with his wife and
children to Miramar Ranch, his windswept mesa home sixteen miles
from San Diego, and from that remote spot became another long-
range publisher like Bennett, Jr., and Pulitzer, managing his enterprises and expanding his chain.

"The loneliness of my life is great," Scripps wrote near the end of it. "I am hated by the rich for being a renegade, and I am hated by the poor for being rich. I am not wise enough or learned enough to be an acceptable member in the highbrow club. I have learned too many things to make me a comfortable companion of the man in the field, on the street and in the shop."

Scripps trained his sons to succeed him, keeping them out of college so that they would not, as he said, acquire a sense of superiority through buying knowledge and training which the common people could not afford; but the eldest, James, broke away from him and died suddenly at thirty-four. It would have been difficult for any son to live with such a father. The lord of Miramar ruled in feudal splendor, like Hearst, but he was a far different kind of man, with his bushy red beard, balding head covered with a skullcap, and trousers tucked into white kid boots. He wanted his papers to be autonomous, but at the same time he wanted his editors to feel and think as he did. "I have one principle," he said, "and that is represented by an effort to make it harder for the rich to grow richer and easier for the poor to keep from growing poorer." Of his papers, he said, "We can hold together, having supporting us the army of our followers, so long as we fight hard and fight and win our battles for them; so long as we fight against privilege and success, by degree transferring some of the privileges from the few to the many." The first Bennett or Pulitzer could not have said it better.

Until nearly his last breath, Scripps was busy. In 1920 he founded Science Service, the first attempt to translate the burgeoning activities of the nation's scientific community into stories the untrained reader could understand. A little later he endowed the Foundation for Research in Population Problems, at Miami University in Ohio, and with his half-sister Ellen established and financed the Scripps Institute of Biological Research at La Jolla, which eventually became the Scripps Institution of Oceanography, part of the University of California.

Like those other eccentrics of the business, Bennett, Sr., and Pulitzer, Scripps was a yachtsman, and at the end of his life he retreated to sea, as they had, to escape the pain of life ashore, roving from place to place, proud and alone. One night in March 1926, he died suddenly of apoplexy at seventy-two, on his yacht as it lay anchored in Monrovia Bay, off Liberia. According to his wishes, he was buried at sea. He left behind him a controlling interest in papers in fifteen states, besides all the subsidiary properties. Robert Paine Scripps, his only surviving son, was in charge, but less and less was heard of him; oddly, he too retired to Miramar and died on his yacht at sea, off Lower California, when he was only forty-two. Until the founder's grandchildren were old enough to take over, Roy Howard, who had been the business manager of the Scripps interests, ran the chain.

Scripps's chief rival in the business of chain journalism—a phrase from which chain operators invariably shudder away—was Hearst. The contrast in both methods and personalities could not have been greater. Where Scripps ran his papers on little money, made them relatively autonomous, and trained the editors himself, Hearst spared no expense to establish his empire, and hired editors to run his newspapers but gave each one of them his daily personal attention.

The Hearst empire began to form in 1904, when he added a Boston paper to those in San Francisco and New York. When he at last rested in 1931, he had either founded or acquired forty-two daily newspapers, with an audience of more than 3 million people on Sunday and perhaps twice that on weekdays. The California papers alone earned more than $5 million a year. Fourteen of these were merged with other Hearst papers, seven others were sold, and four suspended. By 1940 only seventeen remained, and the trimming went on after his death in 1951, until by 1960 only thirteen dailies and nine Sunday editions remained.

In the operation of the Hearst chain, the key word was "crusade." Hearst carried on where the nineteenth-century battles left off, but in a different way. "Crusade" had its own peculiar meaning to him. He told a convention of Hearst executives at San Antonio in 1929, "I feel that it is desirable for the papers not to make enemies by violent attacks; but it is essential for the papers to conduct constructive campaigns for the benefit of the community with which they are associated. . . . Make crusades, but take enough interest in the affairs of your community and give enough thought to the situation existing to be able to make constructive crusades and accomplish results of actual, acknowledged value."

Like so many other things Hearst wrote and said, there is no way of knowing whether he really believed these high-minded words. Certainly the facts are that his crusading was fanatical, unyielding, and ruthless. The unremitting attack he made year after year on the most eminent captains of industry baffled and profoundly irritated these fellow capitalists. He used them and their banks and services when he needed them, but he had little in common with them and let them know it. They had spent their lives in the acquisition of money through the hard discipline of business; Hearst had spent his having fun—working as hard as they, but always at what he liked best and with no particular regard for profit or loss, except at the beginning and end of his career. His crusades reflected his shifting opinions; at one time or another, he was on both sides of nearly every major issue of our times. A former associate once remarked ruefully: "The bankers fought him for years, then he turned around and kissed them. They couldn't figure it out."

But the crusading, the maneuvering, the shouting, and the exposé led relatively nowhere in the end. In 1936, when the Hearst papers had been particularly loud in their attacks on the administration, and again in 1939 and 1940, when they renewed the isolationist policies of *circa* 1916, there were boycotts here and there of Hearst papers, or of his newsreel, which faithfully followed the propaganda line; but these were shadowy reflections of the public rage Hearst had once generated with his policies. As Oswald Garrison Villard noted wryly in the *Nation*, "It is amazing . . . to hear Wall Street men now praising Hearst when they themselves, or their fathers, in 1898 and again at the outbreak of World War I were violently denouncing Hearst and having his newspapers thrown out of their clubs and libraries."

The truth is that the constant reiteration of Hearst policies in his papers for nearly half a century had produced a kind of acceptance. He had become something of an institution, as safe and reliable as the Republican Party. Those who opposed him were no longer particularly afraid of him. Those who agreed with him found him a dependable reassurance in troubled times. A sign of those times was the *Journal-American*, the last of the New York Hearst papers, whose pages represented the largest menagerie of extreme right-wing writers ever gathered under one journalistic tent. They were the chief solace of a great many of the people Hearst had spent most of his life attacking.

Men like Scripps and Hearst were anachronisms in the later years of their lives, and by the sixties, there were new proprietors in the field totally unlike them. S. I. Newhouse, a retiring, publicity-shy man, had quietly built up an empire of thirteen dailies and eight Sunday papers, along with four television and three radio stations, and eleven magazines. His interests were not primarily editorial but financial. The basic technique he employed was to buy an ailing paper and resuscitate it by modern management methods, chiefly cost-cutting and the assiduous promotion of circulation and advertising.

But already in the sixties, Newhouse and the other chain operators were being dwarfed by the vast empire of a hitherto obscure Canadian, Roy Thomson, whose international organization of newspapers, magazines, book-publishing houses, and other enterprises far surpassed everything except his British rival, the International Publishing Corporation. In America, Thomson has become the largest publisher of newspapers, at least numerically, although none of them is a major organ. He has absorbed some smaller chains.

No better indication of the change that has overtaken the media is available than the difference between the two kinds of chain management, new and old. Roy Howard kept a close editorial watch on his newspapers for decades, and Hearst personally directed the editorial operation of his, but the new men had no such intention. "Nobody knows better what to print than the editors on the spot," Newhouse has said. Thomson gives his editors complete editorial autonomy, while holding them responsible financially. He sees no conflict of interest in the fact that he owns a segregationist paper in the American South and is in partnership with black publishers in Nigeria. While the older proprietors disdained the word "chain" and preferred "group," in a public-relations effort to establish the autonomy of their papers, there was no case of a newspaper in a "group" being in violent opposition to the policies or political beliefs of the group's owner or owners. By contrast, there is a wide diversity of political opinion in the Thomson organization, and its owner makes no slightest effort to enforce conformity.

Chain journalism is a solidly established business today. There are well over a hundred of these chains, more than 60 per cent of them organized within the boundaries of single states. About 30 per cent, perhaps more, of the nation's dailies are chain-owned, and the practice of serving two or more suburban communities under a hyphenated name is common.

The personal, individual element disappeared from chain journalism with the passing of Hearst and Scripps, just as it did in the case of single papers with the demise of men like Colonel Robert R. McCormick and his cousins Joseph Patterson and Eleanor "Cissie" Patterson, all of them cast in the nineteenth-century mold of powerful eccentricity.

McCormick and Patterson, taking over where Medill had left off with the Chicago *Tribune*, had co-existed as co-proprietors from 1910 until 1919, but it was a partnership doomed to fail. They could not have been more unlike. Patterson considered himself a man of the people, possibly a socialist, and he had already written two novels of social protest. McCormick thought of himself as an aristocrat, and behaved as though he were the last of the Bourbons. This disparity came to a head during the First World War, in which Patterson enlisted as a private and worked his way up to a captaincy while McCormick began as an officer on Pershing's staff, living in Paris a good part of the time and ultimately becoming a colonel. At a meeting in France, which is said to have occurred on a manure pile to avoid the danger of a farmhouse field headquarters being intermittently shelled, Patterson told his cousin that he had talked in London to Lord Northcliffe, whose tabloid *Daily Mirror* had already recorded more than a million in circulation, and that Northcliffe had urged him to try the formula in America.

After the war, by agreement, Patterson retained his family interest in the *Tribune* but went to New York to live, and began publishing the *Daily News* on June 26, 1919. At first, he found it difficult to attract able newspapermen from other dailies to work for him. Other publishers jeered at his paper as the "servant girl's Bible." But then, almost overnight, the formula Patterson had developed found its audience, and by 1925 the circulation had gone over a million. The *News* had started in last place; now it was first. Moreover, its Sunday edition, begun in 1921, took only four years to lead its field, with a record Sunday circulation in the United States of 1,234,189.

Sex and sensation were the stock-in-trade of the *News*. Observing its phenomenal success, the old master of the art, Hearst, launched a competing tabloid in 1923, the *Mirror,* but it was never more than a dim reflection of the *News*, which went on to become the largest daily in America. Other imitators were no more successful. Bernarr Macfadden attempted to outsensationalize Patterson with his *Evening Graphic,* known in the trade as the *"Pornographic,"* but the numbing effect of its daily assaults on sense and sensibility made it impotent in a short time. It ultimately went insane and was committed to the history books.

The *News* was described accurately as "by turns sobby, dirty, bloody, and glamorous," covering the news in a manner that would "appeal to the more elementary emotions of a truck-driver, and to the truck-driver in everyone." When the crash of 1929 changed the emotional tone of America abruptly, Patterson astutely altered his formula. "We're off on the wrong foot," he told his staff. "The people's major interest is no longer in the playboy, Broadway, and divorces, but in how they're going to eat, and from this time forward we'll pay attention to the struggle for existence that's just beginning."

Patterson's decision resulted in the paper's passionate support of the Roosevelt administration for nearly eight years, while the Chicago *Tribune* became the President's principal enemy. The cousins were united again, however, when the issue of isolationism or intervention in the Second World War found them in the same camp. By that time, too, Patterson was rich and successful enough to have lost his enthusiasm for socialism. In a short while the *Daily News* was quite as far to the right as the *Tribune*.

With the passing of both cousins, Patterson in 1946 and McCormick a few years later, the last of the eccentric personal publishers were gone. Both had exhibited behavior which was, to say the least, peculiar (but no more so than the Bennetts), and they had run their papers in the strong-minded manner of the nineteenth-century giants. Yet they were without any substantial political influence, although imagining themselves as perhaps even more powerful than their predecessors: as arrogant and unyielding and utterly unaware of what was going on in America. Since their departure, the papers have slowly been shifting to more contemporary ground; but the *Tribune* still often thinks of itself editorially as the sole savior of the Republic, and the *News* has never seemed to get itself past the era of Franklin Roosevelt. Cissie Patterson's paper, the Washington *Times-Herald*, has long since disappeared, with its publisher, but it is still remembered for its own particular brand of insanity. All three papers had interlocking financial interests, as the two survivors do today, and their political stances were the same.

Of the numerous other attempts at tabloid journalism, the most interesting was the launching of the newspaper *PM*, a liberal, experimental daily, without advertising, on June 18, 1940. Marshall Field III was its owner, and the editor was Ralph Ingersoll, who had conceived it after a career as vice-president and general manager of Time, Inc., where he had also given birth to *Life* magazine.

The prospectus of *PM* was so exciting, and its promise of a frankly liberal policy so entrancing, that it attracted thousands of applications from some of the best newspapermen in the country. Certainly few papers have ever been launched with such a distinguished staff and such promising prospects. Few, too, have ever lived up to their promise as well. Yet *PM* was, in the end, a failure. The liberals did not support it, as Field and the others had expected. The decision not to take advertising was a major mistake, rectified in 1947 when it was too late. General readers were attracted by *PM*'s outstanding artwork, superlative departments, good writing, excellent editorials, and investigative reporting, but they were disappointed by the inadequacy of its news coverage, which was often as biased on the liberal side (although never pro-Communist, as some of its more excitable enemies charged) as Colonel McCormick was on the opposite end. After suffering losses estimated at as much as $5 million and failing to achieve a circulation of even 200,000, *PM* was sold in April 1948 to Bartley Crum, a noted lawyer who had once been Hearst's attorney, and Joseph Barnes, then foreign editor of the *Herald Tribune*. It had a brief reincarnation as the *Star* before it suspended in January 1949.

It is worth noting that no outspokenly liberal newspaper or magazine in the history of the media has ever been financially successful. All have either been subsidized, failed entirely, or clung to life through sheer persistence and sacrifice on the part of the owners. Those conservatives who see the "great liberal media" as threats to everything they imagine threatened are baying at a paper moon. With only a few exceptions, the media remain solidly conservative—if, of course, words still have any meaning. There are fanatics who think the New York *Times* is operated from the Kremlin.

The Great Adjustment of 1929 and the Great Depression which followed it marked the end of a kind of American newspapering which had existed since James Franklin's *Courant*. Hearst and McCormick were the last flowering. The transition period had been a long one, from the turn of the century through three decades of crusading, war, and tabloidism. The world began to change radically in the thirties, and the Second World War created in its aftermath a wholly new environment for the newspaper business.

19

The Great Transformation: II

IN THE MAGAZINE WORLD, three figures stand out above all the others in transforming this part of the media business. Muckraking was much more sensational, but it was transitory. What Cyrus H. K. Curtis and his two editors, Edward Bok and George Horace Lorimer, created was more lasting, and made a broader impact on American culture.

Curtis was an ambitious boy from Maine whose shrewd business sense made him a fortune, like Munsey, but there the resemblance ended. Munsey's view was limited to the countinghouse, while Curtis possessed a vision that embraced America. Unlike most of his publishing contemporaries, Curtis made no pretense of being an editor. His particular genius lay in knowing how to create magazine properties, and in finding the men to edit them. After that, he had the good sense to leave these editors alone. They rewarded him by producing, in the *Ladies' Home Journal* and the *Saturday Evening Post*, two of the most successful magazines ever turned out in America and, in the case of the *Post*, the one that was most beloved.

The *Journal* began as a women's supplement to a paper Curtis founded in 1879, the *Tribune and Farmer*, but it was so successful that it was clear to the proprietor he should sell the parent publication and keep the supplement. Consequently the supplement became the *Ladies' Home Journal* in 1883.

Starting at 20,000, Curtis built up the *Journal's* circulation by various devices, which were widely copied. The first was to offer four subscriptions for a dollar in a "club," thus making one subscriber a salesman in obtaining the other three. Curtis was a master at this kind of list building; in his first attempt the *Journal*'s circulation doubled in six months. To this he added a newspaper advertising campaign, costing him only $400, that doubled his circulation again in the succeeding six months.

Demonstrating the kind of sensitivity that made him so successful, Curtis now began to improve his magazine, knowing that something more than circulation devices and advertising would be required. A magazine needed a big name to sell it, and Curtis went up to Massachusetts to get one—a writer named Marion Harland, who was then one of the best-known writers for women in America. For $90 he got a short story from her, and spent more money to advertise her presence in the *Journal*. As he had hoped, she attracted many new readers, and circulation reached 270,000 by 1886.

It was not easy to get writers, however. The best ones did not want to write for a women's magazine that was regarded as scarcely above the level of a household-hints organ. Curtis persuaded Louisa May Alcott to add her name to his "List of Famous Contributors" by promising to contribute $100 to her favorite charity if she would do one piece for the *Journal*. There were not many other noteworthy names, however, except perhaps for Marietta Holley, whose "Samantha Allen" by-line had made her well known, and Mary Jane Holmes, the popular novelist.

Nevertheless, circulation climbed steadily, even at a fifty-cent annual price. Curtis declared in 1887 that he meant to have a million subscribers soon, and to achieve this he devised new circulation schemes, along with his cleverly written advertising. In 1889, taking a large gamble, the publisher jumped his subscription price to a dollar a year, increasing the size of the magazine to thirty-two pages and adding a cover. Fortunately, he was able to get $200,000 in advertising credit from F. Wayland Ayer, one of the founders of N. W. Ayer & Son, the noted advertising agency, who also endorsed Curtis' notes in the amount of $100,000 so that he could get the paper he needed.

With such backing, Curtis was able to launch the broad, bold advertising campaign he envisaged, but it still required careful financing for a few years until, in 1891, he established a stock company capitalized at $500,000, and the Curtis Publishing Company was born.

When the *Journal*'s circulation went over 400,000 in 1889, Curtis made the move that elevated the magazine to preeminence. His wife,

Louisa Knapp, had been editing it since its days as a supplement, but now she wanted to leave to spend more time with her children, and Curtis had to find a new editor. It could only have been his peculiar genius for selection that led him to Edward William Bok, a most unlikely candidate. A Dutch immigrant at the age of seven, he had been in book publishing and had edited *Brooklyn* magazine briefly before going into the newspaper syndicate business.

Aside from that, what made his initiation as editor of a women's magazine so remarkable was that Bok had no particular fondness for women, except for his mother, whom he adored. A bachelor, he seemed to have little feeling for the other sex except a kind of idealization. His ideas about them were odd, to say the least. But Curtis may have recalled that the most successful proprietor of a women's magazine until that time, Louis Godey, had many of the same attributes.

More disturbing to those who worked with him was Bok's truly staggering egocentricity. In the manner of similarly self-absorbed men, he often referred to himself in the third person. His autobiography, *The Americanization of Edward Bok*, for many years on every high school reading list, was written in that mode.

Somehow Curtis knew that Bok understood how to talk to women in a magazine. Perhaps, as Dr. Mott suggests, Bok made the magazine in the image of what women wanted to be instead of what they were, or it may be that he simply had a sixth sense about his audience, as the best editors have always had, and knew, by that same "instinct" with which he credited the ladies, what they wanted to read. If that was the case, he knew they wanted to read something more than the cookies-and-patterns pablum they had been fed for so many years.

The other magazines viewed his assumption of the editor's chair as a hilarious event, and he was the victim of a good deal of lampooning in the newspapers and other periodicals. Some of it was cruel and occasionally verged on the libelous. Meanwhile, Bok quietly went about his courtship of Curtis' daughter, whom he married, ending at least some of the gossip about his supposedly defective heterosexuality. Even then he suffered abuse and ridicule as long as he was editor, but more of it was inspired by his success than by his peculiar nature.

Somehow Bok managed to make his readers feel that the magazine was their intimate friend. They told it their problems and were answered in the department "Side Talks with Girls," written for many years by Isabel A. Mallon under the pseudonym "Ruth Ashore"; and in "Heart to Heart Talks," edited by Mrs. Margaret Bottome. There was even a "Side Talks with Boys" department. In articles, readers were given views of the private lives of great men, from P. T. Barnum's "How I Have Grown Old" to Benjamin Harrison's description of family life in the White House.

Bok refused to take patent-medicine advertising, the staple of many magazines, and with the help of Mark Sullivan, one of the most accomplished muckrakers, who joined his staff, carried on a crusade against the manufacturers which was a factor in the passage of the Federal Food and Drug Act in 1906.

As time went on, Bok began to fill the pages of the *Journal* with the best writers of the day, foreign and domestic. By this time he was vice-president of the company, the magazine was highly profitable, and he was visiting England and France in search of new work. Kipling became a friend and contributor, but Bok did not hesitate to edit from his work what he thought might offend the ladies—for instance, he eliminated a drinking scene from Kipling's first contribution to the *Journal*. Bok edited Twain too and, in his sublimely arrogant way, declared that the author had admitted he was right, which hardly seems consistent with Twain's character.

One of the unique features of the *Journal* was its publication of music—everything from Sousa marches to Paderewski, Strauss, Mascagni, and Josef Hofmann, who edited a music department in the magazine for a time. Bok's editorial genius constantly expanded the contents in new directions, pushing back the frontiers that had confined women's periodicals. He began running house plans in 1895, and held contests for best homes. "I firmly believe," said Stanford White, probably the best-known architect of his day in America, "that Edward Bok has more completely influenced American domestic architecture for the better than any other man in this generation." Bok also wanted to improve interior decoration, Pullman cars, and the appearance of cities, and he was one of the first, if not the first, to protest and fight against outdoor advertising.

By the turn of the century, the *Journal* had surpassed every other magazine in circulation. It was 800,000 in 1900, two years later it had climbed to 900,000, and in 1903 it finally passed Curtis' long-sought million mark. People were eagerly reading in its pages serializations of books which were to become famous: Kipling's *Just So Stories* and *Puck of Pook's Hill*, Jean Webster's *Daddy Long Legs*, and the work of Kate Douglas Wiggin. Bok even persuaded Theodore Roosevelt to dictate a column to a newspaperman, in two sessions every month while he was shaving, for a department entitled "The President."

Later, Roosevelt wrote another column, but anonymously—a department called "Men," whose authorship was a closely guarded secret.

Bok kept the *Journal* to the forefront of its field by bold and imaginative editing. Often he was ahead of his time and ahead of his audience. It took real editorial courage, as well as foresight, to come out in favor of sex education. He lost thousands of subscribers by permitting the *Journal* to talk about syphilis, the first time the word had appeared in an American popular magazine. Bok brought to the editing of women's periodicals the concept of service, which later came to dominate all of them. He encouraged his readers to think of the *Journal* as "a great clearing-house for information," as he put it, and by the time this particular service ended in 1917, the yearly tide of letters had reached nearly a million. Bok also instituted the Curtis Advertising Code, which was designed to protect readers from fraudulent or extravagant claims in advertising, and specifically banned financial, tobacco, playing-card, or liquor advertising. The prohibition on liquor was absolute; not even wineglasses or steins could be shown.

Circulation of the magazine was beginning to approach 2 million by 1912, and reached that point in the fall of 1919. It sometimes carried more than $1 million worth of advertising in a single issue, and often ran to more than two hundred pages. As editor of the most valuable magazine property in the world, whose prosperity he had personally created, Bok earned his salary of $100,000 a year.

At the end of the First World War, during which the *Journal* astonished the business by ranking third among the magazines most demanded by soldiers, Bok resigned his editorship. He had created a great magazine and he was rich. Now he wanted to write and pursue his philanthropic interests. His characteristic farewell did not run in the *Journal* but in the *Saturday Evening Post*, its companion publication. There, in 1919, he reviewed his life in the United States since he landed as a penniless immigrant, and entitled it, with his usual sublime assurance, "Where America Fell Short with Me." Nonetheless, he had made magazine history, not only as an editor who created an entirely new kind of magazine but as an advertising genius who joined his extraordinary talents with Curtis' to promote it.

Meanwhile, Curtis had been equally fortunate in finding an editor for his other publication, the *Post*, which he had bought in 1897 for $1000 when it was near death, with no more than 2000 names on its subscription list.

Once in possession, Curtis did not quite know what to do with his property. But the news of his purchase had gone out on the news-service wires, and the announcement was read in the city room of the Boston *Herald* by a restless young reporter named George Horace Lorimer, who had recently come over to the paper from the rival *Post*, where he had been refused a two-dollar raise. The wire-service story said that Curtis was hoping to find an outstanding editor who could make his new property successful, and within an hour Lorimer had wired him asking for the job. Curtis wired back that he would be in Boston the following week, and would be delighted to talk with him. As Lorimer recalled it later: "I expected to go to Philadelphia. Mr. Curtis, however, replied that I should meet him at the Hotel Touraine in Boston. There, on a divan in the lobby, we talked one morning for about ten minutes." Before they shook hands and parted, Lorimer had been hired as the first—and last—literary editor of the *Post*.

Lorimer was not at all what Curtis had been looking for. He was anything but literary; he was obscure, and he had no magazine experience. Curtis wanted the exact opposite, and for the moment did not think of him as editor in chief; but, as in the case of Bok, his sixth sense told him that Lorimer was his man.

As the son of one of the nation's most powerful evangelical ministers, George Claude Lorimer, Curtis' acquisition had grown up in Boston and Chicago, dropped out of Yale after his freshman year, and gone to work for one of his father's richest parishioners, P. D. Armour, the meatpacker, where he worked fourteen hours a day for ten dollars a week. In that job, Lorimer discovered that he loved business, and it remained a lifelong passion with him.

After he had married the daughter of a Chicago judge and appeared about to be named an executive in the company, he made a sudden, uncharacteristic quixotic gesture and quit to go into the wholesale grocery business, which proved to be a disaster.

Casting about for a new occupation, Lorimer deliberately chose writing, as though it was what he had meant to do all along. He wanted to be a writer and editor on magazines, but, believing newspaper work was the best preparation, he had gone to work for the Boston papers—until Curtis hired him.

As literary editor, he served a little less than two years until the publisher fired his temporary editor, William George Jordan, and went to Europe to look for another, leaving Lorimer in charge as managing editor. In a sudden position of power, Lorimer knew he had only a short time to prove himself, and, as he said later, "I had little money to spend and the paper had no reputation."

At once he made two policy changes that revolutionized the maga-

zine business. He promised to pay for manuscripts on acceptance, and
to give a yes or no answer on submitted articles and stories within
seventy-two hours. Nothing could have been better calculated to
attract writers; the common practice was to hold submissions for
weeks, months, or longer, at the editor's convenience, and to pay on
publication, which might be months away. Lorimer began, too, the
practice of making regular trips to New York in search of writers,
another policy that soon bore fruit.

Returning from Europe without finding an editor, Curtis saw what
Lorimer had done and found it good, making him editor in chief on
St. Patrick's Day 1899. When Lorimer left the editor's chair nearly
thirty-nine years later, on the last day of 1936, the *Post* had been for
three decades one of the most successful and significant magazines in
the history of periodicals.

Lorimer left an indelible mark on his times. He was the articulate
voice of millions, the purveyor of entertainment, advice, and political
sentiment to a considerable body of middle-class Americans, for the
most part WASP Republicans. Yet he was almost unknown to the
Post's readers. Of the more than 3 million people who bought the
magazine at the peak of its circulation under his editorship, only a
few knew the editor as more than a name on the masthead. He
remained an anonymous figure until the final issue of the *Post* under
his editorship, when for the first time he signed an editorial. Nevertheless he was a man whom nine presidents recognized as the potent
spokesman for a sizable bloc of voters, and whom thousands of writers, both famous and unknown, looked upon as almost a god. Lorimer
was the *Post*, and the *Post* was Lorimer.

At the start, he knew he had to do two things to save the magazine:
get more advertising, and give his periodical an identity. His business
experience helped him to accomplish the first objective, and in a
sense led to achievement of the second. For Lorimer ardently
believed, as Calvin Coolidge remarked later, that the business of
America was business—and if that was true, a magazine that dealt
with business, both in fiction and in nonfiction, must necessarily
appeal to large masses of Americans. He meant to edit the *Post* for
every adult in America's population of 75 million—a truly mass magazine.

Unable to find anyone to write about business, he wrote in his
spare time his *Letters from a Self-Made Merchant to His Son*, which
ran serially in the *Post* and later was published as a book, to become
a simultaneous bestseller in the United States, England, and Ger-

many. Translated later into a dozen languages, it survived more than forty years, more generally circulated in all parts of the world than any book of American authorship since *Uncle Tom's Cabin.* After this astounding success, everyone wanted to write about business.

Lorimer was overwhelmed with manuscripts on the subject, among them Frank Norris' novel *The Pit,* which the *Post* ran serially. To cover business in articles, Lorimer hired two outstanding reporters, Sam Blythe and Isaac Marcosson, whose names were soon household words. Marcosson became the greatest interviewer of his time, writing about celebrities of every variety all over the world, while Blythe was equally celebrated as a political correspondent, and for years made the *Post's* coverage of domestic politics the best any magazine could boast.

So swiftly and thoroughly had Lorimer created his product that by 1909 the *Post* had taken on, although still in rough form, the distinctive character it would retain for the next quarter of a century. It was already the nation's leading magazine, and was rapidly becoming an American institution as well. The editor had total control of his product, and possessed the genius to take full advantage of it. He personally read and okayed every line of editorial matter and advertising that went into the magazine. Many, if not most, of the editorial ideas came from him, and writers were his personal friends. When the *Post* was the largest carrier of advertising in the business, Lorimer had the character to throw out of his office one day an advertiser who suggested that his ad be tied in with an article. Lorimer insisted that there be absolutely no influence on editorial content by advertisers, and in time that became a novelty in itself in the magazine business. Yet he remained a thorough businessman, and directed the business operations of the magazine himself.

In effect, Lorimer interpreted middle-class America to itself. Since his own interests and attitudes were primarily the same as those of his readers, he had no difficulty editing a magazine for them: he simply put in it what he himself liked. He could sense the national mood with the accuracy of the keenest political leaders. In the twenties, for example, when sports were a national passion, the *Post* carried the life stories of Babe Ruth, Jack Dempsey, Bobby Jones, and other contemporary heroes.

As an ardent Republican, Lorimer was probably the first to recognize Herbert Hoover as a man who could be president, and he and William Allen White did as much as any others behind the scenes to get him elected, a campaign beginning as early as 1919. By the mid-twenties, Lorimer's *Post* editorials were probably more influential than any carried by the newspapers, and they played an important part in pushing public opinion in the direction of Hoover. Once their man was in the White House, however, both White and Lorimer changed their minds about him—leaving intact the latter's record of dissatisfaction with every president he knew.

It is easy to see why Lorimer came to cherish the dangerous illusion that he knew the American people better than anyone. This big, bluff man, who looked the epitome of the business entrepreneur, was speaking for millions of people, as the success of his magazine and his voluminous mail constantly told him. The famous *Post* covers, by Norman Rockwell and others, mirrored an apple-pie middle-class America that was far from being as idealized as it is fashionable to believe today. Those who lived with Rockwell's people identified with them as much in the twenties as they did in the seventies. The fiction and articles in the *Post* were, year after year, a record of their tastes, interests, and aspirations. (Those who say Rockwell painted "an America that never was," the usual phrase, are simply not familiar with rural and small-town life in the America of the teens and twenties. These critics dismiss the content of the drawings as corny and sentimental. Of course. Was that life ever anything else?)

It was all the more shocking to Lorimer then in 1932 when Franklin D. Roosevelt, a man who represented everything he despised except for his wealth, won the presidency. Lorimer felt personally betrayed by this event. The people whom he had loved and trusted and served with all his might had turned on him and made an even worse mistake than electing Wilson. Lorimer could not understand it. He was profoundly shaken, and both he and the *Post* began to decline. The magazine fought Mr. Roosevelt hard for four years, in both editorials and articles, and when he was reelected in 1936, it was the end for Lorimer. He resigned at the close of the year, making it public in the only signed editorial he ever wrote for the *Post*, in the issue of December 26, 1936. Less than a year later, on October 27, 1937, Lorimer was dead, the victim of throat cancer; he had been a heavy smoker all his life.

The man whom everyone called affectionately "the Boss" had created a magazine in his own image. It was not, of course, without critics. Intellectuals generally despised it, although many of them wrote for it. Lorimer himself was regarded by them as hopelessly "square," long before the word was common slang, and indeed he was. There were those who thought him ruthless, in the manner of the business tycoons he admired, but others considered him just, and certainly many of his values were at odds with those of the tycoons.

To Lorimer, publishing was "the business of buying and selling brains; of having ideas and finding men to carry them out." No better definition has been written. He believed correctly that there was a plebiscite on every issue of a periodical, to determine its worthiness, and that no business could so quickly succumb owing to apathy or complaisance on the part of its director. "Drugs may be prepared by formula, steel made true by process, and other commodities standardized," he wrote, "but so long as the word counts for more than the type in which it is fixed, so long as the story counts for more than the picture which draws the eye to it, and so long as literature becomes a lifeless thing in the very act of conforming, the periodical will never be standardized and sold indefinitely on the strength of its pretty package and the uniformity of its contents. Publishing is and always will be a contest of ideas—the last stronghold of unrestricted competition free to all comers."

Lorimer and Bok were the leaders in the transformation of magazines into business institutions. As editors they were solidly in the tradition of the highly individual personalities who had made all of the great magazines and newspapers before them, but they created the first true mass magazines in America and, in doing so, tied them irrevocably to the business of advertising, which had been a negligible part of periodical income before. Curtis' editors were strong-minded men who were able to resist advertising pressures, but these pressures were rapidly becoming too strong for anyone to resist. By the twenties, it was advertising—national in the magazines, local and national in the newspapers—that dominated the media, laying out before the consuming public the most elaborate bazaar in the history of merchandising—the fruits of American industrialization and technology.

For the most part, urban newspapers successfully resisted the natural inclination of advertisers to attempt to influence or control editorial content. Flagrant exceptions could always be cited, but most of the press, especially the major dailies, remained relatively independent of advertising influence, in spite of the popular myth to the contrary. With magazines, the advertisers were in a far stronger position. A magazine's circulation became not so much a primary source of income (in time it cost more to service subscriptions than they were really worth) as a bargaining force in the competitive struggle for the advertising dollar, which had to be spread around among all the media.

The ultimate result was a relationship between advertising and editorial content that virtually ended editorial independence in all but a relatively few magazines. A magazine struggling to retain its share of a soap account, for example, when the manufacturer was already pouring the bulk of his advertising money into competing media, would not be likely to undertake an exposé of the soap industry, if one were demanded. On a more commonplace level, magazines had good reason not to risk offending advertisers if they wanted to survive, and when public relations dictated a particular working arrangement between advertising and editorial matter, no one was likely to question it.

Some magazines, to be sure, clung to their independence, but they were likely to be either the rich and powerful periodicals, which could afford to lose a little, or the small and radical, which either had little to lose or were subsidized. But on the great middle ground, a gradual homogenization occurred as the twentieth century wore on. Most magazines came to reflect the conservative business interests of their advertisers. In belief, they became business institutions themselves—extremely large ones, in the case of group publishing—and behaved like it.

On the positive side, the tidal wave of advertising, with accompanying huge revenues, transformed magazines from relatively drab productions to works of graphic art. The income made it possible for publishers and editors to buy anything that would make a magazine better to look at and more readable. Graphic-arts craftsmanship in illustration and design was matched by craftsmanship in the advertising itself, as the agencies developed their skills. In time, readers found the advertising in a magazine as attractive to look at and as interesting to read as the editorial matter, at least in some periodicals.

Advertising not only provided the lifeblood that made magazines advance and greatly improved their appearance and content, but also (as the publishers and advertisers constantly reminded critics) helped to raise the material quality of living in an increasingly affluent America as consumers chose from the giant smorgasbord laid out before them. They were helped in their choices by numerous home-service departments in the magazines, and by departmental attention to virtually every aspect of daily living—all reflected in the advertising columns.

If advertising was the major factor in transforming magazines into a business, the rapid development in graphic arts that began at the turn of the century was equally important in making them a handsome product the business could sell. The change to photography began to take place as soon as the rapid dry-plate process was invented in the eighties, and in their coverage of the Spanish-American War, magazines and newspapers took as much advantage of the new art as possible. Taking pictures became a national pastime, and photography magazines sprang up by the dozen until there were hundreds of them by 1905. It would be a while, though, before photography substantially replaced hand illustration in the periodical press; meanwhile, there were first-rate artists doing work for the best monthlies and weeklies—men like John La Farge, Joseph Pennell, Howard Pyle, Charles Dana Gibson, Howard Chandler Christy, Harrison Fisher, James Montgomery Flagg, Frederic Remington, and others. These men also drew pictures for novels, which contained illustrations well into this century before such drawings were relegated to the jackets.

Photography was the most exciting new dimension added to magazines as they emerged into the twentieth century. A few were surprisingly slow to use it—the *Post* did not do so until about 1919—but as early as 1905 it was clearly the wave of the future.

It is a commonplace historical fact that wars change the lives of people and nations so much that when they are over, nothing is the same again. In the case of the media, that had been true of the decades following the American Revolution, when magazine and book publishing had suddenly blossomed as growing industries, and after the Civil War, when all the media began to play a role in national life that had only been suggested before. The shock of change after the First World War was much greater. An era that had begun with the Civil War was ended, and the magazines, books, and even newspapers that had reflected it most faithfully were the first to be lost in the postwar struggle for survival in a new world.

Many publishers found themselves unable to alter old formulas in a period of dramatic change. Several periodicals that tried to adapt to the new age failed to do so rapidly enough, and died while they were in transition, for lack of capital to keep operating until new formulas could be established. Old standbys like the *North American Review, Living Age, Forum, Independent, Century, St. Nicholas, Judge,* and *Delineator* began to disappear in a way that shocked older readers.

They were replaced by a new generation of innovative publishers: De Witt Wallace, Henry Luce, and Harold Ross, among the leaders. These men were introducing magazines of a kind never seen before, and winning audiences attracted by their fresh formats. The newcomers were closer to the changing tastes than were the old-line publishers. Still, the stronger voices from the past survived for a while. It would take the further upheaval of the Second World War to finish off the Curtis Publishing Company's magazines and the Crowell-Collier group; and not even that was enough to kill the McCall organization and the Hearst magazines.

The survivors went on because their properties were basically strong, and because new editors were found to carry on in the personal way. Crowell-Collier, however, demonstrated the ultimate result of the new order. One of the first companies to diversify, it did not depend on its three magazines—*Collier's*, the *American*, and *Woman's Home Companion*—for its entire income. Its publishing and distribution of books, particularly *Collier's Encyclopedia*, was a highly profitable part of its business, and so was its Sunday newspaper supplement, *This Week*. In time, too, the company acquired some valuable broadcasting properties. These other divisions looked particularly good to management in 1953, when all the magazines were losing money, producing nearly a $5 million deficit in the company that year.

This situation led to the hiring of Paul C. Smith, who had been general manager of the San Francisco *Chronicle* for seventeen years and was highly advertised as a boy wonder. Smith, by tight management practices, brought the company into the black within two years, but then a new group of twenty-six investors gained control in the summer of 1955, and the handwriting was on the wall. When it came time to make a corporate decision about strengthening the company's profit position, it was clear that by eliminating the magazine division Crowell-Collier would eliminate its primary problem. In the new climate of the fifties and sixties, there was no sentiment involved in killing old and honorable magazines.

Another indication of things to come was the fact that the Hearst Corporation suffered less than the others because so many of its magazines were in specialized rather than general fields. Specialization and diversification: those were obviously the ingredients of survival.

More than anything else, however, the era after the First World War, particularly the twenties and thirties, was characterized by a flood of new ideas that changed the shape of the business. Among the things the new periodicals demonstrated was the fact that when people appear with ideas acceptable to large numbers of readers, they will be successful, everything else being equal, whether times are good or bad. Some of the most notable magazines and magazine empires of our time were launched in the twenties, and some in the thirties—when economic conditions were in the sharpest possible contrast.

The twenties, when many of the old magazines were dying, was a decade in which Henry Luce founded *Time* magazine, Harold Ross began the *New Yorker*, and De Witt Wallace created the *Reader's Digest*. In the thirties, in the somber depths of the Depression, Luce had the courage to start *Fortune* magazine, selling for a dollar, an unheard-of price, and directed to an audience for whom the title was largely a memory. Then, in 1936, when the country was still floundering, he had the audacity to publish *Life*, although the experts told him it was the wrong time and the wrong idea. Earlier, when times were at their worst, David Smart put on the market his new magazine, *Esquire*, selling for fifty cents, double the price of the ordinary periodical.

These magazines were not so much new ideas in themselves as they were fresh approaches to old ideas. Thus *Time* carried the *Literary Digest*'s basic idea to a new level; the *New Yorker* took up where the old *Life* and *Judge* left off; the new *Life* was a contemporary expression of *Leslie's* and its imitators; *Fortune* was a logical extension of *Success, System, World's Work*, and similar periodicals, while the *Reader's Digest* went back to the old clip-and-paste beginnings of magazine publishing, in its original conception. Only *Esquire* came close to being a brand-new idea.

All these magazines had their imitators and rivals, in the traditional manner, and some of those survived in their own right, notably *Look, Newsweek*, and *U.S. News & World Report*.

There was one innovation that was truly new. Bernarr Macfadden, still another eccentric, introduced to the magazine business the confession and the true-detective periodical, both based in different ways on the loneliness and sexual hypocrisy of Americans. Macfadden's *True Story* had more than a dozen imitators, which at one time in the fifties attracted a collective audience of more than 14 million. Macfadden was also capable of reproducing the past, which he did with *Liberty*, a return to the popular, cheap magazines of the turn of the century. As a latter-day Frank Leslie, he established a string of publications which in 1935, at the peak of their circulation, had more than 7 million readers, larger than any other group. Five years later the empire was nearly bankrupt, and the stockholders forced the publisher to retire, after which it was brought into the black under new management.

A significant aspect of magazine publishing in the twenties was the increase in specialization, forecasting the decisive trend that is taking place today. Publishers who could visualize a particular readership for a magazine, to fill a special need, were able to create durable properties. Consequently, the burgeoning mass magazines were accompanied by another group of periodicals with much smaller circulations, which nevertheless virtually saturated their audiences. This included not only those which dealt in specialties, but those that refined what the larger magazines were doing. Intellectual magazines, for example, like the *Atlantic* and *Harper's*, were carrying on a nineteenth-century tradition of serious thinking about matters treated more broadly by the mass magazines. They subdivided into conservative and radical (using those words loosely), the latter coming to include not only the longer-established *Nation* and *New Republic* but newcomers of the twenties like the *American Mercury*, founded by H. L. Mencken and George Jean Nathan in December 1923.

The *Mercury*, whose green cover protruded from the coat pockets of young men all over the country, was the chief organ of iconoclasm in an era of Babbittry. Besides Mencken's attacks on the activities of what he called the "booboisie" of the nation, meaning the Silent Majority, and Nathan's superb theatrical criticism, the magazine printed the work of the sharpest satiric minds extant, and its fiction was outstanding.

Viewed in retrospect, however, Mencken was not exactly what he seemed to be at the time. The *Mercury* delighted the social rebels of that day because it pilloried the establishment, the stuffed shirts who had made a religion out of Wall Street and who exalted Rotarianism to the level of a national philosophy. It was against organized religion, organized politics, and organized everything else. This, together with Mencken's masterful, erudite prose, which made him one of the century's finest stylists, obscured the fact that much of what he wrote and what the *Mercury* advocated, in its reverse way, was not only nonsense but deeply conservative.

There was something authoritarian about Mencken's iconoclasm, something of the savagery of the revolutionary just before he has enough power to raise his own guillotines. All this became somewhat clearer, to the vast disillusionment of Mencken's followers, by that time grown older and wiser, when he appeared on Alf Landon's campaign train in 1936, wearing a large Kansas sunflower in his buttonhole and exhorting the same booboisie he had scorned only a decade before to follow him.

Perhaps the most remarkable development of the century was the proliferation of magazines far beyond those intended for the general audience ("consumer" periodicals, as they are known in the trade). While these general magazines dominated the newsstands, made the headlines, and provided a highly diversified source of information and entertainment, they were increasingly overwhelmed in number by what might be called, for lack of a more accurate word, the business press. Of more than 16,000 magazines published today, fully 10,000 are involved with the business world. About 8000 or so of these are company magazines, known also as house organs, and the remainder are industrial publications. The total circulation of these magazines is well above 60 million. Not only do they dominate magazine publishing, but they also constitute what is probably the greatest reservoir of printed information in the world. Their economic growth has been phenomenal, exceeding statistically the rise in both gross national product and national income.

The primary function of these magazines is to provide information about events in whatever segment of the business world each one covers, and at the same time anticipate changes and advise how to meet them. Thus they are first of all news magazines. Secondarily, they provide how-to information, and also are opinion organs, analyzing the news and evaluating its impact.

All told, the business press puts out more than 800,000 editorial pages per year, the work of 14,000 full-time editors. As a class, these magazines enjoy a far greater longevity than consumer publications, of which only a handful now date from before the beginning of the twentieth century, while scores of business periodicals have observed their centennials. The people who read them do so with an intensity unmatched by consumer-magazine readers. "Survival reading," one steel executive has called it, which sums up the motivation of a large part of the readership. Moreover, the business magazines offer a merchandise mart through their advertising pages that is unmatched by any other medium.

Those who imagine that the business periodical is the kept woman of its particular organization or industry are unaware that it is often a crusading organ, and sometimes is the conscience of the people it serves. An editor-publisher in the vending industry, for example, broke the Bobby Baker story, piecing together random bits of evidence until an anonymous early-morning telephone call led him to the Maryland official records that disclosed Baker's control of vending-machine companies, hotels, and other real estate. Again, it was a business editor who led a campaign against the high-voltage swimming pool light fixtures that were electrocuting unsuspecting swimmers at the rate of one a month, on the average, in 1960. The achievements of business-paper editors in public health and safety alone have been remarkable.

Nor have the editors been content with simple exposés. Examining the causes of hospital-acquired infections, one publication conducted its own original research to trace some infections to mops and mop-bucket water, then developed tests that would help hospitals to evaluate disinfectants and set labeling standards. It was a business magazine, too—one serving the advertising industry—that helped to bring about the Better Business Bureau; and certainly the automotive service magazine that trained 40,000 mechanics by correspondence course in the interest of road safety deserves some kind of special commendation. No other medium, it may be added, has done more to spread scientific knowledge.

When one considers how much the newspaper and magazine media have been transformed in our time, it becomes all the more remarkable that the book-publishing industry has changed so little. In their structure and operation, the houses of today are little different from those of the past century. A new generation of publishers has come on, but descendants of the nineteenth-century founders still control some houses. Computers have been introduced to shipping and billing procedures, but there are still two major seasons for selling books, royalties are still paid twice a year, distribution problems are substantially the same, and much else remains unchanged. The major developments have been the growth of the paperback industry and the wave of mergers, acquisitions by large corporations, and conversion from privately held to publicly held companies that in themselves were accompaniments of the economic madness of the sixties affecting business generally.

What has changed, of course, is public taste, and publishers' lists have changed to accommodate it. The primary shift has been from fiction to nonfiction, as it was in the magazines. We have come a long way from George Barr McCutcheon's *Graustark*, which originated the mythical-European-kingdom genre and sold more than 1.5 million copies after its publication in 1901. It was one of the romantic novels that created huge sales before the First World War, nearly all of them selling more than a million copies—a hard-cover sale unknown today. Publishers eagerly poured out books like *Quo Vadis*, which surpassed its rival in the sex-and-religion formula, *Ben-Hur*; a long list of romantic historical novels, and, most important, the family novel of the early nineteen-hundreds.

The family novel was a publishing phenomenon not equaled before or since. The book business has never seen such hard-cover fiction sales records as were set by two writers alone, Gene Stratton-Porter and Harold Bell Wright. Mrs. Porter, in the years before the First World War, sold between 8 and 9 million copies of her nineteen novels, which were stories of growing children and the love of nature. Wright, an ex-minister, compiled an even more awesome record with his novels, which were intended as social criticism of what he considered the failure of the churches to reach out to the common people, and to deal with the large questions of power, privilege, and corruption that were occupying the magazines and newspapers. His nineteen novels sold a total of more than 10 million copies; one, *The Winning of Barbara Worth*, sold 1,635,000 copies in hard cover, what would be a respectable paperback sale today.

After the war, the success of H. G. Wells's *Outline of History* signaled the shifting of emphasis in publishing from fiction to nonfiction that accelerated rapidly in the thirties. Historical "outlines" were suddenly extremely popular, including Willem van Loon's *Story of Mankind* and Will Durant's *The Story of Philosophy*, the predecessor of the ten-volume *History of Civilization*, only recently completed, which he wrote with his wife, Ariel.

Another publishing phenomenon of the twenties was the immense success of the Little Blue Books, five-cent booklets published in Girard, Kansas, by E. Haldeman-Julius, and advertised in full pages which made it possible to order by numbers on a coupon. The average sale of these books was 150,000 each, and they went out to millions of people in remote towns and on farms who could not afford to buy real books even at the prevailing retail prices, which were still $2.50 on the average for fiction. The titles ranged from the classics in all categories to jokes and home entertainment and self-help books.

The national hypocrisy about sex still hindered the publication of books which dealt with the subject forthrightly in the mass market. *Ulysses* won a victory in the Supreme Court in 1922 which made its distribution possible in America, but there was a relatively small audience for it. The French realistic writers were not subjected to the savage persecution they had suffered at the close of the past century, and no one now had the temerity to censor Tolstoy. Nevertheless, sex in mass-market publishing meant incredible potboilers like Elinor Glyn's *Three Weeks*, which dealt with illicit love on a tiger-skin rug in a manner that seems hilarious today; or Robert Hichens' *The Garden of Allah*, about love in the desert between a beautiful English girl and a runaway priest; or Ethel M. Hull's *The Sheik*, in which another beautiful English girl in the desert is carried away by a handsome sheik, who was embodied on the screen in Rudolph Valentino.

Other books of the twenties were in trouble with the censors and with middle-class morality in general, but they were not big sellers and, except for *Ulysses*, James Branch Cabell's *Jurgen*, and a few others, they were not usually literary.

The Crash and the resulting Depression changed book publishing as it did everything else. Hervey Allen's *Anthony Adverse*, in 1933 the first big seller of the decade, was a historical romance far removed from those of the turn of the century, and the sex in it was equally apart from the coy and mawkish products of an earlier time, or the synthetic product manufactured by Glyn and Dell. Similarly, when *Gone With the Wind* arrived, while Allen's book was still on the bestseller list, the South that Margaret Mitchell created and the characters who moved in it were romantic enough but a long distance from the cardboard plots and figures of earlier novels in that genre.

As the fiction of our time turned more and more to social realism, with John Steinbeck, Ernest Hemingway, and their contemporaries, so did nonfiction become increasingly more popular and finally outstrip fiction on the publishers' lists and in the public's buying patterns. The war years consolidated that trend and later developments broadened it. More and more, information books became the staple of bookstores and publishers. There was said to be an "information explosion," but it was really the result of a long-continuing trend of supplying an increasingly numerous and diverse population with facts and ideas they had never been able to obtain before in such quantity. Since this was also happening to newspapers and magazines, as they broadened their horizons and became more diverse, the great transformation could be said to have been completed by mid-century.

20

Radio and Television: The New Dimension

WE HAVE LIVED so long now with radio and television that only people who were born more than fifty years ago can remember what it was like without them. No other medium has so influenced American life as broadcasting, in little more than a half century, and since its audiences are far larger than those enjoyed by the other media, embracing nearly all of the population, it has raised profound social, political, and cultural questions.

When broadcasting was new, it was viewed as a medium that would unite people as never before, but in fact it has splintered them beyond any real hope of unification. It has been a great educator, as anticipated, but not always in the ways that early theorists imagined. A whole body of law has become attached to it, multiplying the ambiguities of its social role and creating a mythology devoutly believed in by people who have a vested interest in its operations. Worst of all, because of broadcasting's tremendous inherent power to influence public opinion, it is a medium that has become the centerpiece of a gigantic struggle for power in which, as usual, no one's interests are being particularly well served.

The theoreticians of communications argue that the people have an inherent right to the air, that in effect they own it, and therefore the people's representatives have a right to regulate it. Broadcast law is based on that assumption, which has little if any basis in reality.

Naturally, the Constitution has nothing to say on this subject, nor is public ownership of the air among the Declaration's "unalienable rights." Indeed, if "life, liberty, and the pursuit of happiness" are to be taken seriously, government control of broadcasting would never be among these rights. The fact is that the air is controlled by those who have some reason to control it. Governments, recognizing the power such control gives, regulate broadcasting in every country, including ours, exercising varying degrees of repression and censorship.

Government and business together control the air when it is construed as space over real estate, and it is then bought and sold like any other commodity. People, as people, have little to say about this. For the first time, environmentalists are challenging the manipulation of real estate air rights, but they are not making much headway.

As for broadcasting, citizens may imagine that they exert some kind of control over it because, theoretically, they elect the Congress, which funds the Federal Communications Commission and confirms the appointment of its members by the president. Again, theoretically, the voters could use that inherent power, but they never have and are not likely to do so. Instead, the Congress, the President, and the Federal Communications Commission hold the power. The FCC, which is the creature of the other two, is essentially a political body, responsive to pressures that do not necessarily have any relationship to the public welfare. The national networks, caught between a government that holds the threat of license renewal over them and a public whose fickle tastes and passions give them no support whatever, quite naturally devote themselves to making money and trying to stay out of trouble. A few network executives have shown an understanding of this situation and a willingness to go beyond the countinghouse and fight for basic principles, but their enthusiasm is always tempered by the necessity to stay economically viable.

How did broadcasting ever get into this position? Government control was not something that began when the medium grew large and powerful, but was exerted soon after Marconi proved that it was possible to transmit sound through the air without wires. What happened after that was a salmagundi of blunders and power grabs, rather than any kind of sinister conspiracy, or a simple, forthright takeover of the medium—as occurred in even the most liberal governments of Europe, where broadcasting now enjoys a freedom more minimal than exists here.

Marconi's discovery created a small army of amateur radio operators who were soon busy communicating with each other, using equipment that in those primitive days did not enjoy the sharp tuning developed later. Consequently, the air was filled with the excited but nonessential chatter of these amateurs, and that began to annoy the United States armed forces, especially the Navy, which considered themselves the chief beneficiary of the new invention. There is no doubt that the Navy had a just grievance. Its wireless communications were constantly jammed by the amateurs and, if Marconi's little black box was going to have the revolutionary military uses the Navy was certain it had, something had to be done about it. That something, obviously, was control of the air waves. Nothing could have been simpler, or more in the pattern of American political life. The Navy went to its friends in Congress, who passed a radio licensing law in 1912 which President Taft (the armed forces' friend, as his predecessors had been) did not hesitate to sign—the protestations of the amateurs notwithstanding. There was no support for the amateurs from either public or press. No one could foresee the ultimate effect of giving government the right to regulate broadcasting as a matter of national policy.

This was the law that governed broadcasting until the Radio Act of 1927. The restraints it imposed were minor but important. Anyone who wanted to broadcast now had to get a license from the secretary of commerce and labor, not an elected official. Transmission could not be done without an operator's license, or in the presence of someone who had one, and the license could be obtained only by taking an examination. As a gesture toward lost freedom, the law did not permit the secretary of commerce (who had sole power to issue licenses after 1913) to refuse an applicant—even though he could assign wavelengths and set time lengths, another piece of legislative bungling.

As a result, licenses proliferated—almost a thousand in a few months—but the Navy's problem was solved because the amateurs were kept within one band width, and ship and government broadcasting were separated into two other bands. A few amateurs paid no attention to the law, and there were many radio buffs (actually a greater number than those who held licenses) who were engaged in receiving but not sending. There were 8562 transmitting licenses by 1917.

One of the earliest license holders was David Sarnoff, a young immigrant boy who had worked for the American Marconi Company in Nantucket, the Arctic, and Brooklyn before he got a job in 1912 as operator at the John Wanamaker store in New York while he studied engineering at Pratt Institute in Brooklyn. Wanamaker, foreseeing the possibilities of wireless, had equipped both his Philadelphia and his Brooklyn stores with powerful commercial wireless equipment.

Sarnoff was sitting quietly at his Wanamaker instruments on a dull

April afternoon in 1912 when he heard signals in his earphones: "*Titanic* struck an iceberg. Sinking fast." There were no details whatever, and no indication of the message's origin. Sarnoff immediately passed this news on to the world through the press and concentrated on seeking further information from the air. Pounding away with his key, he alerted all ships at sea within range of his signals. One of these, the *Olympic*, gave him the information that the *Titanic* had sunk and that the *Carpathia* was bringing survivors to New York. Sarnoff then established communication with the *Carpathia*, to get the names of survivors. Sitting alone at his receiver for seventy-two hours, he gave the world the only story of this historic tragedy that was available. President Taft ordered every other wireless station in the country to shut down, to eliminate as much interference as possible. Even so, it took remarkable skill and endurance in those days of weak signals, primitive circuits, and deafening atmospheric interference to maintain contact.

Thousands of people milled in the streets outside the Wanamaker store, many of them friends and relatives of those on board the ship; these people were given names of survivors as soon as they could be identified and transmitted. Transferring to the Sea Gate station in Brooklyn, after three days and nights on the key at Wanamaker's, Sarnoff identified the last of the 706 survivors before he rose from his instrument, pale and shaking.

The repercussions of the tragedy were far-reaching. In the investigative clamor that followed, it was pointed out that a ship equipped with wireless was much nearer to the *Titanic* than the *Carpathia*, the chief rescue vessel, but her only operator was in bed. Obviously there must be better wireless service at sea, both the public and the newspapers cried. Congress, pressured to act, soon passed a law requiring wireless equipment and operators on all oceangoing vessels carrying more than fifty passengers. The act also required an around-the-clock watch, with two operators, and an independent auxiliary source of power for the equipment. Within another year, more than five hundred American ships were so equipped.

"Wireless" was a word on everybody's tongue in the aftermath of the tragedy, but, oddly enough, its very usage doomed it as the common word for Marconi's invention. People began to saw off "radio" from its full name "radio wireless telegraphy" and use it as a kind of shorthand. Within a decade "radio" was part of the language. The United States Navy preferred the term radio-telegraphy and adopted it, but in time "telegraphy" was shorn from that usage too.

The effect of the *Titanic*'s sinking on the fortunes of the Marconi Company and on David Sarnoff was nothing less than spectacular. Every newspaper story—and there were thousands of them—constituted free advertising for the company, which was virtually certain to be mentioned in all of them. Wireless was suddenly in the public mind all over the world, and the Marconi Company was soon the largest of its kind in the United States. As for Sarnoff, he was on his way to his career as guiding genius of the Radio Corporation of America, the largest such company in the world.

Before the First World War, the general public knew little or nothing about radio except what the *Titanic*'s sinking had inspired. Those who were informed about communications did not take seriously Lee De Forest's revolutionary invention of the three-element vacuum tube he called the Audion. De Forest, in fact, had gone on trial in 1912, charged with selling fraudulent stock for his wireless system. The validity of this charge could be judged by its language, in which the invention that made De Forest famous and home radio possible was described as "a strange device like an incandescent lamp, which he called an Audion, and which device was proved to be worthless." The inventor barely escaped going to jail and was given a stern lecture by the court on the advisability of "getting a common garden variety of job and sticking to it."

With only a few exceptions, people could not visualize the Audion as what it would shortly become—the heart of radio. In general, the experts still thought of wireless, or radio, as an interesting toy, a comparatively unprofitable service that represented no real challenge to conventional telegraphy. Chief among the exceptions was Sarnoff, who in 1916 proposed the bold and imaginative use of the new medium as a home instrument for mass consumption. In a famous document known in broadcasting history as the "Radio Music Box Memo," he wrote to the vice-president and general manager of the Marconi Company: "I have in mind a plan of development which would make radio a 'household utility' in the same sense as the piano or phonograph. The idea is to bring music into the house by wireless. . . ."

He went on to describe his "Radio Music Box," which would, he prophesied, be able to receive "lectures at home which can be made perfectly audible; also events of national importance can be simultaneously announced and received. Baseball scores can be transmitted in the air by use of one set installed at the Polo Grounds. The same would be true of other cities. This proposition would be especially interesting to farmers and others living in outlying districts removed from cities. By the purchase of a 'Radio Music Box' they could enjoy concerts, lectures, music, recitals, etc. which may be going on in the nearest city within their radius. While I have indicated the most probable fields of usefulness for such a device, yet, there are numerous other fields to which the principle can be extended. . . ."

His idea was received with polite silence by the company. "They considered it a harebrained scheme," Sarnoff remarked years later. But he got his opportunity to promote the idea after November 1919, when the Radio Corporation of America was formed, with Owen D. Young as chairman and the majority ownership residing with General Electric, although in the next two years both Westinghouse and American Telephone & Telegraph became large stockholders. The first act of the new corporation was to buy out the American operations of the Marconi Company, and Sarnoff was at once appointed commercial manager of the new organization. Two months later, he was taking up the Radio Music Box idea with Young, in a new memo which forecast not only home radio but radio programs in magazines and a broadcasting system. This time he was taken seriously.

In 1920, RCA placed its first production order with General Electric for Radio Music Boxes, and a few months later, Dr. Frank Conrad, a Westinghouse engineer, began the first broadcasts as they are known today over station KDKA, in East Pittsburgh. Sarnoff himself pushed the burgeoning radio business over the top and made it a national institution overnight with his proposal to broadcast the heavyweight championship fight between Jack Dempsey and Georges Charpentier from Boyle's Thirty Acres in Jersey City. Nearly 300,000 people heard Major J. Andrew White, the popular editor of *Wireless Age*, describe Dempsey's fourth-round knockout victory. Within a year, radio had become a national craze, and stations were springing up across the country.

In the first two years of radio, between 1920 and 1922, Americans spent an incredible $100,000 for sets, tubes, headphones, and batteries. In another two years, the number of home receivers had reached an astonishing 3 million, most of whose owners in 1924 drew their chairs up close to the gooseneck speakers attached to the new superheterodyne sets so that they might better hear the throaty, fading voice of William Jennings Bryan, in the sunset of his career, speaking from the Democratic National Convention in Madison Square Garden. Broadcasting, Bryan proclaimed, was "a gift of Providence," and so it seemed to those who heard him.

Young Americans today, to whom radio is a commonplace that travels with them anywhere they want to go, can hardly realize what the new medium meant to those who were old enough to listen in the nineteen-twenties. A door to the world had opened for millions of people in small towns and on lonely farms. With a twist of the dial they were transported to Carnegie Hall, to distant football fields, to nightclubs and ballrooms where the new dance music was being played, and eventually to anywhere a microphone and remote transmitting equipment could be placed, which meant that they were vicarious witnesses of news events. It was a transformation in national life perhaps even more remarkable than the one produced later by television.

Inevitably, the death of the other media, particularly books, was freely predicted. These foretellings of doom had begun in the eighteen-nineties, when the craze for bicycles apparently had every able-bodied American pedaling about the landscape, consuming time which might otherwise be spent in reading. Trade journals deplored this development, but even while the craze was going on, the nation went through those "literary fevers," described earlier, which made authors the equivalent of today's rock stars. Then it was the sudden popularity of motion pictures that threatened the existence of established media in the first two decades of the new century; but that new medium only produced a new category of magazines and stimulated the flow of fiction from the publishers.

Radio, and later television, elicited the same gloomy prophecies, but obviously none of them was justified. The other media have grown and thrived under the competition, proving that technologies do not necessarily replace other technologies with which they compete. The analogy of the automobile replacing the horse was never a relevant comparison. Rather than replacing, as history demonstrates, competing technologies adjust to each other and live together.

While this fact seems clear enough, it was not sufficient to deter thousands of people who should have known better from believing an academic spellbinder, Professor Marshall McLuhan, when he told them a few years ago that the "linear media" were about to disappear, to be replaced by electronic communications which would bring mankind together in a "global village." Some people were so caught up in McLuhan's obscure rhetoric that what was virtually a cult began to spring up about his ideas, and he was duly anointed as the leading communications prophet, although relatively few could either read or understand what he wrote.

Since then, the only medium that has seemed in any danger of eclipse is McLuhan himself, about whom not much is heard anymore. It is worth noting, perhaps, that McLuhan was compelled to use the print media to spread his idea that they were irrelevant. As for the "global village" notion, it is not communications that have brought us as uneasily close together as we are, but shared economic and political disasters.

The other media were not extinguished, or even placed in danger of being so, by the advent of radio and television, but they were nevertheless deeply influenced by them. As an entertainment medium, broadcasting offered strong competition to magazines, motion pictures, and fiction book publishing, but there were numerous interrelationships as well. The effect of the competition could best be seen in the hard blow dealt to movies by television, and in the way television changed the character of newspapers.

Newspapers were hardly affected by radio news, even when it struck at the traditional spot-news function by bringing listeners a continuous flow of five-minute newscasts around the clock. People listened to these capsule summaries, and they tuned in, in large numbers, to the news commentaries of pioneers like Lowell Thomas and H. V. Kaltenborn. But the real attrition of big-city newspapers did not begin until television newscasting added the dimension never before achieved—the ability to see news happening. Unless the stories were major, television newscasting did not further curtail the spot-news function of the papers; the damage had already been done there by radio. But it created a successor to Thomas and Kaltenborn in the network news show, which not only built up huge audiences but in the persons of the anchormen established personalities who far surpassed in public recognition anything achieved by print writers or radio commentators. Ironically, the polls showed that they were more believed by the public than the newspapers, although there was no slightest reason why this should be so.

They were believed, that is, unless they brought news the public did not want to hear, as in the turbulent presidential campaign of 1968, when the polls showed that a public which had only just accorded the network anchormen the tribute of being most believed turned on them as "liberals" and "biased" when they reported what was happening in Chicago rather than what people wanted to believe was happening.

Economically, the impact of radio and television on the print media was worse than in other respects. The new media stretched the advertising dollar far beyond even what might have been expected, because of the constantly rising costs of production in broadcasting. Newspaper and magazine costs were rising, too, but broadcasting rose faster, and that industry could claim more of the advertising dollar because it could offer the advertiser a much greater numerical penetration of the mass market.

Yet the other media survived and did well. They lost advertising but they gained some, too, by specializing and doing things television could not do, particularly with local markets. As news purveyors, the newspapers stopped competing with each other on the newsstands in the old way, as mergers and losses contracted the daily field, leaving most cities with only one newspaper, or two at the most. In editorial content, the newspaper concentrated more on giving the detail and background of stories, and in digging out material that television had neither the time nor the motivation to obtain.

Television has not been a crusading medium, by and large, as the newspapers have been and still are, and as magazines from Frank Leslie's *Illustrated News* to *Life* and *Look* have been. The reason, of course, is its relationship to government and the peculiar nature of network operation.

The turning point in government control of broadcasting came in 1926, when the 1912 radio law was tested in court by the Zenith Corporation, and the United States Court for the Northern District of Illinois ruled that the secretary of commerce did not have the authority to regulate the air waves, as he had been doing for fourteen years. The American system of government, said the court, did not permit "the play and action of purely personal and arbitrary power." (One wonders what the honorable justices of those days would have thought of the Watergate era.) Instead of taking an appeal, the Acting Attorney General of the United States agreed with this verdict. Obviously, a new law would have to be passed, but by that time it was July and Congress had gone home.

During that summer, chaos erupted on the air, now that all government restraint had been removed and no force within the broadcasting industry itself was strong enough to replace it. Stations increased their power, moved to better spots on the dial, and broadcast at the hours that suited them best. Moreover, many new stations went on the air, and the result was a deafening clamor as the dials of the superhets moved across the broadcast spectrum. By the time Congress came back in December, there was a universal clamor for a new law, and the demand was led by the broadcasters themselves. As Erik

Barnouw, the historian of the industry, observes, "For broadcasting it was an hour of decision." It was a decision taken in the worst possible circumstances, designed to stave off anarchy rather than to consider the constitutional implications of government control.

In the midst of the argument over a new law, the National Broadcasting System, first of the major networks, was inaugurated with a great show in the Grand Ballroom of the Waldorf-Astoria. As many as 12 million people were estimated in the radio audience that tuned in to hear the New York Symphony, under Walter Damrosch; the New York Oratorio Society; Mary Garden, singing in Chicago; Will Rogers, doing a monologue in Kansas City; remote pickups from various ballrooms of the dance bands of Vincent Lopez, Ben Bernie, George Olsen, and B. A. Rolfe; Edwin Franko Goldman's band; Tito Ruffo, the Metropolitan Opera tenor; and Weber and Fields. Two months later, there were a pair of NBC networks originating in New York—the "red" network emanating from WEAF and the "blue" network from WJZ.

By that time the Radio Act of 1927 was a reality. It was a better law than the 1912 law, but, as Barnouw observes, "it was already obsolete when passed." Its principal provisions were:

To maintain the control of the United States over all channels.

To provide for the use of channels, "but not the ownership thereof," by licensees, but only for limited periods, "and no such license shall be construed to create any right beyond the terms, conditions, and periods of the license."

In granting a license or transfer of a station, the guiding standard would be the "public interest, convenience or necessity," a legal phrase of such splendid ambiguity that it has been a subject of controversy ever since.

Every applicant for a license had to sign "a waiver of any claim to the use of any particular frequency or wave length or of the ether as against the regulatory power of the United States."

Recognizing the growing and already thorny issue of censorship, the law read: "Nothing in this act shall be understood or construed to give the licensing authority the power of censorship over the radio communications or signals transmitted by any radio station, and no regulation or condition shall be promulgated or fixed by the licensing authority which shall interfere with the right of free speech by means of radio communications." Then the act abridged its own promise of free speech by forbidding "obscene, indecent, or profane language."

Anticipating another difficult issue, the act did not require the giving of time to candidates for office but obligated the stations to treat rival candidates equally and gave them "no power of censorship over the material broadcast under the provisions of this paragraph."

Taking a stand against monopoly, the act forbade licensing "any person, firm, company, or corporation, or any subsidiary thereof, which has been finally adjudged guilty by a Federal court of unlawfully monopolizing or attempting unlawfully to monopolize, after the Act takes effect, radio communication, directly or indirectly, through the control of the manufacture or sale of radio apparatus, through exclusive traffic arrangements, or by any other means or to have been using unfair methods of competition."

The most significant error in the bill was the assumption that stations would control their own programing, already nullified by the creation of network broadcasting. The act made only a last-minute promise that the regulatory agency would be authorized to make "special regulations application to radio stations engaged in chain broadcasting." Nor did the act deal specifically with the vital matter of time sales, except to note that broadcast material must be "announced as paid for or furnished, as the case may be, by such person, firm, company or corporation." The imminent impact of radio advertising was thus either unforeseen or evaded.

Who was to enforce these regulations? The act provided for the creation of a Federal Radio Commission, and even before it was fully organized, it was already being subjected to heavy congressional pressure. Secretary of Commerce Herbert Hoover, gladly relinquishing his authority over broadcasting, drew up a list of five appointees which President Coolidge sent along to Congress. They included Admiral W. H. G. Bullard, as chairman; Colonel John F. Dillon; Eugene O. Sykes; Henry A. Bellows, and Orestes H. Caldwell. The first three were confirmed in March, but Admiral Bullard and Colonel Dillon both died within a few months. Consequently, Sykes, a former Mississippi Supreme Court justice, was the only confirmed member until the spring of 1928. Bellows and Caldwell, both unconfirmed, were the only ones in the lot who knew anything about broadcasting. Bellows resigned and went back to the broadcasting business in Minneapolis before he could be confirmed.

Orestes Caldwell, the remaining figure of the original five, was a conservative who had worked for trade periodicals in the electrical-equipment field, particularly *Radio Retailing*, which he had launched for McGraw-Hill in 1926. Considering the editorial sentiments of that magazine, it was widely believed that Caldwell was not really in sympathy with the act he was supposed to administer, specifically its anti-monopoly provision, and in any case was too closely identified with the radio retailing segment of the industry. The Senate refused to confirm him, but he began working anyway under an interim appointment, hoping the next Congress would do so; meanwhile he went on unabashedly collecting his salary from *Radio Retailing*. He was finally confirmed by one vote in March 1928.

The new commission began without funds because Congress had neglected to appropriate any before it disbanded. Hoover gave the members shelter. Two more commissioners joined in November: Harold Lafount, a Salt Lake City hardware dealer who had also done radio manufacturing, and Sam Pickard, who had inaugurated the Kansas State College radio programs before he began to direct radio activities for the Department of Agriculture. In the following March, the commission was complete at last, with the addition of Ira Robinson, of West Virginia, a former judge, who became its chairman.

From the beginning, the commission was under the thumb of Congress and subject to constant pressure from it, as it is today. Louis Caldwell, the commission's first counsel, noted later the "political pressure constantly exercised . . . in all manner of cases."

The act of 1927, administered with varying success by this commission, was the law of the land until 1934, but as soon as Franklin D. Roosevelt was in the White House, there was talk of a new law to replace it. Mr. Roosevelt wanted one as part of his broad-scale reform program, but it was not well understood at the time that he intended nothing more radical than to put telephones and broadcasting in the same jurisdiction, taking the former away from the Interstate Commerce Commission. The impetus for real reform came mostly from educators, who were convinced that radio, which they saw as the best educational resource ever made available to them, had been sold out to the business interests, with the support and connivance of the commission.

Commercial broadcasting was already being depicted as a cultural disaster, and so when the Wagner-Hatfield bill of 1934 advocated, among other things, that the financially hard-pressed educational stations, shoved into a corner by the commercial interests, be permitted to sell enough of their time to make such stations self-supporting, there was wide support for it. But the supporters of the old Radio Act, who were also upholders of the *status quo* with no intention of permitting the commercial broadcasters to suffer competition, held up their hands in pious horror, exclaiming that there was already too much advertising on the air, and here were the educators wanting more of it.

In settling the dispute by compromise, Congress as usual not only failed to satisfy either side but closed the door to any kind of really equitable settlement. The Communications Act of 1934 created a new seven-man Federal Communications Commission, transferred the telephone authority to it, as Mr. Roosevelt had desired, and placed the critical matter of the Wagner-Hatfield bill in the lap of the new commission, which was to hold hearings on it and report back to Congress. The new act was largely a reprise of the old one, and a victory for the *status quo*. The idea of reserved channels for education, the nucleus of the Wagner-Hatfield bill, was quietly buried in the hearings. With only a few low-power stations operating for them, the educators were shunted to the last row in broadcasting.

The former commission had operated on a level only slightly above that of the old-fashioned ward heelers. The new commission suffered from the same disease that still afflicts it; that is, it was a political body and it was, on the whole, conservative. Worse, it was administering a law that was obsolete in 1927 and wholly mythological in the 1934 rewritten version, since its basic premise was wrong—that broadcasting in America was locally responsible since it was comprised of stations individually licensed. It was as though the networks did not exist; and by this time they were the largest fact of life in broadcasting.

But the most important omission in broadcasting legislation and the whole body of law that grew up around it was any recognition that in the increasingly vital matter of news broadcasting, the FCC— in short, the federal government—was given an implicit power of censorship. The idea that the protection of the First Amendment should be extended to broadcasting was not even considered, and is still not taken seriously by Congress, even though television has become the most important and influential of the news media.

The utter irrationality of this attitude is matched only by the 180 degree turn between conservatism and liberalism that has been made since 1946 in the matter of government control of programing in general. In March of that year, the FCC issued a report entitled *Public Service Responsibility of Broadcast Licensees*, soon familiarly known as the blue book. It was an approach to the deterioration of programing, and an attempt to assess promise-and-performance data on the stations.

In short order, the blue book was a center of controversy. It did, indeed, document the melancholy character of local programing, and it was hailed by the public-spirited everywhere as a step toward better radio fare. Justin Miller, new president of the National Association of Broadcasters, was cast as a villain when he said, at least by implication, that he believed broadcasters had been mistaken to allow the FCC any rights whatsoever where programing was concerned. FCC decisions made in that area were "censorship," he said bluntly, and violated the constitutional guarantees of freedom of speech, as well as the guarantees in the Communications Act itself. He also decried as "hooey and nonsense" the notion that the people owned the air. *Broadcasting* magazine, the voice of the industry, began to advance the idea that in exercising the power of censorship over what went on the air the government was emulating the totalitarian regimes so recently defeated.

Miller and the magazine were considered voices of reaction in 1946, but the situation is completely reversed today, now that television has shown us what a powerful national influence visual news presentations can be. The struggle now is to prevent, if possible, an authoritarian-minded government from regulating what goes on the air, as occurs elsewhere in the world. It should be clear in logic and history that the First Amendment gives protection to news broadcasting at least, but because those who want to control the media are in power it is now unpatriotic in some circles to insist that the "press" in "freedom of the press" must include broadcasting—if there is any meaning left in words after the public-relations experts and the lawyers are through with them.

The federal (or state, or local, for that matter) government ought to have no more voice in determining program content than it does in telling magazines or book-publishing houses what they may print, and it ought to have no more control over news on the air than news that is in print. Broadcasting clearly comes within the scope of the First Amendment, and only raw political power, exercised on behalf of purely political interests, keeps it from that protection.

It is often cited that no radio or television station has ever lost its license because of what it put on the air, with the single exception of WHDH in Boston, and only then because the court insisted on it. That, however, is not the result of the government's benevolence, or because it lacks the power, but because of the excessive timidity of the broadcasters. They are timid because, as businesses, they put the defense of their profit-and-loss statements ahead of everything else, including political and moral considerations. They even put up with the nonsense of the equal-time restriction, which is as absurd in its operation as it is unconstitutional. Newspapers are not required to give equal time to political candidates under the First Amendment; there is no rational reason why broadcasters should be compelled to do so.

Julian Goodman, president of NBC, has stated the logic of this issue succinctly. Speaking of a Florida Supreme Court decision (subsequently reversed) requiring any newspaper printing an attack on the character of a political candidate to give equal space for rebuttal, Goodman told a University of Florida graduation audience: "Now that sounds uncomfortably like the equal-time rule that broadcasters have lived with for so many years and that has effectively kept radio and television from providing full journalistic coverage of political campaigns. But whether you call it equal time or equal space; and whether the medium is newsprint or airwaves—no matter how you slice it, it is the people's constitutional right to a free press that is being sliced."

Goodman added, in words that should be heeded by every publisher, particularly those who are too myopic to see what is happening to them, "Our newspaper colleagues have come to realize that when the bell tolls for broadcasting, it also tolls for them."

This viewpoint admittedly makes strange bedfellows. The Reverend Carl McIntire, an extreme right-wing fundamentalist minister, was ordered by the government in 1973 to stop broadcasting from his station, WXUR, in Media, Pennsylvania, on the ground that in obtaining its license the station did not say it intended to broadcast the Reverend McIntire's right-wing sermons unbalanced by other viewpoints. McIntire threatened to continue broadcasting from a pirate radio station, Radio Free America, anchored just beyond the three-mile limit off Cape May, New Jersey, and to crusade for an end to government regulation of broadcasting.

Almost at the same time, oddly enough, the annual Earl Warren Conference of lawyers and journalists, held in Cambridge, Massachusetts, made the same proposal, that radio and television stations be freed at once from all government control over their broadcasts. Paul Porter, a former FCC chairman, in an article in *Center* magazine, published by the Center for the Study of Democratic Institutions, in Santa Barbara, agreed that the time had come to make this change.

"Court decisions are narrowly based on a scarcity doctrine that no longer applies," Porter wrote. "We have the technological sophistication to provide all the channels anybody can use. So why not give broadcasters permanent licenses and hold them responsible in the marketplace?"

As for improving the quality of programing on the commercial networks, a thick jungle of impenetrable prose surrounds the subject. It is an idle and futile exercise for intellectuals to attack the quality of broadcast programs, whether radio or television. Of course, there is a much larger audience for rock music than there is for Beethoven's last quartets, and there is no question that situation comedy and violence have far more mass appeal than serious documentary inquiries into the state of the nation. As this history of the media has shown, the broadening of the mass audience has been accompanied by an inevitable drop in quality. That is an inescapable fact of life.

If broadcasting is to reach a mass audience, it will have to go on doing this kind of programing, which is the kind commercial sponsors will pay for precisely because it does reach the mass audience. No one should be deluded by the occasional complaints from this audience that they are bored with what is given them. They are not bored by the quality, but by the quantity, which is overwhelming, compared with any other nation's output. They are bored by satiety, as they are with everything else in the affluent society, not by a longing for better things.

Nor should there be any delusion that some kind of compromise can be found between the proprietors of commercial television and those who want it to be a great educational and cultural force, as everyone thought it would be at the beginning. The only possible compromise is educational television; and that will never realize its potential until it is adequately funded by the government, and the government is then somehow persuaded to keep its hands off the management and programing—not a very likely possibility in the present climate. The fact that the educational stations have to struggle for their lives is proof that most viewers do not want culture and education from the tube. Nevertheless, those who attack commercial television should not forget that even though the time it spends on documentaries and other cultural materials is extremely limited, a great deal of information has been presented which has helped to educate millions of Americans, particularly in terms of science, the arts, and the knowledge of other cultures.

In terms of what is possible or is likely to happen, any radical change in broadcast programing or regulation seems remote. Attempts at solution are still sought, however. One of the most thoughtful was produced in 1973 by a Brookings Institution study titled "Economic Aspects of Television Regulation." The study takes note of the chief criticisms of television—that it fails to exploit its cultural potential, offers insufficient variety and appeals to the lowest common denominator, offers too limited a choice even among programs of the same kind, and that programing is determined by a few powerful organizations and individuals. Then it proposes a solution, which is essentially to break up local and national monopolies and to end governmental regulation of program content.

The idea of achieving better television through greater competition is a plausible one—social activists have believed since the days of the muckrakers that monopoly must be broken to have a healthy society. But it is not so simple. Any number of monopolies were broken in the era of trustbusting, but few of their evils were ended; most of them have multiplied immeasurably in this era of conglomerates. In any case, monopoly is not necessarily evil in itself. Some of the best newspapers in the United States enjoy local monopolies, while conversely there are cases, as in San Francisco, where two competing newspapers nearly ruined each other.

Again, if a few powerful organizations and individuals are not to control broadcasting programing, who is to do it? Committees? Consumer organizations? Groups of always "concerned" citizens? It would hardly matter because nothing would be changed. Mass audiences would demand mass entertainment, which would be exactly what they are given now; and since it would have to be paid for, advertisers would foot the bill. If private enterprise did not pay, then the government would have to, and we would have even greater governmental control than we do now.

To really end monopoly and to give consumers control of broadcasting would require a radical overturn of the American government, for which there seems not the slightest disposition in a generally conservative population.

The complaints of former Vice-President Agnew about "elitist" broadcasting network owners and commentators can be dismissed as a combination of simple ignorance and political moonshine. Only slightly less irrelevant is the complaint of some social scientists that networks cover only the events that can be handled most easily and cheaply and will attract large audiences. While it is true that the limited number of camera crews—a dozen or more at NBC, for example —curtails the number of events that can be pictured visually, still pictures and the reading of news items fill in the gap.

Critics of network news, scholarly and otherwise, would do well to watch it. They would find that its composition, in the condensed form imposed by time limitations, is exactly the same as a metropolitan newspaper. The major international and domestic events are covered, and if they seem to originate mostly in Washington, New York, and other urban centers, it is because the major news usually occurs in these places. There is a leavening of feature material, some of it investigative and some of it trivial, just as there is in a newspaper.

The overall news judgments as to what is news are the same. That is easily proved by taking the front pages of the major dailies and the three network news shows on any given day and comparing the judgments of what the news managers in these media think is news. It will be a generally uniform judgment, based on a common professional experience, which the critics lack. When these critics say that television or the newspapers are not reporting the news, or they are reporting it in a biased way, what they are really saying is that the news *they* want to see reported is not there, or it is not reported in the way *they* want to see it done. It is simply a question of who makes the decisions; consequently the argument comes down to a matter of personalities and motivations, and on that score there is no possibility whatever of agreement.

There is plenty of room for real criticism of television news, but one seldom sees it in the rhetoric of social and political critics. For example, the quality of interviewing on television is abysmally low. A veteran newspaper reporter would seldom employ that perennial question of the television interviewer, "What was going through your mind when" something happened. It is a silly question matched only by the silly replies it evokes.

Again, there is no excuse for thrusting a microphone into the face of some obscure citizen who has just lost a son or a husband or is facing some overwhelming catastrophe, and asking, "How do you feel about this?" or "What are your thoughts now?" and then having the camera hold on a twisted, teary, helpless face. This is not only a needless invasion of privacy, reminiscent of the days when newspapermen had to do the same thing in the name of competition, but a heartless abuse of privilege against the unprivileged. No one would have dared to put a microphone into the face of Jacqueline Kennedy after the assassination and inquire, "How do you feel about this terrible tragedy, Mrs. Kennedy?" Why is it any more permissible to do it to the widow of a policeman struck down by a thug's bullet?

Other criticisms of television news coverage could be made, but they would be professional, not cries of "Why don't they cover" this or that, or "Walter Cronkite must be a commie liberal or he wouldn't have talked that way about the President," or the somewhat more scholarly complaint that television camera crews film only dramatic events. Like the president getting out of an airplane? one wants to inquire, or a senator sitting at a desk giving an opinion? The fact is that within the limitations imposed by time, economics, government regulation, and the makeup of the mass audience, television news does a remarkable job of capsuling the most important events of the day, and the best local news shows not only cover their towns but often demonstrate more investigative zeal than the local newspapers.

Television's limitations are imposed—unlawfully and wrongly, it is argued here—by the government, but even more so by the mass audience it serves. All criticism of the medium ought to be seen in terms of that audience's composition. Like so much else about the nation, it is a mirror most people don't want to look into. One must remember that 95 per cent of American homes now have television sets, and the people in these homes watch them several hours a day. Consequently this audience, which includes most of us, is an immensely powerful determining factor in consumption of goods, political attitudes and voting, and social attitudes and behavior. What is this audience composed of, then?

Only about 11 per cent over twenty-five have graduated from college.

Two thirds over twenty-five have not completed high school.

From twenty to thirty times more adults read newspaper comic strips than the editorials.

For every intellectual magazine like the *New Yorker, Harper's*, or the *Atlantic*, there are at least thirty on the lowest level of mass readership.

Readership of books is higher than it has ever been before, measured by retail sales figures, publishers' output, and library records, but it has failed to keep pace with the growth of the population, and millions of homes have either no books at all or no more than a few paperbacks and gift books which are seldom opened. Mass-housing developments tell the story: few of these houses have any bookshelves. Worse, according to a recent survey, nearly 50 per cent of the population rarely, if ever, read a book for the purpose of advancing their education or knowledge.

We live in what seems like an age of travel, but there are millions of adults who have never been more than two hundred miles away from home, and millions more who have never spent a night in a hotel or a motel. Americans are not as mobile as some statistics would lead us to believe, and so they tend to a regional and local parochialism. If it were not for the *noblesse oblige* attitude of the rich, and their sometimes honest interest in the arts, no symphony orchestra, opera company, or museum of any consequence could survive—and even so, many would be gone today if it were not for reluctant federal government help, and the only somewhat less reluctant help from state and local governments.

This is the audience for radio and television programing. It is the audience that, according to the Roper Organization poll in 1973, finds television news the most credible among the four major media, at a figure of 48 per cent, while newspapers rate only 21 per cent, magazines 10 per cent, and radio 8 per cent.

The figures and facts above answer a great many of the questions about television as a news and entertainment medium.

21

The Press and Government

IT IS OFTEN SAID that there are only two theories of the press extant, only two kinds of relationship between press and government: the one in totalitarian or authoritarian countries and the one in the "free world." But how free is the free world? When one examines closely the press of every country on a comparative basis, it becomes clear that in reality there are three varieties of relationship: totalitarian or authoritarian; partial control in varying degree; and the American system, with its unique First Amendment and Supreme Court.

Viewed in this light, press freedom in the United States takes on a new importance. The totalitarian or authoritarian theory, stemming from the absolute right of kings and other monarchs, is prevalent in the world today. With variations, it is practiced in the Soviet Union and all of Eastern Europe, and in Yugoslavia and Spain. In South America it is the practice in Brazil, Argentina, Bolivia, Nicaragua, Paraguay, El Salvador, Chile, Peru, Cuba—the list increases every year. In Africa, the press is more or less totally controlled in Algeria, Libya, Egypt, Nigeria, Ghana, Zaïre, Upper Volta, Dahomey, the Central African Republic, Sierra Leone, Togo, Burundi, South Africa, Rhodesia, and Angola; there is, in fact, scarcely a place remaining in Africa where the press is really free. All of the Middle East is under authoritarian rule except Israel, where the press can often be subjected to severe censorship. In Asia, only India retains a free press, and in the Pacific only Australia, New Zealand, and Japan.

Where the press is controlled by government, the control is in greater or lesser degree, ranging from rigid censorship and complete direction of what is printed, to various methods of intimidation, brutally overt or subtle. The semantics of ideology sometimes present this control as the will of the people, and therefore "democratic," but by American standards there is no free press. Even where newspapers and magazines have some degree of freedom, radio and television are state-controlled, as noted previously.

We have seen, during the years of the war in Indochina, the progressive extinction of whatever limited freedom of the press existed there. Wherever the Nixon administration carried its war for "freedom" and "democracy," freedom of the press, upon which any authentic democracy must depend, was one of the first victims. The Philippines, which had only an indirect role in the conflict, had a press widely celebrated as one of the freest and most interesting in the world, but almost overnight it came under authoritarian rule. The excuse there, as it has been everywhere, was that Communism must be resisted. It is resisted, obviously, by establishing authoritarian right-wing regimes which are no more interested in press freedom or civil liberties than the Communists.

One of the most savage ironies of our time is the fact that the United States supports so many regimes which not only totally control their own press but eject our reporters who try to cover the news there. This was not so surprising, however, to those who were aware that the Nixon administration had engaged in a systematic effort to control the press in every way possible within the framework of our system, from backing restrictive laws to arousing and capitalizing on the latent hostility toward the press that always exists in the population. Americans talk a great deal about freedom of the press and the First Amendment, especially in the Watergate era, but there is abundant evidence to show that this is only lip service, ritualistic in character.

Even in Britain, the one place where we might expect to find sympathy and support for the First Amendment idea and the distinctive character it gives our press, some leaders of the press and public opinion find American freedom distasteful and believe it ought to be curbed. Here the British and the Americans have something in common. The British are forever talking about their tradition of justice in the courts and the rule of law in England, but this tradition can hardly have carried much weight in the nineteenth century (see Charles Dickens and several of his contemporaries), and it does not carry much weight today.

True, the British people have a respect for law that is quite unknown in lawless America, and on the whole conduct themselves accordingly. But it is difficult to see the operation of justice in the way the press is controlled in England by a government and a judicial system, working together, which impose their belief about the relationship of press and government whether the press likes it or not.

British authorities behave openly in ways that the Americans practice in secret. Late in December 1972, two Scotland Yard men visited the offices of the *Railway Gazette,* an obscure monthly with a 12,000 circulation, produced a search warrant, and for three hours went through filing cabinets and desks, searching for clues to the leak of a missing government document. Did this document concern nuclear warfare or delicate negotiations with a world power? Not at all. It had to do with changes in the railway network the government had proposed. Later, the *Gazette*'s editor charged that the police were bugging his telephone. Questions were raised in Parliament, but nothing was done. Earlier, a British court had prevented the *Sunday Times* of London from publishing a definitive article on thalidomide, on the ground that it might influence the negotiations for a settlement of damage suits brought by the drug's victims.

Under British law, reporters may report only what is said at a trial, and must not go beyond it. Cases like those in the United States recently, where reporters have refused to disclose their sources, would never get to court; the reporter and possibly his editor would be summarily arrested and thrown into jail for contempt. The source is not often a British official; they are secretive to a degree that would be intolerable here, and speak to the press only with reluctance. They are backed by the Official Secrets Act, enacted more than sixty years ago, which makes no distinction between information protected by "security," as ambiguous and ridiculous a term there as it is here, and any other kind of government document.

When the *Sunday Times* denounced the raid on the *Gazette* as a "sinister farce," police called upon the editor, Harold Evans, and warned him that he, too, might face prosecution under the Official Secrets Act. It is a crime under this act to publish anything at all from official documents unless authorized. Charles Wintour, editor of the *Evening Standard,* who has sought to change the law, notes that the number of trees blown down in a park during a gale would be an official secret, which may be why gardeners who work for the government have to sign a pledge under the act.

The British press also operates under severe libel laws, and it is so easy to collect under them that large damages are often won by public figures. One compelling reason for creating the British Press Council was the size of the awards given by hostile juries to anyone who brought a suit against a newspaper. By contrast, it is extremely difficult to be prosecuted for libeling a public figure in this country, although private persons are reasonably protected.

Under these circumstances, it is hardly surprising that there is little investigative reporting of any consequence in England, particularly when it might involve corrupt officials. A newspaper would not dare to accuse an official of wrongdoing unless the police had already taken some action against him.

It is sometimes pointed out that one reason for official distrust of the press in Britain is the traditional upper-class attitude toward newspapermen, left over from previous centuries. Usually the reporter has not gone to the right schools; he is not really a gentleman. As one editor has said, journalists "are not the types ministers feel they would normally have down for the weekend."

Americans should not dismiss this as British snobbism, because matters are not much better in the United States, where we delude ourselves as to egalitarianism. Reporters often sense the unspoken attitudes of people in power, especially government officials and businessmen. It is an attitude of usually concealed contempt for people whom they consider essentially inferior, and whose implicit power they both fear and resent. It was well expressed by a New York *Times* reporter who walked out of one of Mayor John Lindsay's press conferences observing, "You know what he really thinks of us? 'If you guys are so goddamned smart, how come you're not stockbrokers?'" People in power find it intolerable to be confronted by those whom they regard as inferior, who have the ability to discuss them and their affairs in public, and whom they cannot control. In America, a long tradition of anti-intellectualism is also involved in many cases.

Whether it is envy or myopia, British journalists have displayed a surprising lack of understanding of what is at stake in American press freedom, particularly in the Watergate case and its surrounding phenomena. Some of the adverse comment has come on the heels of a ruling which even British editors described as astonishing. In the summer of 1973, the courts fined a small English weekly $500 for describing a defendant in a preliminary hearing as "bespectacled and dressed in a dark suit," and reporting that the charge was serious and that the accused had been married on New Year's Day. In a country where the press can be treated with such contempt for freedom, it is surprising to find a distinguished journalist like William Rees-Mogg, editor of the London *Times*, charging the New York *Times* and Washington *Post* with "publishing vast quantities of prejudicial matter" on the Watergate affair. "We have the extreme legal position in this country. You have the extreme public position in the United States. The best system is somewhere in the middle."

Rees-Mogg may not realize it, but he is the one in the middle. Except in terms of basic philosophy, there is little difference in practical effect between British judicial control of the press and totalitarian government control. Yet the British press is not directly and absolutely controlled by the government. It has a measure of freedom to print what it likes as long as it does not interfere with the ruling class's concepts of law or reveal government "secrets," and while these restrictions may encompass large areas of news, it is not like the situation in authoritarian countries, where nothing at all may be printed without approval. Consequently, the British press, in company with the Scandinavian press, is in the middle between the remainder of the world and the United States, although the Scandinavians are much closer to the United States.

Those in and out of the American government who criticize the press and long to control it in some way have much more in common with their authoritarian friends than they imagine, or would ever be willing to admit. In a pamphlet on the press published in 1921, Lenin declared: "In the capitalist world, freedom of the press represents the freedom to buy the newspapers and those who edit them as well as the freedom to buy, corrupt and mold public opinion in the interests of the bourgeoisie." By substituting "leftist liberals" for "bourgeoisie," one has the essential attitude of conservative press critics.

Lenin clearly defined the totalitarian theory of the press, and it has not changed under successive Soviet leaders. The prime mission of the press is not to inform but to propagate Communist ideas and popularize the measures of the Soviet government. In America, the critics, especially those in the Nixon government, put it another way: the press should report what's right about America, not what's bad. It should be constructive, not destructive. It should not criticize or attack the government when the President is acting in what he regards as matters of national security, or in what he conceives to be the national interest. The difference is not substantial.

We often hear that the papers print and the television stations show too much news of crime and disaster. The totalitarian press agrees. In both the Soviet and China, this kind of news is seldom seen in any of the media. The policy of the Soviet press, to quote a study made by the International Press Institute, is simple: "A one-sided choice of news, the deliberate holding up of news, silence on certain events, and falsification of others." This was also the policy of the Nixon administration in respect to the news it was able to control, and, still following the Soviet pattern, it labeled as false and attempted to discredit the news it was not able to control.

This was not an invention of the President and his men. It was the culmination of a complex political development that has been taking place in this century. News had always been "managed" to some extent since Washington gave his exclusive on the Farewell Address, but it was done neither well nor often. Presidents fought back against attacks by the press—sometimes unwisely, as in Taft's case—but they were desultory skirmishes.

The modern era in press-government relations began with the Harding administration—paradoxically, since Harding was the only publisher ever to occupy the White House, and his early relations with the press were perhaps the best that had been seen in Washington since Lincoln's day. He was the first of the presidents to make his press conferences both regular and permanent. Yet in time he began to complain strongly that the press was paying too much attention to congressional attacks on his Cabinet members (richly deserved, it may be added), and it was clearly implied that not only would the administration look with disfavor on newspapers and correspondents that did the criticizing but, if the press could not give the White House favorable publicity, none was wanted at all. That was Lenin's idea, rigged out in the rhetoric of a presumed democracy.

Unfortunately, the issue was not confronted but buried in the inevitable political controversy that followed, as the critics in Congress cried out that Harding, an old newspaperman himself, was attempting to muzzle the press. And this was the same president who told William Allen White during a conversation at the White House, "There is nothing in the job here. As a matter of fact, I go to press at the White House every afternoon at three o'clock."

Harding, of course, was spared the scandals of his administration by his sudden death. Viewed from the standpoint of the Watergate era, there is something terribly familiar in Professor James E. Pollard's comment in *The Presidents and the Press*, "There is strong evidence of his growing awareness that men whom he had named to responsible positions had been grossly false to their trust, that others had used him for basely selfish purposes, and that worse was to come." The same thing had been said of Grant, but the question of malfeasance or misfeasance, or both, was never raised except by subsequent historians, and Harding's memory was treated with a kind of professional affection by contemporary newspapermen.

Teapot Dome, like the Watergate burglary, tended to overshadow and minimize the dangerous attitude Harding had taken in virtually demanding good publicity or none, on pain of excommunication by the White House of offending journalists and their papers.

When Franklin Roosevelt arrived, after a decade of blandness in Washington and disaster in the nation, an entirely new atmosphere was created by the extraordinary personality of the man who now occupied the White House. Mr. Roosevelt was subsequently called "the best managing editor in the country" and he deserved the compliment. Instead of fighting the press, the President manipulated it—and in a curious way, the press let itself be manipulated. The working press in general admired and enjoyed the President; some reporters even loved him, in common with a majority of Americans. The publishers, however, were predominately anti-Roosevelt, and many hated him with the pure passion of the rich and privileged whose clubs and social life they shared. The bias of these publishers was so pronounced, and often so vicious, that even as prominent a Republican Party man and publisher as William Allen White was compelled to denounce them at a convention of the American Society of Newspaper Editors.

Reporters believed Mr. Roosevelt even when they disagreed with him—always excepting, of course, the few members of the Washington press corps who worked for the newspapers of the radical right, and who were quite as fanatical as their publishers. The consensus was that the President was sincere and courageous, and that he put the interests of the celebrated "common man" first. Rich and privileged himself, he was, as his upper-class opponents bitterly called him, "a traitor to his class." Besides, he understood the press as no president has before or since. As Heywood Broun said, he was "the best newspaper man who has ever been president of the United States."

Roosevelt used radio as adroitly as he did the newspapers to advance his ideas; the Fireside Chats became famous and provided further ammunition for his frustrated critics. Yet he was careful about overexposure before that word was being used in this sense, and he made rivals like Landon and Willkie look weak and amateurish.

Confronted with a press two thirds of which opposed him editorially in 1936 and 1940, the President frequently counterattacked his more violent critics, particularly the "McCormick-Patterson axis," as it was sometimes called, meaning the Chicago *Tribune*, the New York *Daily News*, and the Washington *Times-Herald*. One can only imagine the conservative anger if President Nixon had been attacked with the viciousness employed by these papers. Hearst, who had been largely responsible for Roosevelt's nomination in 1932 through his control of the California delegation, turned on his choice and became another of the administration's most irrational critics. These and other enemies were always sounding cries of alarm that the administration was endangering freedom of the press—but the press had never been so free since Lincoln's day to say whatever it liked about a president, no matter how unprincipled it might be.

With all of his intelligence and broad understanding of the press, however, in the end Roosevelt fell into the same pattern of thought exhibited by other presidents and, as White put it, "utterly misunderstood and entirely misconstrued and misconstructed the motives underlying the presentation of the news." Editorials were one thing, the Kansas editor was saying, but the news columns were something else; and the President had embraced the common fallacy of believing that news is primarily and deliberately shaped to editorial policy. This is an article of faith among those hostile to the press that seems impossible to dislodge; they single out the relatively few exceptions and ignore the effort to be fair and accurate which is characteristic of most of the press. In fact, the papers which have made the least effort in this direction, or none at all, have been those at the extremes of right and left.

Roosevelt wound up believing, as all presidents have, that the press was unfair to him and did not present "both sides," in spite of the fact that even the papers that opposed him most sharply did not exclude his views from their news columns. His enemies perennially sounded cries of alarm that he meant to curtail freedom of the press by legislation, but he never made any such move and there is no evidence that he intended to do so.

While the media were split apart, in common with the population, over the issue of intervention or isolation, when the Second World War began there was less difficulty between press and government and press and military than in any previous conflict. A system of voluntary censorship was set up and closely adhered to, with only a few exceptions, one of them the ubiquitous Chicago *Tribune*. The accreditation of war correspondents worked well, for the most part, and the press reported the war better than it had any other in history, losing many excellent correspondents as battle casualties in the process. Only in the diplomatic maneuvers behind the lines was there any real conflict, as at the 1941 meeting of Roosevelt and Prime Minister Winston Churchill to draft the Atlantic Charter, and again during the Cairo and Teheran conferences. In these cases the press complained that it had been kept at a distance and told too little.

Through all three Roosevelt administrations, in spite of the overwhelming antagonism on the part of most publishers, it is worth noting that the small corps of his supporters included most of the best newspapers in the country—the same newspapers, by and large, that have fought against the war in Indochina and the Nixonian attempt to discredit and stifle the press along with any other dissenters.

The change since the death of Roosevelt has been remarkable and significant, and it has been conditioned by two factors. One was the advent of television, which gave presidents and other politicians both a powerful new weapon and an instrument which could destroy them as well as advance their fortunes. The other was the use of public-relations techniques in government, of the kind that had been increasingly effective in business and industry.

President Eisenhower took little advantage of these new tools. But then, he did not need them. He was a highly popular president who hardly needed public relations, and who had only to appear on television to command an immense and loyal audience. Dissent in the press was minimal. No doubt Mr. Eisenhower shared the distaste of his predecessor, Harry Truman, for the press. He appeared to believe, with Truman, that the press was sometimes unfair to him and his administration, and that it did not always reflect public opinion. But that has been characteristic of every president, as we have seen. Nor, in the case of both Eisenhower and Truman, did these feelings seriously hamper their relationships with the press. Their administrations ended in an atmosphere of relatively good feeling, in spite of a few disputes.

President John F. Kennedy, however, began a whole new era of government-press relations. Young, politically tough, and culturally knowledgeable in a way that none of his predecessors except FDR had been, he was aware of how important a part television had played in getting him elected. He was aware, too, of his own personal charisma and how effectively it could be projected by the television cameras. It was not surprising, then, that he began at once to televise his press conferences and to use television as a political weapon.

He also sharpened up an old weapon and wielded it more effectively, perhaps, than any president since Lincoln—the device of using correspondents with whom he developed close relationships to leak information, to send up trial balloons, and in general to act as buffers. He was able to use the media shrewdly because he himself was a competent writer. Both he and his wife had been newspaper reporters in earlier days: the President as an INS correspondent covering important international events, including the Potsdam Conference and the organization of the UN in San Francisco, and Jackie as an inquiring photographer for the Washington *Times-Herald*. These two people, who became symbols of liberalism almost as anathematic to conservatives as Franklin Roosevelt had been, were trained, ironically, in the ultraconservative schools of Hearst and "McCormick-Patterson axis" journalism. Apparently it did not rub off. The President's Pulitzer Prize-winning *Profiles in Courage* got bad notices in the conservative press.

As in Harding's case, President Kennedy's familiarity with the news process did not save him from difficulties with the press. These stemmed from two sources. One was the way he used his knowledge to manage news by giving certain stories to favored correspondents who could be guaranteed to present them in the way he wanted them presented. The other was the inevitable result of his slow passage into the Vietnam morass, the war no one was willing to admit was illegal and immoral, nor willing to admit, for a time, that it was even going on.

Only by hindsight can we see now that it was in the term of this idolized and martyred president that the seeds of our present crisis were sown. For the first time, under his administration, we heard it said by the assistant secretary of defense, Arthur Sylvester, a former newspaperman, that it was "the government's inherent right to lie, if necessary." And for the first time, as David Halberstam has documented in *The Best and the Brightest*, this "inherent right," a monstrously false presumption itself, became an unacknowledged governmental policy. Finally, and perhaps worst of all, no one in the administration thought it was wrong either to manage the news with planted exclusives, in the manner of a public-relations flack, or to lie about matters of war and peace which affected the lives of every citizen.

More than one informed American during the Cuban missile crisis must have felt a deep sense of rage and frustration in the knowledge that a few powerful men in government, the President foremost among them, had the power to blow up the world without prior consultation with those who would be blown up with it. "Mozart killers," the furious Viennese musician said of Hitler and his gang of destroyers. Mozart was in constant danger of being killed again for a long time, beginning with Cuba, all in the name of the ultimate absurdity—to "save" the world from one ideology by destroying all ideologies. "Better dead than red," said these toyers with other people's lives.

It was the atmosphere created in the Kennedy administration, as Halberstam has shown, that carried over into the administration of Lyndon Johnson, with immensely destructive effect. In pressing for domestic reform, Mr. Johnson dealt courageously with the portions of the press, both South and North, which fought him savagely on the question of civil rights. In the case of Vietnam, however, he and his administration lost all perspective, lied to press and public without any particular restraint, rationalized their lies with shibboleths that were already obsolete at the end of the nineteenth century, and pressed forward to a chimeric goal with the hot-eyed zeal of a new Inquisition, culminating in the débâcle of 1968, one of the most sordid political spectacles in American history.

Those who thought the Johnson performance could not be surpassed were soon enlightened after the advent of Mr. Nixon. With the help of a small army of public-relations men, the lie was raised to an art, and the secrecy far surpassed even Johnson's passion for it. The vast network of deceit and fraud collected under the name of Watergate has been the most visible symbol of the Nixon administration; but to those who study the relationships of the press and government, something even more subversive of the democratic process has been taking place.

Nixon's intense, outspoken hostility to the press, also expressed by most of those who have been part of the palace entourage, has given the public the impression that he is one man against the media, fighting a brave battle alone. This impression has been created largely by public-relations techniques. People remember the often quoted remark he made in the course of his rambling, hysterical press conference of 1962, after he lost the California governorship, when he told a shocked and embarrassed assemblage of reporters, "You won't have Nixon to kick around any more. . . ." Yet the facts are that most of the state's newspapers backed him in that campaign; and since then, in all three of his presidential campaigns, he was supported editorially by nearly 80 per cent of the country's newspapers—exactly the opposite of Roosevelt's situation.

No better proof could be offered of the essential political fairness of the press in the news columns than this fact. Editorially, Nixon had been able to count on the backing of all but 20 per cent of the nation's press. That 20 per cent included, however, most of the papers that are the best, by any reasonable measurement. But this was not enough for the President. He did not want to be opposed by *any* publisher or writer, and he particularly resented what the reporters wrote about him and his administration in the course of trying to convey the incredible events that had been going on in Washington since 1968. William Shannon, in the New York *Times*, described the Nixonian attitude well:

"Mr. Nixon approaches public life as if it were a succession of selling jobs. He resents reporters asking questions and raising awkward issues which call attention to the fact that whatever he is merchandising at the moment may not be all that he says it is. His attitude is very much like that of some corporation executives who deal with the press only through public relations advisers. . . ."

In the 1972 campaign, one reporter wrote, he behaved "like a touring emperor." As Shannon said, "he was completely insulated from the press and the people, addressing only selected friendly audiences in halls from which the press is excluded. A view on closed-circuit television is as close as most reporters get to him." Six months later, as the Watergate storm broke, his isolation was even more complete: it was eight months afterward before he held another press conference.

The Nixon administration's campaign to descredit the press through official hatchetmen like Agnew, before his fall, and the White House speechwriter Patrick Buchanan, with occasional assistance from Clay T. Whitehead, former director of the Office of Telecommunication, is familiar to everyone and needs no further detailed rehearsal. As any serious student of the press knows, there was little these men said that could be taken seriously by informed people, although there were a handful of Midwestern publishers and editors who contributed their own variety of nonsense on the subject. The kindest thing that could be said of the administration critics is that they were uninformed. But considering the impact of what they said on the large part of the public eager to have its hostilities confirmed, it is doubly unfortunate that these opinions came from men who, if they had not been projected into the upper reaches of public life by accidents of history, would never have been able to command a corporal's guard as an audience. Buchanan's only media experience was writing editorials for a right-wing St. Louis daily. Agnew had no experience or knowledge of the media whatever; he dutifully read what was written for him by his speechwriters.

The kind of thinking, if it could be called that, which went into their diatribes had its roots in the authoritarian mind. When censorship was imposed on Uruguayan news media in June 1973 by the military dictatorship, it was extended to international news agencies operating in that country. These agencies were told that any article emanating from them must be "objective" and that sources of information must be precisely stated. Nothing in the articles, it was added, must contain any element that might endanger the country or be offensive to "good habits." These were the basic ideas embodied in Nixon administration press criticism. Only a single word stands between American press freedom and the concept of the press which that administration shared with authoritarian countries: in this country, it is still said that the press "should"; in the others the "should" becomes "must," and "must" is enforced with the kind of controls that are only talked about here.

Again and again President Nixon expressed his belief that he and his men need not tell the public or Congress anything more than he alone thought they should know—and in the case of Congress, as the secret Cambodian bombing disclosed, only those who would support his position, rather than the leaders. Unabashed lying was justified on the basis of "security," or "saving the lives of our soldiers," or some other euphemism for absolute authority.

When Sinclair Lewis wrote *It Can't Happen Here* in the mid-thirties, he not only gave a phrase to the language but accurately forecast the present situation, as Herbert Mitgang has pointed out. The point Lewis was making, Mitgang noted, was that "home-grown hypocrisy leads to a nice brand of home-grown authoritarianism, as American as Mylai and Watergate."

In *It Can't Happen Here*, President Windrip dreams of retirement cottages in Florida and California. He appoints little-known lawyers to the Supreme Court. He increases defense budgets in the name of peace. His attorney general attacks irresponsible news reporting. About the press, he says: "I know it only too well. Almost all editors hide away in spider-dens, men without thought of Family or Public Interest or the humble delights of jaunts out-of-doors, plotting how they can put over their lies and advance their own positions and fill their greedy pocketbooks by calumniating Statesmen who have given their all for the common good and who are vulnerable because they stand out in the fierce Light that beats around the Throne."

Under the caption "It Can't Happen Here," and illustrated with a picture showing storm troopers burning books in Berlin, the Knight Newspapers in a public-service ad of 1973, placed in their own and other publications, declared: "There is a struggle going on in this country. It is not just a fight by reporters and editors to protect their sources. It is a fight to protect the public's right to know. Even the protection of the First Amendment may not be sufficient to prevent a gradual erosion of this cherished freedom under pressure from courts and government. It can't happen here as long as the press remains an open conduit through which public information flows. But, if the press becomes a tool through which the government informs the public of only those things it thinks the public should know, anything can happen here."

These could hardly be self-serving fears in a country where the highest court in the land has been known to show its contempt for the First Amendment, not only in its decisions but in remarks of its members off the bench. Chief Justice Burger has not taken the trouble to conceal his hostility toward the press, nor have the other three Nixon appointees.

Only two months before he was nominated to the Court, Justice Lewis F. Powell, Jr., urged the United States Chamber of Commerce in a confidential memorandum to counter criticism of free enterprise in schools and the news media in this fashion: "The national television networks should be monitored in the same way that textbooks should be kept under constant surveillance. This applies not merely to so-called educational programs (such as *Selling of the Pentagon*) but to the daily 'news analysis' which so often includes the most insidious type of criticism of the free enterprise system." This from a man shortly to be called upon to judge vital issues affecting both the media and business.

The press, of course, including television, was already being monitored in the White House by Patrick Buchanan, through whose authoritarian mind the President was getting his knowledge of what the media were doing. Buchanan was the writer of the Agnew speeches in 1969 criticizing the television networks, the New York *Times,* and the Washington *Post.* He was the man who talked about an antitrust action to force networks to produce the kind of news coverage and commentary desired by the White House. He was the man who opposed public television and helped to get its budget cut because its news programs dared to criticize the presidency. He was the man who prepared the President's daily summary of what the media were saying because Nixon, unlike his predecessors, was not a devoted reader. A man whose qualifications were three years of media experience, unlimited arrogance, and an appalling ignorance of media and their history, Buchanan was a proper *agitprop* director for an administration characterized by contempt and hatred for the press.

The Nixonian campaign against the press had reached a peak by mid-1972. L. Patrick Gray III, then assistant attorney general and in White House favor, was charging television and newspapers with inaccurate, unfair, and slanted reporting against the administration. Buchanan and Ehrlichman were making similar charges. In *Monday*, the Republican National Committee's publication, Ken W. Clawson, deputy director of communications for the executive branch, accused the New York *Times* of "being a conduit of enemy propaganda to the American people." Other administration figures carried on similar irrational propaganda campaigns.

Known administration sympathizers were deployed in the media themselves in the attempt to discredit an exposure of Nixonian policies and methods that was barely beginning, since Watergate was nearly nine months away. Robert Novak, a syndicated columnist, who at that point could be relied upon to attack his own colleagues, did so. S. I. Hayakawa, the retired president of San Francisco State, a linguistics expert suddenly become an authority on the media, devoted an entire syndicated column to their "onesidedness." John R. Coyne, once an Agnew staff member, published a book called *The Impudent Snobs: Agnew vs. the Intellectual Establishment*, a book that was awesome in its ignorance of the subject. James Keogh, another former Nixon staff member and a former *Time* editor, produced a better-written but no less incredible analysis entitled *President Nixon and the Press*. J. L. Robertson, of the Federal Reserve System, a banker posing as an authority on media problems, wrote in *Air Force* magazine, in words recalling Governor Berkley and the seventeenth century, that "freedom of the press gives anyone who has access to a printing press or a microphone the right to lie and deceive, even if those lies are part of an effort to incite people to perform illegal acts, such as blowing up banks. . . . We find the communications media being used to undermine the credibility of everyone who represents authority. . . ." Or, as Berkeley put it (we can remind ourselves), "for learning has brought disobedience, and heresy, and sects into the world, and printing has divulged them, and libels against the best government. . . ."

Coming from an administration that had already hinted the press might be regulated if it didn't conform, that had already tried to exercise prior restraint in the case of the Pentagon Papers, and that had pursued subpoenas and investigations of reporters in and out of the courts, this subtle campaign of terror had to be taken seriously by the media. It was, said William Small, vice-president of CBS, "insulting to journalists . . . who are not ready to surrender their role in a democracy to bureaucrats and other politicians simply because they wear American flags in their lapels. It's our flag, too—it's our country, too—and if our institutions are being corrupted, it's being done by those who want the news to be bland, innocuous and devoid of any substance other than obeisance to the status quo. . . . Good things don't happen because bad news is not reported. . . . If we give only the good news, only the safe news, only the uncontroversial, then we are only compounding the ignorance of our constituents."

The absurdity to which the attacks were carried, and the intellectual poverty of those who made them, was illustrated in Keogh's book. To take one of many examples, in which he turned on his erstwhile employers, the former *Time* editor wrote: "In one remarkable sentence, [a] *Time* Essay said that when reminded of American progress, 'the young are quick to point out that the most rational and technically accomplished society known to man has led only to racism, repression and a meaningless war in the jungles of Southeast Asia.' The use of 'only' said that there was nothing else—nothing of positive value in U.S. society—and the use of 'point out' accepted the charge as fact. Given this kind of intellectual diet by the country's most prestigious media, young people could be encouraged to turn on and drop out in greater numbers."

Aside from the fact that exactly the opposite has happened, Keogh, whose book constantly complains of media "distortion," fails to understand that the *Time* essay, not always celebrated for accuracy, was in this case entirely accurate. The young did, and do, "point out" these things and *they*, not *Time*, are the ones who accept them as fact. It is *they*, not *Time*, who say there is nothing of positive value in U.S. society. It seems strange, in retrospect, that a man with media experience should make the common error of those outside the media in accepting the idea that a publication, when it is reporting the opinion of someone, either individual or group, is itself advocating that opinion.

People in government generally, whether in this country or elsewhere, seem unable to understand the function of a free press. They see it, as it has been seen by politicians and those in authority since the invention of the printing press, as a hindrance to those in positions of power. They consider the media as pandering to a public hungering for sensation, and newspapers as avid for anything that will make headlines, wholly disregarding the fact that headlines have long since become a relatively unimportant matter to the press, since competition has virtually disappeared.

For example, a letter to the editor of the New York *Times* by Karl L. Rankin, former ambassador to Taiwan and Yugoslavia, asserted: "The news media naturally cater to the public appetite and at the same time fulfill their traditional crusading role. In contrast, the media in many other countries must support their regimes before public opinion. . . . So effective and bitter was the discrediting of the Administration over Vietnam, under two Presidents, that at its culmination last November only the patriotic reaction of American voters forestalled abdication of the country's long-established responsibilities as a world power."

It seems not to occur to such people that it is the administration that discredits itself by its actions, not the media in reporting them. Rankin goes on: "Have we made a fetish of freedom of the press and the public's right to know that may destroy the authority of the executive, pervert the orderly course of justice and transform the legislative branch into a television show?" One would like to hear Jefferson on the subject of making a fetish of press freedom.

Even so urbane and experienced a diplomat as Abba Eban, foreign minister of Israel, shocked at least some of the distinguished congress of world journalists, members of the International Press Institute, in June 1973, when he told them at their convention in Jerusalem that the press was creating difficulties for international diplomacy and was hindering the search for international peace. Eban also reiterated the old and easily disproved charge that the headlines capture only sensational, fleeting images of excitement while the more positive, slow development of human societies goes unrecorded by the mass media.

"There are two kinds of countries to which you will be giving your attention," Eban told the delegates. "There are those countries in which the press is intimidated by governments and there are those countries, including Israel, where everything is the other way round, where the governments are somewhat intimidated by the press." That brought a ripple of disbelieving laughter from some delegates, not only at the notion that the Israeli government was intimidated by the press, but that any other government was in such a condition.

Another speaker on the program was far closer to reality. He was

Quintin Yuyitung, former publisher of the *Chinese Commercial News*, one of the papers suppressed by President Ferdinand Marcos when he took dictatorial control of the Philippine government. Yuyitung was arrested, deported, and detained for two years in Taiwan, and had been released less than a year. "There are many countries in the world," he said, "where politicians have seized absolute power and muzzled the press, but we have yet to find a country in which the press has seized absolute power and muzzled the politicians."

The Philippines had been a classic example of a country with complete press freedom turned upside down overnight. In September 1972, President Marcos declared martial law, suspended the constitution with its pledges of press freedom, closed newspapers, and arrested and jailed many journalists. When some papers were permitted to resume, they did so under strict government control, and none were permitted to be critical of the government. Journalists released from jail found themselves jobless and deprived of freedom of speech. Many of their colleagues remained in jail without hope of trial.

In his report on the Jerusalem assembly, Ernest Meyer, director for the Press Institute, put it succinctly: "It cannot be repeated often enough that the legitimacy of the fight for freedom of the press is founded on the right of citizens to be fully and honestly informed. The health of our democracies depends on the responsible performance of this public service; the very survival of all our liberties depends on it."

Meyer quoted an editorial published in the Gaullist paper *La Nation*, published at a time when a new left-wing daily, *Libération*, had just been founded. It read in part: "If *Libération* should one day cease publication, like most journals of opinion so far, we should be the last to rejoice. And if *La Nation* should in turn encounter difficulties, our best-intentioned colleagues would be most unwise to celebrate. For *Libération* and *La Nation*, both poor, both threatened, are still evidence of that freedom of expression dear to the French people, who may not realize its value until the whole of the press has passed into the hands of a few powerful and unscrupulous groups who can control journalists like docile instruments in the service of brainwashed readers. And then it will be too late."

It may well be that it is already too late. Aroused by the Nixon administration's planned and deliberate assault on the press, the American public's hostility to the media just before Watergate reached a peak at which the overwhelming electoral vote of 1972 (still mistakenly called a mandate, when in terms of the popular vote it was a minority of a minority) was as much a repudiation of what the media had been printing about the administration as it was a testimonial to the deep distrust of George McGovern. Then the explosion of Watergate momentarily restored some of the media's prestige. In the warm afterglow of this landmark display of the power of investigative reporting, the media were seen to be vindicated, and even some of their enemies found kind words to say about them.

But as the events of Watergate and the Ervin committee's work, fully reported by television, developed, so much bad news was more than large segments of the public wanted to take. The mirror had been held up once more, and there were millions who did not like what they saw. Characteristically, some minimized the scandal or even denied its existence, while others blamed the media for bearing the bad news. From that point it was easy to begin blaming the media for the entire thing, and for many of the ills associated with the whole monstrous affair. Nixon himself and those close to him in the government were the leaders in this new flight from reality. As late as August 1973, in his San Clemente press conference at which he answered the press's questions about Watergate for the first time, the President was not only blaming the press for his difficulties but was doing it with a scarcely concealed anger and hostility, masked only by the usual rhetoric which the reporters present had heard many times before.

How ready the public was to accept the Nixonian view was evident in the man-in-the-street interviews carried by the television news shows and in the newspapers. When the *National Observer* ran an institutional advertisement on its plebiscite to determine how its readers felt about a Nixon resignation (35,398 for, 15,841 against), it quoted some of the individual responses, and they showed how thoroughly the public had been indoctrinated. Here are some samples:

From Lake Charles, Louisiana: "Every time I hear the word Watergate I become more convinced that the media, especially the TV newsmen, are the human counterparts of the predatory animals that follow and prey on game herds."

From Dallas: "Look at the facts that for the first time in decades we haven't been at war, the farmers and ranchers never had it so good. Inflation rates the lowest of all free nations, no unemployment, foreign trade balances improving and relations improving everyday with Russia and China. Why don't you write about these things and a President who is doing a good job?"

From Crawfordsville, Indiana: "If they had exhibited one-tenth of their zeal in demanding the real truth about Chappaquiddick, which was obviously swept under a judicial rug a few years back, they would really have a national scandal to write about. Why the hob-nailed treatment of the one compared to the kid-gloved treatment of the other?"

From Clarkston, Michigan: "What is all the fuss about? So they stole the other team's signals. This is as American as the Avon lady. It's like a bunch of cars all going over the limit, only the last one gets a ticket, though they are all guilty."

From Freehold, New Jersey: "This whole thing is ridiculous. Sam Ervin's follies have gone beyond all bounds of senatorial dignity and the damned fools are now playing only to the TV and don't give a damn for the country. It's an affront to the American public."

From Greencastle, Indiana: "No, my wife and I and all our friends firmly agree. It would be utterly ridiculous for the President even to consider resignation. We hired him to do a major series of terribly difficult and significant jobs. We only hope and pray that his enemies and their misguided followers (including large segments of the press) will get this claptrap circus out of the road and let him get on with the important business of running the country."

These responses, which seemed much more typical than the careful balance preserved in the *Observer*'s advertisement, judging by what the other media were printing and showing, inevitably raise again the question that some analysts have raised before—"thinking the unthinkable," as Herman Kahn said in another connection. The question is whether, on the basis of the evidence, Americans really want a free press—whether they would not be happier with the authoritarian variety that makes no one, particularly the government, unhappy, that prints only the good news about America and not the bad, that plays a "constructive," "objective" role, to be judged by what the government considers to be the public interest.

If that question were asked in a poll (properly phrased, of course), the answer would almost certainly be no, although one wonders what the proportions would be. But then, Americans are always quick to give lip service to noble principles in which they do not actually believe in practical terms. It is a serious question, although some may not think it so, whether Americans even deserve to have a free press, whose freedom is guaranteed uniquely by the First Amendment. Large segments of the population do not appear to care. Large elements of the bench and bar appear to be determined to assert judicial superiority over the media. Large numbers of people openly express their hatred of the media.

As Ernest Meyer said in his assembly report, "Threats to the freedom of the press come from all directions: from governments, from financial forces in their most aggressive modern form, from multi-national companies, advertisers, pressure groups, trade unions, and even from within the profession in the form of a confrontation, often more emotional than rational, between publishers and editorial staff."

Alexander Hamilton, opposing Jefferson's comfortable notion that it was only necessary to embody the principle of press freedom in a constitution to make it viable, wrote scornfully and prophetically in 1788: "What signifies a declaration, that 'the liberty of the press shall be inviolably preserved?' What is the liberty of the press? Who can give it any definition which would not leave the utmost latitude for evasion? I hold it to be impracticable; and from this I infer that its security, whatever fine declaration may be inserted in any constitution respecting it, must altogether depend on public opinion, and on the general spirit of the people and of the government."

If the "general spirit of the people and of the government" is the only guarantee of a free press today, its demise is assured unless that spirit changes in both the governed and their governors.

22

Why Media People Are
and Should Be Liberals

CONSERVATIVES ARE CONVINCED that media people are liberal—that is, everlastingly damned. They say this with varying degrees of fervor. James J. Kilpatrick, a syndicated conservative columnist, thinks it is one of the most controversial questions in journalism today, and in 1973 he saluted Walter Cronkite for confirming that "most newscasters are biased against conservatism" and that "television newsmen tend to be left of center."

It would be difficult to find another statement with so many misleading ideas in it. The notion that there is a political "center" is an antiquity going back to the Greeks, but it is an absurdity in itself. A man at the center would have no opinions one way or the other, otherwise he could not be at the center. The "center" is merely a linguistic device for dividing right from left; its only precise meaning is in the physical sciences.

There are, however, varying degrees of ideology right and left. It is the inability to see that there is no difference between the extremes of the right and left that has caused so much trouble in the democracies, particularly ours, where there are many confessed deep thinkers constantly trying to prove that black is white. "Liberals," if this abused word still has any meaning, are certainly on the left, and their opinions cover most of the spectrum up to the extreme, or radical, edge. That they are "biased against conservatism" is simply the view from the right. Rather they see the conservatives differently from the way the conservatives see themselves—and the reverse is true.

There is nothing new or "controversial" in all this, as Kilpatrick seems to think. Anyone who has worked in the media over the last forty or fifty years knows as a truism that even the most conservative newspapers are staffed largely by writers and editors who would regard themselves as liberals, or at least not right-wing. What is believed and set down in ringing prose in the editorial writers' rooms is most often viewed with embarrassment in the city room, if the paper is conservative, as most are.

This is not to say that the working press, including radio and television, is entirely liberal. As would be the case in any body of people so large, every part of the spectrum is bound to be represented. The conservatives, however, are distinctly in the minority. They become conservatives and remain so for a variety of reasons; no clear growth and behavior pattern applies to all or even most of them.

In the case of the liberals, however, it is a different matter. Fitzpatrick believes, as many conservatives do, that young people are indoctrinated in college by professors who are "a little left of center," but that is simply another failure of the conservative mind to understand the difference between left and right. Faculty members in colleges seem to divide in general between liberal and conservative on the basis of the disciplines they teach. Generally speaking, and of course there are always exceptions, those in the humanities, where free inquiry and skepticism are prerequisites, are more likely to be liberal, whereas those in business schools, medical schools, and the physical sciences, where both inquiry and skepticism are governed by codified sets of rules, are more likely to be conservative. At that, in a recent poll by the American Council on Education, 44 per cent of faculty members in colleges and universities describe themselves as conservative.

As for the students, they are not as radical and "left of center" as recent events have led people to believe. At the height of the campus rebellion of the late sixties, there was never more than 5 per cent of the total body of students in America, at the most generous estimate, involved in the trashing and burning and general rebellion. A substantial number went along with the radicals out of conformity—that is, not to have done so would have been like saying that the establishment was right about Vietnam, which was the core of the argument. On that question, there was not much dissent among students, although a small minority was for Nixon even so.

As for journalism students, there is no need for indoctrination. They usually have the sharpest, most inquiring minds in the student body and, like most journalists from the beginnings of the profession, they seem to come equipped with a kind of innate resistance to humbug, a sensory apparatus which informs them that the world is full of people who are solemnly trying to tell them things that aren't so. There are conservatives among them, too, as there are on journalism faculties. One finds nothing monolithic about it, and the liberalism itself is of widely varying degree. Conservatives stand out, however, as political oddities. Patrick Buchanan was not like most of his classmates at the Graduate School of Journalism, Columbia University. On the other hand, those who have taught there and elsewhere can easily remember students who came as conservatives and within a few years were liberal activists. The reverse occurs rarely.

How and why, then, do media people become predominantly liberal (since there is no better word for it)? It should be remembered that "liberal" may mean they are liberal Republicans instead of liberal Democrats. The differences between these two categories are not substantial.

People who work in media come from all kinds of economic and social backgrounds today, unlike the situation up to the time of the First World War, when they came overwhelmingly from the lower end of both scales. In those generations they were predominantly young men (and a few women) who came to the cities from small towns, and sometimes from the farms. Those in upper-class families did not often go into media work because it was not quite respectable, at least not until a category of millionaire publishers had been created in the big cities. Some newspapers, like the Kansas City *Star*, were noted as training grounds for New York and Chicago. Less adventurous aspirants, those with less drive and those who preferred small-town life, stayed behind to staff the dailies and weeklies in smaller communities.

Today the influx of new talent into the media is much more diversified. There are more blacks and more women, although the bars are far from beaten down. The upper economic and social levels are better represented, reflecting the rebellion of the children of the affluent in the sixties. Natives of the metropolis are also much more in evidence—inevitably, since 80 per cent of Americans now live in metropolitan areas. It is, in brief, a more homogeneous mixture of people than it was even as late as the twenties and thirties, and quite different from what it was before 1917.

No matter what level of society they come from, however, and no matter what their previous training—whether in a school or department of journalism, which is increasingly the case, or whether from a background of liberal arts or prelaw, or without any college training —they share a common experience once they are in the media.

In the old days, the pattern for aspirants was to start on a small paper (or a small radio or television station) and work up the ladder. Now many graduates of journalism schools and departments go directly to metropolitan newspapers or broadcasting stations, and into magazines and public-relations work. The latter two occupations provide a different kind of work experience; but those who get jobs in newspapers or broadcast journalism find themselves undergoing a common succession of discoveries about the world.

Reporting, where most people begin, is an educational experience which at once begins to draw a line between those in the media and those outside it. Few of those outside have any idea how the media operate. There are millions of Americans who visualize newspapers, for example, as places where editors are constantly searching for some new sensation, some new way to embarrass the politicians they don't support. They think of reporters as wandering the streets, looking for "headlines" or "scoops," tracking down criminals, digging up "dirt" about political enemies, and writing of these things without regard for anything the average citizen values or believes in.

The reality, of course, is far different. Editors try to find out where news is occurring and attempt to cover what they believe is worth covering. Inevitably that attempt collides with other people's idea of what is worth covering. It is impossible to get into any newspaper everything that people think should be in it, or to write the news in such a way that it will satisfy everyone, much less those who were involved in it and have their own ideas, not necessarily correct by any means, of what actually happened. Reporters and editors try to be accurate and fair, no matter what the public may think, but in any edition of a newspaper containing hundreds of thousands of facts, mistakes are unavoidable. Many people who find something they think or know is wrong conclude that everything else in the paper is at least questionable—a common critical fallacy that afflicts some book reviewers, too.

Editors know it is impossible to satisfy everyone's demands as to what the newspaper should or should not print, and they know that no matter what they print on any subject, however it is treated, there will be someone who doesn't like it, who believes it to be inaccurate or unfair. Not all newspapers make the same effort to be fair and accurate, of course. The best are scrupulous about it and come as close to the ideal as fallible human hands and brains can, which must always fall short. Others try with varying degrees of zeal, and there are some that make little or no effort, but they are in the minority.

Another thing editors know is that readers are forever confusing the editorial page and the news columns. If they hate what the editorials say, they are certain the news is contaminated with the same poison, and they will find it whether it is there or not. Their hostility extends from the editorial page to everyone who works for the newspaper. Reporters who cover labor news for an anti-union paper may have the experience of getting an angry rebuff from a union leader when the reporter announces what paper he is from, even though he himself may be a paid-up member of the American Newspaper Guild and wholly sympathetic to the union in question.

As for the reporters, unless they are specialists working in a relatively narrow field, such as labor or education, or local politics, they will meet an astonishing variety of people in the course of an ordinary day's work. The largest metropolitan dailies are now a collection of specialists, as universities are a community of scholars, but elsewhere reporters still do general-assignment work, covering whatever parts of the day's news are assigned to them from the city desk. Many of the specialists, too, have been on general-assignment work before they come to work only in their specialty.

Being a reporter and talking to such a wide variety of people is educational in a number of ways, and it is the kind of education available nowhere else. In one aspect, it requires dealing with any number of subjects for which the reporter may have had no adequate preparation except his general knowledge, and so in time he learns a little about a great many things and begins to acquire a detailed knowledge about one or two. An experienced reporter learns how to inform himself. Mencken once said that all he needed to be the second best authority on any subject was access to a first-class public library. Not many reporters have Mencken's extraordinary intellectual capacity, but the nature of their work gives them a broader general knowledge than most of the reading public possesses.

Reporters are educated in another and probably more significant way. They learn at an early date that respectable and presumably responsible people, politicians especially, will look them in the eye and lie. They will say something one day and flatly deny it the next. After long experience with this kind of thing at levels from the county courthouse through city hall to the upper reaches of Washington, a good reporter learns not to trust anyone, regardless of party. Consequently, while media people are predominantly liberal, if they have had this kind of training they are skeptical of any politician, regardless of party. If they are registered Democrats, it is more because of their general feeling that, historically and actually, Republicans are likely to be the defenders of power and privilege, rather than from adherence to specific Democratic platforms or doctrines. Thus they were likely to be defensive about Lyndon Johnson even though most opposed his Vietnam policies. Mr. Johnson abused his power, they thought, but he did not exalt privilege and protect it at the expense of the public interest.

The working press sees the world in a very different way from the rest of the population. Reporters know what people in public life are really like. They see events in their raw, unvarnished state—but not a great deal of this gets into the news columns, as it did in the nineteenth century. People and events were treated then in a more uncompromising way because there was much less effort toward fairness and accuracy. Reporting was impressionistic, subjective, and often highly colored by the reporter's own personality, freely expressed in his use of "I," still prevalent in British and some other European reporting. The twentieth-century style has produced a uniformity that some have found drab and bland—one paper reads more or less like another—and this has led to the rebellion which produced the so-called New Journalism, in essence simply a reversion to nineteenth-century style.

Even editors wonder sometimes why only a fraction of what a reporter sees and knows gets into the papers. A news executive from the New York *Times* once spent a day in Washington examining the work of the Washington bureau. He talked to the reporters stationed in various parts of the capital, and to the men who directed them. At the end of the day, leaning back in his chair over a drink at the National Press Club, he asked the news editor of the bureau plaintively, "Why is it I don't see much of what I heard today in the New York *Times*?" It was a rare moment of truth. An executive long removed from the news beats forgets the reality with which the reporters deal from hour to hour. Much of this cannot be reported, sometimes because it can't be proved, sometimes because it would close up valuable sources forever, and sometimes because the reality would be denied both by the people who create it and by those who read it.

Readers could have been told, for instance, about the sex lives of some recent presidents, but they were not because of a feeling on the part of the press that public figures, at this level particularly, have a right to privacy about such matters, unless for some reason it is made a political issue by a rival politician.

In simple human terms, the disparity between the world of the reporter and the world of the ordinary citizen who knows only what he reads is often obvious when the reporter finds himself talking about public affairs to someone who does not have his firsthand knowledge. The ordinary citizen believes what he wants to believe about public events; the reporter believes what he sees and is able to evaluate what he hears. A city editor in an Illinois community once instructed his reporters to reproduce exactly what was said and what went on in one day at city hall, excluding only obscenities (a large exclusion, one might add). The result was so horrifying that it was stopped after that day because of the outcry from the public and the howls of anguish from city hall. Even though they may know better, people apparently want to think that public officials talk the way they do in the newspapers instead of in the often profane and cynical way they actually speak.

In the case of Washington, that vast menagerie, much more emerges than what is experienced by the average city-hall reporter. In this last stronghold of real competition among the media, efforts to get the news are on about the same level as they were in New York when the city had eighteen newspapers. This is not entirely a blessing. One of the worst handicaps a reporter can suffer, and it is epidemic in Washington, is to know his sources so well that he becomes a good friend instead of a critic, which his calling should compel him to be. Every veteran newspaperman is familiar with the reporter who has been so long on the city-hall beat that he is indistinguishable from the aldermen. A story about the corruption of the mayor or his political friends is not likely to come from that reporter.

Washington reporters are acutely dependent on sources, and sometimes they know them far too well. During a period when the columnist Joseph Alsop was little more than a propagandist for the Air Force because of his closeness to the top officers of that command, those who were aware of this situation knew how to evaluate Alsop's writing; but those who were not, which included most of the readers of his nationally syndicated column, had no way of separating fact from advocacy. Alsop was only one of many similar offenders; he appeared to be more prominent because of his unrestrained arrogance. Political columnists of long service almost inevitably—although there are a few exceptions—become so entangled with their sources that everything they write has to be viewed from certain perspectives, which unfortunately their readers do not possess.

It is significant that the Watergate story was not broken by one of the White House correspondents, highly capable journalists who were nearer to it than anyone else in the media, but by two city men on the Washington *Post* who were not handicapped by constant proximity to high office. When you were on a "dear Bob" and "dear John" basis with Messrs. Haldeman and Ehrlichman, and when the President, no matter what you might think of him, knew you by your first name and called you by it, and when you shared to some extent the daily life of these dignitaries, the impulse to question whether they were acting in anybody's interest but their own did not arise. Certainly it did not in the case of Watergate, or if it did it was never acted upon.

There are critics of the press in the profession itself who believe that Washington news would be much better reported if correspondents in the White House and on Capitol Hill were rotated on something like a three-month basis so that no one would be too friendly with the sources of news. That idea, whatever its technical difficulties, would be equally salutary if applied to regular news beats outside Washington—city hall beats, federal beats, police beats, whatever.

In any case, there is a great deal more investigative reporting going on today than there has been for some time, both in Washington and elsewhere. Not that there is any significant increase in corruption, excepting Watergate collectively. It simply rises to the surface and boils over now and then. But the tremendous growth of our society in the past twenty-five years, particularly the government-military-industry complex, reaching out into every aspect of the nation's life, provides many more opportunities for corruption to exist. When public officials and businessmen are dealing with sums of money which dwarf anything known until a quarter of a century ago, the possibilities for corruption become infinite.

The "New Journalism" has played a role in the dramatic growth of investigative reporting, although not the one it thinks it has performed. In their megalomaniacal self-confidence, the New Journalists are convinced they have revolutionized the business, when in fact they have only stimulated it in an indirect way. It is no accident that their reportage, except for Vietnam, has been much more sociological and anthropological than political. Where it has been political, it has been so filtered through the subjective eyes of the observer that it produced no practical effect. None of the Watergate revelations has been the work of a New Journalist, nor have any of the other major media investigations, for that matter.

One of the characteristics which separate the new breed from the old is the extreme seriousness with which the former take themselves. The old breed's view of the world is largely one of tolerant cynicism, based on an innate distaste for pretension, particularly where they themselves are concerned. But the new breed are nothing if not pretentious, writing windy essays about what they are doing and why they are doing it, talking solemnly about "history as the novel and the novel as history," and how fiction has died (again, as it has for a hundred years periodically), and how they are the shining practitioners of a new art form, when in fact it is the form with which journalism began.

When one wades through this mass of pompous rhetoric and gets down to the product itself, the result is depressing. The New Journalists write entertainingly, of course, aided by various gimmicky devices which will seem old-fashioned in another decade or so. It is more fun for the average reader to read about life in the United States through the prose of Norman Mailer and Gay Talese and Tom Wolfe, to name the most celebrated practitioners, but it is less than informative. When one has come back from a trip through Mailer's tangled psyche, and Talese's exotic view of human institutions, and Wolfe's exotic view of exotica, it is obvious that for these "new" writers style is everything and substance is a nuisance. Somehow they contrive to be trivial about the most serious subjects.

"Manners and morals *were* the history of the sixties," Wolfe asserts confidently—certainly one of the most preposterous statements of the century, as any qualified historian could tell him. He sneers at the old journalism, with its "pale beige tone," as though this tone had not produced since 1900 most of the impetus for all the social reforms we enjoy by reporting factually, not fancifully, what has been taking place in American life. No legislation has been passed, no indictments handed down, no crooked politicians removed from office, as a result of the New Journalism.

In ordinary circumstances the New Journalists could be dismissed as a short-lived phenomenon of the times, well out of the mainstream of media history; but they have done some serious damage to the credibility of the media at a time when press freedom is in the greatest danger since the Constitution was written—a time when that credibility, as against that of a government which wants to stifle it, has become a vital issue.

In such a situation, it does not help to have a school of writing arise which purports to re-create the thoughts and feelings of the people it is writing about, and which creates imaginary characters as composites of real people. This is fiction, and no amount of tortured rhetoric will make it fact. Readers have no way of making the distinction and learn to accept speculation, simple opinion, or pure imagination as fact when it is presented to them in a prose that is more entertaining than standard newswriting. Even intellectuals are easily misled by the pretensions of the New Journalism. Wolfe's anthology of the genre was reviewed in the New York *Times Book Review* by the author of a book on Stendhal, an English professor who nevertheless had no hesitation in talking authoritatively as a media expert about how much better the New Journalism is than the old.

No journalist of any experience would argue that the media, print or broadcast, are beyond criticism. Like any other institution, the media have their faults—although seldom the ones the critics insist upon. It is amusing to note that some of the journalism reviews staffed by people either in the media or associated with them academically print letters to the editor accusing them of the same faults the editors attribute to the media they are monitoring. Not even criticism of the press by its own people is above criticism, it appears, and on the same grounds at that—inaccuracy, unfairness, unwillingness to get all the facts, and the rest of the litany.

One should also beware of the kind of criticism that depends on verbal gimmickry, especially coined words. Perhaps the first was *Time's* "nonbook," soon a part of the language but nonetheless quite meaningless. A book is a book. The motivations that went into making it, or whether a particular group or individual approves of it, are irrelevant to the fact of its existence. All books are "nonbooks" or "made books," as the other phrase goes, in the sense that they are conceived as ideas; someone puts them together, and they emerge in bound form to reach a certain market, whatever it may be. Whether someone thinks it is an unnecessary book, or an irrelevant book, or chooses to categorize it in some other way, has nothing to do with it.

Similarly, another recent critic talks about "newsthink," defined as "the rhetorical bias of the news media in favor of turning a non-event into 'news.'" This notion stems from the invention by Professor Daniel Boorstin of "pseudo-news," to describe, one supposes, something that is not hard news. When a man calls a press conference to announce something, it is said, that is pseudo-news because it has been caused to happen and is only news when someone says it is. This is still another flight from reality. If a man calls a press conference and reporters are there to hear him say something, that act in itself is news. Whether what he says is trivial, unnecessary, or irrelevant must remain a matter of individual judgment, but the fact that it is reported makes it news. Reporters and editors are the best judges of whether or not it is news worth printing. There are numerous press conferences to which scarcely anyone comes, and the results of which are spiked on the city editor's desk.

The critic who coined "newsthink" exhumes the hoary arguments about the words headline writers use, contentions that one would think had been decently buried thirty years ago, and gives his readers some further thoughts about "labeling" people (as Bobby Kennedy, "ruthless," and Lyndon Johnson, "power-mad"), as though this were general practice, when if course it is not.

As a sample of such nonthinking by nonexperts, the author of "newsthink" offers us a sample of what he calls "trending," in which "the news media decide that events in a certain area are moving in a uniform direction. All the information on the subject will then reinforce the idea of the trend. A good example is the media's handling of youth. In 1967 the youth trend was away from politics; in 1968 into politics; in 1969 out of politics; in 1970 back again. Now the youth trend is away from politics once more."

Exactly. As anyone who spends time in a college classroom knows, there was a general apathy toward politics in 1967, but a sudden surge forward in 1968 when young people thought they might be able to end the war in Vietnam by getting President Johnson out of office. When that occurred and the war went on, they retreated again into their usual state of disbelief and despair over the democratic process. In 1970 they were back again, inspired to new anger by the Cambodian outrage. When it became perfectly clear that the President meant to do whatever he liked without regard for Constitution, Congress, or anyone who dared to dissent, the opposition on the campuses crumbled in the most sudden way, and not even Watergate was enough to revive any real activist interest in politics. Not "trending" or "newsthink," but fact.

Critics who say "the media" do this or that are now legion. But as Ben Bagdikian, one of the best professional critics, reminds us, "the word 'press' brings so many different images into so many different heads that the contemporary controversies about the news sound like a shouting match between a convention of Pepsi-Cola bottlers and the vintners of St. Emilion."

What do people mean when they say "the media"? Bagdikian points out that there is "a wild conglomeration of organisms (1750 daily papers, over 8000 weeklies, 22,000 periodicals, 850 television and 6400 radio stations) and they range in quality from noble to idiotic. . . . Most press criticism consists of an angry man reading one news item that crosses his desk and firing off a jeremiad about 'The American Press.' "

What the media need now is not what its critics imagine, in their various self-serving ways. They need more bright and dedicated men and women—"liberals," much as it may dismay the conservatives, and not New Journalists who can't distinguish fact from fancy and who in any case, though they may be ideologically liberal, are politically amoral. These liberals need to consider themselves as sworn enemies of pretension, humbug, and lying. People in public office should be presumed guilty unless they are constantly proving themselves to be innocent by serving the people who elected them, honestly and without special favor. The media people ought to report more news, and do it more thoroughly and intelligently. There is enough investigating of American life to do to last all of them for the remainder of the century and beyond. Print and broadcast journalism alike ought to be removed from the grasp of government and the attempts of politicians and the judicial system to destroy or cripple its First Amendment protection. The media ought to pay less attention to their critics, few of whom are worth listening to, and more to improving their product in terms of thoroughness, readability, and accuracy.

Generalizations, one may say. Where are the specifics? The specifics are not the problem; they are readily available from a good many sources within the profession. Specifics will do us no good whatever unless there is a determination on the part of the media to save themselves, to fight government to the end. Most important of all, there must be a determination on the part of their readers, for whose service they exist, to keep them free and viable. Without these qualifications, there is little question but that the United States, the last real stronghold of press freedom, will slip into some kind of authoritarian control before the century is ended.

For Further Reading

Together with my own eleven volumes in the field of communications (listed in the front matter), the following hard-cover titles are recommended:

American Journalism, by Frank Luther Mott (rev. ed., Macmillan, 1967).

The Press and America, by Edwin Emery (3d ed., Prentice-Hall, 1972).

Golden Multitudes, by Frank Luther Mott (Macmillan, 1947).

A Tower in Babel: A History of Broadcasting in the United States to 1933, by Erik Barnouw (Oxford University Press, 1966).

The Golden Web: A History of Broadcasting in the United States, 1933–1953, by Erik Barnouw (Oxford University Press, 1968).

The Image Empire: A History of Broadcasting in the United States from 1953, by Erik Barnouw (Oxford University Press, 1970).

A History of Book Publishing in the United States, vol. I, *The Creation of an Industry, 1630–1865*, by John Tebbel (Bowker, 1972); vol. II, *The Expansion of an Industry, 1854–1919*, to be published in 1975; and vol. III, *An Industry Comes of Age, 1919–*, to be published in 1977.

The Book in America, by Hellmut Lehmann-Haupt *et al.* (Bowker, 1951).

Book Publishing in America, by Charles Madison (McGraw-Hill, 1966).

The Presidents and the Press, by James E. Pollard (Macmillan, 1947).

The Correspondent's War, by Charles H. Brown (Scribner's, 1967).

They Will Be Heard, by Jonathan Daniels (McGraw-Hill, 1965).

Media Power, by Robert Stein (Houghton Mifflin, 1972).

Excellent bibliographies will be found in Mott's *American Journalism* and Emery's *The Press and America*, as well as in the three Barnouw volumes. The notes in my three volumes of the history of book publishing comprise a key to the literature in the field, and an even more extensive (and probably definitive) bibliography in publishing will be found in Thomas Tanselle's *A Guide to American Imprints* (Harvard University, Belknap Press, 2 vols., 1972). For newspapers and magazines particularly, *The Literature of Journalism* (University of Minnesota Press, 1964) is a first-rate bibliographical guide which also evaluates the works.

The following recent paperback titles are also recommended:

Citizen Hearst, by W. A. Swanberg (Bantam, 1971).

Pulitzer, by W. A. Swanberg (Scribner's, 1972).

Publishers on Publishing, by Gerald Gross (Grosset & Dunlap, 1961).

The Mass Media Book, ed. by Rod Holgren and William Norton (Prentice-Hall, 1972).

Mass Culture Revisited, ed. by Bernard Rosenberg and David Manning White (Van Nostrand Reinhold, 1971).

Readings in Mass Communication: Concepts and Issues in the Mass Media, ed. by Michael C. Emery and Ted Curtis Smythe (William C. Brown, 1972).

Mass Media and the National Experience: Essays in Communication History, ed. by Ronald T. Farrar and John D. Stevens (Harper & Row, 1971).

Mass News: Practices, Controversies and Alternatives, ed. by David J. Leroy and Christopher H. Sterling (Prentice-Hall, 1973).

Media, Messages, and Men: New Perspectives in Communication, by John C. Merrill and Ralph L. Lowenstein (McKay, 1971).

The Fourth Estate: An Informal Appraisal of the News and Opinion Media, by John L. Hulteng and Roy Paul Nelson (Harper & Row, 1971).

Survey of Broadcast Journalism, 1968–1969, ed. by Marvin Barrett (Grosset & Dunlap, 1969).

Survey of Broadcast Journalism, 1969–1970, ed. by Marvin Barrett (Grosset & Dunlap, 1970).

TV as Art, ed. by Patrick D. Hazard (National Council of Teachers of English, 1966).

Media Casebook: An Introductory Reader in American Mass Communications, ed. by Peter M. Sandman, David M. Rubin, and David B. Sachsman (Prentice-Hall, 1972).

On the Cable: The Television of Abundance, Report of the Sloan Commission on Cable Communications (McGraw-Hill, 1971).

Wiring the World: The Explosion in Communications (U.S. News & World Report, 1971).

Index